THE INVESTIGATOR'S LITTLE BLACK BOOK 3

by
Robert Scott, P.I.

The Investigative Resource
Used by THOUSANDS
of Private Investigators, Law
Enforcement Agencies, Media
Organizations and Others!

Crime Time Publishing Co.
Beverly Hills, California

The Investigator's Little Black Book 3
© 2002 by Robert Scott, P.I.

Published by
Crime Time Publishing Co., Inc
287 S. Robertson Blvd., #224
Beverly Hills, CA 90211

www.crimetime.com

The Investigator's Little Black Book is a trademark of
Crime Time Publishing Co., Inc

 Printed on Recycled Paper

Printed in the United States of America
10 9 8 7 6 5 4
First edition

Scott, Robert
    The investigator's little black book 3 : the
investigative resource used by thousands of private
investigators, law enforcement agencies, media
organizations and others! / by Robert Scott -- 1st ed
    p. cm
    LCCN 2001135720
    ISBN 0-9652369-4-3

    1 Public records--United States--Telephone
directories 2 Records--United States--Telephone
directories 3 Private investigators--Handbooks,
manuals, etc 4 Investigations--Handbooks, manuals,
etc I Title

JK2445 P82S36 2002   352 3'87
                            QBI01-201308

DISCLAIMER

This book is for informational purposes only. Any reliance upon the information contained herein is at the sole risk of its user.

Inclusion in this book of any individual, company, service, product or governmental agency does not constitute endorsement of the individual, company, service, product or governmental agency by the author or publisher.

Although every reasonable effort has been made to present accurate and complete information in this book, errors or omissions may be contained in the information presented. No warranties, either expressed or implied, are made by the author, publisher or distributors of this book.

—— INTRODUCTION ——

Dear Investigator,

I want to introduce you to my mistress. Well, actually, you're already holding her in your hands. While I've been married to my life as a private investigator since *The Investigator's Little Black Book 2* was published, this new edition has been my mistress. She stole my evenings, my weekends, my vacations and quite a few sick days. I'll let you decide if the end result was worth the effort.

Inside *The Investigator's Little Black Book 3*, you'll find a huge collection of investigative resources that will make you a more informed investigator. Thousands of previously published sources have been updated and thousands of new ones added. Websites have also been added en masse. You'll also find more cross references that should make locating the right information more effortless.

Who uses this book? People like you — private investigators, law enforcement agents, reporters and other investigative professionals. People whose work is to uncover truth. A special job indeed! It's with great pride that I share with you the sources in this book.

I need to express a word of gratitude to some special others. My readers — people like you — have been selfless in sharing new sources that they have come across during their workdays. Hardly a day goes by when I'm not sent something new and for each and every one, Thank You! I also can't leave out the invaluable assistance of my researchers, and most of all chief researcher Annette René, who have toiled tirelessly on behalf of this project. Thanks also to Los Angeles P.I. Bill Schneid for providing invaluable comments on how to make this a better book. Finally, thank you to my friends and investigators who conducted peer review before the book was published.

In closing, I want to share with you my favorite quote about the life of the investigator that was passed along to me by longtime P.I. Richard O'Neil — "It's a front row seat to the Greatest Show on Earth." This perfectly captures the life investigators lead — sitting in the orchestra pit, steady observers to lives gone bad. I hope you'll take this book along with you as a guidebook and companion. And keep an eye out for me — I'll be just a scant few seats away.

Best regards,
Robert Scott, P.I.
Los Angeles, Calif.
January 2002

Reader's Guide

You are now reading the most recent edition of *The Investigator's Little Black Book*! The prior editions of the book — *The Investigator's Little Black Book (1996)* and *The Investigator's Little Black Book 2 (1998)* — are now obsolete and out of print.

About Internet Addresses:

Websites have been added throughout the book. They have *not* been added when their inclusion would create more of a detriment, through clutter, than they would a benefit.

For free Internet-based public record searches, visit our free search site, *Black Book Online*, at *www.crimetime.com*. *Black Book Online* is a free resource for professional investigators and is not meant for use by the general public. Although this book contains many public record sources, it is not meant to be a directory of online public records — especially at the state and local government level.

Outdated Internet Addresses:

If an extended Internet address shown in this book is defunct, use directory "backtracking" to relocate the page. The simple technique of backtracking one directory at a time will turn dead-end web addresses into good ones more often than not. For example, if the following web page is down:

---

www.att.com/traveler/tools/codes.html

Re-enter it, minus the last directory, as follows:

www.att.com/traveler/tools/

If this address is still defunct, go back one more directory, as follows:

www.att.com/traveler/

Once an active page is found, search it for links to take you back to the content you were originally looking for.

Your Sources Wanted:

A great many of the sources in this book come from readers just like you. If you come across a source that would be suitable for inclusion in future editions of this book, please send them to us. By e-mail:

research@crimetime.com

Or by U.S. mail:

> Research Dept.
> Crime Time Publishing Co.
> 289 S. Robertson Blvd., #224
> Beverly Hills, CA 90211

THE INVESTIGATOR'S LITTLE BLACK BOOK 3

Table of Contents

Sources of Information, A - Z   1

Reference Guide   297

Privacy Law Survival Guide   414

New subject headings not appearing in prior editions are noted
with this icon.

Exceptional sources are noted
with this icon.

All material appearing in prior editions has
been updated. Most previously appearing subjects have been greatly expanded. Although not
marked "new," they more often than not contain substantial new information.

ABA ROUTING NUMBERS

■☞ NEW! Every checking account number contains a nine-digit ABA routing number that identifies the financial institution that the account is at. When a check is presented for payment, it's ultimately guided back to the issuing bank for payment. (See *Reference Guide* for *Anatomy of a Check*.) But how can an investigator identify the bank when he just has this nine digit number but not the bank name? Here's three options:

Run ABA numbers online at this Federal Reserve website to identify the banking institution:

www.fedwiredirectory.frb.org/search.cfm

Or you can get the same information by calling the Reference Desk at the *American Bankers Association*:

800/BANKERS

Another way is to purchase the *ABA Key to Routing Numbers*. It's published semi-annually and contains 28,000 ABA routing numbers and their corresponding banks, plus retired numbers from the past five years. Sells for $159.

800/321-3373
847/933-8073
www.tfp.com

ACADEMY OF MOTION PICTURE ARTS & SCIENCES LIBRARY

The *AMPAS* library contains a wealth of information on movie industry credits. Ask for the reference desk.

310/247-3020
www.oscar.org

ACCIDENT RECONSTRUCTION

There are a number of accident reconstruction associations — almost all have an online directory of members.

The *Accident Reconstruction Network* is a web-based professional organization.

858/538-3960
www.accidentreconstruction.com

California Association of Accident
Reconstruction Specialists   925/284-7739
www.accidentreconstructions.com/caars/

International Association of Accident
Reconstruction Specialists   517/622-3135
www.iaars.org

National Association of Profes-
sional Accident Reconstructionists   301/843-0048
www.napars.org

Texas Association of Accident
Reconstructionists   *www.taars.org*

OTHER SOURCES:
NHTSA, Auto Safety Hotline   800/424-9393
NHTSA, Office of Defects
Investigation   202/366-2850
NHTSA, Crash Worthiness Research   202/366-4862
NHTSA, Office of Vehicle Safety
Compliance   202/366-2832
www.nhtsa.dot.gov

Accident Investigation Quarterly
& Accident Reconstruction Journal   301/843-1371

For classes and other information on the science of car
crashes, contact the *Northwestern University Traffic
Institute.*

    800/323-4011
    www.nwu.edu

Investigators who diagram accident scenes will want a
traffic template. *Law Tech Publishing* is one seller of these
handy devices. Price range is $8.95 and up.

    800/498-0911
    www.lawtech-pub.com

ADDRESS CORRECTION REQUESTED

Postal forwarding information is now
officially available only for service of
process when requested by a person who is
entitled in that state to serve legal papers. Sssh — don't tell
the brain trust at the Post Office that you can get the same
information by addressing an envelope to the old address
and writing ADDRESS CORRECTION REQUESTED on
it. If the party has moved and there's a forwarding address
on file, the envelope will be returned to you with the new
address. Cost? One first-class postage stamp. *Update (2-21-
03): The Post office has changed the terminology to
RETURN SERVICE REQUESTED instead of ADDRESS
CORRECTION REQUESTED.*

ADOPTION INVESTIGATIONS

What sets adoption searches apart from
ordinary missing persons searches is that
the name of the person being searched for

is usually unknown. In addition, there are a variety of laws that shield the identity of the birth parent(s) of an adoptee. For these and other reasons, a specialist in these types of cases may be needed. One such firm is *The Adoption & Missing Persons Bureau*, a division of *Worldwide Tracers*. Their work has been featured on numerous TV shows including "Oprah" and "48 Hours."

800/432-FIND
www.worldwidetracers.com

AERIAL & SATELLITE PHOTOGRAPHY

HOT! There's been a major breakthrough in the availability of archived satellite photographs. *MapQuest*, the free Internet mapping website, now offers the option of seeing an archived satellite photograph in most areas of the United States. Most photographs are a couple years or so old. Nevertheless, they provide an instant — and free — means to check land use and surrounding streets. Along with the reverse directory, this will be a first step when conducting an address investigation.

www.mapquest.com

The latest entry into the private spy satellite business is *Space Imaging* of Thornton, Colorado. The company boasts commercial sale of custom satellite pictures of any spot on Earth with one meter resolution — making it the highest resolution photos-from-space available on the free market. Sale of these photos to terrorist-friendly countries is forbidden and other restrictions may apply in time of war or national crisis.

800/232-9037
303/254-2000
www.spaceimaging.com

Earth Science Information Center, a project of the U.S. Geological Survey, has a massive collection of aerial photographs of the entire United States. Both recent and vintage shots are available. Cost ranges between $12 and $50 per shot.

888/ASK-USGS
edc.usgs.gov

Spot Image Corp. sells custom photographs that can be taken from their satellites of any spot on Earth. Resolution is 10 meters — meaning you'll see buildings, not people. Custom shots cost approximately $2500 each. Also available is an extensive library of pre-existing shots taken over the last few years. These go for $750 to $1500 each.

703/715-3100
www.spot.com

The GEMI Store (Geographic Earth Mapping Information) acts as a broker for various sources of archived aerial and satellite photographs.

888/333-GEMI
www.gemistore.com

AIRCRAFT
See...*AVIATION*.

Also see...*FEDERAL AVIATION ADMINISTRATION*.

AIRCRAFT THEFT INVESTIGATIONS
The Aviation Crime Prevention Institute aids in the detection and prevention of aircraft theft. A monthly bulletin of stolen aircraft and aircraft parts is published. Also available is a database of stolen aircraft dating back to 1974.

800/969-5473
301/991-2817
www.acpi.org

AIR FORCE PERSONNEL LOCATOR
The Air Force Worldwide Locator handles all requests for locating an active member of the *Air Force* from the general public, families and government/military officials. Military addresses will be provided for active personnel unless the person is in a "protected" position of sensitive, deployable or overseas duty. In these cases, a letter will be forwarded to the service person, but their address will not be provided.   Parents or spouses may telephone for assistance. All others should mail their requests. Include a fee of $3.50 per name. Provide the subject's full name with middle initial; SSN or Air Force Service Number; and date of birth (or a duty history in the Air Force giving the place, month and year of assignments after June 1970). Send with a check or money order made payable to DAO-DE RAFB to:

HQ AFPC/MSIMDL
550 C Street West, Suite 50
Randolph AFB, TX 78150-4752
Telephone: 210/565-2660

The *Locator* also provides a Certificate of Record of Military Service to substantiate an individual's service in the Air Force. The certificate fee is $5.20 per name. Civilians and representatives of civilian businesses must send a written and properly signed request on official letterhead and pay an additional nonrefundable research fee of $3.50 per name.

Also see...*MILITARY PERSONNEL*.

ALTERNATIVE PRESS INDEX

The Alternative Press Index, published quarterly, offers a subject index to articles appearing in approximately 250 alternative, radical and usually left-wing publications.

Alternative Press Center   410/243-2471
www.altpress.org

AMERICAN INSURANCE SERVICES GROUP, INC.
See...*ISO CLAIMSEARCH*.

Also see...*MARINE INDEX BUREAU*.

AMERICAN SOCIETY FOR INDUSTRIAL SECURITY

ASIS is *the* powerhouse professional organization for corporate security types. Members include corporate security directors, as well as consultants, attorneys, law enforcement agents and others. Its CPP designation (Corporate Protection Professional) is highly respected and has been earned by over 9,000 members.

703/519-6200
www.asisonline.org

AMERICANS WITH DISABILITIES ACT

The United States Department of Justice has oversight over compliance with the Americans with Disability Act. Violations of this law can lead to what's referred to as an "ADA lawsuit." Call the *ADA Information Line* for technical questions and general ADA information.

800/514-0301
www.usdoj.gov/crt/ada

AMERICA ONLINE

To subpoena account records from AOL, the lawsuit must be filed in a federal court or in the Commonwealth of Virginia as AOL will not respond to subpoenas from out of state. Once the subpoena is received by AOL, they will notify the account holder, providing him or her with the opportunity to quash it. If the subpoena is not quashed, AOL will comply within 14 days. To serve a subpoena on AOL, personal service is required at the following address: *America Online, Attn.: Custodian of Records, 22000 AOL Way, Dulles, VA 20166*. Any questions should be directed to the *AOL Legal Department*, which can be reached at their general information phone number.

General Information   703/265-1000
Screen Name/Password Inquiries   888/265-8004

Law enforcement may serve a search warrant to receive the same information. Search warrants to be served on AOL

5

are typically walked through the criminal courts in Leesburg, Virginia by Loudoun County Sheriff's Office Inspector Ron Horack.

703/777-1021

AOL maintains a little known online legal department that posts information on AOL related litigation and other legal issues. Sections include information on online defamation, intellectual property and other cyber-issues.

http://legal.web.aol.com

Photo: The county courthouse in Leesburg, Virginia, where search warrants are filed for AOL account holder information. (Photo courtesy of Michael J. Kacmarcik.)

ANI
ANI stands for *Automatic Number Identification*. Call an ANI from a phone line and you'll be read back the line's telephone number. There are hundreds of local ANIs. Here's three, as of our publication date, that appear to work throughout the U.S.

888/324-8686
800/555-1160
800/532-7486
(then press 1)

Need to know who the long distance carrier is for any given phone line? From that line, call this number and a computer will tell you.

700/555-4141

Also see...*TOLL-FREE CARRIER IDENTIFIER.*

ANSIR
See...*TERRORISTS AND TERRORISM* or *FEDERAL BUREAU OF INVESTIGATION.*

ARMY PERSONNEL LOCATOR

The U.S. Army World Wide Locator provides address information for active-duty Army personnel. All requests must be in writing, except in emergency situations. Send a check or money order for $3.50 per search made payable to the Finance Officer. Include the service person's full name and Social Security Number or date of birth.

Army World Wide Locator
U.S. Army Enlisted Records & Evaluation Center
8899 E. 56th Street
Indianapolis, IN 46249-5301
Telephone: 703/325-3732

Also of interest is an online version of the Army Worldwide Locator, which provides military addresses for active duty personnel. The service is free for military and government users. Otherwise, there's a $3.50 fee, payable by credit card. Also available are Soldiers' and Sailors' Certificates for $5.20 each.

www.erec.army.mil/wwl/

To obtain a certificate of service or nonservice (a Soldiers' and Sailors' Certificate), include a check for $5.20 made payable to the Finance Officer, along with the service person's full name and Social Security Number or date of birth, and send to the address below:

Commander
U.S. Army Enlisted Records & Evaluation Center
ATTN: PCRE-RP
Indianapolis, IN 46249-5301

The National Personnel Records Center will forward a letter to a *former* Army member at his or her last-known address. Send the letter in a sealed and stamped envelope inside a second envelope addressed to the *National Personnel Records Center* with a letter requesting their assistance. Include the service member's name, serial number and/or Social Security Number, and date of birth, if available.

National Personnel Records Center
9700 Page Avenue
St. Louis, MO 63132-5200

Also see...*MILITARY PERSONNEL*.

ARSON INVESTIGATIONS

Pragmatics, Inc. manufactures fire investigation equipment, including accelerant detectors.

800/541-2221
636/255-6787
www.pragmatics-arson.com

Applied Technical Services is a private forensics lab that offers fire causation analysis.

800/544-5117
www.atslab.com

Analytical Forensic Associates, Inc. uses chemical analysis of fire debris to identify accelerants.

770/246-1711

Fire Science & Technologies, Inc. are fire and explosion investigators in Washington State.

425/222-9499
www.doctorfire.com

The Insurance Committee for Arson Control sponsors an annual arson investigation seminar.

317/875-5250
www.arsoncontrol.org

International Association of Arson
Investigators   501/568-3473
www.fire-investigators.com

National Fire Protection Association   800/344-3555
www.nfpa.org

Bureau of Fire & Aviation Management tracks forest fires currently burning in the United States.

202/205-1500
www.fs.fed.us/fire

The U.S. Fire Administration maintains a nationwide database of fire incidents, as submitted by participating local fire agencies. It's known as the Fire Incident Reporting System and is statistical in scope.

301/447-1024
www.usfa.fema.gov

ART – STOLEN

The *FBI* maintains its *National Stolen Art File (NSAF)* which contains photographs and descriptions of stolen works of art with artistic or historical significance. All requests to search the NSAF must be made through a law enforcement agency in support of a criminal investigation. However, select works of art from the NSAF can be viewed on the Internet at the URL below. Individuals wanting to access the full NSAF should contact their local FBI office. The FBI doesn't have an art theft unit, so instead contact your local FBI office and ask to speak with an interstate theft supervisor. The actual NSAF is maintained by the *FBI's Interstate Theft/Government Reservation Crimes Unit*, which is a subsection of the *Violent Crimes and*

Major Offenders Section of the *Criminal Investigation Division*.

202/324-4192
www.fbi.gov/majcases/arttheft/art.htm

On an international level, *INTERPOL* has begun posting stolen works of art on its website as well.

www.interpol.int/Public/WorkOfArt/Default.asp

The U.S. Customs Service *Art Recovery Team* investigates illicit trafficking of art, antiquities and cultural property.

866/LOST ART
www.customs.gov/enforcem/art.htm

Art that was originally plundered by the Nazis in Europe continues to surface at museums in the U.S. and throughout the world; and in private collections. Deciding ownership of the art is a moral and legal dilemma yet to be resolved. Some major museums, including the *Getty*, are posting information on their websites identifying suspected Nazi-looted art. There are a number of websites that delve further into this issue. Here's one:

www.viliniusforum.lt

Trans-Art International is staffed by attorneys who provide legal services to collectors to protect their rights under U.S. law. Company principal Dr. Willie Korte is widely known as an expert in World War II-era art thefts.

202/416-1721
www.trans-art.com

International Foundation for Art Research offers an authentication service to make sure your Picasso *really* is a Picasso. They also publish *IFAReports* with a focus on stolen art.

212/297-0941
www.ifar.org

Art Loss Register has offices in London and New York City. Their database includes 70,000 stolen works of art and art objects and is relied upon by both insurance companies and law enforcement.

212/391-8791
www.artloss.com

Trace Publications, Ltd. circulates a monthly publication of stolen art to collectors, dealers and museums. Company owner Phillip Saunders is an internationally known art theft consultant.

011-44-01983-826000
www.trace.co.uk

ASSASSINATIONS

NEW! One website JFK assassination buffs will want to visit is the website for *The Sixth Floor Museum* at Dealey Plaza. Or if you should find yourself in Dallas, you can visit Lee Harvey Oswald's sniper nest in person.

> 214/747-6660
> *www.jfk.org*

Still can't get enough? You can view a live shot over the Internet, 24 hours a day, from the *Texas School Book Depository*.

> *www.earthcam.com/jfk/*

Also see...*COALITION ON POLITICAL ASSASSINATIONS*.

ASSET FORFEITURE FINANCIAL RECOVERY

Need a collection agency to pursue recovery of a debt on behalf of your agency or a client? *Asset Forfeiture*, a Glendale, California-based collection company, has a set fee of 25% of moneys recovered, with no minimum placement.

> 888/4ASSET4
> *www.socalmall.com/assetfortfeiture/*

ASSOCIATED PRESS

AP is a nonprofit syndicate that feeds news and photos to news organizations throughout the world. *AP* maintains a huge file of photographs of notables and other people in the news. If the subject of your investigation has been in the news, this might be one source of a photograph. Photos are sold through affiliate, *Wide World Photos*.

Headquarters   212/621-1500
                                 www.ap.org

Wide World Photos   212/621-1930

ASSOCIATION OF CERTIFIED FRAUD EXAMINERS

NEW! When the letters CFE follow an investigator's name, there's a good bet you're dealing with a pro. The *Association of Certified Fraud Examiners* is now 25,000 members strong with chapters throughout the U.S. and elsewhere. This is where the anti-white collar crime crowd can be found. Their website includes a free e-mail based newsletter, *FraudInfo*, and membership and fraud training information.

> 800/245-3321
> 512/478-9070
> *www.acfe.org*

ASSOCIATION OF THREAT ASSESSMENT PROFESSIONALS

 ATAP is the premier national organization for threat assessment professionals — those who seek to protect their clients from stalking, harassment and workplace violence. Membership is by sponsorship only (you have to know a current member to join) and consists of law enforcement, corporate security and private investigators. There are currently 6 chapters with locations in Chicago, Denver, Los Angeles, Northern and Southern California, Texas and Washington, D.C.

310/312-0212
http://atap.cc

AT&T "00" INFO

AT&T's directory assistance offers standard business/residential lookups as well as reverse lookups when an address is needed from a published phone number. (They don't provide phone number to address matches.) Cost is $1.99 per call for up to two listings. They'll connect the second listing for free. There are two ways to reach AT&T "00" Info. If AT&T is your long distance company, just dial zero twice. If not, dial 10-10-ATT-00.

AT&T Customers   00
Non-AT&T Customers   10-10-ATT-00

AT&T LANGUAGE LINE

HOT! *Language Line Services* offers interpreters by phone in more than 140 languages. No appointment is necessary. You call them, they connect you to an interpreter, then to the subject of your interview. Payment accepted by credit card. Cost ranges from $3.50 per minute (Spanish) to $4.00 per minute (all other languages) during business hours. Fees range from $4.00 to $4.50 per minute during non-business hours.

800/752-0093
www.languageline.com

AT&T TELE-CONFERENCING

Need to have a phone call with up to fourteen other parties at once? *AT&T Tele-Conferencing* will connect all of you. Charge based on the number of lines and length of call.

800/232-1234
700/456-1000

AT&T TRUE MESSAGES

You might think of *AT&T True Messages* as a "Reverse Answering Machine." You record a message for the person you're trying to contact. AT&T will then call the unanswered phone once every half hour for the next ten hours. If they're successful, there's a $2.25 charge. If they're not successful, there's no charge.

800/562-6275

ATTORNEYS
See...*STATE BAR ASSOCIATIONS*.

■☞ [NEW!] AUDIO/VIDEO ENHANCEMENT

Applied Forensic Technologies   877/TAPE-EXPERT
262/245-1313
www.tapeenhancment.com

Electronic Services Agency   937/644-2170
www.1esa.com

Forensic Audio Lab   310/859-8755
www.forensicaudiosleuth.net

Team Audio   419/243-3000
www.audiorestoration.com

Audio Forensic Center   415/397-0442

AUDIT BUREAU OF CIRCULATIONS

■☞ [NEW!] Magazines and other periodicals are required by federal law to publish audited information on their circulation. The largest provider of this service is the *Audit Bureau of Circulations*, a private company.

847/605-0909
www.accessabc.com

AUTOMATIC NUMBER IDENTIFICATION
See...*ANI*.

AUTOPSIES
See...*DEATH INVESTIGATIONS*.

Also see...*CORONERS*.

AUTO REPOSSESSION
Repossessors can be found through these professional associations.

Time Finance Adjusters   800/874-0510
904/274-4210
www.tfaguide.net

National Finance Adjusters   410/728-2400
www.nfa.org

American Recovery Association   504/366-7377
                                       www.repo.org

California Association of Licensed
Repossessors   916/781-6633
                                       www.calr.org

Professional Repossessor magazine is a nicely done magazine that includes how-to-tips, product reviews and war
stories.

                                       888/REPONEWS
                                    www.prorepomag.com

AUTO SAFETY HOTLINE
Auto Safety Hotline, Dept. of Transportation, maintains
information on auto safety, including recalls.

                                       800/424-9393
                                       www.dot.gov

AUTOTRACKXP
See...*DATABASE PROVIDERS*.

AVIATION
The International Society of Air Safety Investigators is an
organization of air accident investigators with members in 35
countries. The Society maintains a technical library with
copies of 600 plus air accident reports and information on
over 9,000 accidents in its computerized databases.

                                       703/430-9668
                                       www.isasi.org

NASA Headquarters Library is a good starting point for
space and flight related inquiries.
                                       202/358-0168
                           www.hq.nasa.gov/office/hqlibrary/

Aircraft Owners & Pilots Association is the world's largest
aviation association with over 340,000 pilots and aircraft
owners as members.
                                       301/695-2000
                                       www.aopa.org

Databases of FAA registered pilots and airplanes are
available for free on the Internet, and at a low cost through
many online database providers. *Aviation Research Group*
has produced a CD-ROM containing this information as
well. Sells for around $113.
                                       513/852-5110
                                       800/361-2216
                                www.aviationresearch.com

Jane's World Airlines is available in book form, diskette, or
CD-ROM (Price range $890 - $1,500). Inside you'll find

detailed data on the world's major airlines, including financial associations, fleet sizes, aircraft type and names of key decision makers.

Jane's Information Group   703/683-3700
www.janes.com

Insured Aircraft Title Service, Inc. has information on aircraft owners, pilots, mechanics and manufacturers.

800/654-4882
405/681-6663
www.insuredaircraft.com

Aviation Information
Research Corporation   703/823-1264

Search the National Transportation Safety Board database of aviation accidents and selected incidents on the Internet.

www.ntsb.gov/NTSB/query.asp

For FAA databases on the Internet, click the "Aviation" button at *Black Book Online*.

www.crimetime.com/online.htm

Also see...*FEDERAL AVIATION ADMINISTRATION*.

BANK ACCOUNTS
See article *Lawful Bank Account Sources* in our *Reference Guide*.

BANK ROUTING NUMBERS
See...*ABA ROUTING NUMBERS*.

BANKRUPTCY COURTS
Many listed courts have a 24-hour touch-tone automated information system called Voice Case Information System (VCIS). Punch in the name or Social Security Number of a person and the computer will tell if there has been a bankruptcy filing. Courts without VCIS must be contacted by phone during normal business hours.

Also see....*PACER* for computer access.

Alabama, Northern District:

Decatur Division		256/355-2349
	vcis	877/466-8879
Birmingham Division		205/731-3746
	vcis	877/466-0796
Anniston Division		256/238-0456
	vcis	877/466-0795
Tuscaloosa Divison		205/758-1309

Alabama, Middle District:		334/223-7486
Alabama, Southern District:		334/441-5638
	vcis	334/441-5637
Alaska:		907/271-2695
	vcis	907/271-2658
Arizona:		
Phoenix Division		602/640-5832
	vcis	602/640-5820
Tucson Division		520/620-7470
	vcis	520/620-7475
Yuma Division		520/783-9535
Arkansas, Eastern District:		501/918-5565
	vcis	800/891-6741
Arkansas, Western District:		501/918-5565
	vcis	800/891-6741
California, Northern District:		
San Jose Division		408/535-5118
	vcis	800/457-0604
San Francisco Division		415/268-2300
	vcis	800/570-9819
	vcis	415/705-3160
Oakland Division		510/879-3600
Santa Rosa Division		707/525-8539
	vcis	800/570-9819
California, Eastern District:		
Fresno Division		559/498-7217
	vcis	800/736-0158
Modesto Division		209/521-5160
	vcis	800/736-0158
Sacramento Division		916/498-5525
	vcis	916/551-2989
California, Central District:		
Los Angeles Division		213/620-0031
	vcis	213/894-4111
San Fernando Division		818/587-2932
	vcis	818/587-2936
Santa Ana Division		714/338-5406
	vcis	714/836-2278
Santa Barbara Division	vcis	805/884-4806
Riverside Division		909/276-2914
	vcis	909/774-1150
California, Southern District:		
San Diego Division		619/557-6875
	vcis	619/557-6521
Colorado:		303/844-0263
	vcis	303/844-0267
Connecticut:		860/240-3570
	vcis	800/800-5113
Delaware:		888/667-5530
		302/573-6243
	vcis	888/667-5530
	vcis	302/573-6233
District of Columbia:		202/273-0630
	vcis	202/273-0048

Florida, Northern District:
Pensacola Division 850/444-0189
Tallahassee Division 904/942-8815
Florida, Middle District:
Jacksonville Division 904/232-1311
vcis 904/232-1313
Orlando Division 407/648-6212
vcis 407/648-6800
Tampa Division 813/301-5206
vcis 813/243-5210
Florida, Southern District: 305/536-7492
vcis 800/473-0226
vcis 305/536-5979
Georgia, Northern District: 404/730-3264
vcis 404/730-2866
vcis 404/730-2867
Georgia, Middle District: 912/752-3551
vcis 912/752-8183
Georgia, Southern District:
Augusta Division 800/295-8679
Savannah Division 912/650-4190
Hawaii: 808/522-8118
vcis 808/522-8122
Idaho: 208/334-9895
vcis 208/334-9386
Illinois, Northern District:
Chicago Division 312/408-5101
vcis 312/408-5089
Rockford Division 815/987-4489
vcis 815/987-4487
Illinois, Central District: 217/492-4260
vcis 217/492-4550
vcis 800/827-9005
Illinois, Southern District: 618/482-9114
vcis 618/482-9365
vcis 800/726-5622
Indiana, Northern District: 219/968-2270
vcis 800/726-5622
vcis 219/236-8814
Indiana, Southern District: 317/226-5146
vcis 800/335-8003
Iowa, Northern District: 319/286-2287
vcis 800/249-9859
vcis 319/362-9906
Iowa, Southern District: 515/284-6427
vcis 800/597-5917
vcis 515/284-6230
Kansas: 800/613-7052
vcis 800/827-9028
vcis 316/269-6668
Kentucky, Eastern: 859/233-2777
vcis 800/998-2650
Kentucky, Western: 800/263-9389
vcis 800/263-9385

	vcis	502/625-7391
Louisiana, Eastern:		504/589-6961
	vcis	504/589-7879
Louisiana, Middle:		225/382-2176
	vcis	504/382-2175
Louisiana, Western:		800/523-1976
	vcis	800/326-4026
	vcis	318/676-4234
Maine:		207/780-3268
	vcis	888/201-3572
	vcis	207/780-3755
Maryland:		410/962-0776
	vcis	410/962-0733
Massachusetts:		617/565-6021
	vcis	617/565-6025
Michigan, Eastern District (includes Detroit):		313/961-4934
	vcis	313/961-4940
Michigan, Western District:		616/456-2415
	vcis	616/456-2075
Minnesota:		651/848-1096
	vcis	800/959-9002
	vcis	612/664-5302
Mississippi, Northern District:		662/369-9805
	vcis	662/369-8147
Mississippi, Southern District:		
Biloxi Division		228/432-5542
	vcis	800/293-2723
	vcis	601/435-2905
Jackson Division		601/965-5301
	vcis	800/601-8859
	vcis	601/965-6106
Missouri, Eastern District (includes St. Louis):		314/425-6935
	vcis	314/425-4054
Missouri, Western District:		816/512-5115
	vcis	816/842-7985
Montana:		406/782-1051
	vcis	406/782-1060
Nebraska:		402/221-4882
	vcis	800/829-0112
	vcis	402/221-3757
Nevada:		
Las Vegas Division		702/388-6633
	vcis	800/314-3436
	vcis	702/388-6708
Reno Division		775/784-5559
	vcis	800/314-3436
New Hampshire:		603/666-7923
	vcis	800/851-8954
	vcis	603/666-7424
New Jersey:		973/645-3555
	vcis	877/239-8547
	vcis	973/645-6044

New Mexico:		505/348-2496
	vcis	888/435-7822
	vcis	505/248-6536
New York, Northern District:		518/257-1669
	vcis	800/206-1952
New York, Southern District:		
New York City Division		212/668-2896
	vcis	212/668-2772
White Plains Division		914/390-4060
	vcis	212/668-2772
New York, Eastern District:		718/488-7012
	vcis	800/252-2537
	vcis	718/852-5726
New York, Western District:		716/551-3155
	vcis	800/776-9578
	vcis	716/551-5311
North Carolina, Eastern District:		919/856-4752
	vcis	919/234-7655
North Carolina, Middle District:		336/333-5389
	vcis	910/333-5532
North Carolina, Western District:		704/350-7509
	vcis	704/350-7505
North Dakota:		701/297-7165
	vcis	701/239-5641
Ohio, Northern District:		330/489-4779
	vcis	800/898-6899
	vcis	330/489-4731
	vcis	216/489-4771
Ohio, Southern District:		
Columbus Division		614/469-6638
	vcis	800/726-1006
Dayton Division		937/225-2516
	vcis	800/726-1004
Oklahoma, Northern District:		918/669-4033
	vcis	888/501-6977
Oklahoma, Eastern District:		918/756-4812
	vcis	918/756-8617
Oklahoma, Western District:		405/231-4955
	vcis	405/231-4768
Oregon:		800/610-9315
	vcis	800/726-2227
	vcis	503/326-2249
Pennsylvania, Eastern District:		215/597-3501
	vcis	215/597-2244
Pennsylvania, Middle District:		
Harrisburg Division		570/901-2835
	vcis	877/440-2690
Wilkes-Barre Division		570/821-4033
	vcis	877/440-2690
Pennsylvania, Western District:		412/355-2588
	vcis	412/355-3210
Rhode Island:		401/528-4062
	vcis	401/528-4476
South Carolina:		800/410-2988

	vcis	800/669-8767
	vcis	803/765-5211
South Dakota:		800/261-3167
	vcis	800/768-6218
	vcis	605/330-4559
Tennessee, Eastern District:		888/833-9512
	vcis	800/767-1512
	vcis	423/752-5272
Tennessee, Middle District:		615/254-5290
Tennessee, Western District:		901/328-3617
	vcis	888/381-4961
	vcis	800/406-0190
Texas, Northern District:		
Amarillo Division		806/324-2302
	vcis	800/886-9008
Dallas Division		214/767-3616
	vcis	214/767-8092
Fort Worth Division		817/978-3802
	vcis	800/886-9008
Lubbock Division		806/472-7336
	vcis	214/767-8092
Texas, Southern District:		800/998-9037
	vcis	800/745-4459
	vcis	713/250-5049
Texas, Eastern District:		903/590-1220
	vcis	903/590-1217
Texas, Western District (includes San Antonio and El Paso):		210/472-6262
	vcis	210/229-4023
Utah:		800/718-1188
	vcis	800/733-6740
	vcis	801/524-3107
Vermont:		800/260-9968
	vcis	800/260-9956
	vcis	802/747-7627
Virginia, Eastern District:		
Richmond Division		804/916-2484
	vcis	800/890-2829
Alexandria Division		703/258-1234
	vcis	800/890-2858
Newport News		757/595-1365
	vcis	800/890-2785
Norfolk		757/222-7441
	vcis	800/890-2954
Virginia, Western District:		
Harrisonburg Division		540/434-8373
Lynchburg Division		804/528-9003
Roanoke Division		540/857-2319
Washington, Eastern District (includes Spokane):		509/353-2404
	vcis	509/353-2404
Washington, Western District (includes Seattle):		206/553-0600

	vcis	800/409-4662
	vcis	206/553-8543
	vcis	206/442-6504
West Virginia, Northern District:		304/233-2871
	vcis	304/233-7318
West Virginia, Southern District:		304/347-5678
	vcis	304/347-5680
Wisconsin, Eastern District:		414/297-1400
	vcis	414/297-3582
Wisconsin, Western District:		608/264-5630
	vcis	800/743-8247
Wyoming:		307/772-2036

BANKS AND BANKING

The Federal Deposit Insurance Corporation (FDIC) insures and monitors funds at FDIC insured banks, savings associations and bank holding companies. Areas of interest at the agency's website includes its Institution Directory, a searchable database of every FDIC-insured institution and an Online Banks directory of illegal websites that may be misrepresenting themselves as legally chartered. Also of note is OTS Summary of Deposit reports that contain balances for more than 85,000 FDIC-insured branches.

877/ASKFDIC
www.fdic.gov

The Office of the Comptroller of the Currency (OCC) charters, regulates and supervises all national banks. Of particular interest to investigators is an *Enforcement Actions* search which identifies past actions against banks, officers, directors and employees. Search it on the Internet.

Headquarters — 202/874-5000
www.occ.treas.gov

For Enforcement Actions:

www.occ.treas.gov/enforce/enf_search.htm

Office of Thrift Supervision — 202/906-6000
www.ots.treas.gov
Complaint Hotline — 202/906-6237
800/842-6929

Board of Governors of the
Federal Reserve — 202/452-3000
www.federalreserve.gov

Also see...*OFFSHOREBUSINESS.COM*.

Also see...*ABA ROUTING NUMBERS*.

Also see...*THOMPSON FINANCIAL PUBLISHING*.

BAR ASSOCIATIONS, STATE
See...*STATE BAR ASSOCIATIONS*.

BIO-TERRORISM
See...*TERRORISTS AND TERRORISM*.

BLACK BOOK ONLINE
Black Book Online is the Internet companion to this book. It features a vast selection of free public record (and other) database searches. Use is restricted to private investigators, law enforcement, collectors, skiptracers, journalists and other professional investigators. Free.

www.crimetime.com/online.htm

BODILY INJURY CLAIMS
See...*ISO CLAIMSEARCH*.

Also see...*MARINE INDEX BUREAU*.

For statistical information on injuries, including such information as costs, frequency and demographics, consider obtaining an annual publication from the *National Safety Council* called *Accident Facts*. The current book is 160 pages and sells for $29.95.

800/621-7619
www.nsc.org

Consumer Product Safety Commission, National Inquiry Information Clearinghouse maintains a database on product-related injuries.

800/638-2772
301/504-0424
www.cpsc.gov/about/clrnghse

BOOKS

Books in Print is *the* database of books currently in print and is relied upon as an authoritative source by both bookstores and libraries. BIP now has its own website. Although membership is required, as of our publication date, a free trial membership was available. Most libraries and major bookstores also have access to *Book in Print*.

813/855-4635
www.booksinprint.com

Looking for an out of print book? You could spend the day calling used bookstores or you could use *Harvest Book-search*. There's no charge for the search and no obligation to buy.

800/563-1222
www.harvestbooks.com

Also useful in finding hard-to-find books is *bibliofind.com*. In collaboration with *Amazon.com* and various nationwide booksellers, *bibliofind.com* can locate rare, used and out-of-print books.

www.bibliofind.com

Want to know how many copies a particular book has sold? *The Ingram Stock Status System* is a good place to start. Ingram is one of two major book distributors that distribute product to conventional bookstores. Overall they account for roughly half of all books distributed in the U.S. By calling this number and punching in a book's ISBN one can learn how many copies have been shipped last year and so far this year to book outlets through Ingram. (ISBN stands for International Standard Book Number and can be found on the copyright page of nearly all books.) Some books, such as *The Investigator's Little Black Book*, won't be reflected much here as the majority of these sales are sold through specialty catalogs that don't use Ingram as a middleman.

615/213-6803

BOXING

 Nearly every state has a boxing commission that regulates fighters and promoters. Under the auspices of the *Association of Boxing Commissioners*, a fighter who has been suspended by one commission is placed on a nationwide suspension list and cannot fight in other states. View this suspension list online at the website of the *Association of Boxing Commissioners*.

717/787-5720
www.boxingcommission.com

Information on individually licensed boxers is also available from state boxing commissions. For contact information on the individual state boxing commissions, visit this website:

www.boxingcommission.com/comltg.htm

BRB PUBLICATIONS

BRB is *the* leading publisher of public record reference materials — you'll find at least one of their books on the bookshelf of just about every P.I. agency in America. Their flagship product is *The Sourcebook to Public Record Information*. Other titles include *The National Directory of Public Records Vendors*; *The MVR Book; The MVR Decoder Digest* and *Public Records Online*. Also check out their subscription-based website, *publicrecordsources.com*.

800/929-3811
www.brbpub.com

BROADCAST TRANSCRIPTS

CNN transcripts	800/CNN-NEWS
ABC News transcripts	800/CALL-ABC
NPR (National Public Radio) transcripts	888/NPR-TEXT
CBS News transcripts	800/777-TEXT

BUREAU OF ALCOHOL, TOBACCO & FIREARMS

Headquarters	202/927-7777
	www.atf.treas.gov

ATF HOTLINES:

Arson Hotline	888/ATF-FIRE
Bomb Hotline	888/ATF-BOMB
Illegal Firearm Activity	800/ATF-GUNS
Firearms Theft Hotline	800/800-3855
Cigarettes	800/659-6242
Other Criminal Activity	888/ATF-TIPS

Anyone who encounters a stranger or suspicious person who is attempting to purchase ammonium nitrate for criminal purposes is requested to discreetly obtain the person's physical description and vehicle license plate number and immediately call:

800/800-3855

Direct Freedom of Information Act Requests to *Bureau of Alcohol, Tobacco, and Firearms, Freedom of Information Request, 650 Massachusetts Ave. N.W., Washington, D.C. 20226.*

OTHER ATF PHONES:

ATF Academy	912/267-2251
Press Office	202/927-8500
National Laboratory Center	301/762-9800
Atlanta Forensic Science Lab	404/679-5100
San Francisco Laboratory Center	510/486-3170
Explosive Enforcement Branch	202/927-8030

FEDERAL FIREARM LICENSES:

There are approximately 93,000 federal firearms licenses issued in the U.S. which allow a person or business to function as a gun dealer. To determine if an individual or business maintains a Federal Firearms License, call the *ATF Licensing Center*:

404/679-5040
877/560-2435

To verify that a Federal Firearm License number is valid, visit this website:

www.atf.treas.gov/firearms.nlc

FIREARM HISTORIES:
National Tracing Center aids law enforcement agencies by tracing the history of firearms from manufacture through current ownership:

800/788-7133
304/274-4100

 Need a serial number for a lost or stolen firearm? Then contact the gun dealer from whom the firearm was originally purchased. If the gun dealer is out of business, contact the *ATF*, which will search its records for a fee of $37.50. Include the name of the person who purchased the firearm; the name of the out-of-business dealer; the dealer's city, state and zip code; date of purchase or at least a three-year time span when the purchase was made; make, model and gauge of firearm. Include both your name and address as well as a daytime phone number. Direct your request to *ATF, Disclosure Division, 650 Massachusetts Avenue, Washington, D.C. 20226.*

800/788-7133
202/927-8480

ATF FIELD OFFICES:
Atlanta Field Division:

Atlanta, GA	404/679-5170
Macon, GA	912/474-0477
Savannah, GA	912/652-4251

Baltimore Field Division:

Baltimore, MD	410/962-0897
Hyattsville, MD	202/927-3200
Wilmington, DE	302/573-6102

Boston Field Division:

Albany, NY	518/431-4182
Boston, MA	617/565-7050
Buffalo, NY	716/551-4041
Burlington, VT	802/951-6593
Concord, NH	603/223-0071
Hartford, CT	203/240-3400
New Haven, CT	203/773-2060
Portland, ME	207/780-3324
Providence, RI	401/528-4366
Rochester, NY	716/263-5720
Syracuse, NY	315/448-0889
Springfield, MA	413/785-0007
Worcester, MA	508/793-0240

Charlotte Field Division:

Charleston, SC	843/727-4275
Charlotte, NC	704/716-1800
Columbia, SC	803/765-5723
Fayetteville, NC	910/483-3030

Greensboro, NC	336/347-4224
Greenville, SC	864/232-3221
Raleigh, NC	919/856-4366
Wilmington, NC	910/815-4936

Columbus Field Division:
Cleveland, OH	216/522-3080
Cincinnati, OH	513/684-3354
Columbus, OH	614/469-5303
Fort Wayne, IN	219/424-4440
Indianapolis, IN	317/226-7464
Merrillville, IN	219/791-0702
Toledo, OH	419/259-7520
South Bend, IN	219/236-8352
Youngstown, OH	910/815-4936

Chicago Field Division:
Chicago, IL	312/353-6935
Oakbrook, IL	708/268-0986
Springfield, IL	217/492-4273

Dallas Field Division:
Dallas, TX	214/767-2250
El Paso, TX	915/534-6449
Fort Worth, TX	817/978-2771
Lubbock, TX	806/798-1030
Oklahoma, TX	405/297-5060
Tulsa, OK	918/581-7731
Tyler, TX	903/590-1475

Detroit Field Division:
Detroit	313/393-6000
Flint, MI	810/766-5010
Grand Rapids, MI	616/456-2566

Houston Field Division:
Austin, TX	512/349-4545
Beaumont, TX	409/835-0062
Corpus Christi, TX	361/888-3392
Houston, TX	218/449-2073
McAllen, TX	956/687-5207
San Antonio, TX	210/805-2727
Waco, TX	254/741-9900

Kansas City Field Division:
Des Moines, IA	515/284-4857
Kansas City, MO	816/421-3440
Omaha, NE	402/221-3651
Springfield, MO	417/864-4707
Wichita, KS	316/269-6229

Los Angeles Field Division:
Los Angeles, CA	213/894-4812
Riverside, CA	909/276-6031

San Diego, CA	619/557-6046
Van Nuys, CA	818/756-4350

Louisville Field Division:

Ashland, KY	606/329-8092
Bowling Green, KY	270/781-7090
Ft. Wayne, IN	219/424-4440
Indianapolis, IN	317/226-7464
Lexington, KY	606/233-2771
Louisville, KY	502/582-5211
Wheeling, WV	304/232-4170

Miami Field Division:

Ft. Lauderdale, FL	954/356-7369
Ft. Myers, FL	941/334-8086
Hato Rey San Juan, PR	787/277-8734
Jacksonville, FL	904/232-3468
Miami, FL	305/597-4800
Orlando, FL	407/648-6136
Pensacola, FL	850/435-8485
St. Thomas, VI	340/774-2398
Tallahassee, FL	850/942-9660
Tampa, FL	813/228-2184
West Palm Beach, FL	561/835-8878

Nashville Field Division:

Birmingham, AL	205/731-1111
Chattanooga, TN	423/855-6422
Huntsville, AL	256/539-0623
Knoxville, TN	865/545-4505
Memphis, TN	901/544-0321
Mobile, AL	334/441-5338
Montgomery, AL	334/223-7507
Nashville, TN	615/781-5364

New Orleans Field Division:

Baton Rouge, LA	225/389-0485
Biloxi, MS	601/863-4871
Jackson, MS	601/965-4205
Little Rock, AR	501/324-6181
New Orleans, LA	504/841-7000
Oxford, MS	601/234-3751
Shreveport, LA	318/676-3301

New York Field Division:

Melville, NY	631/694-8372
Newark, NJ	201/357-4070
New York, NY	212/466-5145

Philadelphia Field Division:

Atlantic City, NJ	609/625-2228
Camden, NJ	609/968-4884
Harrisburg, PA	717/221-3402
Philadelphia, PA	215/597-7266

Pittsburgh, PA	412/395-6911
Reading, PA	610/320-5222
Trenton, NJ	609/989-2155

Phoenix Field Division:

Albuquerque, NM	505/346-6910
Cheyenne, WY	307/772-2346
Colorado Springs, CO	719/473-0166
Denver, CO	303/866-1173
Phoenix, AZ	602/776-5400
Salt Lake City, UT	801/524-5853
Tucson, AZ	520/670-4725

San Francisco Field Division:

Bakersfield, CA	805/861-4420
Fresno, CA	559/487-5393
Las Vegas, NV	702/388-6584
Oakland, CA	510/637-3431
Reno, NV	775/784-5251
Sacramento, CA	916/498-5100
San Francisco, CA	415/744-7001

Seattle Field Division:

Anchorage, AK	907/271-5701
Billings, MT	406/657-6886
Boise, ID	208/334-1983
Helena, MT	406/441-1100
Honolulu, HI	808/541-2670
Portland, OR	503/326-2171
Seattle, WA	206/220-6440
Spokane, WA	509/324-7866
Yakima, WA	509/454-4404

St. Paul Field Division:

Fargo, ND	701/239-5176
Milwaukee, WI	414/297-3937
Sioux Falls, SD	605/330-4368
St. Paul, MN	651/290-3092

Washington Field Division:

Bristol, VA	540/466-2727
Falls Church, VA	703/285-2551
Norfolk, VA	757/441-3190
Richmond, VA	804/560-0005
Roanoke, VA	540/857-2300
Washington, D.C.	202/927-8810

Also see...*NATIONAL INSTANT CRIMINAL BACK-GROUND CHECK SYSTEM.*

BUREAU OF PRISONS (FEDERAL)
See...*PRISON HISTORIES, FEDERAL.*

Also see...*STATE PRISONS.*

BUSINESS BACKGROUND INVESTIGATIONS

Experian Online Services sells "Snapshot Reports" on more than 13 million U.S. companies. Information returned includes credit risk data. The basic search is free. If a hit is obtained, a full report costs $14.95.

www.experian.com

The U.S. Dept. of Commerce Library reference desk will check standard business reference publications for basic background information on businesses.

202/482-5511

Dun & Bradstreet is the leading business credit reporting company. Their business information reports typically contain limited information on trade accounts and public records, such as tax liens. Dollar for dollar, not a great deal.

Customer Service   800/234-3867
                                    www.dnb.com

Standard & Poor's Online Registry provides information on public and private companies, their owners and key executives.

800/237-8552
www.standardandpoor.com

For $100, this *U.S. Dept. of Commerce* unit will provide a credit report and background info on foreign companies. Ask for *World Trade Data Reports.*

202/482-4204
www.doc.gov

Graydon America offers online business credit reports on overseas companies to its registered users.

800/466-3163
www.graydonamerica.com

CreditRiskMonitor.com offers real-time financial information 24 hours a day. It provides detailed analytical company reports, a real-time news service and an e-mail notification service that automatically e-mails you a news headline on any company in your profile within minutes of the article's release. Their database is updated continuously and monitors more than 8,400 U.S. public companies.

www.creditriskmonitor.com

The Export-Import Bank of the United States will provide credit data on foreign companies to whom it has extended credit. It can also provide loan repayment statistics for countries as a whole.

202/565-3960
www.exim.gov

Also see...*CORPORATIONS*.

Also see...*CANADIAN CORPORATIONS*.

Also see...*ECONOMIC NEWS*.

Also see...*COMMODITY FUTURES*.

Also see...*BUSINESSCREDITUSA.COM*.

BUSINESSCREDITUSA.COM

When information is needed on a business, $3 will get you off to a good start with a business profile from *BusinessCreditUSA. com*. Information returned includes location, names of key management, approximate number of employees, business type and years in business. Also included are bankruptcies, tax liens and judgments. Look for photographs of company store fronts to be added in the future. There's no charge for conducting the initial search to identify the company. No subscription is necessary; pay online with a credit card.

www.businesscreditusa.com

BUSINESS ESPIONAGE

Business Espionage Controls & Countermeasures Association is a professional organization of investigators specializing in the detection of "bugs" as well as more conventional snooping methods.

301/292-6430

Also see...*FEDERAL BUREAU OF INVESTIGATION* for information on ANSIR.

Also see...*DEBUGGING*.

Also see...*NATIONAL COUNTERINTELLIGENCE CEN-TER*.

Also see...*OVERSEAS SECURITY ADVISORY COUNCIL*.

CALIBRE PRESS

Calibre Press puts out a unique and interesting book/video catalog that many investigators will find worthwhile. Primarily targeting police officers, the catalog includes such titles as *Pocket Partner*, *The Counterterrorism Handbook* and *First Response Guide to Street Drugs*.

800/323-0037
www.calibrepress.com

CANADIAN CORPORATIONS

Infomart Online is an online information service focusing on Canadian business. Includes newspapers, newswires, corporate profiles, more.

800/668-9215
www.infomart.ca

CANADIAN GOVERNMENT
Reference Canada   800/667-3355
www.canada.gc.ca

Revenue Canada   800/622-6232

Ministry of Corporate and Consumer
Relations   416/326-8555

Ministry of Justice and Attorney
General   613/992-4621

American Consulate, Toronto   416/595-1700

For information on Canadian Motor Vehicle Licensing, see
DRIVER RECORDS.

For information on obtaining vital records in Canada:

www.archives.ca

CANADIAN INVESTIGATIONS
Nationwide directory assistance in Canada
can be searched on the Internet at *Canada
411.*

http://canada411.sympatico.ca

Private investigators in Canada can be located through the
following organizations:

Alberta Association of Private
Investigators   403/257-5703
www.alberta-investigators.org

Canadian Private Investigators
Resource Centre   *www.cpirc.com*

Council of Private Investigators
– Ontario   519/471-4681
www.cpi-ontario.com

Private Investigators Association
of British Columbia   877/319-3388
                                    604/878-4388

CAP INDEX
The CAP Index is a computer driven
model which purports to be an accurate
predictor of crime vulnerability for any
given location. It includes not only actual crime reports, but

also elements of "social disorder" such as nearby poverty. It's used by companies to grade the crime risk of potential locations and by insurance companies, attorneys and others in connection with crime-related civil litigation. A report for any given address can be ordered at their website for $150. They also offer expert witness testimony to back up the reports.

800/227-7475
610/903-3000
www.capindex.com

CARFAX

NEW! Designed for consumer use, *Carfax* may occasionally be of use to investigators who otherwise have access to their own state's official motor vehicle records. The service lets the user submit a VIN (Vehicle Identification Number) and receive back a title history of the vehicle sans ownership information. (Their data is for cars and light trucks only — commercial trucks are not included.) The site may be useful to investigators in a couple of ways. First, it includes a free VIN decoder. By entering a VIN number, the model year, make and model will be returned instantly and at no cost. The second use is more obscure, but may be of interest to investigators who need to determine the out-of-state registration history of a vehicle. For example, has a stolen or repossession-designated vehicle been taken to another state and re-plated? If it has been re-registered out of state; the state where it has been registered should be indicated. There's generally a two to three-month reporting lag time. The cost is $14.95 to run the VIN and receive its *Carfax* history. *Carfax* is not the end-all for a vehicle investigation, but it may be useful from time to time.

www.carfax.com

CASINOS

NEW! *World Gaming Network* is an employment screening company used by casinos and other gaming interests. The company maintains a proprietary Employment History Database collected from member casinos with employee hire/fire information. The information is restricted under the Fair Credit Reporting Act. It's available to member firms only.

877/224-9134
www.wgnscreen.com

International Casino Monitoring provides intelligence on casino cheats.

609/499-7378
www.intcasmon.ndirect.co.uk

The Nevada State Gaming Control Board publishes its "Black Book" of cheats barred from the state's casinos. Free upon request.

702/687-6500
www.gaming.state.nv.us

New Jersey Division of
Gaming Enforcement   609/292-9394
www.state.nj.us/lps/ge/index

New Jersey Casino Control
Commission   609/441-3200
www.state.nj.us/casinos

The largest collection of gambling-related literature in the world can be found at the *University of Nevada, Las Vegas Special Collections Department.*

702/895-2234
www.library.nevada.edu/speccol

The Indian Gaming Management Staff at the *Bureau of Indian Affairs* maintains information on Indian tribes with gaming interests. There are currently compacts with 157 tribes in 24 states.

202/219-4066
www.doi.gov/bia

The National Indian Gaming Association is a trade group representing over 142 Indian nations who operate casinos or other gaming interests.

202/546-7711
www.indiangaming.org

CELEBRITY LOCATES

HOT! Locating celebrities and other high profile persons from the worlds of entertainment or sports is fraught with peril for private investigators. First comes the issue of the client and his or her intent — does the investigator *absolutely* know that the client is not a celebrity stalker? Secondly comes another difficult question: Can the investigator find the privacy-seeking celebrity or will he find dead-ends at publicity offices, fan mail clubs and mail drops? A smart solution to both problems is to subcontract your work to Los Angeles private investigator *John Grogan* who maintains a 10,000 name file containing address and other vital information on celebrities. He'll accomplish your mission in a manner that does not risk the safety of the celebrity. He's typically used for service of process but also acts as a go-between to deliver fan mail, scripts and other items.

818/883-6969
www.johngrogan.com

Book publisher *Axiom Information Resources* publishes several books containing celebrity contact information and dates of birth. Look to receive mostly fan club, mail drop and agent addresses here.

734/761-4842
www.celebritylocator.com

Contact information for actors and other celebrities who are members of the *Screen Actors Guild* (SAG) can be obtained at the SAG actor's location line. You'll get an agent's name and phone number.

323/549-6737
www.sag.org

Similar information for television and radio talent may be found through their union, *AFTRA*.

212/532-0800
323/634-8100
www.aftra.org

CELL PHONE COMPANIES

AT&T Wireless:
Customer Service	800/888-7600
Prepaid Wireless	800/761-9878
Fraud Department	800/504-2096
Subpoenas/Search Warrants	800/635-6840

www.attws.com

Cingular Wireless:
Customer Service	866/CINGULAR
Subpoenas/Search Warrants	866-254-3277

www.cingular.com

Nextel:
Customer Service	800/639-6111
Subpoena Compliance	703/433-8860

www.nextel.com

Sprint PCS:
Customer Service	800/480-4727
Consumers	888/211-4727
Business	888/788-4727
Subpoenas/Electronic Surveillance	800/877-7330
Call Trace Bureau (To report harassing calls)	877/451-1980

www.sprintpcs.com

Verizon Wireless:
Customer Service	888-466-4646
	800/247-8682
Paging Customer Service	888-247-7890
Subpoenas, Court Orders, Wiretaps	908/429-3885

verizonwireless.com

CELL PHONE FRAUD
See...*COMMUNICATIONS FRAUD CONTROL ASSOCIATION*.

CENSUS BUREAU, U.S.
Public Information Office   301/457-3030
www.census.gov

CENTERS FOR DISEASE CONTROL
General Information   404/639-3311
www.cdc.gov

Centers for Disease Control,
Travelers' Health Hotline   877/FYI-TRIP

Press Office, CDC   404/639-3286

CENTRAL INTELLIGENCE AGENCY
Headquarters   703/482-1100
www.cia.gov

For background information on select current and former operatives, see...*NAMEBASE*.

CERTIFIED PUBLIC ACCOUNTANTS
"CPA" means *Certified Public Accountant*. Among other things, requirements to be a CPA include a college degree, passage of a national exam and continuing education on changes in tax law. To check if a person is really a CPA, call your state's Board of Accountancy:

Alabama	334/242-5700
Alaska	907/465-2580
Arizona	602/255-3648
Arkansas	501/682-1520
California	916/263-3680
Colorado	303/894-7800
Connecticut	203/566-7835
Delaware	302/739-4522
District of Columbia	202/727-7468
Florida	352/955-2165
Georgia	404/656-3941
Guam Territorial	671/646-3884
Hawaii	808/586-2694
Idaho	208/334-2490
Illinois	217/333-1565
Indiana	317/232-5987
Iowa	515/281-4126
Kansas	913/296-2162
Kentucky	502/595-3037
Louisiana	504/566-1244
Maine	207/582-8723
Maryland	410/333-6322

Massachusetts	617/727-1806
Michigan	517/241-9249
Minnesota	612/296-7937
Mississippi	601/354-7320
Missouri	314/751-0012
Montana	406/444-3739
Nebraska	402/471-3595
Nevada	702/786-0231
New Hampshire	603/271-3286
New Jersey	973/504-6380
New Mexico	505/841-9109
New York	518/474-3836
North Carolina	919/733-4222
North Dakota	701/775-7100
Ohio	614/466-4135
Oklahoma	405/521-2397
Oregon	503/378-4181
Pennsylvania	717/783-1404
Puerto Rico	809/722-2122
Rhode Island	401/277-3185
South Carolina	803/734-4228
South Dakota	605/367-5770
Tennessee	615/741-2550
Texas	512/305-7850
Utah	801/530-6456
Vermont	802/828-2837
Virgin Islands	809/773-4305
Virginia	804/367-8590
Washington	360/558-3557
West Virginia	304/558-3557
Wisconsin	608/266-1397
Wyoming	307/777-7551

CHARITABLE ORGANIZATIONS

Start a background check of a tax-exempt organization at *GuideStar.com*, a privately run website rich with IRS tax-exempt organization information. Information returned usually includes income and expense data as well as the organization's Employer Identification Number.

www.guidestar.com

Or to learn much of the same information by telephone, contact the IRS at its tax-exempt organization customer service number. They'll tell you whether or not an organization has tax-exempt status, as well as its EIN and other information.

877/829-5500

Tax-exempt organizations with a minimum annual gross income of $25,000 or more are required to file IRS form 990. This is their tax return, so to speak. Form 990's are public record and can be obtained from the IRS. Use IRS Form 4506A and fax or mail your request. There's a copy charge of $1 for the first page and 15 cents for each additional page. They'll bill you.

Fax 801/775-8803

Internal Revenue Service
Attn.: Stop# 6716/EO Photocopy Unit
P.O. Box 9953
Ogden, UT 84409

If you don't have a blank copy of IRS Form 4506A, go to the IRS website and then scroll down to 4506A.

www.irs.gov/forms_pubs/forms.html

The BBB Wise Giving Alliance is a provider of information on charitable organizations. Mini-dossiers are currently available for free on the Internet.

703/276-0100
www.give.org

The American Institute of Philanthropy is another watchdog group focusing on charitable groups. They publish a quarterly guide to charities which includes rankings based on openness and cost of fundraising.

301/913-5200
www.charitywatch.org

All states register charitable organizations. Contact one of these numbers to receive background information on charitable organizations:

Alabama	334/242-7335
Alaska	907/562-0704
Arizona	602/542-4285
Arkansas	501/682-2007
California	916/445-2021
Colorado	303/894-2680
Connecticut	860/808-5030
Delaware	302/577-8400
District of Columbia	202/442-4400
Florida	850/488-2221
Georgia	404/656-3920
Hawaii	808/586-2727
Idaho	208/334-2300
Illinois	312/814-2595
Indiana	317/232-6201
Iowa	515/281-5926
Kansas	785/296-4564
Kentucky	502/696-5389
Louisiana	225/342-9638
Maine	207/624-8624
Maryland	410/974-5534
Massachusetts	617/727-2200
Michigan	517/373-1152

Minnesota	651/296-3353
Mississippi	888/236-6167
Missouri	573/751-4936
Montana	406/444-2034
Nebraska	402/471-2554
Nevada	775/684-5708
New Hampshire	603/271-3591
New Jersey	973/504-6262
New Mexico	505/222-9092
New York	212/416-8401
North Carolina	919/733-4510
North Dakota	701/328-2900
Ohio	614/466-3180
Oklahoma	405/521-3049
Oregon	503/229-5548
Pennsylvania	800/732-0999
Rhode Island	401/222-3048
South Carolina	803/734-1790
South Dakota	605/773-4400
Tennessee	615/741-2555
Texas	512/463-2185
Utah	801/530-6601
Vermont	802/828-2386
Virginia	804/786-1343
Washington	800/332-4483
West Virginia	304/558-6000
Wisconsin	608/266-5511
Wyoming	307/777-7311

CHECK FRAUD

These companies maintain databases of persons who have written checks with insufficient funds or on closed accounts. These aren't databases set up for investigators, though. Rather, they're geared toward merchants who must typically open an account and pay a monthly minimum charge:

TeleCheck	713/599-7600
	800/710-9898
	www.telecheck.com

Equifax	404/885-8000
Equifax Check Systems	800/437-5120
	www.equifax.com

| National Check Fraud Service | 843/571-2143 |

| SCAN | 800/262-7771 |

| CrossCheck | 707/586-0551 |

| International Check Services | 800/526-5380 |

One highly knowledgeable source of how counterfeit and other bad check schemes are run is *Frank Abagnale* — who himself is a former convicted check forger. Today, he's relied upon by the FBI, major banks and corporations to stem losses from check schemes.

800/237-7443
www.abagnale.com

CHEMICAL SPILLS - EMERGENCY HOTLINES
Chemtrec is the chemical industry's emergency hotline for chemical and hazardous substance spills.

800/424-9300
www.chemtrec.com

To report an oil or chemical spill, call the Coast Guard's *National Response Center*.

800/424-8802
202/267-2675
www.nrc.uscg.mil

Chemical Accident Reconstruction Services is an Arizona based firm specializing in analysis of chemical spills.

800/645-3369
www.chemaxx.com

Also see...*TOXIC CHEMICALS*.

Also see...*NFPA Hazardous Material Symbols* in our *Reference Guide*.

CHICAGO CRIME COMMISSION
The Chicago Crime Commission is a not-for-profit organization that has been gathering information on mobsters since 1919. *CCC* maintains an extensive library of local news clippings on mobsters, going back decades.

312/372-0101
www.chicagocrimecommission.org

CHILD ABDUCTION
See...*INTERNATIONAL CHILD ABDUCTION*.

Also see...*NATIONAL CENTER FOR MISSING & EX-PLOITED CHILDREN*.

Also see...*MISSING CHILDREN*.

CHILD ABUSE
There are many organizations set up to aid in the search for missing children. Only one has quasi-governmental status which includes partial access to NCIC and other usually law-enforcement-only resources. *The National Center for*

Missing and Exploited Children is active in not only the recovery of abducted children, but also in the prevention of various types of sexual exploitation. Assistance offered to law enforcement includes photograph and poster preparation, technical case assistance and forensic services. *NCMEC* collaborates with the U.S. Secret Service's Forensic Division to provide handwriting, polygraph, fingerprint and other technical forensic assistance.

800/THE-LOST
703/235-3900
www.missingkids.org

For assistance in reporting child abuse, nationwide, contact the *Childhelp USA National Child Abuse Hotline.*

800/4-A-CHILD
(TDD) 800/2-A-CHILD

Or contact these statewide offices to report abuse. Not all states have a statewide reporting office. In these states, contact local law enforcement or the above listed *National Child Abuse Hotline.*

Alabama		334/242-9500
Alaska		800/478-4444
Arizona		888/SOS-CHILD
Arkansas		800/482-5964
California		916/445-2832
Colorado		303/866-3003
Connecticut		800/842-2288
		800/624-5518
	(TDD)	800/842-2288
Delaware		800/292-9582
		302/577-6550
District of Columbia		202/671-7233
Florida		800/962-2873
Georgia		N/A
Hawaii		N/A
Idaho		N/A
Illinois		800/252-2873
		217/524-2606
Indiana		800/562-2407
		800/800-5556
Iowa		800/362-2178
		515/281-3240
Kansas		800/922-5330
		785/296-0044
Kentucky		800/752-6200
		502/564-2136
Louisiana		225/342-6832
Maine		800/452-1999
		207/287-2983
	(TTY)	207/287-3492

Maryland		800/332-6347
Massachusetts		800/792-5200
		617/232-4882
Michigan		800/942-4357
		517/373-3572
Minnesota		N/A
Mississippi		800/222-8000
		601/359-4991
Missouri		800/392-3738
		573/751-3448
Montana		800/332-6100
		406/444-5900
Nebraska		800/652-1999
		402/471-9196
Nevada		800/992-5757
		775/684-4400
New Hampshire		800/894-5533
		603/225-9000
New Jersey		800/792-8610
	(TDD)	800/835-5510
New Mexico		800/797-3260
		505/841-6100
New York		800/342-3720
		518/474-8740
North Carolina		800/354-KIDS
North Dakota		701/328-2316
		800/245-3736
Ohio		614/466-9824
Oklahoma		800/522-3511
		405/841-0800
Oregon		800/854-3508
		ext. 2402
		503/378-5414
	(TTY)	503/378-6704
Pennsylvania		800/932-0313
		717/783-8744
Rhode Island		800/RI-CHILD
		800/742-4453
		401/222-4996
South Carolina		803/898-7318
South Dakota		605/773-3227
Tennessee		615/532-3545
Texas		800/252-5400
		512/834-3784
Utah		800/678-9399
Vermont		802/241-2131
		800/649-5285
Virginia		800/552-7096
		804/786-8536
Washington		800/562-5624
West Virginia		800/352-6513
		304/558-7980
Wisconsin		608/266-3036
Wyoming		800/457-3659

CHILD SUPPORT ENFORCEMENT
State agencies who enforce child support orders:

Alabama	334/242-9300
Alaska	907/269-6800
Arizona	602/252-4045
Arkansas	501/682-6047
California	916/654-1556
Colorado	303/866-5700
Connecticut	800/842-1508
Delaware	302/577-4807
District of Columbia	202/724-1444
Florida	800/622-5437
Georgia	404/657-3851
Hawaii	888/317-9081
Idaho	800/926-2588
Illinois	447/526-5812
Indiana	800/840-8757
Iowa	515/242-5530
Kansas	800/537-7072
Kentucky	800/248-1163
Louisiana	225/342-4780
Maine	207/287-2826
Maryland	800/332-6347
Massachusetts	800/332-2733
Michigan	517/373-7570
Minnesota	651/296-2542
Mississippi	601/359-4863
Missouri	800/859-7999
Montana	406/444-3338
Nebraska	402/479-5555
Nevada	702/455-4755
New Hampshire	800/852-3345
New Jersey	609/588-2401
New Mexico	800/585-7631
New York	518/474-9081
North Carolina	919/571-4120
North Dakota	701/328-3582
Ohio	614/752-6561
Oklahoma	405/522-5871
Oregon	503/986-6083
Pennsylvania	717/787-3672
Rhode Island	401/222-3845
South Carolina	800/768-5858
South Dakota	605/773-3641
Tennessee	615/313-4880
Texas	806/765-0094
Utah	801/536-8911
Vermont	802/241-2319
Virginia	804/692-1501
Washington	800/442-KIDS
West Virginia	304/558-3780
Wisconsin	608/339-4428
Wyoming	307/777-7193

Tip: The *U.S. Department of Health and Human Services* maintains a list of deadbeat parents who owe more than $5,000 in back child support. Persons named on this list will not be issued a passport for travel outside of the U.S. until the arrears are satisfied. (Code of Federal Regulations, Title 22, Section 51.70 (a) (8))

Also see...*FEDERAL PARENT LOCATOR SERVICE*.

CHOICEPOINT
See...*DATABASE PROVIDERS*.

CITY NEWS SERVICE

An investigator who goes undercover as a member of the press may want to know about *City News Service*. The company provides press credentials to freelance reporters looking for respectability. Their catalog offers "City News Service" press passes, auto press cards, business cards, baseball caps and other useful props. Call for their catalog.

417/469-2423

Looking to step up in the world? You might want to know that the *Associated Press* sells AP baseball caps and Polo shirts. Visit their website and click the Company Store button.

www.ap.org

COALITION ON POLITICAL ASSASSINATIONS
Comprised of medical and forensic experts, academics, authors and investigators, *COPA* has led the charge into reopening the investigations of the murders of the Kennedys, Martin Luther King, Jr. and others. Their primary focus is on unlocking secret government files through legal action.

415/563-4453

COAST GUARD, U.S.
Headquarters   202/267-2229
                                    www.uscg.mil

Coast Guard Investigative Service   202/493-6600

U.S. Coast Guard National Vessel Documentation Center maintains information on vessel ownership. Title papers are available for $25.

800/799-8362
304/271-2400

USCG Office of Boating Safety
Infoline   800/368-5647

Coast Guard World Wide Locator provides duty stations for active duty personnel.

202/267-0581
www.uscg.mil/locator.html

SOS — for Maritime search and rescue emergencies:
Great Lakes, Gulf and East Coasts: 757/398-6231
Hawaiian, Alaskan and Pacific Coasts: 510/437-3701

For information on past search and rescue missions, call:

202/267-1948

Coast Guard records of vessel registrations are viewable on the Internet. Go to *Black Book Online* and click the "Vessels" button.

www.crimetime.com/online.htm

Also see...*MARITIME INFORMATION SYSTEM*.

Also see...*SHIP INFORMATION*.

COMBINED DNA INDEX SYSTEM (CODIS)
CODIS is the little known but rapidly growing database of DNA samples taken from hundreds of thousands of convicted violent offenders. The system is installed in 104 laboratories in 43 states and the District of Columbia. All 50 states have enacted DNA database laws requiring the collection of a DNA sample from specified categories of convicted offenders.

202/324-3000
www.fbi.gov/hq/lab/org/systems.htm
www.fbi.gov/hq/lab/codis/program.htm

COMMODITY FUTURES
To report fraud and/or make complaints, contact the *Commodity Futures Trading Commission.*

202/418-5000
www.cftc.gov

The National Futures Association is the commodity futures industry's self-regulatory organization. Disciplinary and background information are kept on persons and firms involved in commodity futures trading. Includes an online background search.

800/621-3570
312/781-1410
www.nfa.futures.org

COMMUNICATIONS FRAUD CONTROL ASSOCIATION

NEW! Association to combat telecommunications fraud. Members include phone company security personnel, law enforcement agents and others. A weekly faxed fraud alert, quarterly journal and member directory are included with membership.

602/265-CFCA
www.cfca.org

COMPUTER CRIME

The U.S. Department of Justice has set up a portal for computer crime information, located on the web at *cybercrime.gov*. The site includes relevant laws, cases, and policy. The DOJ unit that operates the site is called the *Computer Crime and Intellectual Property Section*. The unit is staffed during business hours by CCIPS attorneys who will provide expertise on computer crime cases to authorized government agencies.

202/514-1026
www.cybercrime.gov

The FBI's *National Infrastructure Protection Center* is the government's primary command and control center for the investigation of major computer crimes including hacking attempts, Denial of Service attacks and viruses. When the Melissa virus spread across the Internet, shutting down computers and networks, NIPC led the investigation. Contact NIPC at FBI headquarters in Washington, D.C. or at any of the 16 FBI field offices that currently have computer crime squads.

202/323-3205
www.nipc.gov

Technically advanced investigators will want to read and learn from *CyberNotes*, the bi-weekly online newsletter of the *National Infrastructure Protection Center*. Find it online:

www.nipc.gov/cybernotes/cybernotes.htm

Local FBI Computer Crime Squads:

Atlanta	404/679-9000
Baltimore	410/265-8080
Boston	617/742-5533
Charlotte, NC	704/377-9200
Chicago	312/431-1333
Dallas	214/720-2200
Houston	713/693-5000
Los Angeles	310/477-6565
Miami	305/944-9101
Newark, NJ	973/792-3000
New Orleans	504/816-3000

New York	212/384-1000
San Diego	619/565-1255
San Francisco	415/553-7400
Seattle	206/622-0460
Washington, D.C.	202/278-2000

When the FBI seizes and searches computers as forensic evidence, look for its *Computer Analysis and Response Team* (CART) to be involved. This is a division of the FBI Crime Lab.

202/324-9307
www.fbi.gov/programs/lab/org/cart.htm

In the near future, you'll be hearing more and more about CART's new secret weapon — *ACES* (Automated Computer Examination System). It's a high tech automation of computer examination procedures that were formerly tedious and time consuming. It combines hardware with software to conduct many routine examinations in a self-documenting, automated method. It's currently being distributed to all FBI field offices.

Carnivore is the FBI's much publicized *and* criticized black box for snooping on e-mail. Installed at an ISP, it's the Internet version of a traditional phone company wiretap placed at a telco building. An FBI spokesperson has described the device, which is software driven, as nothing more than a specialized sniffer. "Sniffer" refers to hacker software set to filter large amounts of data for keywords or passwords.

www.fbi.gov/programs/carnivore/carnivore2.htm

The FBI's *Computer Training Unit*, located at the FBI Academy in Quantico, Virginia, trains new agents, non-federal law enforcement agents, CART personnel and NIPC personnel.

703/632-1939
www.fbi.gov/programs/academy/ctu/ctu.htm

The Customs *Cyber-Smuggling Center* is a Virginia-based unit that focuses on Internet-related crimes such a money laundering, child pornography and intellectual property rights theft.

703/293-8005
www.customs.gov/enforcem/cyber.htm

The National Computer Security Center is a section of the National Security Agency that sets security standards for government computer systems.

301/975-2934
www.nsa.gov/isso/partners/ncsc.htm

U.S. Secret Service, Electronic
Crimes Branch   202/406-5850
                          www.ustreas.gov/usss

Information on computer viruses and how to recognize and
defeat them can be found on the web at *McAfee's Virus
Information Library*. Has over 75,000 viruses cataloged as
of our publication date.

http://vil.mcaffee.com

Password theft is a threat to web-based businesses who sell
access to their products. *Password Cop* is software aimed at
protecting these sites.

www.passwdcop.com

Past hacker-attacks against high profile websites are cataloged by website *attrition.org*. To date, they've profiled
over 2,000 such attacks.

www.attrition.org

Looking to determine the vulnerability of an existing
computer system or network? *Rent-A-Hacker* is a fee-based
firm that hires reformed hackers. They'll be turned loose on
your system without malicious intent to search for security
holes. Minnesota-based.

888/309-9300
218/739-9300
www.rent-a-hacker.com

Have a computer security problem along the lines of
hacking, counterfeit e-mail or other security breaches?
Consider seeking assistance from *Talon Executive Services,
Inc.*

714/434-7476
www.talonexec.com

Information Systems Security Association has a
membership of persons who protect computerized
information.

414/768-8000
www.issa.org

Janus Associates provides information security, computer
forensics, and business recovery consulting services. They
audit computer systems for vulnerability to intrusion and
fraud. They also offer data recovery services for legal
purposes in situations where the data has been "deleted."

203/964-1150
www.janusassociates.com

The *National Institute of Standards and Technology Computer Security Lab* offers publications and a BBS on computer security.

301/975-2920
www.nist.gov

If you want to know what's on the collective mind of the hacker community, check out *2600: The Hacker Quarterly*. It's also referred to as "The Hacker's Bible" by some. Can be gotten through subscription and also at many bookstores.

516/751-2600
www.2600.com

High Technology Crime Investigation Association is for the investigation of computer crime and the security of computer systems. Membership is limited to law enforcement officers and management level security professional in the private sector. Twenty-seven local chapters throughout the country. Check their website for locations.

540/937-5019
www.htcia.org

Metropolitan Police Service (known also as New Scotland Yard) has a *Computer Crime Unit*, which deals with crimes such as hacking and computer-based fraud.

011-44-207-230-1177

The Department of Defense Computer Forensics Laboratory conducts computer examinations, intrusion analysis, data recovery and more for the military.

877/981-3235
410/981-0100
www.dcfl.gov

Also see...*INTERNET FRAUD*.

Also see...*SCAMBUSTERS.ORG*.

Also see...*DATA RECOVERY*.

Also see...*SPYWARE*.

Also see...the *Computer Crime* section in our *Privacy Law Survival Guide*.

COMPUTER PRIVACY DIGEST

Computer Privacy Digest is a weekly e-mail newsletter that will be of interest to investigators who want to keep an ear to what is being said by the privacy underground. It focuses on computerized personal information that is kept by big brother in his many disguises. Some of the information is urban legend; some is insightful and cutting edge. Look for plenty of paranoia about SSNs and cookies (the computer kind, not the chocolate-chip kind) here, too. Free. To subscribe, send an e-mail to *comp-privacy-request@uwm. edu*. In both the subject line and body of the e-mail type the word "subscribe."

CONCEALED WEAPON LICENSES

 Information on concealed weapon permits in all states can be found at the *Packing.org* website.

www.packing.org

Also see our *Reference Guide* for a state-by-state list.

Data company *AutoTrackXP* includes information on concealed weapon permits that have been issued in Florida. See...*DATABASE PROVIDERS*.

Also see...*BUREAU OF ALCOHOL, TOBACCO & FIRE-ARMS*.

CONGRESSIONAL INFO

Pending legislation in the U.S. House of Representatives and Senate can be identified through the *Bill Status Office*. Computerized searching can be done by topic or keyword.

202/225-1772
www.congress.gov

For hourly recorded updates of activity on the House or Senate floor, use these numbers:

House Cloakroom (Republicans)	202/225-7430
House Cloakroom (Democrats)	202/225-7400
Senate Cloakroom (Republicans)	202/224-8601
Senate Cloakroom (Democrats)	202/224-8541

CONSUMER SENTINEL

The Federal Trade Commission rears its ugly big brother head again in the name of consumer protection with the Consumer Sentinel database. It collects information from the Better Business Bureau, Postal Inspectors and law enforcement agencies to catalog fraud schemes on the Internet and elsewhere. Problem is, there's no access to this information by the public and it's not used to initiate criminal investigations. They'll let us know what they think we need to know.

www.ftc.gov/sentinel/index

COPERNIC

Sifting through the billion or so pages of information on the Internet with conventional directories (like Yahoo) and search engines (like Lycos) remains a hit or miss proposition — usually miss *Copernic* is a software solution that results in more effective searching in less time You'll enter your search criteria on the *Copernic* search screen and then it will simultaneously send the search to leading search engines and organize the returns in quick-to-use order after eliminating duplicates and dead links. *2-10-04 Reprint Update Copernic was great until the advent of google search technology Forget Copernic and go to google com*

www google com

COPYRIGHT INFORMATION
U S Copyright Office,
Library of Congress   202/707-3000
www lcweb.loc gov/copyright

Copyright filings made since January 1978 can now be searched on the Internet Unfortunately, the search system, called LOCIS, is an awkward-to-use Telnet interface Visit the web address below and you'll be walked through the process For pre-1978 filings, obtain Circular 22, "How to Investigate the Copyright Status of a Work "

www loc gov/copyright/rb html

CORONERS
Coroners, also known a *Medical Examiners*, are an early source of information in any death investigation

National Association of Medical Examiners	314/577-8298
	www.thename org
Anchorage	907/269-5090
Atlanta	404/730-4400
Baltimore	410/333-3226
Boston	617/267-6767
Charlotte	919/962-6263
Chicago	312/666-0500
Cincinnati	513/221-4524
Cleveland	216/721-5610
Columbus	614/462-5290
Dallas	214/920-5900
Denver	303/436-7711
Detroit	810/469-5214
Honolulu	808/527-6777
Houston	713/796-9292
Kansas City	913/299-1474

Las Vegas	702/455-3210
Los Angeles	323/343-0512
Miami	305/545-2400
Milwaukee	414/223-1200
Minneapolis	612/347-2125
New Orleans	504/524-6763
New York	212/447-2034
Oakland	510/268-7300
Philadelphia	215/823-7457
Phoenix	602/506-3322
Pittsburgh	412/350-4800
Portland	503/248-3746
St. Louis	314/622-4971
Salt Lake City	801/584-8435
San Antonio	210/615-2100
San Diego	858/694-2895
San Francisco	415/553-1694
San Jose	408/793-1900
Seattle	206/223-3232
Washington, D.C.	202/698-9000

CORPORATIONS

CorporateInformation.com is a free web-based search engine that provides links to over 350,000 corporate profiles.

www.corporateinformation.com

Each state has a department of corporations that registers corporations doing business in that state. Information typically includes corporate officers, registered agents, location and history:

Alabama	334/242-5324
Alaska	907/465-2521
Arizona	602/542-4251
Arkansas	501/682-3409
California	916/657-5448
Colorado	303/894-2251
Connecticut	860/270-8000
Delaware	302/739-3073
D.C.	202/727-3400
Florida	904/487-6053
Georgia	404/656-2817
Hawaii	808/586-2744
Idaho	208/334-2300
Illinois	217/782-7880
Indiana	317/232-6576
Iowa	515/281-8993
Kansas	785/296-4564
Kentucky	502/564-2848
Louisiana	225/925-4704
Maine	207/287-3676
Maryland	410/767-1184
Massachusetts	617/727-9640

Michigan	517/373-1820
Minnesota	651/296-2830
Mississippi	601/359-1633
Missouri	573/751-4153
Montana	406/444-2034
Nebraska	402/471-4080
Nevada	775/684-5708
New Hampshire	603/271-3244
New Jersey	609/292-9292
New Mexico	850/487-9000
New York	518/473-2492
(faster, pay-per-call line)	900/835-2677
North Carolina	919/807-2225
North Dakota	701/328-3662
Ohio	614/466-3910
Oklahoma	
($5 charge for up to 3 searches)	900/555-2424
Oregon	503/986-2200
Pennsylvania	717/787-1057
Rhode Island	401/222-3040
South Carolina	803/734-2158
South Dakota	605/773-4845
Tennessee	615/741-2286
Texas	512/475-2700
Utah	801/530-4849
Vermont	802/828-2386
Virginia	804/371-9733
Washington	360/753-7115
West Virginia	304/558-8000
Wisconsin	608/266-3590
Wyoming	307/777-7311

Many states have their data on the Internet, for free. For links to these sites, visit the corporation section at *Black Book Online.*

www.crimetime.com/online.htm

For states who do not offer this information for free, see... *DATABASE PROVIDERS.*

COUNTERFEIT CURRENCY
The U.S. Secret Service,
Counterfeit Division   202/406-8300
www.treas.gov/usss

Office of the Comptroller of the
Currency, Enforcement and
Compliance Division   202/874-4800
www.occ.treas.gov

COUNTERFEIT PRODUCTS
Counterfeit products are big business — there's no advertising costs, quality control is low, and often, the sales are in cash and no taxes are paid. It was only inevitable that

this would attract the interest of organized crime groups, including the Vietnamese gang BTK (Born to Kill) and the Wah Ching organized crime syndicate out of China. Investigators who specialize in counterfeit goods and IP (Intellectual Property) investigations will want to know about the *International Anti-Counterfeiting Coalition*. The group combats various forms of IP piracy through awareness, education, law enforcement training and the promotion of laws that serve as a deterrent to counterfeiting.

202/223-6667
www.iacc.org

To report suspected counterfeit Microsoft products, call the *Microsoft Anit-Piracy Hotline*:

800/RU-LEGIT
www.microsoft.com/piracy

To report counterfeit music tapes and CDs, contact the *Recording Industry of America Piracy Hotline*.

800/BAD-BEAT
www.riaa.com

Also see...*NATIONAL ANTI-PIRACY ASSOCIATION*.

Also see...*VIDEOTAPE PIRACY*.

COUNTRY CODE LOOKUPS
The *Reference Guide* of this book contains dialing codes for most nations worldwide.

For information on both country codes and city codes, visit the *AT&T Worldwide Traveler* website:

www.att.com/traveler/tools/codes.html

Speaking of AT&T, if you're a customer of this company and will be traveling abroad, you'll want to take along their free pocket guide to foreign access codes. Visit this web address and select the pocket guide. You'll be taken to a pdf page to download and print out this useful mini-guide.

www.att.com/traveler/global/global.html

CPAs
See...*CERTIFIED PUBLIC ACCOUNTANTS*.

CREDIT BUREAUS
Three "Super Bureaus" collect and disseminate personal financial information on millions of Americans. Release of the information is regulated by the Fair Credit Reporting Act and various state statutes. Note: Subpoenas must be signed by a judge. All three bureaus accept service by mail

at the addresses below. None charge a fee. Be sure to include the subject's social security number and current address when requesting a credit report by subpoena or search warrant.

EQUIFAX:

Equifax	800/685-5000
	800/685-1111
Subpoenas/Search Warrants	770/375-2613
	www.equifax.com

Mail subpoenas/search warrants to: *Equifax, Attn.: Custodian of Records, 1600 Peachtree Street, Atlanta, GA 30309.*

EXPERIAN:

Experian	888/397-3742
Subpoenas/Search Warrants	972/390-4016
	www.experian.com

Mail subpoenas/search warrants to: *Experian, Attn.: Custodian of Records, P.O. Box 1240, Allen, TX 75013.*

TRANSUNION:

TransUnion	800/888-4213
	800/916-8800
Subpoenas/Search Warrants	312/466-6401
	312/985-3821
	www.transunion.com

Mail subpoenas/search warrants to: *TransUnion, Attn.: Custodian of Records, 555 West Adams Street, Chicago, IL 60661.*

CREDIT CARD & FINANCE COMPANIES

American Express Card	954/503-3787
American General	909/884-1101
American Honda	800/408-6132
Associates Capital Bank	800/253-5710
AT&T Universal Bank	904/954-7500
Auto One Finance Corporation	800/725-4480
Bank Card Services	503/245-5595
Bank of America	800/423-3811
Bank of Hoven	605/948-2278

Bank of New York (DE)	800/777-9379
Bank One	202/833-6620
Bank One of Detroit	616/771-7000
BMW Financial Services	800/398-3939
BMW / Land Rover	800/578-5000
	800/398-3939
BP Oil / Amaco	800/227-3329
Broadway	800/531-7650
Cathay Bank	626/281-8808
Chase Bank	480/731-3009
Chemical Bank	517/839-5350
Chevron	800/243-8766
Chevy Chase	800/987-BANK
Chrysler Credit	800/289-1243
Chrysler Financial	949/788-4400
Citibank	800/843-0777
CitiFinancial	925/689-6620
City Capital	714/704-6236
Consecofin	605/355-7000
Countrywide Funding	626/304-8400
Countrywide Home Loans	805/520-5100
Diner's Card (Merchant Verification)	800/525-9040
Discover Card	800/DISCOVER
	800/347-2683
Diversified Ventures Inc.	847/564-5180
First Card	847/888-6000
	800/862-9356
First USA Bank	800/622-6528
Fleet Credit Card Service	215/956-0482
Ford Motor Credit	800/727-7000
	877/873-0085

GE Capital Auto Financial Services	800/488-5208
GMAC	800/200-4622
HSBC	800/975-4722
Home Depot	800/677-0232
Household Bank	800/477-6000
	800/685-1000
JC Penny	503/652-4700
	800/542-0800
Lord & Taylor	800/654-0520
Macys West	800/949-1800
MBNA America	302/456-8926
Mercedes Benz Credit	800/654-6222
	503/293-6100
Mellon Bank	800/753-7011
Neiman Marcus	800/753-0407
Nextel	303/721-3400
Nordstrom	206/233-6800
OSI Collection Service	206/315-1200
Primus Financial	800/945-8000
Providian Financial	800/356-0011
Sanwa Bank	310/278-3410
Sears	800/877-8691
Standard Oil (CA)	559/924-2064
	800/544-2064
Student Loan Marketing Association	888/272-5543
Toyota Motor Credit	626/821-3300
Union Bank / California	800/237-0561
United Mortgage Company	714/960-0722
Union Planters Bank of Miami	800/585-5361

VISA:

Customer Service	800/847-2911
Law Enforcement Assistance	800/367-8472
Washington Mutual	800/788-7000
Wells Fargo Bank	800/642-4720
WFNNB / Victoria Secret	800/695-1526
Wilshire State Bank	213/387-3200
Zales Jewelers	800/586-6923

CREDIT CARD FRAUD

International Association of Financial Crimes Investigators	415/884-6600
	www.iafci.org
Mastercard - Law Enforcement Assistance	800/231-1750
Visa Law Enforcement Assistance	800/367-8472
Discover Card Law Enforcement Assistance	800/347-3102

CREDIT CARD IDENTIFIER

Have a credit card number, but don't know the bank of issuance? By calling *Chase Merchant Service's* toll-free number, authorized users can identify the bank of issuance. Authorized users should choose option 2, then enter the first six digits of the credit card number, then hit the * key. The phone number of the bank which issued the credit card will be read by an automatic attendant.

800/326-7991

CREDIT REPORTS

See...*Credit Reports* in our *Privacy Law Survival Guide*.

Also see...*CREDIT BUREAUS*.

CRIME LABS

National Medical Services offers crime lab services including identification of poisons, drugs and food contaminants. In addition to criminal casework, consider them for use in product tampering and food poisoning matters as well. Also offered is a 24/7/365 STAT toxicology lab for urgent identification of the toxic agent in poisoning cases. Pennsylvania-based.

800/522-6671
24-hour *STAT Toxicological Lab* 877/782-8869
www.nmslab.com

The American Society of Crime Lab Directors is a professional organization which also provides accreditation for crime labs. Their website features an extensive list of accredited, government crime labs.

919/773-2600
www.ascld-lab.org

The Society of Forensic Toxicologists is limited to the study and identification of various types of poisons, including drugs. For a referral to a forensic toxicologist in your area, call:

480/839-9106
www.sof-tox.org

PoisonLab is a lab specializing in forensic toxicology. They'll identify drugs, poison and other toxins from biological specimens.

858/279-2600
www.poisonlab.com

ChemaTox Laboratory, Inc. is a Colorado based lab that offers a number of services, including drug identification, soil pollutants and arson (accelerant) testing.

800/334-1685
www.chematox.com

Forensic Science Consulting Group is a private crime/ forensics lab whose specialties include crime scene analysis, ballistics, fingerprints and trace evidence.

760/436-7714

Chemical Toxicology Institute is located in Northern California and focuses on drug and other laboratory tests.

650/573-6222
www.chemtoxinst.com

U.S. Department of Fish & Game's National Fish & Wildlife Forensic Lab has been called the first full-service wildlife crime lab in the world.

541/482-4191
www.lab.fws.gov

Also see...*FORENSIC SCIENCE COMMUNICATIONS*.

Also see...*DNA*.

Also see...*DRUG DETECTION*.

📷 NEW! CRIME MUSEUMS

*Al Capone's Hideaway and Steak
House*, St. Charles, IL   888/SCARFACE

Alcatraz Island,
San Francisco, CA   415/705-5555
www.nps.gov/alcatraz/

Bonnie and Clyde Museum,
Gibsland, LA   318/843-6141

Casino Legends Hall of Fame Museum at the Tropicana
Hotel and Casino in Las Vegas features an extensive exhibit
on the history of organized crime in Las Vegas.

888/826-8767
www.lvbegins.com/hof.cfm

The Conspiracy Museum, Dallas, TX   214/741-3040
800/535-8044
www.conspiracymuseum.com

The FBI Tour in Washington, D.C., runs daily Monday
through Friday between 8:45 a.m. and 11:45 a.m. on a first-
come, first-served basis. See a virtual tour online.

202/737-3759
www.fbi.gov/fbinbrief/tour/slide01.htm

The P.I. Museum, in San Diego, is a must-see for its
collection of rare historical artifacts relating to the field of
private investigation. See legendary P.I. Hal Lipset's 1972
Citroen SM and other neat stuff.

619/238-1985
www.pimuseum.com

Historical Museum of Lawmen,
Las Cruces, NM   505/525-1911

International Spy Museum,
Washington, D.C.   *www.spymuseum.org*

Jesse James Farm and Museum,
Kearney, MO   816/628-6065

*New York State Prison
(Sing Sing),* Ossining, NY   914/941-0108

*Oklahoma Prisons Historical
Museum*, McAlester, OK   918/423-4700

Old Idaho Penitentiary, Boise, ID   208/334-2844

Old St. Johns County Jail,
St. Augustine, FL   800/847-2330
                                     904/826-4218

Sherlock Holmes Museum,
London, England   *www.sherlock-holmes.co.uk*

The Sixth Floor Museum
School Book Depository, Dallas, TX   888/485-4854
                                     214/747-6660
                                     www.jfk.org

Texas State Prison Museum,
Huntsville, TX   409/295-2155

Tuol Sleng Genocide Museum,
S-21 Prison, Cambodia

        www.cambodia-web.net/camtourist/toulsleng/

Wyoming Territorial Prison and
Old West Park (U.S. Marshals
Museum), Laramie, WY   800/845-2287
                                     307/745-6161
                               www.wyoprisonpark.org

CRIME SCENE CLEANUP SERVICES
In California, trauma scene management **NEW!** practitioners are licensed by the state's Department of Health Services. A complete list of these services can be obtained online.

                                     916/327-6904
        www.dhs.ca.gov/ps/ddwem/environmental/
                          med_waste/practitioners.pdf

Trauma Crime Cleanup (Nevada; Southern California; Phoenix, Arizona; Atlanta, Georgia; Houston and Galveston, Texas; and Miami, Dayton Beach and surrounding areas in Florida)

                                     888/305-1198
                      www.traumacrimecleanup.com

Crime Scene Cleaners, Inc.
(Nationwide)   800/357-6731
                       www.crimescenecleaners.com

All Covered Bio Recovery
(Washington)   206/568-0789
                                     425/576-1471
                      www.allcoveredbiorecovery.com

Asepsis Technology
(Northern California)   800/593-2737
                       www.asepsistechnology.com

Bio Clean LLC
(Washington, Oregon) 888/412-6300
www.biocleanllc.com

Bio-Recovery Services of America
(Ohio, Michigan and Indiana) 800/699-6522
419/381-8255
www.biorecovery.net

Bio-Scene Recovery, Inc.
(Ohio, Pennsylvania, W. Virginia) 877/380-5500
www.bioscene.com

Clean Scene Services
(Southern California) 877/BIO-HAZARD
www.cleansceneservices.com

Crime Scene Clean-up
(Maryland) 800/295-5460
www.crimeclean-up.com

Great Lakes Restorative Drying
(Michigan) 800/883-7987
www.grtlks.net/Trauma/

HAR-BRO Interiors
(Southern California) 800/266-5677
www.harbro.com

Mayhem and Mishaps
(Florida, North and South Carolina) 803/419-9118
www.mayhemandmishaps.com

Pro-Tech Services
(Northern California/Nevada) 877/581-0235
www.pro-tech-services.com

Red Alert
(Southeast Texas) 800/570-1833
281/993-0016
www.wecleanall.com

ServiceMaster
(Kansas) 316/685-2325
800/646-2325
www.svmwichita.com

CRIME STATISTICS
Uniform Crime Reports from the FBI can be accessed online at the Bureau's website.
202/324-3000
www.fbi.gov/ucr

Also see...*CAP INDEX, THE.*

Juvenile Justice Clearinghouse maintains statistics and data on juvenile justice.

850/644-7113

www.fsu.edu/~crimdo/jjclearinghouse

U.S. Department of Justice,
Bureau of Justice Statistics   800/732-3277

www.ojp.usdoj.gov

CRIMINAL RECORDS
FEDERAL:

NCIC 2000 (National Crime Information Center) is law enforcement's massive nationwide criminal history database. Although operated by the FBI, it is used by virtually every federal, state and local law enforcement agency. *NCIC 2000* has over 39 million records and is available, nationwide, to over 80,000 federal, state and local authorized users. Access to *NCIC* is through a tightly monitored computer system over high security telephone lines. Access by unauthorized users is a federal crime.

NCIC currently consists of seventeen separate databases or "files." By far the largest file is the *Interstate Identification Index* (also commonly known as the "Triple I") which has criminal records from all 50 states. Most of these are felonies, but some serious misdemeanors are also included. The *"Triple I"* is only as complete as the records that are supplied to the FBI by the states. Felony arrests could have occurred which would not be reflected in a person's *Interstate Identification Index* record due to shortcomings in the reporting process.

The remaining files are Stolen Articles; Foreign Fugitives; Stolen Guns; Stolen License Plates; Deported Felons; Missing Persons; Criminal Justice Agency Identifier; Stolen Securities; Stolen Boats; Gang and Terrorist Members; Unidentified Persons; U.S. Secret Service Protective file; Stolen Vehicles; Persons Subject to Protection Orders; Wanted Persons and Canadian Police Information Center.

Additional NCIC 2000 features include mug shots; right index fingerprints; sex offenders; and persons on probation or parole.

304/625-6200

www.fbi.gov/hq/cjisd/ncic.htm

www.foia.fbi.gov/ncic552.htm

Anyone can request a copy of their own criminal record. Contact this *FBI* number for more information. However, be forewarned that the process is cumbersome.

202/324-5454

For information on current and past federal inmates, see...
PRISON HISTORIES, FEDERAL.

For criminal filings in federal courts, see...*PACER.* Or see...
FEDERAL DISTRICT COURTS.

STATEWIDE CRIMINAL CHECKS:
Statewide criminal checks can be run in 43 of 50 states by
non-law enforcement persons. This includes states that offer
statewide criminal conviction data and/or state prison
histories. State prison histories as a rule will detect
convictions for serious felonies, but not for less serious
crimes which may have resulted in local jail time, probation
or both.

Several commercial data vendors make criminal record
information available to their customers as well. See...
DATABASE PROVIDERS. Also see our *Reference Guide* for
our *Master List of Commercially Available Public Record
Databases* which details what criminal records are available
through these services in which state.

Also see...*SEX OFFENDER REGISTRIES.*

Also see...*WANTS AND WARRANTS.*

ALABAMA
Statewide criminal histories are maintained by the Alabama
Bureau of Investigation. They're available to the public only
with the signed consent of the person being investigated.

800/228-7688

The Alabama Department of Corrections makes information
on previously incarcerated felons available to the public. By
phone, a name check can be done for felons released within
the past five years.

334/240-9550

Prison history information going back ten years or more can
be obtained by mailing a written request. There's no fee, but
a SASE should be included. Send to: *Alabama Department
of Corrections, Attn.: Central Records Office, P.O. Box
301501, Montgomery, AL 36130.*

ALASKA
The Alaska Department of Public Safety maintains the
state's criminal records repository. Statewide criminal
records are not open to the public.

The Alaska Department of Corrections' official policy is
that incarceration history information on previously held
persons is not public record.

For information on inmates currently incarcerated in the state's prison system, call the Jail Access Information Line (JAIL) to learn charges, bail information, scheduled parole hearings and more. The cost is $1.25 for the first minute and 95¢ for each additional minute.

900/226-5040

ARIZONA
Arizona is a closed-record state — statewide criminal histories are not available to the public.

The Arizona Department of Corrections' Offender Services Bureau has information on previously incarcerated persons going back to 1986. Call 602/542-5586. When the automated attendant provides choices, select the Public Access option. This same information can be obtained over the Internet for free.

602/542-5586
http://adcprisoninfo.az.gov/ISearch.htm

Also available from the Arizona DOC is its Inmate Information Line, a pay-per-call service for information on currently held inmates. Operates 24 hours a day. Cost is $1.25 for the first minute and 95¢ for each additional.

900/226-8682

ARKANSAS
Statewide criminal checks are not available in Arkansas without the signed consent of the person being investigated. However, the Arkansas Department of Corrections will release information on previously convicted felons who were incarcerated from the mid-1980's through the present. There's no fee, but inquiries must be mailed. Include a SASE along with the name and DOB of the person being checked to: *Arkansas Department of Corrections, Attn.: Diagnostics Unit, 7500 Correction Circle, Pine Bluff, AR 71603.*

Also from the Arkansas Department of Corrections is a searchable database of current state prison inmates. Find it on the Internet.

www.state.ar.us/doc/inmate_info/

CALIFORNIA
In California, statewide criminal checks are limited to law enforcement only unless the person being investigated gives his or her signed consent. Other requirements also apply.

By calling the California Department of Corrections with a person's name and DOB, you can learn if he or she has a history of incarceration in the state's prison system since 1977. The line is operated 24 hours a day, 7 days a week.

916/445-6713

Available through a number of commercial database vendors, such as *Merlin Information Services (www. merlindata.com)* and *ChoicePoint (www.choicepointonline. com)*, is access to criminal court indices in key counties throughout the state. Although not a true statewide check because not all of the state's counties are included, the most populous counties are. Accounts with these commercial data vendors are not available to the general public.

A list of the state's prisoners who are condemned to die is relatively small — with 600 names — but can be viewed on the Internet. See the death row list here:

www.cdc.state.ca.us/issues/capital/capital9.htm

COLORADO
Colorado makes rap sheets (arrests and convictions) available to the public. This is one of the few states where arrest information (when there is not necessarily a following conviction) can be obtained. You'll need to pay a $7 fee per name checked and complete a form called Public Request for Information. Call the Colorado Bureau of Investigation Information Line for details at 303/239-4680. Further details and a request form can also be obtained on the Internet.

http://cdpsweb.state.co.us/cbi/Identification/identmain.htm

The Colorado Department of Corrections will release information on persons previously incarcerated in its state prison system. Their records span from 1976 through the present. You'll need a name and DOB to conduct a name check. Call the Colorado DOC at 719/579-9580 and ask for Records.

CONNECTICUT
Connecticut offers statewide criminal conviction histories for $25 per name. Their data goes back to the 1960's. Turnaround time is approximately two weeks. Includes both felony and misdemeanor convictions. Send your request including the fee, name and DOB of the person being checked to *Connecticut Department of Public Safety, Bureau of Identification, P.O. Box 2794, Middleton, CT 06457*. Checks should be made payable to "The Commissioner of Public Safety." Requests are filled by mail only. For further information, call 860/685-8480.

In addition, the Connecticut Department of Corrections keeps track of persons who were previously incarcerated in the state's prison system. They'll do name lookups by phone when provided with a name and DOB. Their computerized data goes back to the 1980's. Call 860/692-7480.

DELAWARE
Neither statewide criminal histories nor prison history

checks are available in Delaware, unless you're law enforcement.

DISTRICT OF COLUMBIA
District of Columbia criminal checks can be done through the D.C. Superior Court by telephone. Includes felony and some misdemeanor convictions since 1978. Have the subject's name and DOB ready when you call.

202/879-1373

FLORIDA
No state has a more outstanding availability of criminal history information than Florida. The state allows statewide criminal history checks without the permission of the person being investigated. Information returned includes arrests for serious crimes. Unlike most other states, no conviction needs to arise from the arrest to allow the release of the information. Information is available by mail or over the Internet. Phone lookups are no longer available.

The fee is $15 to run a name on the Florida Department of Law Enforcement's website. You'll need a credit card. Results are returned instantly. If problems are encountered with the website, call 800/292-3242 or 850/410-8110.

www2.fdle.state.fl.us

To request the same information by mail, start by obtaining the state's Criminal History Information Request form. The form can be found on the Internet at *www.fdle.state.fl.us*. Then click the Criminal History Info button. The form can also be requested by sending a SASE to *Florida Department of Law Enforcement, USB/Public Records, P. O. Box 1489, Tallahassee, FL 32302*; 850/410-8109. Complete the form and remit with a fee of $15 per name checked.

On the Internet, information on currently incarcerated persons can be obtained at the Florida Department of Corrections' Inmate Population Information Search form.

www.dc.state.fl.us/activeinmates/inmatesearch.asp

GEORGIA
Although Georgia doesn't have a statewide criminal check available to non-law-enforcement parties, the Georgia Department of Corrections will release information on any person who has previously been incarcerated in a state prison. Their database goes back decades. To conduct a name search by telephone, call Inmate Information at 404/656-4569. Be ready to provide the name, race and DOB of the person.

The same information can be obtained over the Internet:

www.dcor.state.ga.us/OffenderQuery/asp/
OffenderQueryForm.asp

The state will also release information about a person who is under active parole supervision. Call the Georgia Board of Pardons & Parole.

404/656-5330

HAWAII
Hawaii will release a person's adult criminal history, including both felonies and misdemeanors. Send the person's name, DOB and SSN plus a $15 fee. (They prefer payment by money order or cashier's check.) Send your request to *Department of Attorney General, Hawaii Criminal Justice Data Center, Room 101, 465 S. King Street, Honolulu, HI 96813*; 808/587-3106.

The Hawaii Department of Public Safety's Inmate Classification Department maintains information on persons who have been incarcerated in state prison going back to the 1960's. They can search by name or Social Security Number, but both are preferred. Date of birth is also helpful. Here are three direct numbers into Inmate Classification: 808/587-1337; 808/587-1336; and 808/587-2566.

IDAHO
Idaho will not release a person's criminal history without the signed consent of the person whose name is being checked.

However, the Idaho Department of Corrections will release information on convicted felons who have served time in a state penal institution. Their database goes back to 1979. In addition to the person's name, also be prepared to provide a DOB and SSN. Call 208/658-2000 and ask for Records.

ILLINOIS
Statewide criminal histories are available to law enforcement only in Illinois.

The Illinois Department of Corrections will release information on previously incarcerated felons, going back to the early 1990's. The information can be accessed by phone or over the Internet. By phone, call 217/522-2666 and ask for extension 2008. Online, go to *www.idoc.state.il.us* and use the inmate search feature. If a hit is made, substantial background information is returned on the offender.

INDIANA
The Indiana State Police maintain statewide criminal records in Indiana. They are available to law enforcement and to employers who complete State Form 8053. Call

317/232-8262 for the form and further details.

However, the Indiana Department of Corrections will release information by phone on persons who have been incarcerated in a state prison going back to the middle of 1989. The main switchboard number for the Indiana Department of Corrections is 317/232-5715. When the automated attendant answers, try hitting option 1, then option 2. Or better yet, try these direct lines into the Records Department: 317/232-5716; 317/232-5765; 317/232-5772. The same information can also be found on the Internet:

www.in.gov/indcorrection/ODSdisclaim.html

IOWA
Iowa will release the adult criminal conviction history of a subject, including both felonies and serious misdemeanors. Arrest information without a disposition will also be included for the past 18 months. The fee is $13 per name checked. Your request must be made on a special state-provided form. If you want a person checked under two names (e.g., a married name and maiden name), two fees and two request forms must be submitted. The forms and further instructions can be obtained by calling this number and asking for a "Non-Law-Enforcement Record Check Request" form and a Billing form. They'll fax you what you need. The same form can also be obtained over the Internet at *www.state.ia.us/government/dps/dci*. Call 515/281-5138 for further details.

The Iowa Department of Corrections will also release information on previously incarcerated felons. Their data goes back at least 20 years. Information is available by phone.

515/281-4811

KANSAS
In Kansas, statewide criminal histories are available to the public. A user agreement, called the Criminal History Record Request and Agreement, must be requested from the Kansas Bureau of Investigation. After executing the agreement, names can be checked for $10 each. Turnaround time is eight to ten weeks.

785/296-8200
www.kbi.state.ks.us

A much easier avenue is to telephone the Kansas Department of Corrections. Adult felony conviction information which resulted in state prison incarceration is public record in Kansas. Their database includes persons incarcerated from 1978 to the present. Call the Records Department directly.

785/296-0521

KENTUCKY

Kentucky is one of the few states with centralized collection of criminal court conviction records. The person whose record is being checked is notified, however. Name checks are done by mail only. Cost is $10 each and they take a week to fulfill. Call 502/573-2350, ask for Records, and then request to be faxed a Record Request Form.

The Kentucky D.O.C. will release information on previously incarcerated felons. Their records go back to the early 1980's. Call Offender Information directly.

502/564-2433

Names of inmates currently held by the Kentucky Department of Corrections can be viewed on the Internet:

www.cor.state.ky.us/~kool/ioffsrch.asp

LOUISIANA

The Louisiana State Police maintain the state's repository of criminal records. However, this information is available to the public only with the signed release of the person being investigated. Call 225/925-6095 for further details.

The Louisiana Department of Corrections maintains a database going back to the 1980's of previously incarcerated persons. Call 225/319-4223 to run a name.

MAINE

Maine offers adult criminal conviction histories to anyone requesting the information. The state's criminal records aren't computerized yet, so there's a slow turnaround time — possibly three months. Send $7.00 with the subject's name and date of birth to: *Maine State Police, Bureau of Identification, 3600 Hospital Street, Augusta, ME 04330;* 207/624-7009.

The Maine Department of Corrections will release information on persons incarcerated going back to 1959. You'll need the person's name and DOB. The direct line for doing a name check is 207/287-4381. If this is busy, try the main switchboard at 207/287-2711 and tell the operator you need to check if a person was previously incarcerated.

MARYLAND

The primary source for statewide criminal records in Maryland is the state's Criminal Justice Information System (CJIS). The CJIS includes all misdemeanors statewide and felonies from three jurisdictions, including Baltimore. The system is open only to qualified subscribers. Single searches are not available directly from CJIS. Call 888/795-0011 for details. This is an option for private investigation agencies but not the public.

The Maryland Department of Corrections' Data Processing Unit will release information on previously incarcerated persons. They need a name and DOB to do the search. Their data goes back 20 years. Here are two direct lines to the unit: 410/585-3351; 410/585-3352.

MASSACHUSETTS
Massachusetts is a state that puts the rights of convicted criminals over the public's right to know. However, some criminal history information is available on a restricted basis through the state's CORI system. For details on this convoluted approach, visit the official website: *www.state. ma.us/chsb/CORI.html* or call 617/660-4600 for further details.

The Massachusetts Department of Corrections doesn't release information on past or present inmates to the public.

MICHIGAN
Commercial users, including private investigation agencies, can obtain an account with Michigan's Criminal Justice Information Center to run criminal histories. Both felony and misdemeanor convictions are included and no release is necessary from the subject of the investigation. After being issued an agency I.D. number and password, searches can be run over the Internet for $5 each. Results are instant. There is no sign up fee and requirements to establish an account are minimal.

517/322-1956
www.state.mi.us/msp/cjic/

Once an account has been obtained with the Michigan CJIC, go to this web address to run actual criminal histories. User identification number and password required.

http://ichat.state.mi.us

Statewide criminal records are available to the public in Michigan on a mail-in basis. Information returned will be all felony and misdemeanor convictions going back to the 1950's. Send a letter and $5 per name to the Michigan State Police requesting a "Criminal History Record." Include the full name, DOB, race and sex of the person being investigated. If available, also include the person's Social Security Number and Michigan driver's license number. There's a two-to-three-week turnaround time. Mail your request to: *Michigan State Police, Central Records Division, 7150 Harris Drive, Lansing, MI 48913*.

517/322-1955

The Michigan D.O.C. maintains a database of previously incarcerated persons going back to the mid-1950's. They'll do a lookup over the phone if provided with the person's full legal name and either a DOB or SSN.

517/373-0284

The Michigan Department of Corrections also maintains a website with public access to its Offender Tracking Information System (OTIS). It's a database of offenders incarcerated after July 1, 1995.

www.state.mi.us/mdoc/asp/otis1.html

MINNESOTA
Minnesota will release felony and certain misdemeanor conviction information without the permission of the person being investigated. Information released will be for the last 15 years only. Send the subject's full name and DOB with a SASE to: *Bureau of Criminal Apprehension, 1246 University Ave., St. Paul, MN 55104*. Include a fee of $4 per name checked. Indicate that you are requesting a Public Record Criminal History Check. Payment accepted by money order, company check or personal check. Call 651/642-0670 for further details.

Information on persons previously incarcerated by the Minnesota Department of Corrections is available by phone. Their information goes back over 20 years. Call Records at 651/642-0322.

Information on currently incarcerated prisoners and parolees still under supervision can also be obtained on the Internet at the Minnesota Department of Corrections' offender locator website:

www.doc.state.mn.us/publicviewer/

MISSISSIPPI
Neither statewide criminal histories nor inmate history information are available in Mississippi.

MISSOURI
Missouri statewide criminal record checks are available without the subject's consent. Send a check or money order for $5 per name to: *Missouri State Highway Patrol, Attn.: Criminal Records, P.O. Box 568, Jefferson City, MO 65102*. Include the subject's name, DOB and SSN. All convictions, pending charges and a 30-day arrest history will be released. Records date back to the 1960's. To obtain a request form, visit www.mshp.state.mo.us. Call 573/526-6153 for further information.

Also in Missouri, the Department of Corrections maintains information on previously incarcerated persons going back decades. There's no charge and the results are given by phone. Have the person's name, DOB and SSN available when calling. Inquiries are handled by the Probation and Parole Department, 573/751-8488.

MONTANA
Montana will provide criminal history information. Included are felony criminal convictions going back to the subject's 18th birthday, plus misdemeanor convictions for the past five years. Turnaround time is seven to ten days. Fee is $5 per name checked. Include the subject's name, any known aliases, DOB, SSN and a SASE. Mail request to: *Montana Department of Justice, Identification Bureau, 303 N. Roberts, #374, Helena, MT 59620*; 406/444-3625.

The Montana Department of Corrections maintains information on persons incarcerated in state prisons going back to 1978. The information is public record. Contact the Montana DOC Records Department directly at 406/444-9521.

NEBRASKA
Nebraska allows criminal history checks without the consent of the subject. Records returned include all arrests and convictions when the arrestee's fingerprints have been taken. In practical terms, this means felonies and serious misdemeanors. There's a 15-day turnaround time. Fee is $10 per name checked. Send the fee and the person's name, DOB, SSN and any aliases to: *Nebraska State Patrol, Attn.: CID, P.O. Box 94907, Lincoln, NE 68509-4907*; 402/471-4545.

The Nebraska Department of Correctional Services maintains information on all persons who have been incarcerated in state penal institutions at any time going back to mid-1977. They'll do a name check by phone. The direct line for the Records Department is 402/479-5661. If the line is busy, try the main switchboard at 402/471-2654 and ask for Records.

NEVADA
The Nevada Highway Patrol maintains the state's criminal record repository. However, information will be released only if they are provided with both the signed consent of the person being investigated and a set of his or her fingerprints.

The Nevada Department of Corrections will release information on persons previously incarcerated in state prison. Their records go back many decades. In addition to the person's name, they also prefer to have a SSN and/or DOB. Turnaround time for information is usually prompt. They prefer inquiries to be faxed to 775/687-6715. If no fax machine is available, call them directly at 775/887-3285 and tell the operator you want to check a name to see if a person was previously incarcerated.

Robert Scott, P.I.

NEW HAMPSHIRE
Statewide criminal histories are released in New Hampshire only with the signed consent of the subject of the investigation.

However, the state's Department of Corrections' Offender Records section will release information on persons previously or currently incarcerated. Their computer name check, which can be done by phone, goes back to 1994. Manual checks of prior years are also available if requested. They'll release information on the person's crime and the sentence received.

603/271-1823

NEW JERSEY
The New Jersey State Police maintain statewide criminal records. They are available on a restricted basis to employers, attorneys and private detectives. Visit the New Jersey State Police website at *www.njsp.org* for full details.

The New Jersey Department of Corrections' Inmate Locator line is very hard to get through on. However, when you finally bust through the busy signals, you can learn if a person was previously incarcerated in state prison going back to 1976.

609/777-5753

Also of interest in New Jersey are postings on the Internet of Parole Eligibility Notices by the State Parole Board. Find it online:

www.state.nj.us/parole/elig.htm

NEW MEXICO
The New Mexico Department of Public Safety maintains statewide criminal record histories. Information is released only with the signed consent of the person being investigated.

The New Mexico Department of Corrections will tell you if a person has been incarcerated in a state prison at any time in the last 25 years. Call 505/827-8709 and ask for Records. They'll provide results over the phone; be prepared to provide the name of the person being checked and as many personal identifiers as possible.

NEW YORK
Statewide criminal records are not available to the public in the state of New York without a court order.

The New York City area maintains a somewhat centralized search system called the Unified Court System, with 13 counties included. However, they can only search one county at a time. (The counties are Bronx, Dutchess, Erie, Kings, Nassau, New York, Orange, Putnam, Queens,

Richmond, Rockland, Suffolk, and Westchester.) Cost is $16 per name per county. Name checks return information on convictions and pending prosecutions and can be conducted by mail-in or walk-in request. Name searches by phone are not available. Turnaround time is one to two business days. Requests must be submitted on their Criminal History Record Search (CHRS) form. Call 212/428-2810 to request a CHRS form and further instructions. They'll fax it to you if asked nicely.

The New York State Department of Correctional Services maintains a database of currently and previously incarcerated persons going back 25 years. After release, a convict will remain in the system for a minimum of 15 years. The information is available by phone at 518/457-5000 or on the web at *www.docs.state.ny.us*. Once at the page, scroll down to the "inmate lookup" link to be taken to the search page.

Also worthy of note in the state of New York is the Victim Information and Notification Everyday (VINE) system. The system allows crime victims and members of the public to obtain information on the release date of currently incarcerated inmates. You'll need the inmate's name and DOB or his Department of Corrections Identification Number (DIN) or his New York State Identification Number (NYSID) which can be obtained by calling the prosecuting district attorney's office. Your call must be made from a touch-tone phone. Call 888/846-3469.

NORTH CAROLINA
Statewide criminal histories are not available to the public in North Carolina.

However, the North Carolina Department of Corrections maintains a database of previously incarcerated persons going back to 1974. It's open to the public and they'll do a name search over the phone. Call the Combined Records unit at 919/716-3200. They can also search their records by Social Security Number.

In addition, the North Carolina Department of Corrections' website contains additional searchable databases. The Inmate Releases file contains state prison system parolees who were released since January 1, 1998. A second searchable database, Public Access Information System, contains information on inmates incarcerated since July 1, 1995. Both can be accessed at *www.doc.state.nc.us*.

Also in North Carolina is SAVAN (Statewide Automated Victim Assistance & Notification), which allows crime victims to obtain up-to-date information on offenders by calling 877/NCSAVAN.

NORTH DAKOTA

North Dakota will release a person's statewide history for felony and some misdemeanor convictions. Also included are certain events from the preceding 12 months, including arrests. Call 701/328-5500 and request a "Non-Criminal Justice Records Release" form. After completing the form, return it with a $20 fee to the North Dakota Bureau of Criminal Investigation. (Note: The person whose name is checked is notified by the state that his or her criminal history has been requested. However, the identity of the requester is kept confidential.)

The North Dakota Department of Correction and Rehabilitation keeps track of persons incarcerated in state prison going back to 1965. They'll do a name check by phone. Call Inmate Records directly at 701/328-6125. If the line is busy, try the central office at 701/328-6390 and ask for Inmate Records.

OHIO

Statewide criminal records are available in Ohio only with the signed consent of the person being investigated. A set of fingerprints from the person being investigated is also required.

Ohio Professional Electronic Network (OPEN) offers a computerized database of county arrest records from 82 of Ohio's 88 counties. The data comes from jail bookings — if the arrestee wasn't booked into jail, there will be no record. Some of the information goes as far back as 1967. The information is available online, on a subscription basis. Call 800/366-0106 or 614/481-6980.

If you'd like to access the OPEN database of Ohio arrest records on an as-needed basis without subscribing, you can contact Ohio private investigation agency, FYI Investigations at 614/890-1330. They accept credit cards and will do a search of the Ohio arrest record database for a flat fee of $25 per name.

The Ohio Department of Rehabilitation and Correction maintains information on previously incarcerated persons going back to the 1970's. The only persons not included are "hideaways" who have been extracted from the system for reasons including witness protection. Preferred search criteria are a name and SSN, but a DOB is also useful. Call the Records Retention Center directly at 614/752-1073. The same information is available on the Internet:

www.drc.state.oh.us/CFDOCS/inmate/search.htm

OKLAHOMA

Oklahoma has an open criminal record policy. For a fee of $15 per name, the Oklahoma State Bureau of Investigation

(OSBI) will conduct a statewide criminal arrest history. Their records go back to 1925 and include any person who was arrested and fingerprinted. The searches are available by mail or fax. To request an OSBI statewide criminal check by mail, send a letter stating the reason for the request, the subject's full legal name, any aliases, race, sex, DOB and SSN and a SASE. The fee of $15 per name checked must be paid by business check or money order only. Personal checks are not accepted. Turnaround time for mail requests is approximately two weeks. Mail to: *Oklahoma State Bureau of Investigation, Criminal History Reporting, 6600 North Harvey, Building 6, Suite 140, Oklahoma City, OK 73116*; 405/848-6724.

OSBI searches can also be done by fax using a credit card. Turnaround time for fax/credit card requests is approximately two days. Call 405/848-6724, ask for Records, and then ask that a blank fax search form be faxed to you.

The Oklahoma Department of Corrections maintains records on previously incarcerated persons going back to approximately 1984. The information is available to the public. Call Records directly at 405/425-2624 to run a name check. If this line is busy, call the Oklahoma DOC main switchboard at 405/425-2500 and ask for Records.

A check of currently incarcerated inmates with the Oklahoma Department of Corrections can be done over the Internet at the below URL. Click the Offender Lookup option.

www.doc.state.ok.us/DOCS/offender_info.htm

OREGON

Oregon statewide criminal histories are available without the subject's consent — but there's one catch: The subject of the inquiry is sent a letter and told that you have requested his or her criminal history. Felony and misdemeanor conviction information going back to the subject's 18th birthday is included. Limit requests to one name per letter and include the person's name, DOB and last known address. Send payment in the amount of $15 per name to: *Oregon State Police, Attn: Open Records, Unit 11, P.O. Box 4395, Portland, OR 97208*; 503/378-3070.

Another option for statewide criminal checks in Oregon is the *Oregon Judicial Information Network* which maintains civil and criminal court indices from all 36 counties. A subscription is required. There's a $295 set-up fee, plus hourly fees of $10-$13 and a $10 monthly user fee.

877/826-5010
www.ojd.state.or.us/ojin

Just need a small number of OJIN lookups and don't want to become a subscriber? Oregon P.I. Max Whittington offers single lookups for $50 each.

503/644-6678
www.oregonpi.com/OJIN.htm

The Oregon Department of Corrections will run a name check by phone to determine if a person was previously incarcerated in the state prison system. Their computerized records cover 1983 through the present. Call 503/945-0920. After an SID number is obtained, further information can be obtained through Records at 503/373-1515.

PENNSYLVANIA
The Pennsylvania State Police offers felony conviction data from its central repository. The information is available by mail or over the Internet after registration has been completed. No consent is necessary from the person being investigated. There is a $10 fee per name searched. To do a search by mail, you'll need to use their form, "Request for Criminal Record Check." To obtain the form, call 717/783-5494 and ask that it be mailed or faxed to you. Complete the form and mail back with a $10 fee per name checked. To check the status on submitted forms, call 717/783-9222.

The information can also now be obtained on the Internet. However, a registration form must be completed and a user name and password issued. The Pennsylvania Access to Criminal History (PATCH) system can be found at

http://patch.state.pa.us/psp/Overview.htm

The Pennsylvania Department of Correction's Inmate Records unit will release information on persons previously incarcerated. Their records go back to at least the 1970's. You'll need a name and at least one personal identifier to do a name check. Call Inmate Records directly.

717/730-2721

Inmates currently incarcerated in the state's prison system can be identified through an online search available at

www.cor.state.pa.us/cgi-bin/locator.pl

RHODE ISLAND
Statewide criminal histories are available only with the signed consent of the person being investigated. The Rhode Island Department of Corrections maintains a database of persons who have been incarcerated since 1992. They'll conduct a name check by phone. Call the Records Department directly.

401/462-3900

SOUTH CAROLINA

South Carolina will release criminal conviction information from all years and arrest information that is less than one year old. Information is available by mail or over the Internet. By mail, send payment in the amount of $25 per name checked, payable by money order or company check only. Include the subject's name, DOB and SSN (if available). Also include a SASE. Mail request to: *South Carolina Law Enforcement Division, Attn: Records, P.O. Box 21398, Columbia, SC 29221*; 803/737-9000.

Over the Internet, have a credit card handy (there's still the $25 charge) and go to *www.sled.state.sc.us/* and follow the links for "State Criminal Records Check." To run a name, you'll need not only the name, but also the subject's date of birth, gender and race.

The South Carolina Department of Corrections will do a name check by phone to determine if a person was previously incarcerated. Goes back to the 1970's. Call 803/896-8531.

SOUTH DAKOTA

Statewide criminal histories can be obtained only with the signed consent of the person being investigated.

The South Dakota Department of Corrections maintains a database of current and past prisoners, going back approximately ten years. The information is available to the public and they'll do a name check by phone. Call 605/773-3478.

TENNESSEE

Statewide criminal records are off limits to the public in Tennessee, unless you're a subscriber to Lexis-Nexis. This data provider offers the Tennessee Criminal Case Index which includes misdemeanor and felony docket filings, statewide, from 1995 to the present. See...*DATABASE PROVIDERS*...for more details on Lexis-Nexis.

However, the Tennessee Department of Corrections' Sentence Information unit will provide information on previously incarcerated persons. Their computerized records go back to February of 1992. However, a manual search of earlier records is available upon request. You'll need both a name and DOB to run a check: 615/741-1000

Persons who were placed on parole or probation in other states but who are residing in Tennessee can be identified at the Tennessee Internet Crime Information Center website, located at *www.ticic.state.tn.us* or by calling 888/837-4170.

TEXAS

Texas statewide criminal histories are publicly available. A person's misdemeanor and felony conviction criminal history and/or felony deferral record will be released without his or her consent. Send a $10 fee, plus as many identifiers as possible on the subject, including name, DOB, SSN, race and sex. Requests are currently turned around in about 48 hours. Send your request to: *Texas Department of Public Safety, Attn: Crime Records Service, P.O. Box 15999, Austin, TX 78761-5999*; 512/424-2474.

The same information can also be found on the state's website. The cost is $3.15 per name. Use your credit card.

http://records.txdps.state.tx.us/dps/default.cfm

But wait...there's another way to check statewide criminal records in Texas. A private firm called Quick Search has the same information and will run a name for $7.00. Credit card payment accepted by phone.

214/358-2840

The Texas Department of Corrections (TDC) won't do phone checks but they will search their records if a mail-in request is made. Their records go back to the 1850's. The service is free, but takes approximately two weeks to complete. Send your request including the subject's name and either DOB or TDC number and a SASE to: *Inmate Records, Texas Department of Corrections, P.O. Box 99, Huntsville, TX 77340*; 409/294-6509.

UTAH

In Utah, statewide criminal records are not public record.

Records on currently incarcerated persons and those on probation or parole are public information. However, persons previously incarcerated and no longer or probation or parole will not be indicated. Call the Utah State Department of Corrections, 801/265-5500.

VERMONT

Statewide criminal records can be obtained in Vermont only with the signed consent of the person being investigated. Other restrictions also apply. Call 802/244-8727 for further details.

Incarceration histories are not public record in Vermont. However, persons currently incarcerated can be viewed at the Vermont Department of Correction's website.

http://public.doc.state.vt.us/cgi-bin/public.cgi/query

VIRGINIA

Statewide criminal histories are maintained by the Virginia State Police and are available only with the signed consent of the person being investigated. Other requirements also apply.

The Virginia Department of Corrections will check their records to determine if a person was previously incarcerated. Their records go back to the 1980's. The requester must have the person's full name and DOB. Call 804/674-3209. If this line is busy, try the main switchboard at 804/674-3000 and ask for Inmate Intake.

To learn if a person is presently incarcerated by the Virginia Department of Corrections, visit their website:

www.vipnet.org/cgi-bin/vadoc/doc.cgi

Virginia has broken new ground with a program that releases information on offenders who are currently under parole supervision. (It's known informally as the Know Thy Neighbor Law.) For a fee of $5 any person can request a printout of all persons on parole within a given zip code. For $37.50, you can receive a similar list (on paper or computer disk) for the entire state. For 24-hour information, call 804/674-3243. To obtain the list, mail your payment and request to: *Virginia Department of Corrections, Attn: Victim Services Unit, 6900 Atmore Dr, Richmond, VA 23225.*

WASHINGTON

In the state of Washington, statewide criminal conviction histories are public record. Information returned includes criminal convictions; arrests from the past year when there is no disposition; and whether the person is a registered sex offender or kidnapper. The information is available both by mail and over the Internet.

To request a criminal check by mail, you'll need to obtain Form 3000-240-569 (also known as "Request for Conviction Criminal History Record") by calling the Washington State Patrol at 360/705-5100. Ask for Customer Service — they can either fax or mail the form to you. After the form has been completed, return it with a $10 fee per name to: *Identification and Criminal History Section, Washington State Patrol, P.O. Box 42633, Olympia, WA 98504-2633.* Turnaround time for mail requests is approximately 7 to 14 working days.

The same information is available over the Internet with a credit card. Results are instantaneous. The fee is still $10 per name. The online system, known as WATCH (Washington Access to Criminal History) can be found here:

http://watch.wsp.wa.gov/WATCHOPEN/default.asp

The Washington D.O.C. has information on persons incarcerated going back to the 1970's. They'll do a name check by phone. They prefer the caller to have the name, DOB and SSN of the person being checked. Call 360/753-6454.

WEST VIRGINIA

The West Virginia State Police maintain the state's criminal record repository. However, statewide criminal histories are available only with the signed consent of the person being investigated. Other requirements also apply. Call 304/746-2100 for further details.

The West Virginia Division of Corrections will conduct a name check by phone to determine if a person has been previously incarcerated. Their computerized records go back five years; their file card index system goes back decades. Call 304/558-2037 and select extension 40 or 42 to be connected to Records.

WISCONSIN

Wisconsin arrest and conviction information from 1971 through the present is available without the subject's consent. Required information is the subject's name, DOB, sex, and race. Send a SASE, and payment in the amount of $13 per name checked. Mail your request to: *Crime Information Bureau, Attn: Record Check Unit, P.O. Box 2688, Madison, WI 53701-2688*; 608/266-5764.

In addition, the Wisconsin Department of Corrections makes incarceration history information available by phone. Their records go back to 1962. Records between 1962 and 1982 contain minimal information. Records since 1982 contain details such as charges and length of incarceration. To check a name, call the Master Record Check unit directly.

608/266-2097

WYOMING

Statewide criminal records are available in Wyoming only with the signed consent and fingerprints of the person being checked. Prison name checks are not available in the state, either.

MULTI-STATE SOURCES:
Criminal Information Services, Inc. (CRIS) specializes in providing criminal history searches. Current states where immediate results can be obtained are Arizona, Arkansas, California (15 counties), Connecticut, Florida, Georgia, Idaho, Illinois, Indiana, Kentucky, Michigan, Minnesota, Mississippi, Missouri, New Jersey, New York, North Carolina, Ohio, Oregon, Texas, Utah and Washington. Information in many of the states comes from department of

corrections records, not criminal court indices.

> 800/973-5500
> 503/649-1486
> *www.criminalinfo.com*

G.A. Public Record Services offers hand searches of criminal court records throughout the United States. Fees vary, but rarely exceed $20. Typical turnaround time is under 72 hours. Sign up online.

> 800/760-2468
> 214/320-9836
> *www.gaprs.com*

FOREIGN:
The U.S. Department of State monitors the arrests/trials of U.S. citizens in foreign lands through its *Overseas Citizens Services Unit*.

> 202/647-5226

Also see...*CANADIAN INVESTIGATIONS*.

Also see...*MEXICAN INVESTIGATIONS*.

Also see...*ENGLAND INVESTIGATORS*.

Also see...*INTERPOL*.

CT CORPORATION

Every investigator who serves legal papers **NEW!** should know about CT Corporation. This nationwide firm serves as the registered agent for more than 250,000 businesses. If you need to serve legal documents on a large-sized business, don't waste your time tracking down its executives. Go online to the CT Corporation website and obtain the phone number of their branch office in the state in question. Call them and ask if they represent the corporation for service of process. If they do, your service will be as easy as delivering a newspaper.

> 518/451-8000
> 800/624-0909
> *www.ctcorporation.com*

CURRENCY EXCHANGE RATES

To determine current exchange rates, call *Thomas Cook*.

> 800/287-7362
> *www.us.thomascook.com*

Or visit the *Universal Currency Converter*, a free website, to convert any currency to another.

> *www.xe.com/ucc/*

For historical monetary conversion rates, visit this page:

www.xe.com/ict/

CUSTOMS SERVICE, U.S.
Headquarters   202/927-1000
                                      www.customs.gov

Drug Smuggling Tips   800/BE ALERT
Investigations (Headquarters)   202/927-1600
Press Office   202/927-8727
Art Recovery Team   866/LOST ART

The Customs *Cyber-Smuggling Center* is a Virginia-based
unit that focuses on Internet-related crimes such a money
laundering, child pornography and intellectual property
rights theft.

703/293-8005
www.customs.gov/enforcem/cyber.htm

U.S. Customs tracks and maintains information on persons
exiting and entering the U.S. for law enforcement purposes
through the *El Paso Intelligence Center.*

888/873-3742
www.usdoj.gov/dea/programs/epic

Direct Freedom of Information Act Requests to: *United
States Customs Service, Freedom of Information Request,
1099 14th Street NW, Washington, D.C. 20229.*

Association of Former Customs
Special Agents   877/954-7646
                                      www.afcsa.org

*Photo: A U.S. Customs Blackhawk helicopter patrols the
Southern Florida shoreline. (Photo courtesy of U.S.
Customs Service. Photo by James R. Tourtellotte.)*

DAC SERVICES

DAC Services is a background checking firm/data provider that maintains some very hard-to-find information on truckers. This data includes an employment history file with employment histories for terminated drivers from over 2,500 truck companies. There's a total of 4 million records here alone. The company also maintains a database of past drug and alcohol test results on truck drivers as required by the Department of Transportation. (A signed release from the driver is needed before this information can be released.) Another unique product offered is their driver *Locator Bulletin* that scans new inquiries for a driver's name and passes any new information that comes up back to the requestor. *DAC Services* is a restricted service and is generally available to truck companies only.

Customer Service	800/322-9651
Sales	800/331-9175
Consumer Inquiries	800/381-0645

www.dacservices.com

For an opposing viewpoint of *DAC Services*, read the uncensored comments of truckers at this site:

www.dacsucks.com

DATABASE PROVIDERS

Since the last edition of this book, there has been a consolidation among the many providers of computerized public record databases. Subscription to these services is generally restricted to private investigators, law firms, collection agencies, law enforcement agencies, insurance companies and the media.

Presently, the data landscape consists of a handful of dominant, proven information providers. Close on their heels is a pack of smaller, less well known firms. All make their information available over secured Internet connections. As a rule of thumb, the dominant firms tend to offer more comprehensive data on more reliable systems. As well, their customer service departments are usually more professionally run. Some include 24-hours-a-day support.

In the universe of data providers, *Lexis-Nexis, ChoicePoint* and *AutoTrackXP* are the major planets. Close on their heels comes the smaller but still popular *Merlin Information Services. AutoTrackXP* (formerly *DBT Online*) is now owned by *ChoicePoint* (formerly *CDB Infotek*). In the *Reference Guide* of this book, see our exclusive *Master List of Commercially Available Public Record Databases* that lists the individual data files available on *Lexis-Nexis, ChoicePoint, AutoTrackXP* and *Merlin*.

Lexis-Nexis offers the largest selection of public record databases available. Presently, there's a $150 monthly minimum to maintain an account. *Lexis-Nexis* enjoys widespread use at law firms, government agencies and by the news media. In addition to state and federal public records, the service also includes some foreign public records, news extracts, legal citations and more. As a side note, don't be fooled by the "use your credit card" option at *Lexis-Nexis.com*. This allows access to a limited menu of searches that represent just a tiny fraction of what is available through a bona fide subscription.

General Information	800/227-9597
New Sales	800/227-4908

www.lexis-nexis.com

ChoicePoint remains a top-quality provider of public record data that is used by many private investigation agencies as well as the FBI, DEA and other federal agencies. An extensive menu of data is available from all fifty states and the data generally has an excellent freshness date. Don't look for bargain prices here, though — quality comes at a price. Nationwide searches include Employer Identification Numbers and business credit reports. There's presently a $25 monthly service charge plus a per search fee.

888/333-3365
www.choicepointonline.com

Information on the company's corporate structure and other products and services can be obtained at:

www.choicepoint.net

Law enforcement and other government agencies interested in *ChoicePoint* should use this site:

800/547-5512
www.choicepointgov.com

AutoTrackXP is also widely used for public record searches by law enforcement agencies and private investigators. You'll find a number of interesting searches here that can't be found at the other major data providers, such as U.S. military personnel lookups. You'll also find exceptionally strong coverage of Florida public records including concealed weapon permits and workers compensation claims. There's presently a $25 monthly service charge plus a per search fee.

800/279-7710
www.atxp.com

Merlin Information Services is the little guy on the data-block that offers affordable prices for the bread and butter searches used most often by investigators. There's a strong tilt toward California public records The firm's Ultimate Weapon search remains one of the best deals around — a number of databases can be searched at once for one dollar. Data is purchased only if there's a hit with a small preview first being given Available searches include civil and criminal indices for most major California counties as well as corporation, fictitious business name, UCC and other searches In addition, there's no monthly service fee — you just pay for the searches you run They also offer special flat rate pricing for law enforcement and government agencies

800/367-6646
www merlindata com

Among the lesser known but still credible data providers, you might want to consider

Accurint	888/332-8244
	www accurint com
DCS Information Services	800/299-3647
	www dcs-amerifind com
Flat Rate Info	303/381-2260
	888/259-6173
	www flatrateinfo com
IRB Search	800/447-2112
	www irbsearch com
Locate Fast	877/203-0058
	www loc8fast com
LocatePlus	978/921-2727
	www locateplus com

Ohio Professional Electronic Network (Open) features strong Ohio coverage.

800/935-OPEN
www openonline com

QuickInfo features strong Colorado coverage

303/381-2260
888/259-6173
www quickinfo net

Skipsmasher, Inc , designed by the author of this book, sells data strictly for professional skiptracers

www skipsmasher com

Tracers Information Specialists	877/723-2689
	www tracersinfo com

Criminal Information Services, Inc. (CRIS) specializes in providing criminal history searches. Current states where immediate results can be obtained are Arizona, Arkansas, California (15 counties), Connecticut, Florida, Georgia, Idaho, Illinois, Indiana, Kentucky, Michigan, Minnesota, Mississippi, Missouri, New Jersey, New York, North Carolina, Ohio, Oregon, Texas, Utah and Washington. Information in many of the states comes from department of corrections records, not criminal court indices.

800/973-5500
503/649-1486
www.criminalinfo.com

DATAQUICK
See...*REAL ESTATE INFORMATION.*

DATA RECOVERY
DriveSavers is a well known and respected leader in the field of data recovery. Their process is largely automated and software driven. Their engineers don't testify in court. Cost depends on size of drive to be recovered and turnaround time desired. Rush service is available. Price range is $375 to $3,800.

800/440-1904
415/382-2000
www.drivesavers.com

The Chelsea Group, Inc. specializes in retrieving information from computers when the access code is not available.

208/765-9181
www.computerlegal.com

Access Data Recovery Service also recovers data from computers where the password is missing or not available.

801/377-5410
www.accessdata.com

If the password to an important program has been lost or stolen, and you have legal right to the data, consider the services of *Password Crackers, Inc.*

877/PWCRACK
www.pwcrack.com

Computer Forensics specializes in computer evidence/information recovery, including e-mail as physical evidence. Are you sure that was deleted?

206/324-6232
www.forensics.com

Electronic Evidence Discovery also specializes in data

recovery.

206/343-0131
www.eedinc.com

Ontrack also offers data recovery including a unique Remote Data Recovery Service where they'll connect to your computer through your modem to recover data. Sending in your hard drive not required.

800/872-2599
www.ontrack.com

DATATREE

Once you subscribe to *DataTree*, you can **NEW!** forget about making trips to the county recorder's office to obtain copies of deeds and other public filings. DataTree has optically scanned over 800 million recordings and delivers them instantly via the Internet. A typical charge is $3 for a 3 page document. Coverage areas include most California counties as well as key counties in Arizona, Florida, Hawaii, Illinois, Maryland, Massachusetts, Michigan, Missouri, Nevada, New Jersey, New York, Ohio, Oklahoma, Texas, Utah and Washington state. The Philadelphia metro area (5 counties) is also included. *Update (2-21-03): Datatree no longer sells direct to small users; however the same info can be obtained at courthousedirect.com.*

800/789-7244
www.courthousedirect.com

DBT ONLINE

DBT Online is now called AutoTrackXP. See...*DATABASE PROVIDERS.*

DEATH INVESTIGATIONS

A very good guide to conducting death investigations is *Death Investigator's Handbook* by Louis N. Eliopulos. Available through these publishers, the book is nearly 900 pages long and sells for $40.00.

Paladin Press	800/392-2400
Thomas Investigative Publications	512/719-3595

The John Hopkins Autopsy Resource is a free, online knowledge bank drawn from summaries of over 50,000 autopsies. Names of the dearly departed have been removed — the material is for research purposes only.

www.med.jhu.edu/pathology/iad.html

Once a person has died and appears in the *Social Security Death Index* (also known as the Death Master File), some personal information, previously protected by the Freedom of Information Act, becomes public record. Included in this is Social Security Administration's Form SS-5. This is the original application for a Social Security Number. It contains the decedent's full legal name at birth, date of birth, place of birth, mother and father's full legal name and more. To obtain it, send a $27 fee and a Freedom of Information Act request to: *Social Security Administration, Office of Earnings Operations, FOIA Workgroup, 300 N. Greene Street, P.O. Box 33022, Baltimore, MD 21290.*

Not familiar with how to file a FOIA request? There's a template for a sample request in our *Reference Guide.* Also include a sentence indicating that the person is deceased and appears in the SSA's Death Master File.

When an American citizen dies abroad, the death will often be reported to the nearest U.S. consulate. If the report of the death is accompanied by evidence of the decedent's United States citizenship and a local death certificate, the U.S. consul will prepare Form OF-180, "Report of the Death of an American Citizen Abroad." This report is then permanently filed with the *Department of State* and can be obtained for a twenty-dollar fee. Mail the request to *Passport Services, Correspondence Branch, U.S. Department of State, Washington, D.C. 20522-1705.* WARNING: The State Department may notify the next of kin when a request for a Form OF-180 is made.

If the death occurred abroad, but was not reported to the nearest U.S. consulate, local authorities may have record of the death. Contact the nearest U.S. consulate or embassy (See...*EMBASSIES*) and ask for contact information for local death records.

If an American dies on the high seas, whether in an aircraft or on a vessel, the death record will usually be filed in the next port of call. If the port of call is on foreign soil, requests for copies of the record should be made to *U.S. Department of State, Washington, D.C. 20522-1705.*

Forensic anthropology is the science of obtaining information from human remains. Contact *The American Board of Forensic Anthropology.*

419/213-3908
www.csuchico.edu/anth/ABFA

Also see...*FATAL ACCIDENTS.*

Also see...*HOMICIDE INVESTIGATIONS.*

Also see...*HUMAN REMAINS.*

Also see...*CORONERS.*

Also see...*FORENSIC ENTOMOLOGY*.

Also see...*NECROSEARCH*.

DEATH PENALTY
Statistical information on persons under the sentence of death are maintained by the *U.S. Department of Justice's Bureau of Justice Statistics*.

www.ojp.usdoj.gov/bjs

A somewhat shocking site on the more gruesome side effects of electrocution can be found at this website:

www.theelectricchair.com

Death Penalty Information
Center   202/675-2319
www.deathpenaltyinfo.org

Published annually, *Death Row* is a large format, soft cover book ($20) that includes the name of every prisoner currently on death row in the United States, plus other vital information.

310/553-2400
www.bobit.com

Capital Punishment
Project/ ACLU   205/675-2319
www.aclu.org

See the *Reference Guide* of this book for a chart on which states implement the death penalty, and by which mode of execution.

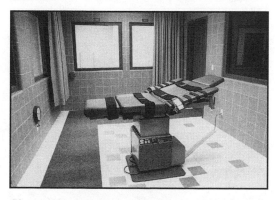

Photo: The execution room at the United States Penitentiary in Terre Haute, Indiana. The life of Oklahoma City bomber Timothy McVeigh ended on this gurney. (Photo courtesy of Federal Bureau of Prisons.)

DEBT COLLECTION

 The Federal Trade Commission regulates debt collectors and enforces the *Fair Debt Collections Practices Act*. Their website has a special section devoted to the FDCPA.

202/326-2222
www.ftc.gov/ftc/consumer

The American Collectors Association offers networking, educational and other benefits to their members.

612/926-6547
www.collector.com

California Association of Judgment Professionals is a new and growing educational and professional association for judgment collectors.

661/664-0767
www.cajp.org

For a analysis of the *Fair Debt Collection Practices Act* and its impact on the activities of private investigators, see the *Privacy Law Survival Guide* at the end of this book.

DEBUGGING

Communication Security, Inc.	979/244-4920
	www.bugsweep.com
Comsec	800/990-0911
	818/502-0000
	www.comsecsolutions.com
Future Focus	425/489-0446
	www.bug-killer.com
Granite Island Group	978/546-3803
	www.tscm.com
Information Security Associates, Inc.	203/357-8051
Intelcom, Inc.	859/263-9425
	www.intelcommunique.com
Microsearch	714/952-3812
Murray Associates	908/832-7900
	www.spybusters.com
RCM and Associates	888/990-6265
SWS Security	410/879-4035
	www.swssec.com

TekSpek Services   315/363-0202
                                 www.tekspek.com

TSCM Technical Services   203/354-9040
                                 www.tscmtech.com

For statistical information on the number and location of federal wiretaps, visit the website of the Federal Judiciary:

www.uscourts.gov/publications.html

Also see...*BUSINESS ESPIONAGE CONTROLS & COUNTERMEASURES ASSOCIATION.*

Also see the *Reference Guide* of this book for *26 Warning Signs of Electronic Eavesdropping.*

DECEPTION DETECTION
See...*JOHN E. REID & ASSOCIATES.*

Also see...*POLYGRAPH.*

DEERS SYSTEM
Most investigators know about the "locator services" that each branch of the U.S. military maintains to aid family members and others in locating active service personnel. However few investigators know that there is one single master database that contains information on all active service personnel, regardless of branch. DEERS stands for *Defense Enrollment Eligibility Reporting System.* In short, it's how the government knows who's entitled to military related benefits, primarily for health care. DEERS is name and Social Security Number driven.

From California   800/334-4162
From Alaska & Hawaii   800/527-5602
All other states   800/538-9552

DEGREECHK.COM
Here's an unfortunate idea whose time has apparently come. Remember the good old days when college degree verification just meant a phone call to the school's registrar? A new service called *Credentials, Inc.* is now relieving schools of this burden — and charging a fee to the person who needs to verify the degree. Price ranges from $2.50 (for 4-day service) to $15.00 (for priority service). Registration is required and an audit trail is created.

                                 847/446-7422
                                 www.degreechk.com

DEMOGRAPHICS
See...*CENSUS BUREAU, U.S.*

DEPARTMENT OF JUSTICE
See...*JUSTICE DEPARTMENT, U.S.*

DETECTION DOGS
Global Training Academy, Inc. trains canines for drug, explosives and arson detection.

800/777-5984
www.globalcorp.com/trainingacademy

Canine Academy trains dogs to detect narcotics. DEA certified.

512/267-2275
www.k9-academy.com

Canine Training Center, U.S. Customs trains dogs to work for Uncle Sam.

540/631-2600
www.customs.ustreas.gov

Drug Detection Dogs is a Southern California based company specializing in drug-sniffing canines.

800/NARC DOG

United States Police
K-9 Association   888/371-4014
www.uspcak9.com

The National Police Bloodhound
Association   570/538-2936
www.icubed.com/~npba

DETECTIVE SCHOOLS
CORRESPONDENCE SCHOOLS:
Detective Training Institute   888/425-9338
www.detectivetraining.com

Global School of Investigation   888/337-8839
                                   413/584-1221
www.pvteye.com

Lion Investigation Academy   877/PI SCHOOL
                                   570/420-9852
www.advsearch.com/lionacademy.htm

National Investigation Academy   818/883-6969
www.nationalinvestigationacademy.com

United States Academy of
Private Investigation   310/657-6333
www.spytechagency.com

TRADITIONAL SCHOOLS:
Center for Professional Investigative
Training (Pleasant Hill, California)   925/927-6620
www.jps.net/cpit/index.html

Central Training Academy
(Chantilly, Virginia)   703/818-0552
www.centraltrainingacademy.org

City College
(Casselberry, Florida)   407/831-8466
www.citycollege.edu

Green River Community College
(Auburn, Washington)   253/833-9111
www.grcc.ctc.edu

Nick Harris Detective Academy
(Los Angeles)   818/343-6611
www.nickharrisdetectives.com

West Coast Detective Academy
(Los Angeles)   818/894-0787
www.wcdetective.com

Henry Ford Community College
(Dearborn, Michigan)   313/845-9605
www.hfcc.net

Academy of Legal Investigators   800/842-7421
(Portland, Oregon)   503/393-8488

DIPLOMATIC SECURITY
Department of State, Diplomatic
Security   202/647-7277

DIPLOMATS

 The Department of State maintains a list of the names of the diplomatic staffs of all missions and their spouses. These persons enjoy diplomatic immunity under the *Vienna Convention on Diplomatic Relations*. The list is updated four times a year and can be obtained on the web or in hard copy. On the web, find it here:

www.state.gov/www/about_state/contacts/diplist

To order a hard copy of the list, contact the Government Printing Office and ask to order the *Diplomatic List,* Department of State Publication 10424.
866/512-1800
202/512-1800
http://bookstore.gpo.gov

Over 118,000 foreign representatives in the United States enjoy either partial or total diplomatic immunity against criminal prosecution. See...*Diplomatic Immunity* in our *Reference Guide* for further details. *The Department of State* offers the following numbers to verify the validity of the status of diplomatic and consular personnel.

202/647-4000
www.state.gov

For Diplomatic Agents and their family members and Consular Personnel and their families:
202/647-1664

For administrative, technical and service staff:

202/647-1405

For *International Organizations* other than the U.N.:

202/647-1402

For current status of diplomatic license plates and motor vehicle registration:
202/895-3532

For current status of *Department of State Driver's Licenses*, which are issued to diplomatic/consular personnel:

202/895-3521

For *Reporting Traffic Accidents and Citations* involving diplomatic personnel:
202/895-3521

U.N. License Plates and motor vehicle registration	212/826-4500

U.N. Personnel Verification:

Diplomatic Agents and family	212/415-4131
U.N. Mission Staff and family	212/415-4168
U.N. Secretariat Employees	212/415-4131
	212/415-4168
After Hours Information	212/826-4500

Also see...*EMBASSIES*.

DISASTERS

Federal Emergency Management Agency	800/462-9029
	www.fema.gov
Staff Locator	www.fema.gov/staff/

National Association for Search and Rescue is an

organization of paid and volunteer searchers dedicated to finding and aiding people in distress. They're known to assist in missing and abducted children investigations.

> 703/222-6277
> *www.nasar.org*

Information on avalanches and avalanche-danger in the Western United States can be obtained at the website of the *Westwide Avalanche Network.*

> *www.avalanche.org*

For the phone numbers of other Avalanche Centers in North America, visit:

> *www.avalanche.org/phonenum.htm*

American Association of
Avalanche Professionals   801/694-9585

The National Geophysical Data Center tracks earthquakes and other earth movements.

> 303/497-6477
> *www.ngdc.noaa.gov*

USGS National Earthquake
Information Center   800/525-7848
> *www.usgs.gov*

The Natural Hazards Research and Applications Information Center studies natural disasters.

> 303/492-6819
Library   303/492-5787
> *www.colorado.edu/hazards*

The Office of Hydrology is the federal agency that tracks flooding.

> 301/713-0006
> *www.nws.noaa.gov/oh*

Bureau of Fire & Aviation Management tracks forest fires currently burning in the United States.

> 202/205-1500
> *www.fs.fed.us/fire*

The Federal Railroad Administration maintains a database of railway accidents.

> 202/366-4000
> *www.fra.dot.gov*

FAA Accident & Incident Histories:

> 405/954-4173
> *www.faa.gov*

DNA

One DNA lab that has an open door policy to private investigators is *Genetic Technologies, Inc.* This Midwest-based lab recently identified the DNA off of an envelope that had been licked shut—25 years ago. They also do work for the FBI and other law enforcement agencies. The firm's literature points out that most investigators ignore DNA testing when conducting fidelity investigations. In fact, bodily fluids recovered off cushions, underwear and elsewhere may be genetically sampled and matched or not matched to those of a spouse. Other services include paternity testing and simple identification (without DNA analysis) of semen, blood and saliva.

877/451-GENE
636/451-GENE
www.genetictechnologies.com

Other DNA labs who offer paternity and/or forensic testing:

GeneScreen	800/DNA-TEST
	ww.genescreen.com
DNA Diagnostics Center	800/613-5768
	www.dnacenter.com
Alpha Genetics	513/475-6667
Cellmark Diagnostics	301/428-4980
	800/USA-LABS
	www.cellmark-labs.com
DNA Paternity Services	800/DNA-1005
DNA Testing Laboratories	513/662-9231
	800/786-9543
	www.dnapaternitytest.com
ReliaGene Tech Inc.	800/256-4106
Genetest	877/404-4363
	www.genetestlabs.com
Identigene	800/DNA-TYPE
	www.identigene.com

The National Commission on the Future of DNA Evidence has been empanelled to study the use of DNA evidence in the criminal justice system, with a focus on setting policy for the use of DNA in post-conviction relief matters. Essentially a policy-drafting think tank, this may be of interest to criminal defense investigators working to appeal wrongful convictions. Administered by the *National Institute of Justice.*

202/307-2942
www.ojp.usdoj.gov/nij/dna/welcome.html

DOCTORS
See...*MEDICAL DOCTORS*.

DOMESTIC VIOLENCE
Dr. Lenore Walker is a leading expert in Battered Woman's Syndrome who frequently testifies in court. She has been a consultant on high profile cases including the O.J. case.

303/322-3444
www.dviworld.org

DRIVER RECORDS
See...our *Privacy Law Survival Guide* for information on the *Driver's Privacy Protection Act*.

Also see our *Drivers License Formats* section in the *Reference Guide*.

There are several online information providers (see *DATABASE PROVIDERS*) from whom authorized users can obtain driver's license information in certain states. This information is generally restricted by the *Driver's Privacy Protection Act*.

STATE MVR AGENCIES:

Alabama	334/242-4400
Alaska	907/465-4335
Arizona	800/251-5866
Arkansas	501/682-7207
California	916/657-6525
Colorado	303/205-5613
Connecticut	860/263-5700
Delaware	302/744-2680
District of Columbia	202/727-6761
Florida	904/695-4115

Georgia: Hit "1," then "3" for status, then follow the prompts. You'll have the option of entering a DL number to learn status: 404/657-9300

Hawaii	808/532-7700
Idaho	208/334-8736
Illinois	217/782-2720
Indiana	317/232-2894
Iowa	515/244-9124
Kansas	785/296-3671
Kentucky	502/564-6800
Louisiana	225/922-1175
Maine	207/624-9000
Maryland	410/787-7758
Massachusetts	617/351-9213

Michigan: This number includes an option to obtain DL information through an automated attendant, 24 hours per day. Cost is $6.55 each and is payable by credit card. Certified copies are $1 each copy. 517/322-1624

Minnesota	651/296-6911

Mississippi	601/987-1200
Missouri	573/751-4300
Montana	406/444-3292
Nebraska	402/471-3918
Nevada	877/368-7828
New Hampshire	603/271-2251
New Jersey	609/292-6500
New Mexico	505/827-2234
New York	518/473-3595
North Carolina	919/715-7000
North Dakota	701/328-2500
Ohio	614/752-7600
Oklahoma	405/521-3344
Oregon	503/945-5000
Pennsylvania	717/391-6190
Rhode Island	401/588-3020
South Carolina	803/896-7839
South Dakota	605/773-6883
Tennessee	615/741-3954
Texas: For the status of a DL, call:	512/424-2600
Utah	801/965-4437
Vermont	802/828-2000
Virginia	804/367-0538
Washington	360/902-3900
West Virginia	304/558-0238
Wisconsin	608/266-2353
Wyoming	307/777-4800

Insurance Information Exchange offers computerized driver's license information on a nationwide basis. Subject to *Driver's Privacy Protection Act* restrictions.

800/683-8553
www.iix.com

CANADIAN MOTOR VEHICLE
LICENSING AUTHORITIES:

Alberta	403/643-7620
British Columbia	604/661-2800
Manitoba	204/945-6945
New Brunswick	506/453-3939
Nova Scotia	902/424-4597
Newfoundland	709/729-2518
Ontario	800/268-4686
Prince Edward Island	902/368-5100
Quebec	418/643-7620
Saskatchewan	306/787-4800
Yukon	867/667-5644
Northwest Territories	867/920-8822

Also see...*MVR DECODER DIGEST/MVR BOOK.*

Also see...*DATABASE PROVIDERS.*

Also see ... *NATIONAL DRIVER REGISTRY*.

DRIVERS LICENSE GUIDE CO.

Publisher of reference books showing real copies of identification cards. Used by retailers to spot bogus identification used by under-age customers and others. The U.S. edition sells for $21.95 and includes copies of driver's licenses from all 50 states. The international edition includes foreign I.D.'s ($24.94). Also check out the company's U.S. Identification Manual. See *U.S. IDENTIFICATION MANUAL* for further details.

800/227-8827
www.driverslicenseguide.com

DRUG DETECTION

STAUnited, Inc. offers drug and alcohol testing for corporate clients. In addition to the tests themselves, the company offers additional support such as legal guidelines to follow, employee notification information, and referral to substance abuse professionals when needed. Unlike some of the below listed companies, these tests are primarily mail-in. (The specimen is sent in an overnight envelope.) Tests meet government guidelines for certain types of employees; some of the instant tests below may not.

800/288-8504
402/483-6600
www.staunited.com

TIG Labs sells do-it-yourself drug test panels that give instant results. Substances tested for include THC (Marijuana), cocaine, heroine, morphine, Speed, Ecstasy and Angel Dust. Prices range from $10 for a single substance test to $35 for multi-panel tests.

316/262-5779
www.tiglabs.com

When any one of several different illegal drugs are used, trace amounts of the substance are left deposited in the cortex of the hair of the user. *Psychemedics* has developed a patented process to detect these trace amounts. Results will be available in around 5 days through a confidential and anonymous 800 number.

Psychemedics, Customer Service   800/800-5447
Psychemedics, Corporate Office   800/628-8073
www.psychemedics.com

Drug Detection Services, Inc. offers mail-in kits.

800/748-2742
www.drugdetection.com

3D Ltd. Drug Detection Devices offers drug-screening services, too.

> 888/768-6786
> 770/886-6226
> *www.3dl.net*

F. Morton Pitt Co. offers law enforcement products, including drug and alcohol test kits.

> 800/533-2838
> 805/658-5133
> *www.fmortonpitt.com*

Alcohol Countermeasure Systems sells breath alcohol analyzers.

> 950/670-2288
> 303/366-5699
> *www.acs-corp.com*

Mistral Security makes a handy collection of presumptive field tests for various drug substances, explosives and fingerprints.

> 800/9MISTRAL
> *www.mistralgroup.com/security.asp*

Also see...*DRUG IDENTIFICATION SERVICE.*

Also see...*DETECTION DOGS.*

Also see...*CRIME LABS.*

DRUG ENFORCEMENT ADMINISTRATION

National Headquarters   202/307-1000
> *www.dea.gov*

DEA Employment Information   800/DEA-4288

DEA FOIA Office   202/307-7709

DEA Controlled Substances Act Registration Records is a little known database of the *DEA* which registers doctors, dentists, veterinarians, pharmaceutical manufacturers and others who are authorized to prescribe controlled substances. (Take a look at the next prescription you receive from your doctor. In small print there should be a DEA number.) Available through select *DATABASE PROVIDERS* including:

AutoTrackXP   800/279-7710
> *www.atxp.com*

Whether or not a doctor has an active DEA registration and the effective date of the registration can also be obtained for free as part of SearchPointe.com's physician profile.

> *www.searchpointe.com*

For the *DEA Schedule of Controlled Substances*, see our *Reference Guide*.

Report sale of illegal drugs to the *Enforcement Section:*

	202/633-1151
El Paso Intelligence Division	888/873-3742
Aviation Unit	817/837-2000

One powerful *DEA* tool is the *National Drug Pointer Index* (NDPIX) which is a relatively new system for information sharing by federal, state and local law enforcement agencies. The system doesn't maintain criminal record information, but it does act as a switchboard so that law enforcement agencies can know if they are investigating common targets. The focus is on drug traffickers here. The system went online in 1997. It's available to law enforcement only through NLETS.

DEA Field Offices:

ATLANTA DIVISION:
Atlanta, GA	404/763-5861
Columbia, SC	803/253-3441
Greensboro, NC	336/547-4219
Nashville, TN	615/736-2559
Savannah, GA	912/447-1035

BOSTON DIVISION:
(Jurisdiction: ME, MA, RI, NH)
Boston, MA	617/424-5715
Hartford, CT	860/240-3700

CARIBBEAN DIVISION:
(Jurisdiction: Caribbean Islands)
Santurce, PR	787/775-1815

CHICAGO DIVISION:
(Jurisdiction: Central and Northern IL)
Chicago, IL	312/353-4391
Indianapolis, IN	317/226-7977
Merrillville, IN	219/681-7000
Milwaukee, WI	414/297-3395
Minneapolis / St. Paul, MN	612/348-1729
Springfield, IL	217/241-6750

DALLAS DIVISION:
(Jurisdiction: Eastern & Northern TX, OK)
Dallas, TX	214/655-8175
Ft. Worth, TX	817/978-3455
Oklahoma City, OK	405/475-7556
Tulsa, OK	918/459-9600
Tyler, TX	903/534-0472

DENVER DIVISION:
(Jurisdiction: CO, UT, WY)
Colorado Springs, CO   719/471-1749
Denver, CO   303/784-6300
Salt Lake City, UT   801/524-4156

DETROIT DIVISION:
Cincinnati, OH   513/684-3671
Cleveland, OH   216/522-3705
Columbus, OH   614/469-2595
Detroit, MI   313/226-4010
London,KY   606/862-4500
Louisville, KY   502/582-5908

EL PASO DIVISION:
(Jurisdiction: West TX, NM)
Albuquerque, NM   505/346-7419
El Paso, TX   915/832-6000

HOUSTON DIVISION:
(Jurisdiction: Eastern, Central, Southern TX)
Houston, TX   713/718-4861
San Antonio, TX   210/525-2900
Waco, TX   254/741-1920

LOS ANGELES DIVISION:
(Jurisdiction: South Central CA, HI, NV)
Honolulu, HI   808/541-1930
Las Vegas, NV   702/388-6635
Los Angeles, CA   213/894-2941
Riverside, CA   909/328-6000

MIAMI DIVISION:
(Jurisdiction: FL)
Miami, FL   305/536-5206
Orlando, FL   407/333-7046
Tallahassee, FL   850/942-8417
Tampa, FL   813/288-1290

NEWARK DIVISION:
(Jurisdiction: NJ)
Camden, NJ   856/968-4899
Newark, NJ   973/273-5000

NEW ORLEANS DIVISION:
(Jurisdiction: LA, MS)
Birmingham, AL   205/290-7150
Jackson, MS   601/965-4400
Little Rock, AR   501/324-5981
Mobile, AL   205/441-5831
New Orleans, LA   504/840-1100

NEW YORK DIVISION:
Buffalo, NY   716/551-3391

Long Island, NY	631/420-4540
New York, NY	212/264-0700

PHILADELPHIA DIVISION:
(Jurisdiction: DE, PA)

Philadelphia, PA	215/597-2344
Pittsburgh, PA	412/395-4502

PHOENIX DIVISION:
(Northern & Central AZ)

Phoenix, AZ	602/664-5600
Tucson, AZ	520/573-5500

SAN DIEGO DIVISION:
(Jurisdiction: Southern CA)

San Diego, CA	619/616-4100

SAN FRANCISCO DIVISION:
(Jurisdiction: Central Coastal CA)

Fresno, CA	415/436-7854
Oakland, CA	510/637-5600
Sacramento, CA	916/566-7401
San Francisco, CA	415/744-6565
San Jose, CA	408/291-7235

SEATTLE DIVISION:
(Jurisdiction: AK, ID, OR, WA)

Anchorage, AK	907/271-5033
Boise, ID	208/334-1620
Portland, OR	503/326-2447
Seattle, WA	206/220-6700

ST. LOUIS DIVISION:
(Jurisdiction: MO, IA, KS)

Des Moines, IA	515/284-4709
Kansas City, KS	913/652-9127
St. Louis, MO	314/538-4600

WASHINGTON, D.C. DIVISION:
(Jurisdiction: D.C., Southern MD, WV, VA)

Baltimore, MD	410/962-4800
Charleston, WV	304/347-5209
Richmond, VA	804/771-8163
Washington, D.C.	202/305-8500

Laboratories:

Special Testing & Research Lab	703/873-3742
Mid-Atlantic Lab	202/275-6478
Northeast Lab	212/620-4932
Southeast Lab	305/590-4830
North Central Lab	312/353-3640
South Central Lab	214/240-0964
Southwest Lab	619/498-0005
Western Lab	415/744-7051

DEA FOREIGN OFFICES:

Ankara, Turkey	011-90-41-265-47
Istanbul	011-90-11-61-3602
Asuncion, Paraguay	011-505-21-201041
Athens, Greece	011-30-1-721-2951
Bangkok, Thailand	011-66-2-253-2917
Chiang Mai	011-66-53-221509
Songkhla	011-66-074-313-523
Bern, Switzerland	011-41-31-43-7367
Bogota, Colombia	011-571-285-1300
Barranquilla	011-57-845-9353
Bonn, Germany	011-49-228-339-2307
Frankfurt, Germany	011-49-69-56002-771
Brasilia, Brazil	011-55-61-321-7272
Sao Paulo, Brazil	011-55-11-881-6511
Bridgetown, Barbados	809/436-4950
Brussels, Belgium	011-32-2-513-3830
Buenos Aires, Argentina	011-541-774-7611
Canberra, Australia	011-6162-7333-470
Cairo, Egypt	011-20-2-355-7371
Caracas, Venezuela	011-58-2-285-3111
Copenhagen, Denmark	011-45-1-42-31-44
Curacao, Netherlands	011-599-9-613066
Guatemala City. Guatemala	011-502-231-8563
Hong Kong	011-852-5-239011
Islamabad, Pakistan	011-92-51-826161
Karachi	011-92-21-515081
Lahore	011-92-42-870-221
Peshawar	011-92-521-42424
Kingston, Jamaica	809/829-4850
Kuala Lumpur, Malaysia	011-60-3-248-9011
La Paz, Bolivia	011-591-2-322-925
Santa Cruz, Bolivia	011-591-333-485
Cochabamba, Bolivia	011-591-42-40476
Lagos, Nigeria	011-234-1-619837
Lima, Peru	011-51-14-24-4236
London, England	011-44-1-499-9000
Madrid, Spain	011-34-1-274-3400
Manila, Phillipines	011-632-521-7116
Mexico City, Mexico	011-525-211-00422
Guadalajara, Mexico	011-52-36-2530-84
Hermosillo, Mexico	011-52-621-7-4732
Mazatlan, Mexico	011-52-678-21760
Tegucigalpa	011-504-323121
Merida, Mexico	011-52-99-25-5742
Monterrey. Mexico	011-52-83-44-5261
Nassau, Bahamas	809/322-8179
New Delhi, India	011-91-11-600-651
Bombay, India	011-91-22-822-3611
Nicosia, Cyprus	011-357-2465-182
Ottawa, Canada	613/238-5633
Montreal, Canada	514/261-1461
Paris, France	011-33-14-296-1202
Marseilles, France	011-38-91-54-92-90

Port-Au-Prince, Haiti	011-509-120-868
Quito, Ecuador	011-593-2-230053
Guayaquil, Ecuador	011-593-4-323-715
Rome, Italy	011-39-6-4674-2225
Milan, Italy	011-39-2-652-841
San Jose, Costa Rica	011-506-20-3939
Santiago, Chile	011-562-71-0133
Santo Domingo, Dominican Republic	809/541-2171
Seoul, South Korea	011-82-2-732-2601
Singapore	011-65-338-0251
The Hague, Netherlands	011-31-70-62-4911
Tokyo, Japan	011-81-3-224-5000
Vienna, Austria	011-43-222-514-2251

DRUG IDENTIFICATION SERVICE

Have a pill and don't know what drug it is? **NEW!** *Patient Prescription Information, Inc.* has pharmacists that are trained to make tablet and capsule identification over the telephone. You'll receive back a fax report which identifies the drug type and its legal status (controlled/over-the-counter), signed by a registered pharmacist. The service has a 50,000 record database that includes prescription, OTC, veterinary, investigational and new drugs.

800/4DRUG ID
www.drugid.net

For photographs of street drugs, visit the authoritative website at *StreetDrugs.org*.

www.streetdrugs.org

Identa-A-Drug is a handbook which uses a three-step identification system to identify street drugs. Sells for around $30.

800/477-7766
www.gallsinc.com

The Food & Drug Administration maintains a database of pharmaceuticals. Provides information on a cost basis.

888/463-6332
301/827-8101
www.fda.gov

DTMF TONES

Free software called *WinTone 2.0* can be found on the Internet to decode taped touch-tones. You'll install it on your computer. Microphone not included.

www.steaksandwich.com

Most spy shops sell DTMF decoders. See...*SPY GEAR*.

An old fashioned pager can also work as a poor man's DTMF decoder. Call your own pager number and then play the recorded tones over the phone. The decoded tones should appear on your pager display.

DUN & BRADSTREET

Dun & Bradstreet is the leading business credit reporting company. Their business information reports typically contain limited information on trade accounts and public records, such as tax liens. Dollar for dollar, not a great deal.

Customer Service   800/234-3867
                                              www.dnb.com

EARTHQUAKES

See...*DISASTERS*.

ECONOMIC NEWS

Need to know about fast-breaking economic news...like whether or not the Fed is going to raise interest rates, or what Treasury cash balances are? *Dow Jones Telerate* is a subscription service, delivered electronically, that posts government and market information direct from the source.

                                              800/444-1068
In Canada: 403/264-1974
                                              www.telerate.com

Need current or historical cost of living information, also known as Consumer Price Index? *The Bureau of Labor Statistics* collects such data for much of the federal government.

                                              202/691-7000
                                              www.bls.gov

EDGAR ONLINE

Edgar Online has the same information contained in the Security and Exchange Commission's EDGAR database, but at a much more user-friendly website. The data is mined from the financial statements of publicly owned companies that are filed with the SEC. Of particular interest is a search called EDGAR Online People which lets you search information, including compensation packages, on over 37,000 corporate executives. Information is updated daily.

                                 www.edgar-online.com

800# DIRECTORY ASSISTANCE

A simple and often effective way to locate any business is to call *800 Directory Assistance*. If the company has a toll-free 800 number, the operator should be able to provide their location.

                                              800/555-1212

EIN IDENTIFIER

[NEW!] EINs (Employer Identification Numbers), also commonly known as FEINs, are *not* automatically public record. Like social security numbers, they are nine digits in length. The first two digits indicate the IRS office where the number was issued. (See *Reference Guide* for *Employer Identification Number Decoder*.) Some commercial database providers have mined an assortment of public records for EINs as well. (See *Master List of Commercially Available Public Record Databases* in our *Reference Guide*.)

(HOT!) Another valuable source of EINs is *FreeERISA.com*. This is a website that mines information from publicly disclosed ERISA reports. (ERISA stands for Employee Retirement Income Security Act.) ERISA reports contain information on money held in the retirement plans of businesses and *must* be filed with the IRS. The government then releases the reports so that people will know where their pension money has been vested. At the same time, the company's EIN becomes public record, along with other data. The company behind the website also offers research services where information on actual assets of the retirement funds can be obtained on a fee basis. The website itself is free, although registration is required.

202/728-0111
www.freeerisa.com

To obtain the EIN of a tax-exempt organization, visit the *GuideStar* website.

www.guidestar.com

ELECTION FRAUD

The Federal Election Commission and its state-level counterparts keep track of who contributes how much to which politicians. This data has been crunched into easy-to-use form by website, *opensecrets.org*. Data is searchable by money donor or by politician.

www.opensecrets.org

William C. Kimberling, Deputy Director of the *Office of Election Administration, Federal Election Commission,* is a recognized expert in election fraud, voter registration and election procedures.

202/694-1095
www.fec.gov

Craig C. Donsanto is Director of the *Election Crimes Branch* of the *United States Department of Justice*. He both investigates and prosecutes election fraud and campaign finance law violations.

202/514-1421
www.doj.gov

ELECTIONS
See ... *POLITICIANS*.

Also see... *FEDERAL ELECTION COMMISSION*.

ELECTRONIC EAVESDROPPING
See... *Electronic Eavesdropping* in our *Privacy Law Survival Guide*.

Also see... *26 Warning Signs of Electronic Eavesdropping* in the *Reference Guide* of this book.

Also see... *DEBUGGING*.

EL PASO INTELLIGENCE CENTER
U.S. Customs tracks and maintains information on persons exiting and entering the U.S. for law enforcement purposes through the *El Paso Intelligence Center*.

888/873-3742
www.usdoj.gov/dea/programs/epic

EMBASSIES
For a comprehensive list of U.S. embassies and consulates abroad, visit this State Department website. When calling a foreign embassy for information or assistance, as for the RSO.

www.usembassy.state.gov

These are major foreign embassies in the U.S. Most will provide information about their countries and many maintain phone books for their homelands.

Afghanistan	202/234-3770
Albania	202/223-4942
Algeria	202/265-2800
Angola	202/785-1156
Antigua and Barbuda	202/362-5211
Argentina	202/939-6400
Armenia	202/296-9076
Australia	202/797-3000
Austria	202/895-6700
Azerbaijan	202/842-0001
Bahamas	202/319-2660
Bahrain	202/342-0741
Bangladesh	202/342-8372
Barbados	202/939-9200
Belarus	202/986-1604
Belgium	202/333-6900
Belize	202/332-9636

Benin	202/232-6656
Bolivia	202/483-4410
Bosnia and Herzegovina	202/833-3612
Botswana	202/244-4990
Brazil	202/797-0200
Brunei	202/342-0159
Bulgaria	202/387-7969
Burkina Faso	202/332-5577
Burundi	202/342-2574
Cambodia	202/726-7742
Cameroon	202/265-8790
Canada	202/682-1740
Cape Verde	202/965-6820
Central African Republic	202/483-7800
Chad	202/462-4009
Chile	202/785-1746
China	202/328-2500
Colombia	202/332-7573
Congo, Republic of	202/726-5500
Costa Rica	202/234-2945
Cote D'Ivorie	202/797-0300
Croatia	202/588-5899
Cuba c/o Swiss Embassy	202/797-8518
Cyprus	202/462-5772
Czech Republic	202/363-6315
Denmark	202/234-4300
Djibouti	202/331-0270
Dominica	202/332-6280
Ecuador	202/234-7200
Egypt	202/895-5400
El Salvador	202/265-9671
Equatorial Guinea	202/518-5700
Eritrea	202/312-1991
Estonia	202/588-0101
Ethiopia	202/234-2281
Fiji	202/337-8320
Finland	202/298-5800
France	202/944-6000
Gabon	202/797-1000
Gambia	202/785-1399
Germany	202/298-4000
Ghana	202/686-4520
Greece	202/939-5800
Grenada	202/265-2561
Guatemala	202/745-4952
Guinea	202/483-9420
Guinea-Bissau	202/872-4222
Guyana	202/265-6900
Haiti	202/332-4090
Holy See	202/333-7121
Honduras	202/966-7702
Hungary	202/362-6730
Iceland	202/265-6653
India	202/939-7000

Indonesia	202/775-5200
Iraq c/o Algerian Embassy	202/483-7500
Iran	202/965-4990
Ireland	202/462-3939
Israel	202/364-5500
Italy	202/328-5500
Jamaica	202/452-0660
Japan	202/238-6700
Jordan	202/966-2664
Kazakhstan	202/333-4504
Kenya	202/387-6101
Korea	202/939-5600
Kuwait	202/966-0702
Kyrgyzstin	202/347-3732
Laos	202/332-6416
Latvia	202/726-8213
Lebanon	202/939-6300
Lesotito	202/797-5533
Liberia	202/723-0437
Lithuania	202/234-5860
Luxembourg	202/265-4171
Madagascar	202/265-5525
Malawi	202/797-1007
Malaysia	202/328-2700
Mali	202/332-2249
Malta	202/462-3611
Marshall Islands	202/234-5414
Mauritania	202/232-5700
Mauritius	202/244-1491
Mexico	202/728-1600
Micronesia	202/223-4383
Moldora	202/783-3012
Mongolia	202/333-7117
Morocco	202/462-7979
Mozambique	202/293-7146
Myanmar	202/332-9044
Namibia	202/986-0540
Nepal	202/667-4550
Netherlands	202/244-5300
New Zealand	202/328-4800
Nicaragua	202/939-6570
Niger	202/483-4224
Nigeria	202/986-8400
Norway	202/333-6000
Oman	202/387-1980
Pakistan	202/939-6200
Panama	202/483-1407
Papua New Guinea	202/745-3680
Paraguay	202/483-6960
Peru	202/833-9860
Phillipines	202/467-9300
Poland	202/234-3800
Portugal	202/328-8610
Qatar	202/338-0111

Republic of Congo (formerly Zaire)	202/234-7690
Romania	202/232-4747
Russia	202/298-5700
Rwanda	202/232-2882
Saint Kitts and Nevis	202/833-3550
Saint Lucia	202/463-7378
Saudi Arabia	202/342-3800
Senegal	202/234-0540
Sierra Leone	202/939-9261
Singapore	202/537-3100
Slovakia	202/965-5161
Slovenia	202/667-5363
South Africa	202/232-4400
Spain	202/265-0190
Sri Lanka	202/483-4025
Sudan	202/338-8565
Suriname	202/244-7488
Swaziland	202/362-6683
Sweden	202/467-2600
Switzerland	202/745-7900
Syria	202/232-6313
Taiwan	202/895-1800
Tanzania	202/939-6125
Thailand	202/944-3600
Togo	202/234-4212
Trinidad and Tobago	202/467-6490
Tunisia	202/862-1850
Turkey	202/659-8200
Uganda	202/726-7100
Ukraine	202/333-0606
United Arab Emirates	202/338-6500
United Kingdom	202/462-1340
Uruguay	202/331-1313
Uzbekistan	202/638-4266
Vatican City	202/333-7121
Venezuela	202/342-2214
Vietnam	202/861-0737
Western Samoa	212/599-6196
Yemen	202/965-4760
Yugoslavia	202/462-6566
Zaire (See Republic of Congo)	
Zambia	202/265-9717
Zimbabwe	202/332-7100

EMPLOYER IDENTIFICATION NUMBERS
See...*EIN IDENTIFIER*.

EMPLOYMENT VERIFICATIONS
See...*WORK NUMBER, THE*.

ENCYCLOPEDIA OF ASSOCIATIONS
Published by *Gale Research*, the *Encyclopedia of Associations* is widely used for locating and profiling special interest associations. Profiles include names of

Robert Scott, P.I.

officials. Includes over 22,000 organizations. Sells for around $2500 in a three volume set. Or you can contact your local library. Or heck, if it's three in the morning you might even want to try the 24-hour reference desk listed in the *LIBRARIES* section of this book. Available through *marketresearch.com*.

800/298-5699
212/807-2716
www.marketresearch.com

ENGLAND INVESTIGATORS
Association of British
Investigators, Ltd.   011-44-2085-463368
www.assoc-britishinvestigators.org.uk

ENGLAND – REAL PROPERTY RECORDS
Land Registry Information does real property ownership searches throughout England.

011-44-1812-881418

ENVIROFACTS
NEW! The Environmental Protection Agency has bundled many of its most vital databases into one super-search called *Envirofacts*. Databases include information culled from EPA inspections and permits. The data is searchable by company name, geographic area, SIC code and pollutant.

www.epa.gov/enviro

ENVIRONMENTAL INVESTIGATIONS
See...*ENVIRONMENTAL PROTECTION AGENCY.*

Department of Energy Environmental Compliance Violations data can be searched on the Internet. Most of the information arises from inspection of energy related facilities and laboratories.

http://homer.ornl.gov/oepa/data/violations.cfm

The *Right To Know Network* makes EPA Enforcement Dockets available over the Internet. The filings arise from DOJ legal action against polluters on behalf of the EPA. Free.

202/234-8494
www.rtk.net/rtkdata.html

Conservation Directory is published by the National Wildlife Federation and contains a comprehensive listing of environmental agencies and groups.

800/836-0510
www.nwf.org/printandfilm

VISTA Information Solutions, Inc. offers databases compiled from state and federal environmental records.

> 800/767-0403
> *www.esri.com/data/online/vista/*

National Radon Hotline   800/SOS-RADON
> *www.nsc.org*

National Pesticides Telecommunications Network maintains information on pesticides, including their effects on health and what to do when a spill occurs.

> 800/858-PEST
> *nptn.orst.edu*

Society of Environmental Journalists

> 215/884-8174
> *www.sej.org*

Also see...*CHEMICAL SPILLS - EMERGENCY HOTLINES.*

Also see...*TOXIC CHEMICALS.*

Also see...*ENVIROFACTS.*

Also see...*NATIONAL FISH & WILDLIFE FORENSIC LAB.*

ENVIRONMENTAL PROTECTION AGENCY
Headquarters   202/260-2090
> *www.epa.gov*

REGIONAL OFFICES:
Region 1
(CT, MA, ME, NH, RI, VT)   617/918-1111
Region 2
(NJ, NY, PR, VI)   212/637-3000
Region 3
(D.C., DE, MD, PA, VA, WV)   215/814-5103
Region 4
(AL, FL, GA, KY, MS, NC, SC, TN)   404/562-9900
Region 5
(IL, IN, MI, MN, OH, WI)   312/353-2000
Region 6
(AR, LA, NM, OK, TX)   214/665-2200
Region 7
(IA, KS, MO, NE)   913/551-7003
Region 8
(CO, MT, ND, SD, UT, WY)   303/312-6312
Region 9
(AZ, CA, HI, NV)   415/744-1305
Region 10
(AK, ID, OR, WA)   206/553-1200

Robert Scott, P.I.

EPA HOTLINES:

Acid Rain Hotline	202/564-9620
Air Risk Information Center Hotline	919/541-0888
Asbestos Abatement	800/368-5888
Clean Air Technology Center Infoline	919/541-0800
Clearinghouse for Inventories and Emission Factors Help Desk	919/541-5285
Climate Wise Wise-Line	800/459-WISE
Emergency Planning and Community Right-To-Know Act Hotline	800/424-9346
Endangered Species Hotline	800/447-3813
Environmental Financing Information Network	202/564-4994
Environmental Justice Hotline	800/962-6215
EPA Grants and Fellowships Hotline	800/490-9194
Federal Facilities Docket Hotline	800/548-1016
Indoor Air Quality Information	800/438-4318
Information Resource Center	202/260-5922
Inspector General Hotline	888/546-8740
Mexico Border Hotline (English/Spanish)	800/334-0741
National Antimicrobial Information	800/447-6349
Environmental Publications	800/490-9198
National Lead Information Center	800/424-LEAD
National Pesticide Telecommunications Network	800/858-7378
National Radon Hotline	800/SOS-RADON
National Response Center Hotline	800/424-8802
Ozone Protection Hotline	800/296-1996
Pay-As-You-Throw Helpline	888/EPA-PAYT
Pollution Prevention Information	202/260-1023
RCRA, Superfund and EPCRA Hotline	800/424-9346
(TDD)	800/553-7672
Safe Drinking Water Hotline	800/426-4791
Storet Water Quality System Hotline	800/424-9067
Toxic Release Inventory - Community Right To Know - EPCRA Hotline	800/535-0202
Toxic Substances Control Act Hotline	202/554-1404
WasteWise Helpline	800/EPA-WISE
Wetlands Information Hotline	800/832-7828

EPA Office of Investigations keeps watch over EPA administered programs for fraud, bribery, and false claims.

303/236-5111
703/308-8283

The *Right To Know Network* makes EPA Enforcement Dockets available over the Internet. The filings arise from DOJ legal action against polluters on behalf of the EPA. Free.

202/234-8494
www.rtk.net/rtkdata.html

The Environmental Protection Agency's *Public Information Center* publishes an annual directory of agency personnel situated at its headquarters.

202/260-5922

EPA
See...*ENVIRONMENTAL PROTECTION AGENCY*.

EQUIFAX
See...*CREDIT BUREAUS*.

EVIDENCE PHOTOGRAPHERS
Evidence Photographers International Council is a professional group of crime scene and civil evidence photographers. Referral service available.

800/356-3742
570/253-5450
www.epic-photo.org

EXCLUDED PARTY LIST SYSTEM

 Technically known as the *List of Parties Excluded from Federal Procurement and Nonprocurement Programs*, this is the federal government's list of banned persons and businesses. Once on the list, they can't do further business with the federal government. Includes everything from doctors who have defrauded a government benefit system to crooked defense contractors to corporate polluters. Over forty federal agencies contribute. Searchable on the Internet without government clearance.

202/501-4873
202/501-4740
http://epls.arnet.gov

EXECUTIVE PROTECTION INSTITUTE

The Virginia-based *Executive Protection Institute* is situated on an 85-acre campus and features a seven-day training course to earn a P.P.S. (Personal Protection Specialist) designation. Other courses offered include Corporate Aircraft Security and Advance Maritime Work (for water-based protection). *EPI* has trained the protection detail of numerous celebrities, government officials and corporate executives.

540/955-1128
www.personalprotection.com

EXECUTIVES

 Pay and bonuses received by top executives at over 9,000 public U.S. companies can be viewed online at *eComp*.

The information is derived from SEC filings. Free.

212/730-4636
www.ecomponline.htm

Also of note is the People Tracker feature on the *Forbes.com* website. It includes profiles on over 120,000 executives and celebrities. Information returned includes executive compensation as well as biographical information. Amazingly, it's free. Registration required.

www.forbes.com

Also...*EDGAR ONLINE*.

Also see...*BUSINESSCREDITUSA.COM*.

Also see...*NAMEBASE*.

Also see...*CORPORATIONS*.

Also see...*FACTIVA.COM*.

EXPERIAN
See...*CREDIT BUREAUS*.

EXPERT WITNESSES
Expert Technologies International specializes in finding experts for every conceivable field.

800/800-4341

An Internet-based option is *exp.com*. The site features thousands of experts who are available to answer questions, often for free or at a nominal cost.

877/968-7397
www.exp.com

Expert Resources, Inc. specializes in providing expert witnesses for court cases:

800/383-4857
www.expertresources.com

Atlanta	404/577-3592
Boston	617/451-5351
Chicago	713/327-2830
Cincinnati	513/241-8648
Dallas	214/698-1881
Detroit	313/964-0505
Honolulu	808/531-5464
Houston	713/223-2330
Los Angeles	213/669-1660
Miami	305/372-5259
Minneapolis	612/338-2788
New Orleans	504/525-8806
New York	212/288-1120

Peoria, IL	309/688-4857
Philadelphia	215/829-9570
San Diego	619/232-4618
San Francisco	415/398-8854
Seattle	206/587-0745
St. Louis	314/241-9669
Washington, D.C.	202/397-1177

Profnet is a network of university research professionals available as background sources, technical consultants and expert witnesses.

800/PROFNET
561/223-7547
www.profnet.com

American Academy of Forensic Sciences is a professional organization that offers an expert referral service. Also maintains a reference library.

719/636-1100
www.aafs.org

National Consultant Referrals, Inc. is another company that specializes in providing expert witnesses.

888/777-5636
www.4expert-witnesses.com

National Forensic Center provides expert witnesses and litigation consultants. They also train consultants to serve as expert witnesses.

609/883-0550
www.expertindex.com

The National Reference Center is a free program of the Library of Congress which maintains a huge database of experts and organizations on virtually any technical or scientific subject.

202/707-5522
www.loc.gov

EXTRATERRESTRIAL INTELLIGENCE

If you ever felt that there was no intelligence here on Earth and wanted to look elsewhere, try the *Center for the Study of Extraterrestrial Intelligence (CSETI)*. The organization is especially focused on ET-Human encounters. CSETI's Disclosure Project focuses on bringing forward government witnesses who have encountered evidence of ETs.

888/ET-CSETI
301/249-3915
www.cseti.org
www.disclosureproject.org

EXTREME COVERT CATALOG

■☞ NEW! *Lee ("The Whole Spy Catalog") Lapin* has assembled a mammoth book on currently available spy gear including everything from fax interception devices to cell phone jammers to asphalt video transmitters. Many of the items are restricted for sale to law enforcement only. Includes manufacturer contacts. If I was stranded on a desert island and could take just one book — it wouldn't be this one. However, I'd sure miss it.

www.intelligencehere.com

FACTIVA.COM

■☞ NEW! *Factiva.com* is the home base for the sweeping and powerful Dow Jones Interactive Publications Library. Includes online access to the electronic archives of over 6,600 publications with a single search. (Publications include *The Wall Street Journal*, major dailies like *The New York Times, The Globe, The Washington Post* and *The Chicago Tribune*; and scores of business journals.) It's free to sign up and free to receive brief summaries of articles found. Full articles cost $2.95 each. Excellent source for conducting background investigations, especially when the subject may be newsworthy or high profile.

www.factiva.com

Also see...*NEWSPAPERS*.

FAIR CREDIT REPORTING ACT

See...the *Credit Reports* section in our *Privacy Law Survival Guide*.

FATAL ACCIDENTS

The U.S. Department of Transportation maintains a computerized database of fatal motor vehicle accidents from all 50 states, called the *Fatal Accident Reporting System*. The information is chiefly statistical and does not provide identifying information on persons involved in the accidents.

202/366-4820
www.dot.gov

FEDERAL AGENTS – FORMER
See...*FEDERAL INVESTIGATORS – FORMER*.

FEDERAL AVIATION ADMINISTRATION

Hotline Information Center	800/322-7873
	www.faa.gov
Accident & Incident Histories	405/954-4173
Airmen Registry	405/954-3205
	registry.faa.gov
Investigations Division	202/366-4000

Aviation Safety Hotline   800/255-1111

Kolbenschlag Aviation Services is an aviation information service that offers customized searching of the FAA's databases.

503/787-8700

A lesser-known aviation database at the FAA is the certificate holder list of government-licensed airlines. Information returned includes number and make of aircraft owned and operated.

http://av-info.faa.gov/opcert.asp

The FAA issues Airworthiness Directives when an unsafe condition exists in an aircraft, aircraft engine or propeller. No person may operate a product to which an AD applies, except in accordance with the AD requirements. Airworthiness Directives issued since 1999 can be viewed on the Internet.

http://av-info.faa.gov/ad/ad.htm

Landings.com is a very useful free website that offers access to a variety of FAA and other aviation-related database lookups. You'll also find links to some foreign aircraft registration databases here.

www.landings.com

Also see...*AVIATION*.

Also see...*Black Book Online* and click the "Aviation" button.

FEDERAL BUREAU OF INVESTIGATION
National Headquarters   202/324-3000
www.fbi.gov

FBI FIELD OFFICES:

Albany, NY	518/465-7551
Albuquerque, NM	505/224-2000
Anchorage, AK	907/258-5322
Atlanta, GA	404/679-9000
Baltimore, MD	410/265-8080
Birmingham, AL	205/326-6166
Boston, MA	617/742-5533
Buffalo, NY	716/856-7800
Charlotte, NC	704/377-9200
Chicago, IL	312/431-1333
Cincinnati, OH	513/421-4310
Cleveland, OH	216/522-1400
Columbia, SC	803/551-4200
Dallas, TX	214/720-2200
Denver, CO	303/629-7171
Detroit, MI	313/965-2323
El Paso, TX	915/832-5000

Robert Scott, P.I.

Honolulu, HI	808/521-1411
Houston, TX	713/693-5000
Indianapolis, IN	317/639-3301
Jackson, MS	601/948-5000
Jacksonville, FL	904/721-1211
Kansas City, MO	816/512-8200
Knoxville, TN	865/544-0751
Las Vegas, NV	702/385-1281
Little Rock, AR	501/221-9100
Los Angeles, CA	310/477-6565
Louisville, KY	502/583-3941
Memphis, TN	901/747-4300
North Miami Beach, FL	305/944-9101
Milwaukee, WI	414/276-4684
Minneapolis, MN	612/376-3200
Mobile, AL	334/438-3674
Newark, NJ	973/792-3000
New Haven, CT	203/777-6311
New Orleans, LA	504/816-3000
New York, NY	212/384-1000
Norfolk, VA	757/455-0100
Oklahoma City, OK	405/290-7770
Omaha, NE	402/493-8688
Philadelphia, PA	215/418-4000
Phoenix, AZ	602/279-5511
Pittsburgh, PA	412/471-2000
Portland, OR	503/224-4181
Richmond, VA	804/261-1044
Sacramento, CA	916/481-9110
St. Louis, MO	314/231-4324
Salt Lake City, UT	801/579-1400
San Antonio, TX	210/225-6741
San Diego, CA	619/565-1255
San Francisco, CA	415/553-7400
San Juan, PR	787/754-6000
Seattle, WA	206/622-0460
Springfield, IL	217/522-9675
Tampa, FL	813/273-4566
Washington, D.C.	202/278-2000

Photo: FBI Headquarters in Washington, D.C. — home to nearly 10,000 employees. (Photo courtesy of FBI.)

FBI FOREIGN ATTACHES:

Athens	011-30-1-721-2951
Bangkok	011-66-2-205-4366
Bern	011-41-31-357-7011
Bogota, Colombia	011-57-1-315-0811
Bonn	011-49-228-3391
Bonn, Berlin Suboffice	011-49-30-238-5174
Bonn, Frankfurt Suboffice	011-49-69-7535-3780
Brazilia	55-61-321-7272
Bridgetown, Barbados	246/436-4950
Brussels, Belgium	011-32-2-508-2111
Budapest, Hungary	011-36-1-267-4400
Cairo, Egypt	011-202-355-7371
Canberra	011-61-6-270-5000
Caracas	011-58-2-977-2011
Hong Kong	011-852-2841-2282
Interpol	011-33-4-7244-7213
Islamabad	011-92-51-826-161
Kiev	011-380-44-244-7345
London	011-44-171-499-9000
Madrid	011-34-1-587-2200
Manila	011-63-2-523-1323
Mexico City	011-52-5-211-0042
Mexico City, Guadalajara Suboffice	011-52-38-25-2998
Mexico City, Monterrey Suboffice	011-52-83-43-2120
Montevideo	011-598-2-48-77-77
Moscow	011-7-095-252-2459
Ottawa	613/238-5335
Panama	011-507-227-1777
Paris	011-33-1-4312-2222
Pretoria	011-27-12-342-1048
Riyadh	011-966-1488-3800
Rome	011-39-6-4674-2710
Santiago	011-56-2-232-2600
Tallinn	011-372-6-312-021
Tel Aviv	011-9723-519-7575
Tokyo	011-81-3-3224-5000
Vienna	011-43-1-31-339
Warsaw	011-4822-628-3041

FBI CRIME LAB:
The FBI Crime Lab is the largest and most comprehensive crime lab in the world. Its services are limited to FBI offices, U.S. Attorneys, military tribunals, other federal agencies for both civil and criminal matters, and all state, county and local law enforcement agencies when a violent crime is involved. (Simple property crimes, such as arson of an unoccupied building, are routinely rejected.) The services are free, however there are certain limitations on which cases are accepted. These include no re-examination of evidence that has already been examined by another

crime lab (unless there are special reasons for re-examination); no examination from crime labs who have the capability of conducting the test; and no testing will be done for non-federal law enforcement agencies in civil matters.

202/324-4410
www.fbi.gov/programs/lab/labhome.htm

Crime Lab Sections:

Abrasives Examinations	202/324-4344
Anthropology and Odontology	202/324-4344
Arson	202/324-4318
Audio	703/632-6191
	707/632-6222
Bank Security Dye	202/324-4318
Building Materials	202/324-4344
Computer Examinations	202/324-9307
Controlled Substance Examinations	202/324-4318
DNA Examinations	202/324-5436
	202/324-4354
Electronic Device Examinations (includes personal digital assistants, eavesdropping devices, etc.)	703/632-6191
Elemental Analysis	202/324-4341
Explosives Examinations (Don't send unexploded bombs!)	202/324-4341
Explosives Residues	202/324-4318
Firearms	202/324-4378
Glass Examinations	202/324-4344
Hairs and Fibers	202/324-4344
Ink Examinations	303/324-4318
Latent Prints	202/324-2163
Metallurgy Examinations	202/324-4341
Paints, Polymers and Adhesives	202/324-4318
Pharmaceutical Examinations	202/324-4318
Photographic Examinations (includes bank robbery footage, automobile make and model identification, and child pornography examination)	202/324-4483
Polygraph Examinations	202/324-2985
Questioned Documents	202/324-4454
Racketeering Records	202/324-2500
Ropes and Cords	202/324-4344
Safe Insulation Examinations	202/324-4344
Scientific Analysis	202/324-4416
Serial Number Examinations (recovery of obliterated identification numbers)	202/324-4374
Shoeprint and Tire Tread Examinations	202/324-4492
Soil Examinations	202/324-4344
Special Projects	202/324-4220
Toolmark Examinations	202/324-4378
Toxicology Examinations	202/324-4318

| Video Examinations | 703/632-6222 |
| Wood Examinations | 202/324-4344 |

The *FBI's Computer Analysis and Response Team* (CART) provides assistance to field office when computers are seized and searched for evidence.

202/324-9307

Also see...*FORENSIC SCIENCE COMMUNICATIONS* for information on the FBI's online forensic science publication.

Also see...*COMBINED DNA INDEX SYSTEM*.

MAJOR INFORMATION SYSTEMS:
NCIC 2000 *(National Crime Information Center)* contains 17 databases covering missing persons, gang and terrorist members, wanted persons and more. See...*CRIMINAL RECORDS*.

CODIS is the *Combined DNA Index System*; the FBI's growing database of DNA from known criminal offenders. When DNA from an unknown subject is recovered at a crime scene, it may be checked against the known offender database for hits. See...*COMBINED DNA INDEX SYSTEM*.

The Criminalistics Laboratory Information System is a computer database of the FBI Crime Lab that identifies the weapon type used to fire a recovered bullet or casing.

202/324-4410

IAFIS is the *Integrated Automated Fingerprint Identification System*. Begun in March of 1997, it's the FBI's computerized database of over 35 million fingerprints. When fingerprints from an unknown subject are recovered from a crime scene, they may be checked here to identify the perpetrator.

202/324-2163
www.fbi.gov/hq/cjisd/iafis.htm

The Forensic Science Information Resource System is a computerized database of forensic evidence, including tire tracks, shoe prints and ballistics.

202/324-4384

MAJOR UNITS/SECTIONS:
ANSIR (Awareness of National Security Issues and Response) is the FBI's public voice for issues of national security including terrorism and espionage. Each FBI field office has an assigned ANSIR coordinator. ANSIR provides non-classified threat information to private sector security directors and others via e-mail and fax. To request inclusion,

send an e-mail containing your name and firm contact information to *ansir@leo.gov*.

www.fbi.gov/hq/nsd/ansir/ansir.htm

The FBI's *Financial Crimes Section* is composed of 6 different units: Health Care Fraud; Governmental Fraud Unit; Financial Institution Fraud Unit; Economic Crimes Unit; Money Laundering Unit; and the Internet Fraud Complaint Center.

202/324-5590
www.fbi.gov/programs/fc/fchome/default.htm

The FBI's *Economic Crimes Unit* focuses on these areas: Telemarketing Fraud; Securities/Commodities; Insurance Fraud; and Bankruptcy Fraud.

202/324-5590
www.fbi.gov/programs/fc/ec/ec_index.htm

The Internet Fraud Complaint Center is a partnership between the FBI and the National White Collar Crime Center. Website includes an online form for reporting online fraud and crime. Unfortunately, the reports aren't intended as a referral for prosecution. Rather, they're for identifying trends.

www.ifccfbi.gov

Also see...*COMPUTER CRIME* for additional FBI resources dedicated to combating cybercrime.

The Child Abduction and Serial Killer Unit (CASKU) consults on major violent crime investigations with local police. Services include profiling.

540/720-4700

When suspects cross state lines to avoid prosecution they may end up a subject of the *FBI's Violent Crimes and Fugitive Unit*, located at FBI headquarters.

202/324-4294

Violent Criminal Apprehension Program (VICAP) is a little known FBI data collection center that catalogs information relating to serial murder and other crimes of violence. Information collected focuses on unsolved, apparently random killings. The purpose is to cross index the data to identify signature aspects of the homicides, hopefully pointing to a single suspect.

800/634-4097

Explosives Unit - Bomb Data Center	202/324-2696
Forensic Science Training Unit	703/632-4576

Domestic Terrorism Unit   202/324-4656

The FBI investigates large scale health care fraud and maintains a *Health Care Fraud Unit* at its Financial Crimes Division in Washington, D.C. However, actual reports of health care fraud are to be made to local FBI offices. Contact your local FBI office and ask to speak with the Health Care Fraud Supervisor.

FBI ACADEMY:
The *FBI Academy*, located on a high-security Marine Corps base in Quantico, Virginia, was established in 1972 and is situated on 385 wooded acres. In addition to class rooms, the facility has Hogan's Alley, the façade of a small town street for agent training, and a 1.1 mile pursuit/defensive driving track. The Academy is closed to the public; no tours are available. Units at the FBI Academy include the Behavioral Science Unit; the Field Police Training Unit; the International Training Program; the FBI National Academy; the Firearms Training Unit; the Forensic Science Research and Training Center; the Investigative Training Unit; the Physical Training Unit; the New Agents Training Unit; the Practical Applications Unit; and the Computer Training Unit. To inquire about a career as an FBI agent, contact your local field office.

703/632-4576
www.fbi.gov/programs/academy/academy.htm

MEDIA INQUIRIES:
The FBI's *Fugitive Publicity Office* leads the PR charge on high-profile Most Wanted cases. It's also the agency's contact point for book authors needing information.

202/324-5348

Photo: The FBI Academy in Quantico, Virginia. It's an exclusive place to be educated — each class has 270 graduates. (Photo courtesy of FBI.)

Non-book media should direct inquiries to the FBI *Press Office*.

202/324-3691

FOIA REQUESTS:
Freedom of Information Act requests to the FBI are seriously backlogged, with fulfillment taking years. However, hundreds of pre-processed files (on well-known persons) are available for viewing without a wait. To view one of these files, call the *FBI FOIA Reading Room* at least 48 hours in advance.

202/324-5520

The *FBI* has started to post some of its most requested FOIA files on the Internet. FBI files on Amelia Earhart, Elvis Presley, Jackie Robinson and others can now be viewed.

www.foia.fbi.gov

FOIA requests to the FBI should be directed to: *FBI FOIA Unit, Records Resources Division, Federal Bureau of Investigation, 9th & Pennsylvania Avenue N.W., Washington, D.C. 20535.*

Anyone can request a copy of their own criminal record from the FBI's Criminal Records Check. The procedure for doing so is somewhat cumbersome, though.

304/625-3878

CURRENT AGENTS:
The *FBI Agents Association* is the largest professional association for active FBI agents. Approximately 70 percent of all agents belong.

914/235-7580
www.fbiaa.org

FORMER AGENTS:
The *Society of Former Special Agents of the FBI* provides networking and other support for Special Agents in their post-bureau life. The organization also assists in job placement of former agents in the private sector.

703/640-6469
www.socxfbi.org

The *Registry of Former Federal Investigators* is a website for the benefit of ex-federal agents (FBI, DEA, IRS, INS, etc.) who are available as expert witnesses or for contract investigative services.

www.rffi.com

TOURS:
Tours of *FBI headquarters* in Washington are still available. Keep your hands off the computers, please! The

tour takes about an hour and includes a walk through the *FBI Crime Lab*. Also included is a new Gangster exhibit.

202/324-3447
www.fbi.gov/fbinbrief/tour/tour.htm

FEDERAL COMMUNICATIONS COMMISSION
The FCC regulates the air waves — TV, radio, ham radio, cell phones.

888/CALL FCC
www.fcc.gov

FEDERAL CONTRACTS
See...*FEDERAL PROCUREMENT DATABASE*.

FEDERAL DISTRICT COURTS
This is a non-exhaustive list of key U.S. District Courts. Contact the court nearest your search area to determine its jurisdiction.

Alabama, Northern	205/278-1700
Alabama, Middle	334/223-7308
Alabama, Southern	334/441-5391
Alaska	907/677-6100
Arizona, Phoenix Div.	602/514-7101
Arizona, Tucson Div.	520/205-4200
Arkansas, Eastern	501/521-6980
Arkansas, Western	501/862-1202
California, Northern	415/556-9800
California, Eastern	916/930-4000
California, Central	213/894-8521
California, Southern	619/557-5600
Colorado	303/844-3433
Connecticut	860/240-3200
Delaware	302/573-6170
District of Columbia	202/354-3000
Florida, Northern	850/435-8440
Florida, Central	407/835-4200
Florida, Southern	305/523-5100
Georgia, Northern	404/215-1660
Georgia, Central	912/752-3497
Georgia, Southern	912/650-4020
Hawaii	808/541-1300
Idaho	208/334-1361
Illinois, Northern	312/435-5670
Illinois, Central	217/492-4020
Illinois, Southern	618/482-9371
Indiana, Northern	219/424-7360
Indiana, Southern	317/226-3700
Iowa, Northern	319/286-2300
Iowa, Southern	515/284-6284
Kansas	785/295-2610
Kentucky, Eastern	336/233-2625
Kentucky, Western	502/625-3501

Louisiana, Eastern	504/589-7650
Louisiana, Central	225/389-3500
Louisiana, Western	318/676-4273
Maine	207/780-3356
Maryland	301/344-0660
Massachusetts	617/748-9152
Michigan, Eastern	313/234-5000
Michigan, Western	616/456-2381
Minnesota	612/664-5000
Mississippi, Northern	662/234-1971
Mississippi, Southern	601/965-4439
Missouri, Eastern	314/244-7900
Missouri, Western	816/426-2811
Montana	406/782-0432
Nebraska	402/661-7350
Nevada	702/464-5430
New Hampshire	603/225-1423
New Jersey	973/645-3730
New Mexico	505/348-2000
New York, Northern	518/257-1800
New York, Southern	212/805-0136
New York, Eastern	718/260-2600
New York, Western	716/551-4211
North Carolina, Eastern	252/830-6009
North Carolina, Central	336/332-6000
North Carolina, Western	704/350-7400
North Dakota	701/530-2300
Ohio, Northern	216/522-4355
Ohio, Southern	614/719-3000
Oklahoma, Northern	918/699-4700
Oklahoma, Western	405/231-5141
Oregon	503/326-8008
Pennsylvania, Eastern	215/597-7704
Pennsylvania, Central	570/207-5680
Pennsylvania, Western	412/208-7500
Puerto Rico	787/772-3011
Rhode Island	401/528-4477
South Carolina	803/765-5816
South Dakota	605/342-3066
Tennessee	901/495-1200
Texas, Northern	214/753-2201
Texas, Southern	713/250-5500
Texas, Eastern	903/590-1000
Texas, Western	210/472-6550
Utah	801/524-6100
Vermont	802/388-4237
Virginia, Eastern	757/222-7201
Virginia, Western	804/296-9284
Washington, Eastern	509/353-2150
Washington, Western	206/553-5598
West Virginia, Northern	304/636-1445
West Virginia, Southern	615/340-2000
Wisconsin, Eastern	414/297-3372
Wisconsin, Western	608/264-5156

Wyoming	307/772-2149
Guam (territorial court)	671/473-9152
Virgin Islands (territorial court)	340/774-0640

☞ [NEW!] FEDERAL ELECTION COMMISSION

Headquarters	800/424-9530
	202/694-1100
Hearing Impaired TTY	202/219-3336
	www.fec.gov

The best site on the Internet with FEC information on political donations is *Political Money Line*. Includes a search to look up campaign donations by donor.

www.tray.com

Also see...*ELECTION FRAUD*.

Also see...*POLITICIANS*.

FEDERAL EMERGENCY MANAGEMENT AGENCY
U.S. government agency that responds to natural and manmade disasters.

800/462-9029
www.fema.gov

Also see...*DISASTERS*.

FEDERAL EMPLOYEES
See...*U.S. MERIT SYSTEMS PROTECTION BOARD*.

FEDERAL EMPLOYER IDENTIFICATION NUMBERS
See...*EIN IDENTIFIER*.

FEDERAL FIREARM LICENSES
See...*BUREAU OF ALCOHOL, TOBACCO & FIREARMS*.

FEDERAL GOVERNMENT FRAUD HOTLINE
Fraud Prevention, General
Accounting Office   800/424-5454
www.gao.gov

FEDERAL INFORMATION CENTER
The Federal Information Center is the general information operator for the entire U.S. government. The center maintains an impressive computerized database of federal government agencies, departments, sections and units. A good place to start when trying to locate a government agency, section or unit.

	800/688-9889
TTY (For hearing impaired)	800/326-2996
	www.info.gov

FEDERAL INVESTIGATORS – FORMER

The Registry of Former Federal Investigators NEW! is a website for the benefit of ex-federal agents (FBI, DEA, IRS, INS, etc.) who are available as expert witnesses or for contract investigative services.

www.rffi.com

The Society of Former Special Agents of the FBI provides networking and other support for Special Agents in their post-bureau life.

703/640-6469
www.socxfbi.org

The Association of Former OSI Special Agents are retired Air Force Office of Special Investigations investigators.

703/978-6198
http://members.aol.com/foremaw/

Association of Former Customs
Special Agents   877/954-7646
www.afcsa.org

FEDERAL LAW ENFORCEMENT TRAINING CENTER

Sixty-three separate federal agencies with law enforcement status train at the *Federal Law Enforcement Training Center* in Glynco, Georgia.

800/74-FLETC
912/267-2100
www.fletc.gov

Also see...*FINANCIAL FRAUD INSTITUTE*.

FEDERAL LICENSE PLATE CHECK

License plates aren't federal – they're issued by states! Right? Yes...with some exceptions, such as consulate plates. But there's a large number of state-issued license plates that contain a federal code: amateur radio and land mobile call signs. The call signs are issued by the *Federal Communication Commission* and people who receive them typically will have either a license plate made with the call sign, or their call sign will be on their license plate holder. There's not a set configuration for the call signs, but here's a typical amateur radio call sign, which I recently saw on a license plate – KD6JWI. By calling the Federal Communications Commission, you can learn the name, address and date of birth of the person to whom a call sign is registered.

888/CALL-FCC
www.fcc.gov

FEDERAL PARENT LOCATOR SERVICE

The Federal Parent Locator Service (FPLS) is a federal program designed to help locate missing parents in child support, child custody, and parental kidnapping cases. Run by the *Office of Child Support Enforcement* (U.S. Department of Health and Human Services), the program relies upon the computerized records of the IRS, Social Security Administration, Department of Defense and state employment security agencies to find a current address for the wanted parent. The agency does not accept requests for assistance from the general public.

202/724-1444
www.acf.dhhs.gov/programs/cse

Also see...*CHILD SUPPORT ENFORCEMENT.*

FEDERAL PRISONS

See...*PRISON HISTORIES, FEDERAL.*

FEDERAL PROCUREMENT SYSTEM

The Federal Procurement System contains information on federal contracts for private services and goods ordered by the executive branch. Only contracts in excess of $25,000 are recorded. The information is collected by the *Federal Procurement Data Center* of the *General Services Administration.*

202/401-1529
www.fpdc.gov
http://fpds.gsa.gov

A second source of the same information is the *CampaignFinance.org* website from *Investigative Reporters & Editors:*

www.campaignfinance.org/fpds/

FEDERAL PROSECUTORS

See...*U.S. ATTORNEY OFFICES.*

FEDERAL RECORD CENTERS

Ultimately federal criminal, civil and bankruptcy files end up in one of 13 *Federal Record Centers:*

301/457-7000
www.nara.gov

Anchorage (covers Alaska)   907/271-2441

Atlanta (covers Alabama, Florida,
Georgia, Kentucky, Mississippi,
North Carolina, South Carolina,
Tennessee)   404/763-7474

Boston (covers Connecticut, Maine,
Massachusetts, New Hampshire,
Rhode Island, Vermont)   877/616-4599

131

Chicago (covers Illinois, Indiana, Michigan, Minnesota, Ohio, Wisconsin)	773/581-7816
Denver (covers Colorado, Montana, New Mexico, North Dakota, South Dakota, Utah, Wyoming)	303/236-0804
Fort Worth (covers Arkansas, Louisiana, Oklahoma, Texas)	817/334-5515
Kansas City (covers Iowa, Kansas, Missouri, Nebraska)	816/926-7272
Los Angeles (covers Arizona, Clark County, Nevada, 11 Southern California counties)	949/360-2641
New York (covers New Jersey, New York, Puerto Rico, Virgin Islands)	212/337-1300
Philadelphia (covers Delaware, Maryland, Pennsylvania, Virginia, West Virginia)	215/597-3000
San Francisco (covers California, except 11 Southern California counties, Nevada, except Clark County, Hawaii, Pacific Ocean territories)	650/876-9001
Seattle (covers some of Alaska, Idaho, Oregon, Washington)	206/526-6501
Washington, D.C.	301/457-7010

FEDERAL TRADE COMMISSION

Federal agency seeks to enforce fair business practices through civil actions. Areas of interest include telemarketing scams, debt collection and, of late, the activities of private investigators.

FTC Headquarters	202/326-2222
	www.ftc.gov
FTC Personnel Locator	202/326-2000

REGIONAL OFFICES:

Atlanta	404/656-1399
Chicago	312/960-5633
Cleveland	216/263-3410
Dallas	214/979-0213
Los Angeles	310/824-4200
New York	212/607-2800
San Francisco	415/356-5270
Seattle	260/220-6363

The FTC's *Consumer Response Center* takes reports of consumer fraud, including Internet and mail sweepstake scams. They share the information with law enforcement for trend identification purposes.

877/FTC-HELP

The FTC issues "RN" numbers which are placed on clothing, fur, textile and other tags to identify the manufacturer of the item. You can look up an RN number on the Internet to see to whom it is registered:

www.ftc.gov/bcp/rn/

Or you can fax a request to: 202/326-3197

FEDERAL WITNESS PROTECTION PROGRAM
Department of Justice, Witness
Protection Office   202/514-3684
www.usdoj.gov/marshals/witsec.html

FEIN
See...*EIN IDENTIFIER*.

FINANCIAL AND INSURANCE CONSULTANTS
Some financial and insurance consultants have more letters *after* their names than they have *in* their names. For instance, John Doe, CLU, or Mary Doe, CPCU. This list will help you decode them — and check their authenticity:

"ATA" stands for Accredited Tax Advisor. The holder of this certification has passed the *College for Financial Planning's Accredited Tax Preparer Program* and has passed a test from the Accreditation Council on Accountancy on taxation. To verify credentials call them or visit their website.

888/289-2228
703/549-2228
www.acatcredentials.org

"APA" stands for Accredited Tax Preparer. As with "ATA," the holder of this certification has passed the *College for Financial Planning's Accredited Tax Preparer Program* and has passed a test from the Accreditation Council for Accountancy on Taxation. To verify credentials call them or visit their website.

888/289-2228
703/549-2228
www.acatcredentials.org

"CPA" stands for *Certified Public Accountant*. See... *CERTIFIED PUBLIC ACCOUNTANTS*.

"CFP" stands for Certified Financial Planner, a designation earned from the *Certified Financial Planner Board of Standards.* Standards include educational requirements, examination and at least five years experience as a financial planner. For up-to-date license information or to learn of any past public disciplinary actions against CFP licensees:

303/830-7500
www.cfp-board.org

"CLU" stands for *Chartered Life Underwriter.* It's the highest professional certification for life insurance agents. To check status contact *The Society of Financial Service Professionals.*

610/526-2500
www.financialpro.org

"CMFC" stands for *Chartered Mutual Fund Consultant.* Designees have completed a 72-hour course on mutual funds. To verify certification, contact the *College for Financial Planning and Investment Company Institute.*

800/237-1200
www.fp.edu

"CPCU" is an acronym for *Chartered Property Casualty Underwriter.* The designation is administered by the American Institute for Chartered Property Casualty Underwriters. Certified members will have knowledge in a broad range of insurance, risk management, and general business topics, building on a foundation of ethical principles and systematic analysis of insurance contracts.

800/644-2101
www.aicpcu.org

"EA" stands for *Enrolled Agent.* This will be a tax preparer who either worked for the *IRS* for 5 years or passed a two-day test on tax law. To learn if a person is an "Enrolled Agent," contact the *National Association of Enrolled Agents.* However, their data only includes enrolled agents who are a member of their organization.

301/212-9608
www.naea.org

Another, more inclusive check can be done through data provider *ChoicePoint.* See...*DATA PROVIDERS.*

"PFA" stands for *Personal Financial Advisor.* This certification comes from membership in the National Association of *Personal Financial Advisors* — a group for planners who are compensated only by clients who pay fees.

888/FEE-ONLY
www.napfa.org

"PFS" stands for *Personal Financial Specialist* and is earned from *The American Institute of Certified Public Accountants*.

888/777-7077
www.cpapfs.org

FINANCIAL CRIMES ENFORCEMENT NETWORK
Financial Crimes Enforcement Network ("FinCEN") is a Department of Treasury division charged with assisting authorized law enforcement agencies in the investigation of financial crime, especially drug money laundering. *FinCEN's* agents and computer analysts rely heavily upon computer databases to identify criminal activity, including the Treasury's Financial Database, containing reports filed under the Bank Secrecy Act, identifying currency transactions over $10,000.

703/905-6096
800/SOS-BUCK
www.ustreas.gov/fincen

FINANCIAL FRAUD INSTITUTE
Special school at the *Federal Law Enforcement Training Center* in Georgia. Classes are available to law enforcement agents only, although the private sector makes input into the curriculum to maintain relevancy.

912/267-2314
www.fletc.gov

FINANCIAL INVESTIGATIONS
See...*BUSINESS BACKGROUND INVESTIGATIONS*.

Also see...*BANKRUPTCY COURTS*.

Also see...*REAL ESTATE INFORMATION*.

Also see...*CORPORATIONS*.

Also see...*INSIDER TRADING*.

Also see...*STOCK DETECTIVE*.

Also see...*OFFSHOREBUSINESS.COM*.

Also see...*EXECUTIVES*.

Also see...*ABA ROUTING NUMBERS*.

■🖝 NEW! FINGERPRINT EXPERTS

Gerald S. Cole	301/230-2909
Ivan Futrell	540/659-6450
Kenneth R. Moses	*www.forensicidservices.com*
Michael J. Sweedo	*www.dakotacom.net/~fingers/*
Robert D. Whritenour	770/218-3555

For more fingerprint consultants,
see website: *www.onin.com/fp/*

IAFIS is the *Integrated Automated Fingerprint Identification System*. Begun in March of 1997, it's the FBI's computerized database of over 35 million fingerprints. When fingerprints from an unknown subject are recovered from a crime scene, they may be checked here to identify the perpetrator.

202/324-2163
www.fbi.gov/hq/cjisd/iafis.htm

Sirchie Corporation sells a large line of fingerprinting supplies.

800/356-7311
www.sirchie.com

Another respected supplier of fingerprinting supplies is *Lightning Powder Company*. There website also includes a free informational newsletter, *Minutiae*.

800/852-0300
503/585-9900
www.redwop.com

FIREARM FORENSICS
The Bureau of Alcohol, Tobacco, and Firearm's National Tracing Center aids law enforcement agencies by tracing the history of firearms from manufacture through current ownership.

304/260-3640
www.atf.treas.gov

 Need a serial number for a lost or stolen firearm? Then contact the gun dealer from whom the firearm was originally purchased. If the gun dealer is out of business, contact the *ATF*, which will search its records for a fee of $37.50. Include the name of the person who purchased the firearm; the name of the out-of-business dealer; the dealer's city, state and zip code; date of purchase or at least a three year time span when the purchase was made; make, model and gauge of firearm. Include both your name and address where the information should be sent as well as a daytime phone number. Direct your request to *ATF, Disclosure Division, 650 Massachusetts Avenue, Washington, D.C. 20226.*

800/788-7133
202/927-8480

The National Integrated Ballistics Information Network is a high tech bullet identification system designed to match up bullets recovered from random crimes to the same weapon. A joint effort of the FBI and ATF, NIBIN is the successor to the DRUGFIRE and IBIS programs.

202/927-5660
www.atf.treas.gov/firearms/nibin/

The Criminalistics Laboratory Information System is a computer database of the FBI Crime Lab that identifies the weapon type used to fire a recovered bullet or casing.

202/324-4410
www.fbi.gov

Forensic Science Consulting Group is a privately owned crime lab whose specialties includes ballistics.

760/436-7714
www.access1.net/fscg

The Association of Firearm and Toolmark Examiners specializes in giving voice to physical evidence that might otherwise stand mute. Started in 1969, this professional group stresses training and research in the scientific analysis of firearms and tools from an evidence standpoint.

815/987-7419
www.afte.org

SecurityArms.com has an extensive free online directory of firearm photographs.

www.securityarms.com

Also see...*BUREAU OF ALCOHOL, TOBACCO & FIREARMS.*

FIREARM LICENSES
See...*BUREAU OF ALCOHOL, TOBACCO & FIREARMS.*

Also see...*CONCEALED WEAPON LICENSES.*

FIRE INVESTIGATIONS
See...*ARSON INVESTIGATIONS.*

FOOD TAMPERING

The FDA Forensic Chemistry Center investigates food tampering cases and unauthorized/counterfeit drugs.

513/679-2700
www.fda.gov/fdac/features/695_forensic.html

Forensic psychiatrist *Dr. Park Dietz* is a recognized expert in food tampering cases, including the Chicago Tylenol murders some years back.

949/644-3537
www.taginc.com

FONE FINDER

This is one of the most useful sites on the Internet for investigating a phone number. Enter a telephone number's area code and three digit prefix and you'll learn the geographic area the phone is in as well as who the phone company is. This will tell you if it's a cell phone or land-line. Over 35,000 cities and 220 countries worldwide are included. It's also used by many law enforcement agencies to figure out who to serve a search warrant on for phone records or a phone tap. Find it at *Black Book Online* (under the "Skiptrace" button), or access it directly:

http://fonefinder.net

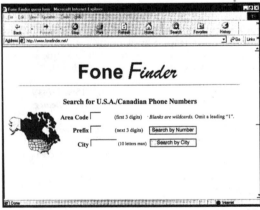

Screenshot: The Fone Finder website — a valuable tool for the investigation of phone numbers.

FOREIGN AGENT REGISTRATIONS

Persons, associations, law firms and others who lobby on behalf of a foreign power must register with the United States government under a statute dating back to World War II. The law was originally designed to unmask Nazi propagandists working on the behalf of Adolf Hitler. Today, this information is received and maintained by the Criminal Division of the U.S. Department of Justice. The information is public record.

202/514-1145
www.usdoj.gov/criminal/fara/

FOREIGN INVESTIGATIONS

The U.S. State Department has a Country Officer assigned to every foreign country. The Country Officers are knowledgeable of their assigned country's affairs and institutions.

202/647-4000
www.state.gov

Contact the State Department's *Overseas Citizen Services* for any situation involving the death, robbery, arrest or disappearance of an American abroad.

202/647-5225

Landing in a foreign country without local currency to catch a taxi, tip a baggage handler or bribe a local official sure is inconvenient. Sure, you could go to an airport currency exchange office...but who likes to wait in line at a foreign airport when there are more important things to be done? *Chase Currency To Go* has a better way. A day or two before you depart, they'll overnight to you a package with any one of 75 foreign currencies. It'll be charged to your credit card.

888/CHASE84
www.currency-to-go.com

The U.S. State Department offers a hotline and a website with travel warnings about areas that are considered a risk to Americans.

202/647-5225
www.travel.state.gov

The Centers for Disease Control offer a travel advisory hotline for assessing health threats to travelers in foreign countries.

877/FYI-TRIP
www.cdc.gov/travel/travel.html

For passport information, including obtaining an emergency passport, contact the *National Passport Information Center*. (Pay per use service, billed to your phone at 35 cents per minute.)

Billed to your phone: 900/225-5674
Billed to your credit card: 888/362-8668

Contact the *Office of Children's Issues* for matters involving international parental child abduction and international

139

adoptions. There's also recorded information on custody and adoptions.

202/736-7000

The State Department also operates the *Children's Passport Issuance Alert Program* which will alert a parent if a passport is applied for his or her child, or if a currently valid passport exists. A Passport Alert form can be downloaded off the Internet.

202/736-7000
http://travel.state.gov/paf_print.html

Need an English-speaking doctor in a foreign land? Contact the *International Association for Medical Assistance to Travellers.*

716/754-4883
www.iamat.org

The Political Risk Assessment Company offers consulting in security and terrorism matters. Company principals include former RAND Corporation researchers and FBI scientists.

310/395-8798

Pinkerton Risk Assessment Services monitors political, terrorist and other threats in foreign lands and publishes a daily bulletin.

703/525-6111
pgis.pinkerton.com

For information on obtaining death certificates of Americans who have died abroad or on the high seas, see... *DEATH INVESTIGATIONS.*

Also see...*AT&T LANGUAGE LINE.*

Also see...*OVERSEAS SECURITY ADVISORY COUNCIL.*

Also see...*FOREIGN WITNESSES.*

Also see...*COUNTRY CODE LOOKUPS.*

Also see...*CURRENCY EXCHANGE RATES.*

Also see...*FOREIGN SERVICE OF PROCESS.*

Also see...*INTERPOL.*

Also see...*INTERNATIONAL DIRECTORY ASSISTANCE.*

Also see...*MEXICAN INVESTIGATIONS...CANADIAN INVESTIGATIONS...ENGLAND INVESTIGATORS.*

Also see...*EMBASSIES.*

Also see...*WORLD FACTBOOK, THE.*

FOREIGN SERVICE OF PROCESS

 For questions regarding the Hague Convention, contact the *U.S. Department of Justice's Office of International Judicial Assistance.*

202/307-0983

For general reference information on implementation of the *Hague Convention*, visit this State Department website:

www.travel.state.gov/hague_service.html

IJS is an American company that specializes in service of process overseas. They know the ins and outs of the Hague Service Convention and will work directly with your client or as your agent.

503/646-5180
www.intlsvcs.com

For help in serving legal documents overseas, contact *Legal Language Services International.*

800/755-5775

FOREIGN WITNESSES

 When the testimony of witnesses from outside of the United States is needed, special government cooperation (here and abroad) and plenty of advance planning are required. Obstacles to be encountered include foreign bureaucracies as well as visas for the entry into the U.S. Here's two key contacts:

The Department of State's *Office of Citizens Consular Services* provides assistance in coordinating with foreign governments and service via U.S. consulates.

202/647-5225

The U.S. Department of Justice,
Special Authorizations Unit   202/307-1954

Also see...*FOREIGN SERVICE OF PROCESS.*

FORENSIC ACCOUNTANTS

Although not technically an organization for forensic accounts, the esteemed *Association of Certified Fraud Examiners* includes many forensic accountants among its members. Members can be found online in the organization's membership directory.

800/245-3321
512/478-9070
www.cfenet.com

Arthur Andersen Business Fraud Risk Management Services maintains offices throughout the U.S. and overseas manned with forensic accounts. Call their headquarters for a local referral.

312/580-0033
www.arthurandersen.com

FORENSIC ENTOMOLOGY

Forensic entomology is the study of what bugs do to dead bodies and what that tells us about time, place and method of death.

M. Lee Goff	808/956-6741
Rob Hall	573/884-2511
Richard W. Merritt, Ph.D.	517/355-8309
Gail S. Anderson, Ph.D.	604/291-3589

FORENSIC SCIENCE COMMUNICATIONS

Official online publication of the FBI for forensic scientists. Technical in nature, covers a wide variety of topics including DNA analysis, Facial Reconstruction and Handwriting Analysis. This is the successor to the FBI's previous publication, *Crime Laboratory Digest*. Free.

www.fbi.gov/hq/lab/fsc/current/index

FORENSIC SCIENCE ORGANIZATIONS

Most, if not all, of the following groups can provide referral to a locally based expert in their field:

American Academy of Forensic Sciences is a professional organization that offers an expert referral service. Also maintains a reference library.

719/636-1100
www.aafs.org

American Society of Questioned
Document Examiners 901/759-0729
www.asqde.org

American Board of Forensic
Document Examiners 713/784-9537
www.asqde.org/abrefpg.htm

American Board of Forensic
Odontology 719/636-1100
www.aafs.org

American College of Forensic
Examiners 417/881-3818
www.acfe.com

Forensic anthropology is the science of obtaining information from human remains. Contact *The American Board of Forensic Anthropology*.

419/213-3908
www.csuchico.edu/anth/ABFA

Mass spectometry is the identification of substances based on the mass of ionized molecules. For more information, contact the *American Society for Mass Spectrometry*.

505/989-4517
www.asms.org

International Association for Identification

651/681-8566
www.theiai.org

International Association of Blood Stain Pattern Analysts

520/760-5590
www.iabpa.org

FORENSIC TOXICOLOGY
See...*CRIME LABS*.

4-1-9 FRAUD

4-1-9 Fraud (pronounced "four one nine") has, unfortunately, become one of the main exports of Nigeria. Although it comes in different variations, it invariably involves its victim forwarding advance loan, wire transfer, tax or other fees to Nigerian nationals who promise big returns to follow the advance payment. Official-looking Nigerian government documents typically are produced, helping to sucker in the victim. The fees are never seen again. "419" refers to the Nigerian penal code section for fraud.

In the United States, the *Financial Crimes Division* of the U.S. Secret Service is aware of the schemes, tracks them, and prosecutes when appropriate.

202/406-6930

The U.S. Department of State has produced an informational publication on 419 scams. DOS Publication 1045 can be downloaded off the Internet for free.

www.state.gov/www/regions/africa/naffpub.pdf

FRAUD TRAINING

The Investigation Training Institute is associated with the highly respected *Association of Certified Fraud Examiners*. They offer continuing education in fraud training and offer classes throughout the country. Visit their website for a schedule of classes.

407/816-7273
www.investigationtraining.com

Sworn law enforcement officers interested in fraud training will want to know about the *Financial Fraud Institute*, a department of the Federal Law Enforcement Training Center in Georgia.

912/267-2314
www.fletc.gov

FREEDOM OF INFORMATION ACT

NEW! For instructions, tips and other information on obtaining information from federal agencies through the *Freedom of Information Act*, see the FOIA section in the *Privacy Law Survival Guide* at the end of this book.

Each federal agency has a FOIA office that FOIA requests must be directed to. Here is a non-exhaustive list of key federal agencies and their FOIA contact numbers.

DEPARTMENT OF JUSTICE:

Office of the Attorney General	202/514-FOIA
Antitrust Division	202/514-2692
Civil Division	202/514-3319
Civil Rights Division	202/514-4209
Criminal Division	202/616-0307
Drug Enforcement Administration	202/307-7596
United States Attorneys	202/616-6757
FBI	202/324-5520
Federal Bureau of Prisons	202/514-6655
INS	202/514-1722
INTERPOL-U.S. Nat'l Central Bureau	202/616-9000
Office of the Inspector General	202/616-0646
Office of the Pardon Attorney	202/616-6070
Tax Division	202/307-0462
U.S. Marshals Service	202/307-9054
U.S. Parole Commission	301/492-5959

For agencies not listed above, or for address or fax information, visit the Department of Justice website and click on the FOIA link which will take you to further information on agencies within and outside the DOJ.

www.usdoj.gov

OTHER FEDERAL FOIA CONTACTS:

Department of Agriculture	202/720-8164
Department of Commerce	202/482-4115
N.O.A.A.	202/482-2621
Department of Defense	703/697-1160
Air Force	703/588-6187
Army	703/806-5698
Marine Corps	703/614-3685

National Security Agency	301/688-6527
Navy	202/685-6545
Office of the Inspector General	703/604-9775
Department of Education	202/708-4753
Department of Energy	202/586-5955
Dept. of Health and Human Services	202/690-7453
Food and Drug Administration	301/827-6567
Department of Housing and Urban Development	202/708-3866
Department of the Interior	202/208-5342
Department of Labor	202/219-8188
Department of State	202/261-8314
Department of Transportation	202/366-4542
United States Coast Guard	202/267-1086
Federal Aviation Administration	202/267-9165
Department of the Treasury	202/622-0930
Bureau of Alcohol, Tobacco, and Firearms	202/927-8480
Comptroller of the Currency	202/874-4700
United States Customs Service	202/927-1805
Internal Revenue Service	202/622-6250
United States Secret Service	202/406-6370
Department of Veterans Affairs	202/273-8135
Amtrak (National Railroad Passenger Corporation)	202/906-2728
Central Intelligence Agency	703/613-1287
Commission on Civil Rights	202/376-8351
Commodity Futures Trading Commission	202/418-5101
Consumer Product Safety Commission	301/504-0785
Environmental Protection Agency	202/260-4048
Equal Employment Opportunity Commission	202/663-4669
Federal Communications Commission	202/418-0212
Federal Deposit Insurance Corporation	202/898-3819
Federal Election Commission	202/694-1220
Federal Emergency Management Agency	202/646-3840
Federal Trade Commission	202/326-2013
General Accounting Office	202/512-2958
Library of Congress (Copyright Office)	202/707-6800
National Aeronautics and Space Administration	202/358-0205
National Archives and Records Administration	301/713-6025
National Indian Gaming Commission	202/632-7003
National Labor Relations Board	202/273-1944
National Transportation Safety Board	202/314-6551
Nuclear Regulatory Commission	301/415-7169
Occupational Safety and Health Review Commission	202/606-5398
Securities and Exchange Commission	202/942-4320
Selective Service System	703/605-4012
Small Business Administration	202/401-8203

Social Security Administration   410/965-1727
United States Postal Service   202/268-2608

OTHER SOURCES:
These companies specialize in assisting Freedom of Information Act requests in Washington, D.C.:

Washington Researchers   202/333-3499
                    www.washingtonresearchers.com

FOIA Clearinghouse   202/785-3704
                    www.citizen.org/litigation/foic/foic.html

The Reporters Committee for Freedom of the Press offers a hotline and publications to assist journalists in obtaining government records through the Freedom of Information Act.
                                   703/807-2100
                                   www.rcfp.org

FUGITIVES, FEDERAL
Contact the *Communications Center* of the *U.S. Marshals Service* to report federal fugitives from justice.

                                   202/307-9100
                                   www.usdoj.gov/marshals

When suspects cross state lines to avoid prosecution they may end up a subject of the *FBI's Violent Crimes and Fugitive Unit,* located at FBI headquarters.

                                   202/324-4294

Also see...*WANTS AND WARRANTS*.

GAMBLING
See...*CASINOS*.

Also see...*HORSES AND HORSERACING*.

GANG INVESTIGATIONS
Here's some useful books:

Gang Slanging by Russell Flores contains over 5,400 gang words and phrases from around the country.

                                   800/498-0911

The Street Gang Identification Manual, identifies gang trademarks, insignias, tattoos, graffiti and hand signs.

                                   800/295-4264
                    www.gangpreventioninc.com

Former Nevada State Prison gang intelligence officer Bill Valentine's book *Gang Intelligence Manual* contains both gang identifiers and behind the scenes information on gang inner-workings.

800/392-2400

GEMOLOGICAL INSTITUTE OF AMERICA
See...*JEWELRY AND GEMS*.

GEMS
See...*JEWELRY AND GEMS*.

GENEALOGY RESEARCH
There are roughly 1600 *Family History Centers* throughout the U.S. They're funded by The Church of Jesus Christ of Latter-Day Saints (aka the Mormons) and are staffed by volunteers. Several computerized databases are available, free of charge, for genealogical research. Non-members of the church are always welcome. Databases available include the *Social Security Administration Master Death Index*; a *Military Records* index of pre-Korean war service; and a third called the *International Genealogical Index*. Due to staff shortage, phone lookups are discouraged. To find your nearest *Family History Center*, call this number:

800/346-6044
www.familysearch.org

GLL Genealogical Services publishes books and software to aid in genealogical investigations. Sample computerized titles available include Utah Death Index 1898-1905 and How to Research American Indian Bloodlines.

800/760-AGLL
www.heritagequest.com

Harvey E. Morse, P.A. specializes in international genea-logical research.

904/706-5000

The Immigrant Genealogical
Society   818/848-3122
www.feefhs.org/igs

International Genealogical Search, Inc. specializes in locating missing heirs.

800/663-2255
www.heirsearch.com

At the website for *American Family Immigration History Center*, you can search passenger records from the ships that brought the immigrants to Ellis Island and the Port of New York.

www.ellisislandrecords.com

Robert Scott, P.I.

GENERAL ACCOUNTING OFFICE
The *GAO* serves as the noncriminal investigative branch for the federal government. Ever hear a congressman talking in-depth on a complex subject like computer security at the Defense Department? There's a good chance that what you are hearing is a regurgitation of a *GAO* report.

GAO, General Information	202/512-3000
Inspector General, GAO	800/424-5454
GAO Publications	202/512-6000
	www.gao.gov

GEOGRAPHIC NAMES DATABASE
The United States Geological Survey has a database called the *Geographic Names Data System* (aka National Geographic Names Database), which stores the names of over two million places in the United States. If you have the name of a place, but don't know the state or region, they'll find it for you.

703/648-4550
nsdi.usgs.gov

GOVERNMENT PRINTING OFFICE
Thousands of government funded publications are available through the *GPO*.

202/512-1200
www.access.gpo.gov

GOVERNMENT BOOKSTORES:

Atlanta	404/347-1900
Birmingham	205/731-1056
Boston	617/720-4180
Chicago	312/353-5133
Cleveland	216/522-4922
Columbus	614/469-6956
Dallas	214/767-0076
Denver	303/844-3964
Detroit	313/226-7816
Houston	713/228-1187
Jacksonville	904/353-0569
Kansas City (open 7 days)	816/765-2256
Laurel, MD	301/953-7974
Los Angeles	213/239-9844
Milwaukee	414/297-1304
New York	212/264-3825
Philadelphia	215/636-1900
Pittsburgh	412/395-5021
Portland	503/221-6217
Pueblo, CO	719/544-3142
San Francisco	415/355-4930
Seattle	206/553-4270
Washington, D.C	202/653-5075

HAGUE CONVENTION
See...*FOREIGN SERVICE OF PROCESS.*

HATE GROUP INVESTIGATIONS
The Southern Poverty Law Center remains a definitive source of information on domestic hate groups such as racist skinheads and the Ku Klux Klan. Information products include a quarterly Intelligence Report and lists of hate and militia groups. They currently track over 600 such organizations.

> 334/956-8200
> *www.splcenter.org*
> *www.tolerance.org*

The Simon Wiesenthal Center will provide information on various forms of racial intolerance. Also available is Digital Hate 2001, a CD-ROM that catalogs over 2,000 hate websites.

> 310/553-8403
> *www.wiesenthal.com*

An extensive list of militia group and related "patriot" sites can be found at the *Anti-Defamation League's* website.

> *www.militia-watchdog.org*

HEALTH CARE FRAUD
The FBI investigates large-scale health care fraud and maintains a *Health Care Fraud Unit* at its Financial Crimes Division in Washington, D.C.

> 202/324-3000
> *www.fbi.gov*

However, actual reports of health care fraud are to be made to local FBI offices. Contact your local FBI office and ask to speak with the Health Care Fraud Supervisor. See... *FEDERAL BUREAU OF INVESTIGATION.*

Doctors, health clinics and others who have been caught cheating Medicare or Medicaid may end up on the *Department of Health and Human Services* List of Excluded Parties. There's currently over 20,000 names on the list and it can be searched for free on the Internet:

> *http://exclusions.oig.hhs.gov/search.html*

To report health care fraud when government funds are involved, such as Medicare and Medicaid, contact the *Office of Inspector General of the Department of Health and Human Services.*

> 800/HHS-TIPS

HIDDEN CAMERAS

Looking for micro-video cameras and related accessories? Excellent selection *and* prices can be found at *Super Circuits*. Their catalog is extensive and worth requesting.

800/335-9777
www.supercircuits.com

Go SOS Security offers ready made hidden cameras in a variety of household items (clocks, boom boxes, books) and wearable items (ties, pagers, cell phones).

888/495-1250
719/592-9376
www.gosossecurity.com

Private Eye Enterprises (in Texas) offers a variety of hidden camera and other covert-use products. You'll find motion-activated video recording systems here, too.

972/960-2266
www.pidallas.com

Kalatel has put together a clever catalog of hidden cameras. One is a working telephone, called the "phone cam," which sends a video signal through a phone line. Others come in smoke detectors, wall mounted pictures and thermostats.

800/343-3358
www.kalatel.com

One of the most unique...and frankly...obscure offerings comes from *Dave Parry*, who specializes in custom building concealment devices for surveillance gear. His primary offerings are psuedo trees and rocks with compartments to hold electronics.

215/657-1909

First Witness Video Surveillance Systems offers an impressive catalog of hidden camera systems. One looks like a VCR, but a hidden camera mounted in the control panel sees and captures everything nearby. They also sell time-lapse video recorders.

800/880-1521
www.firstwitness.com

CrimEye, Inc. offers a catalog of hidden cameras, time lapse recorders, and video transmitters.

800/835-1661
www.crimeye.com

Also see...*SPY GEAR.*

HIGH TECHNOLOGY CRIME INVESTIGATION ASSOCIATION

Association for the investigation of computer crime and the security of computer systems. Membership is limited to law enforcement officers and management level security professional in the private sector. Twenty-six local chapters throughout the country. Check their website for locations.

540/937-5019
www.htcia.org

HOMICIDE INVESTIGATIONS

LAPD homicide detective *Tom Lange* became a household name during the OJ Simpson murder trial. He's now a homicide consultant.

805/526-2305

Also see...*DEATH INVESTIGATION*.

HORSES AND HORSERACING

Thoroughbred Racing Protective Bureau (TRPB) is the investigative agency of the horse racing industry. Members include most major horse tracks around the country. The focus is on defeating corruption in the guise of race fixing, horse doping, horse switching, hidden ownership and organized crime influences. TRPB also maintains a computerized database of information on race track and horse-industry personnel that is used for employment screening and other purposes. (The information is tightly restricted and available to members only.) TRPB also offers horse identification research when the horse has a lip tattoo. Ouch — that has to hurt!

Headquarters   410/398-2261
Tip Line   866/TIP-TRPB
                       www.trpb.com

Associated with the Thoroughbred Racing Protective Bureau is its harness-racing counterpart, *Standardbred Investigative Services* which provides investigative and information services to its members.

410/392-2287
www.trpb.com/sis.htm

The Thoroughbred Times covers the horsebreeding world and also publishes the Stallion directory with information on over 6,500 stallions.

606/260-9800
www.thoroughbredtimes.com

Bloodstock Research Information Services sells a number of informational products containing data on horses, their pedigree and sales stats. Also provides research services.

606/223-4444
www.brisnet.com

The American Quarterhorse Association promotes horse-racing but also offers parentage verification for horses.

800/414-RIDE
www.aqha.com

The Jockey Club maintains the American Stud Book (pedigree records of thoroughbred horses bred in the U.S.) and also maintains a database of all thoroughbred races run in the U.S. Some of the data is free and some is on a pay basis.

212/371-5970
www.jockeyclub.com

Equine Online is an information service with information on every registered thoroughbred and American quarter horse in the U.S. Data includes prize winnings by individual horses — a potentially useful lookup when doing an asset search on a subject that owns race horses. Fee-based service.

www.equineonline.com

Also of interest is the *Equibase Company* which bills itself as the thoroughbred industry's official database of racing information.

www.equibase.com

Conducting a financial investigation of a subject who owns race horses? Did you know that winnings from an owner's horses are public record? *American Racing Manual* (put out by the same people behind the Daily Racing Form) is a CD-ROM which shows amounts paid to owners of winning horses. Published annually, sells for $20.

800/306-3676
www.drf2000.com

OTHER HORSE INDUSTRY RESOURCES:

United States Trotting Association	614/224-2291
Thoroughbred Owners and Breeders Association	606/276-2291
The Jockey's Guild	606/259-3211
Harness Horsemen International	609/259-3717

HOT SITES

When new sources of information become available on the Internet, word spreads first like wild fire through Internet list-serve

"*Hot Sites.*" Membership is free, but restricted to professional investigators — mostly private investigators, cops and corporate security types. Visit this URL to request membership.

http://groups.yahoo.com/group/Hotsites

HOW TO GET ANYTHING ON ANYBODY – THE NEWSLETTER

From Lee Lapin, the author of *The Whole Spy Catalog* and *How to Get Anything on Anyone (Books I and II)*. Now he's back 10 times a year with a newsletter disseminating information that will send shivers up the spine of privacy rights advocates. See a free copy at their website.

www.intelligencehere.com

HUMAN REMAINS

Forensic anthropology is the science of obtaining information from human remains. Contact the *American Board of Forensic Anthropology*.

419/213-3908
www.csuchico.edu/anth/ABFA

Forensic odontologists identify the dead through dental examination. Contact the *American Board of Forensic Odontology* for a local referral.

719/636-1100
www.abfo.org

Also see...*FORENSIC ENTOMOLOGY*.

Also see...*NECROSEARCH*.

IDENTITY THEFT

NEW! Step one for victims of identity theft is to report the matter to the three major credit bureaus so their Social Security Number can be flagged.

Equifax   800/685-1111
                        www.equifax.com

Experian   888/EXPERIAN
                        www.experian.com

TransUnion   800/916-8800
                        www.transunion.com

If checks have been stolen or counterfeited, contact these major check verification companies to request that they notify retailers using their databases not to accept the checks.

National Check Fraud Service   843/571-2143

TeleCheck	800/710-9898
CrossCheck	707/586-0551
Equifax Check Systems	800/437-5120
International Check Services	800/526-5380

If your having trouble getting fraudulent phone calls removed from your account, contact your state Public Utilities Commission or the *Federal Communications Commission.*

888/CALL-FCC
www.fcc.gov/ccb/enforce/complaints.html

If you believe that someone is using your SSN to apply for a job, report it to the *SSA's Fraud Hotline.*

800/269-0271

To report identity theft, call the *FTC's Identity Theft Hotline.* Don't expect a federal investigation, though.

877/ID THEFT
www.consumer.gov/idtheft

IMMIGRATION & NATURALIZATION SERVICE, U.S.
General Information   202/514-1900
Intelligence Division   202/514-4402
www.ins.usdoj.gov

The Employers Sanction Database contains information from INS fines against companies found to have employed illegal aliens. The information was obtained through FOIA and can be searched online. Provided by the Center for Immigration Studies.

202/466-8185
www.cis.org

Foreign nationals who have been issued an "A" Number (short for Alien) can check the status of their hearing at the *INS Immigration Court.* This line is an automated attendant that requires entry of the "A" number.

800/898-7180

When the *INS* screens foreign nationals to verify their admissibility, the NAILS II *(National Automated Immigration Lookout System II)* system is checked. Persons formerly deported and other undesirables are identified and refused entry. Restricted to law enforcement only.

INDEX SYSTEM, THE
Now extinct, *The Index System* was the insurance industry's mega-database of bodily injury claims. This information is now part of *ISO ClaimSearch*. See...*ISO CLAIMSEARCH*.

INDIAN CASINOS AND GAMING
See...*CASINOS*.

INDIVIDUAL REFERENCE SERVICES GROUP
 Trade group formed by the Data Fat Cats to help save credit headers and other data from FTC banishment.

www.irsg.org

INJURY CLAIMS
See...*BODILY INJURY CLAIMS*.

INS
See...*IMMIGRATION & NATURALIZATION SERVICE, U.S.*

INSIDER TRADING
The Division of Enforcement, Securities & Exchange Commission investigates illegal insider trading in the financial markets.

202/942-4000
www.sec.gov

Also see...*STOCK BROKERS*.

Also see...*STANFORD SECURITIES CLASS ACTION CLEARINGHOUSE*.

INSURANCE
See...*LIFE INSURANCE LOCATOR*.

INSURANCE FOR INVESTIGATORS
These companies offer insurance coverage to private investigators:

Alliance Management & Insurance
Services
800/843-8550
760/471-7116
www.amiscorp.com

El Dorado Insurance Agency
800/221-3386
713/521-9251
www.eldoradoinsurance.com

U.S. Risk Underwriters
800/232-5830
214/265-7090
www.usrisk.com

Alliance of Investigative and
Security Services   800/258-7600
                                    www.aiass.org

Mechanic Insurance   800/214-0207
                                www.mechanicgroup.com

INSURANCE IDENTIFIERS

Probable Carrier database is not exhaustive, but may contain useful leads of identifying insurance coverage. Available through two database providers:

ChoicePoint Online   888/333-3365
                                www.choicepointonline.com

AutoTrackXP   800/279-7710
                                      www.atxp.com

Also see...*ISO CLAIMSEARCH*.

Also see...*LIFE INSURANCE LOCATOR*.

Also see...*SAFER DATABASE*...to identify insurance for interstate trucking companies.

INSURANCE INVESTIGATIONS

The National Insurance Crime Bureau (NICB) is *the* insurance industry funded investigative agency formed to combat insurance fraud. Although it is a private agency without law enforcement status, most of its agents are former law enforcement officers.

Headquarters   708/430-2430
Report Fraud Hotline   800/TEL-NICB
                                      www.nicb.org

Producer Database is the first national database of licensing information on insurance agents and brokers, including disciplinary information from state licensing authorities.

                                         816/783-8459
                                www.licenseregistry.com

National Association of Fraud Control Units is a national organization for state government insurance fraud agencies.

                                         202/434-8020
                                      www.naswa.org

Coalition Against Insurance Fraud   202/393-7330
                                www.insurancefraud.org

National Association of Independent
Insurance Adjusters   312/853-0808
www.naiia.com

Also see...*ISO CLAIMSEARCH.*

INTEL BULLETIN

 Informative and well organized Internet-based newsletter for spy-watchers. Features news clippings on recent spy and espionage cases, as well as new product and book reviews. Free. Subscribe online.

www.spytechagency.com

INTERACTIVE INFORMATION SYSTEMS (IIS)

IIS is a well kept secret of both investigators, collectors and law enforcement agencies. Services available include 800 ID "trap lines," "sting cards" and a "Blindline" which allows its user to make untraceable calls. Need a temporary 800 line for a reward offer? They'll handle that, too.

800/495-0888
www.iisnet.com

INTERNAL REVENUE SERVICE

General Information   800/829-1040
www.irs.gov

Criminal Investigations,
Headquarters   202/622-3200

The *Internal Revenue Service* employs nearly 3,200 Special Agents nationwide. Here's their field offices:

Alabama	205/912-5631
Alaska	907/271-6877
Arizona	602/207-8240
Arkansas	501/324-6269
California	714/360-2084
	213/894-2670
	916/974-5294
	415/522-6017
	408/494-7900
Colorado	303/446-1012
Connecticut	860/756-4655
Delaware	302/791-4502
District of Columbia	202/874-0155
Florida	305/423-7280
	904/232-2514
Georgia	404/338-8099
Hawaii	808/539-2870
Idaho	208/334-1324
Illinois	312/886-9183
	217/527-6366

Indiana	317/226-6332
Iowa	515/284-4780
Kansas	316/352-7506
Kentucky	502/582-6030
Louisiana	504/558-3001
Maine	207/622-8528
Maryland	410/962-2082
Massachusetts	617/316-2690
Michigan	313/688-3670
Minnesota	651/312-8023
Mississippi	504/588-3007
Missouri	314/539-3660
Montana	406/441-1022
Nebraska	402/221-4181
Nevada	702/455-1241
New Hampshire	603/433-0571
New Jersey	973/921-4043
New Mexico	505/837-5505
New York	212/436-1021
	718/488-3655
	716/686-4777
North Carolina	336/378-2180
North Dakota	701/239-5141
Ohio	513/263-3260
	216/522-7134
Oklahoma	405/297-4055
Oregon	503/326-2333
Pennsylvania	215/861-1304
	412/395-6504
Rhode Island	401/525-4200
South Carolina	803/253-3029
South Dakota	605/226-7269
Tennessee	615/250-5000
Texas	512/499-5439
	214/767-1428
	713/209-3660
Utah	801/799-6958
Vermont	802/860-2008
Virginia	804/916-3501
Washington	206/220-6037
West Virginia	304/420-6616
Wisconsin	414/297-3046
Wyoming	307/633-0800

IRS Internal Security maintains watch over IRS employees who might be tempted by bribery, fraud or other shortcomings.

202/622-4610

Did you know that the *Internal Revenue Service* has a reward program for snitching on tax cheats?   See... *REWARDS OFFERED*.

Direct Freedom of Information Act requests to: *Internal Revenue Service, Freedom of Information Request, P.O. Box 795 - Ben Franklin Station, Washington, D.C. 20044.*

For information on obtaining the tax returns of tax exempt organizations, see...*CHARITABLE ORGANIZATIONS.*

Also see...*U.S. TAX COURT.*

An *IRS* form investigators may want to know about is IRS Form 4684, Casualties and Thefts. Victims of crime or other unfortunate circumstances (such as a house fire) may recoup some of their losses as a tax deduction.

Investigators who do divorce work and family law cases will want to update themselves with IRS changes called *Innocent Spouse Relief.* Generally, husband and wife are responsible for each other's taxes, individually and jointly. However, a married person may sometimes escape the tax burden of his or her partner. For more information, request IRS publication 971, *Innocent Spouse Relief* and Form 8857, *Request for Innocent Spouse Relief.*

Did you know that the Internal Revenue Service will release a person's tax return to a third party? They will — with the signed authorization of the tax filer on a completed *Form 4506.* Why have *Form 4506* handy at your interviews, statements and depositions? One reason is because many subjects may promise to deliver a prior year's tax returns, only to later renege, or to produce fraudulent documents. With *Form 4506,* the return does directly from the IRS to the third party named on the form. There's a $23 charge for each tax period received. Also included are copies of attachments, including W-2 forms. Don't wait until you need this form to request it. Call this IRS number now and request *Form 4506,* then keep it in your briefcase.

800/829-3676

Form 4506 can also be downloaded directly off the Internet from the IRS website.

www.irs.ustreas.gov/forms_pubs/forms.html

Also see our *Privacy Law Survival Guide* (page 467) for further IRS guidelines on release of tax return information as allowable under the Internal Revenue Code.

INTERNATIONAL ASSOCIATION FOR PROPERTY AND EVIDENCE

Law enforcement-tilted professional association which promotes sound evidence handling procedures through training events and other means. Based in Burbank, California.

800/449-IAPE

Robert Scott, P.I.

INTERNATIONAL ASSOCIATION OF COMPUTER INVESTIGATION SPECIALISTS

Computer crime association whose membership is limited to law enforcement personnel and fulltime civilian employees of law enforcement agencies. Focus is on forensic aspects of seizing and processing computer systems.

503/557-1506
www.iacis.com

INTERNATIONAL CHILD ABDUCTION

For assistance on matters of international parental child abduction, contact the *U.S. State Department's Office of Children's Issues*. There's also recorded information on custody and adoptions.

202/736-7000
http://travel.state.gov/children's_issues.html

The State Department also operates the *Children's Passport Issuance Alert Program* which will alert a parent if a passport is applied for for his or her child, or if a currently valid passport exists. A Passport Alert form can be downloaded off the Internet.

202/736-7000
http://travel.state.gov/cipassportalert.html

Also see...*MISSING CHILDREN*.

INTERNATIONAL CRIME SCENE INVESTIGATORS ASSOCIATION

Internet-based professional organization for crime scene processors. Active (law enforcement), Associate (non-law enforcement) and Student memberships available.

708/460-8082
www.icsia.com

INTERNATIONAL DIRECTORY ASSISTANCE

HOT!

Do you need to locate a business or person in a foreign land? For just $7.95 per lookup, *International Directory Assistance* will provide published address and phone number information in any one of 42 foreign lands. If you haven't used *International Directory Assistance* before, you'd probably imagine that after dialing double zero, one ends up getting patched through to foreign-based operators who speak little or no English. Not true! The operators are American and have access to the published phone numbers of 42 countries. Making a call to them is as effortless as calling your local directory assistance.

00

INTERNET ADDRESSES

Until 1999, *Internic* had a lock on the registration of Internet domain name registrations. Now, there are several organizations which are authorized to register domain names. However the Internic website remains the best centralized place to look up the owner of a domain name.

www.internic.net/whois.html

Or access it through *Black Book Online*, where military, European and Asian domain names can also be researched. Go to this address and click the "Internet" button.

www.crimetime.com/online.htm

Also see the *Reference Guide* of this book where *Internet Abbreviations* further identifies information contained in Internet addresses.

INTERNET ARCHIVES

The Internet is constantly morphing — so how does an investigator learn what a website looked like two, three or more years back? *The Internet Archive Wayback Machine* has archived the Internet going back to 1996. By entering a web address, a user receives back an option of seeing how the site looked during any given year dating back to this time. Over ten billion web pages are stored in the project's massive underground computer facility in San Francisco.

www.archive.org

INTERNET FRAUD

The Internet Fraud Complaint Center is a partnership between the FBI and the National White Collar Crime Center. Website includes an online form for reporting online fraud and crime. Unfortunately, the reports aren't intended as a referral for prosecution. Rather, they're for identifying trends.

www.ifccfbi.gov

Also see...*COMPUTER CRIME*.

Also see...*SCAMBUSTERS.ORG*.

INTERPOL

Short for the International Criminal Police Organization, *INTERPOL* brokers the cooperation of police agencies in

178 countries. It's the only international police organization. Headquartered in Lyon, France. For a list of the 178 member nations, see our *Reference Guide*.

011-33-044-72-44-70-00
www.interpol.int

When American law enforcement needs assistance in foreign lands, the request is routed through the *U.S. National Central Bureau*, the American interface of INTERPOL. (*USNCB* is prohibited from processing requests from non-law enforcement persons or organizations.)

202/616-7827
www.usdoj.gov/usncb

Each of the fifty states and the District of Columbia have a *INTERPOL State Liaison Office* which serves as a point of contact for international investigations including child kidnapping/abductions. Local and state law enforcement agencies should make requests for help to their state liaison office which in turn will forward the request to the USNCB for transmission to appropriate foreign police authorities.

STATE LIAISON OFFICES:

Alabama Bureau of Investigations	334/260-1170
Alaska State Troopers	907/265-9583
Arizona Department of Public Safety	602/223-2608
Arkansas State Police	501/221-8213
California Department of Justice	916/227-4186
Colorado Bureau of Investigation	303/239-4310
Connecticut Central Crim. Intelligence	203/238-6561
Delaware State Police	302/739-5998
District of Columbia Metro P.D.	202/724-1426
Florida Dept. of Law Enforcement	904/488-6933
Georgia Bureau of Investigation	404/244-2554
Hawaii Dept. of Attorney General	808/586-1249
Idaho State Police	208/884-7110
Illinois State Police	217/782-8760
Indiana State Police	317/232-7796
Iowa Department of Public Safety	515/242-6124
Kansas Bureau of Investigation	913/296-8261
Kentucky State Police Intelligence	502/227-8708
Louisiana State Police	504/925-6213
Maine State Police	207/624-8787
Maryland State Police	410/290-0780
Massachusetts State Police	508/820-2129
Michigan State Police	517/336-6235
Minnesota State Crim. Apprehension	612/642-0610
Mississippi Dept. of Public Safety	601/987-1592
Missouri State Highway Patrol	573/751-3452
Montana Department of Justice	406/444-3874
Nebraska State Patrol	402/479-4957
Nevada Division of Investigation	775/687-4408

New Hampshire State Police	603/271-2663
New Jersey State Police	609/882-2000
New Mexico Dept. of Public Safety	505/841-8053
New York State Police	518/485-1518
N. Carolina State Bureau Investigation	800/334-3000
N. Dakota Bureau Crim. Investigation	701/221-5500
Ohio BCI&I, Criminal Intelligence	800/282-3784
Oklahoma State Bureau Investigation	405/848-6724
Oregon State Police	503/378-3720
Pennsylvania AG Intelligence Unit	717/787-0834
Rhode Island State Police	401/444-1006
S. Carolina Law Enforcement Div.	803/896-7008
S. Dakota Div. of Crim. Investigation	605/773-3331
Tennessee Bureau of Investigation	615/741-0430
Texas Department of Public Safety	512/424-2200
Utah Department of Public Safety	801/284-6200
Vermont State Police	802/244-8781
Virginia Department of State Police	804/323-2493
Washington State Patrol	206/753-3277
West Virginia State Police	304/558-3324
Wisconsin Department of Justice	608/266-1671
Wyoming Div. of Crim. Investigation	307/777-6615

INTERPRETERS
See...*AT&T LANGUAGE LINE*.

Also see...*TRANSLATORS*.

INTERSTATE IDENTIFICATION INDEX
The *Interstate Identification Index* is the largest file in NCIC, the FBI's nationwide criminal history system. Also commonly referred to as *"Triple I."* See *CRIMINAL RECORDS* for more details.

INVESTIGATIVE REPORTERS & EDITORS
Professional group, largely concerned with the usage of computerized information for reporting.

573/882-2042
www.ire.org

INVESTIGATOR'S OPEN NETWORK
ION is a well established private investigator's referral service with members throughout America and in many countries abroad.

800/338-3463
www.investigatorsanywhere.com

INVESTIGATORS – PROFESSIONAL ASSOCIATIONS
STATE ORGANIZATIONS:
Alaska Investigators Association   907/373-5453
www.akcache.com/alaskapi/AIA

Northern Alabama Investigators Association — 205/533-1413 — *www.hsv.tis.net/~pvteye.naia*

Arizona Association of Licensed Private Investigators — 602/231-6837 — *www.aalpi.com*

California Association of Licensed Investigators — 800/350-CALI, 916/441-5444 — *www.cali-pi.org*

California Institute for Professional Investigators — 800/400-CIPI — *www.cipi.org*

Los Angeles County Investigators Association — 818/883-6969 — *www.lacia.org*

California Association of Polygraph Examiners — 800/593-8598 — *www.californiapolygraph.com*

California Conference of Arson Investigators — 909/865-5004 — *www.arson.org*

Southern California Fraud Investigators Association — 310/549-1314 — *www.home.earthlink.net/~scfia*

Professional Private Investigators Association of Colorado — 303/430-4802 — *www.ppiac.org*

Connecticut Association of Licensed Private Detectives — 860/651-4200

Delaware Association of Detective Agencies — 302/652-2700

Florida Association of Licensed Investigators — 888/845-FALI — *www.fali.com*

Florida Association of Licensed Recovery Agents — 800/99-FALRA — *www.falra.org*

Private Investigator's Association of Florida — 407/282-3735

South Florida Investigators
Association   954/771-6900
                        www.sofloridainvestigators.org

Investigative Professional Associa-
tion of Georgia   800/675-7616

Georgia Association of Professional
Private Investigators   *www.gappi.org*

Idaho Private Investigators
Association   208/375-1906

Associated Detectives of Illinois   847/352-9900
                                    www.the-adi.com

Indiana Society of Professional
Investigators (formerly Indiana
Association of Private Detectives) 812/334-8857
                        www.indianainvestigators.com

Iowa Association of Private
Investigators   515/546-6353
                        www.iowa-investigators.com

Kansas Association of Licensed
Investigators   913/671-7500
                                    www.k-a-l-i.org

Kansas Association of Private
Investigators   913/362-0104
                                    www.kapi.org

Kentucky Professional
Investigators Assn.   *www.kpia.org*

Louisiana Private Investigators
Association   504/275-0796
                        www.intersurf.com/~lpia

Maine Licensed Private
Investigators Assn.   207/772-3999
                                    www.mlpia.org

Maryland Investigators and Security
Association   800/414-MISA
                                    www.spybbs.com/misa

Professional Investigators Alliance
of Maryland   800/774-7426
                                    www.olg.com/piam

Licensed Private Detective Associa-
tion of Massachusetts   508/586-6417
                                    www.lpdam.com

Association of Massachusetts Licensed Private Investigators	508/587-8100
	508/586-8057
	www.lpdam.org

Michigan Council of Private Investigation, Inc.
313/782-2600
http://lpconline.com/assocations_MCPI.html

Minnesota Association of Private Investigators
612/941-1040
www.edenprarie.com/MAPI

Mississippi Professional Investigators Association
662/424-9524
www.mpia.com

Missouri Professional Investigators Association
573/562-1235

Montana Association of Private Investigators & Security Operators
406/442-2790

Nebraska Association of Private Investigators
402/333-2820
www.napi.org

Nevada Investigative and Protective Services Association
775/772-4429
www.nipsanet.org

New Hampshire League of Investigators
603/753-6734
www.mvcom/ipusers/magee

Association of Professional Investigators (New Jersey)
908/494-1266

New Jersey Licensed Private Investigators Association
973/808-1004

Private Investigators Association of New Mexico
505/255-1425

Associated Licensed Detectives of New York State
212/947-3700
www.aldonys.org

The Society of Professional Investigators (New York)
516/781-1000

North Carolina Association of
Private Investigators   919/878-5001
                                         www.ncapi.org

Ohio Association of Investigative &
Security Services   614/227-4595
                              www.jhanda.com/oasis

Oklahoma Private Investigators
Association   800/299-2241
                                         405/235-0214
                                         www.opia.com

Oregon Association of Licensed
Investigators   503/224-3531
                                         www.oali.org

Pennsylvania Association of
Licensed Investigators   800/443-0824
                                         www.pali.org

Society of Private Detectives of
Puerto Rico   787/745-1930
                              home.coqui.net/pi4upr

South Carolina Association of
Legal Investigators   864/231-8446
                                         www.scalinv.com

Tennessee Professional Investigators
Association   423/577-0999
                                         www.tpia.com

Texas Association of Legal
Investigators   877/444-TALI
                                         www.tali.org

North Texas Process Server's
Association   214/373-3177
                                         www.ntpsa.com

South Texas Private Investigators
Association   281/351-0530
                                         www.ntpsa.com

North Texas Private Investigators
Association   214/226-9100
                                         www.ntpsa.com

Private Investigators Association
of Utah   801/467-9500
                                            www.piau.com

Private Investigators Association of
Virginia   703/960-2810
                              www.pimall.com/piav

Coalition of Virginia Private
Investigators & Security Association   703/360-4848

Virginia Security Association   804/746-7717

Professional Investigators & Security
Association of Virginia   703/521-3262

Virginia Association of Professional
Process Servers   540/342-0300
                     www.members.tripod.com/~covapps

Pacific Northwest Association of
Investigators, Inc. (Washington)   206/624-3910
                                            www.pnai.com

Washington Association of Legal
Investigators   206/625-9254
                                            www.wali.org

Professional Association of
Wisconsin Licensed Investigators   414/875-9991
                                            www.pawli.com

OTHER INVESTIGATIVE ASSOCIATIONS:
Alberta Association of Private
Investigators   403/257-5703
                          www.alberta-investigators.org

American Polygraph Association   800/APA-8037
                                            423/892-3992
                                            www.polygraph.org

American Society for Industrial
Security   703/519-6200
                                            www.asisonline.org

Association of British
Investigators, Ltd.   011-44-0181-546-3368
                    www.assoc-britishinvestigators.org.uk

Association of Certified Fraud
Examiners   800/245-3321
                                            512/478-9070
                                            www.acfe.org

Association of Christian Investigators
210/342-0509
www.a-c-i.org

Business Espionage Controls &
Countermeasures Association
301/292-6430

Council of International
Investigators
215/657-6247
www.cii2.org

Evidence Photographers
International Council
800/356-3742
www.epic-photo.org

Global Investigators Network
708/579-1776
www.glnetwork.com

Information Systems Security
Association
414/768-8000
www.issa-intl.org

Intelnet is a professional association of mostly former
agents from the U.S. intelligence community, now working
in the public sector.
610/687-2999
www.intelnetwork.org

International Association of Arson
Investigators
800/468-4224
www.firearson.com

International Association of Auto
Theft Investigators
941/697-2480
www.iaati.org

International Association of Counterterrorism & Security Professionals
703/243-0993
www.iacsp.com

International Association of Financial
Crimes Investigators
415/884-6600
www.iafci.org

International Association of Marine
Investigators
978/392-9292
www.iamimarine.org

International Association of Special
Investigation Units
410/933-3480
www.iasiu.com

International Bodyguard Association   780/461-5700
www.ibabodyguards.com

International Livestock Identification
and Theft Investigators   303/294-0895

Investigators of America   562-869-2535
www.investigatorsofamerica.com

Investigator's Open Network (ION)   800/338-3463
www.ioninc.com

International Society of Air Safety
Investigators   703/430-9668
www.aviationnow.com

Jewelers Security Alliance of the
United States   212/687-0328

National Association of Bunco
Investigators   410/752-8150

National Association of Fraud
Control Units   202/434-8020

National Association of Fraud
Investigators   386/274-5538
www.nafraud.com

National Association of
Investigative Specialists   512/719-3595
www.pimall.com/nais

National Association of
Legal Investigators   800/266-6254
www.nali.com

National Association of Professional
Process Servers   800/477-8211
www.napps.com

National Association of Railroad
Safety Consultants and
Investigators   248/689-4289
www.narsci.com

National Constable Association   215/547-6400
www.angelfire.com/la/nationalconstable

National Council of Investigative and
Security Services   800/445-8408
www.nciss.com

National Finance Adjusters   410/728-2400
www.nfa.org

I/J

| National Investigation Academy | 818/883-6969 |
| | *www.nationalinvestigationacademy.com* |

| Society of Competitive Intelligence Professionals | 703/739-0696 |
| | *www.scip.org* |

| Southeastern Association of Private Investigation | 954/474-8829 |
| | *www.seapi.com* |

| Texas Association of Accident Reconstruction Specialists | 281/893-9673 |
| | *www.taars.org* |

| Time Finance Adjusters | 800/874-0510 |
| | *www.tfaguide.com* |

| Women Investigators Association | 800/603-3524 |
| | *www.w-i-a.org* |

| World Association of Detectives | 800/962-0516 |
| | *www.wad.net* |

IRS
See...*INTERNAL REVENUE SERVICE.*

IRSG
See...*INDIVIDUAL REFERENCE SERVICES GROUP.*

ISO CLAIMSEARCH
NEW! *ISO ClaimSearch* is the new, super-mega colossal insurance industry database of claims and claimants. It contains the data formerly comprising the Index System (bodily injury claims); the Property Insurance Loss Registry (property claims); and the National Insurance Crime Bureau (auto theft/fraud claims). Health insurance claims are *not* included. Access is limited to insurance companies, fraud bureaus, self-insured entities and third-party administrators. This will be among the first searches run by investigators looking into suspicious insurance claims. Owned and operated by American Insurance Services Group, Inc. of Jersey City, New Jersey, a unit of Insurance Services Office, Inc.

888/778-4102
201/469-3139
www.claimsearch.iso.com

Also see....*MARINE INDEX BUREAU.*

JANE'S INFORMATION GROUP, LTD.
"Sixty Minutes" has described *Jane's* as a private Central Intelligence Agency. *Jane's Information Group* collects and

publishes information on the military capabilities of most of the world's nations. Their books, magazines and CD-ROMs are a good starting point for obtaining information on virtually any military weapon or armed forces.

703/683-3700
www.janes.com

JEWELRY AND GEMS

NEW! The FBI maintains its *Jewelry and Gems Database* as reported by law enforcement agencies and the jewelry industry. Information collected includes suspect descriptions and images, modus operandi, and stolen jewelry descriptions and photos. Located at its Major Theft/Transportation Crimes Unit at FBI headquarters in Washington.

202/324-3000
www.fbi.gov/programs/jag/jagpage.htm

The Gemological Institute of America (GIA) is a safe haven of sound information in the often deception-riddled world of gems. GIA offers several items of interest to investigators. Its Gem Trade Laboratory functions as a respected, independent service for grading diamonds and identifying gemstones. Need to know the value of a diamond or gem? This is the place to go. Its Gemological Library contains related hard-to-find information. There's also an Alumni Association Directory that contains biographical information on GIA graduates. World headquarters are in Carlsbad, California, with locations in several cities worldwide.

World Headquarters	800/421-7250
	760/603-4000
	www.gia.edu
Gem Trade Lab (Carlsbad)	760/603-4500
Gem Trade Lab (NYC)	212/221-5858

Jewelers Board of Trade is a jewelry trade organization that maintains a database of background information on persons in the jewelry business. Access to the database is restricted to subscribers.

213/627-4238
www.jewelersboard.com

JOHN E. REID & ASSOCIATES
John E. Reid & Associates has made a science of detecting deception. They've studied thousands of investigative interviews and have developed a profile of how guilty subjects unconsciously might indicate their guilt through physical and verbal behavior.

800/255-5747
312/876-1600
www.reid.com

173

JOURNALISTS
Society for Professional Journalists   317/927-8000
www.spj.com

National Institute for Computer-Assisted Reporting (NICAR) is a joint project of Investigative Reporters and Editors and the University of Missouri School of Journalism, aimed at furthering the journalistic usage of computer-assisted reporting. Includes newsletter, seminars, website and e-mail list.

573/882-0684
www.nicar.org

The Center for Investigative Reporting is a nonprofit group that, among other things, funds the investigation of hard-to-tackle stories and issues that the mainstream media tends to shy away from.

415/543-1200
www.muckraker.org

Also see...*INVESTIGATIVE REPORTERS & EDITORS*.

JURY VERDICT SUMMARIES
◼☞ NEW! Jury verdict summaries are used by law firms and insurance companies to evaluate the potential exposure of pending lawsuits. Jury verdict publishers from throughout the United States can be found at the website of the National Association of State Jury Verdict Publishers.

www.juryverdicts.com

Jury Verdict Research has profiled over 100,000 personal injury cases' verdicts and settlements on CD-ROM.

800/341-7874
www.lrb.com

Or try *VerdictSearch:*   800/832-1900
215/784-0860
www.moranlaw.com/services

These companies will let you research nationwide verdicts for free on their websites:

More Law   *www.morelaw.com*
Law Journal EXTRA!   *www.ljextra.com/cgi-bin*

JUSTICE DEPARTMENT, U.S.
General Information   202/514-2000
www.doj.gov

U.S. Department of Justice Phone Book is now on the Internet:
www.usdoj.gov/cgi-bin/phonebook/db.cgi

Also see...*U.S. ATTORNEY OFFICES.*

KOREANDETECTIVE.COM

The Korean population in the United States is growing; but Korean-speaking investigators seem to be harder and harder to find. Perhaps one reason is because private investigation is not a fully legal profession in South Korea. Regardless, if your subject is in the U.S. or Korea, *KoreanDetective.com* may be the help you've been looking for. This private agency is run by respected Korean-American P.I. and former journalist Bruce Kang. Chicago based.

847/293-0909
www.koreandetective.com

LABOR UNIONS

Disclosure Room, Office of Labor Management Standards Enforcement, U.S. Dept. of Labor maintains background information on labor unions, their officials, by-laws and financial reports.

202/693-0125
www.dol.gov
DOL, Labor Union Investigations   202/693-0143

LAS VEGAS, NEVADA

Las Vegas, Nevada — a city with more scams and scammers than hotel rooms. Certainly a place worth special mention in this book!

Divorce Records   702/455-2590
Marriage Licenses   702/455-3156
Police Department   702/795-3111
www.lvmpd.com

Photo: Las Vegas, Nevada — one of the few cities in the world to have a street named after a gangster. Inset: Mob-guy Bugsy Siegel. Yes, his name is misspelled on the street sign! (Photo by author; inset courtesy of AP/Wide World Photos.)

For Internet lookups of Clark County, Nevada public records including marriage licenses, court records and more, visit *Black Book Online* and click on the State Records button.

www.crimetime.com/online.htm

LAW ENFORCEMENT DIRECTORIES
See...*NATIONAL DIRECTORY OF LAW ENFORCEMENT ADMINISTRATORS*.

LAW ENFORCEMENT PRODUCT NEWS
Need to keep abreast of the latest law enforcement gadgets, supplies and equipment? Then a free subscription to *Law Enforcement Product News* is a must. This bi-monthly, glossy tabloid-format publication contains wall-to-wall ads for the latest available gear. Available to both law enforcement and private-sector security companies.

800/547-7377
www.law-enforcement.com

LAW ENFORCEMENT – PROFESSIONAL ASSOCIATIONS

American Federation of Police   305/573-0070

Association for Crime Scene
Reconstruction   503/656-0953
                                     www.acsr.com

Black Law Enforcement Association   301/702-2507
                                     www.moblenatl.org

California Gang Investigators
Association   888/229-CGIA
                                     www.cgiaonline.org

Florida Sex Crimes Investigators
Association   954/321-4240
                                     www.fscia.org

International Association of Bomb
Technicians and Investigators   941/353-6843
                                     www.iabti.org

International Association of Campus
Law Enforcement   860/586-7517
                                     www.iaclea.org

International Association of Chiefs
of Police   703/836-6767
                                     www.theiacp.org

Hispanic Police Officers Association   305/594-1173

International Association of Crime
Analysts   408/261-5337
                                           www.iaci.net

International Association of
Financial Crimes Investigators   415/884-6600
                                          www.iafci.org

International Association of Law
Enforcement Intelligence Analysts   609/896-9577
                              www.inteltec.com/IALEIA

International Association of
Railway Police   800/366-6979
                                          www.iarpolice.org

International Association of
Undercover Officers   877/662-6225
                               www.undercovercops.org

International Crime Scene
Investigators   708/460-8082
                                          www.icsia.com

International Narcotic Enforcement
Officers Association   518/463-6232
                                          www.ineoa.org

International Narcotics Interdiction
Association   954/491-5056
                                          www.inia.org

International Police
Association   44-0-115945-5985
                                          www.ipa-iac.org

Marine Patrol Association   617/479-8292
                            www.marinepatrolassoc.org

National Association of Chiefs of
Police   305/573-0070

National Association of Fire
Investigators   312/427-6320

National Association of Property
Recovery Investigators   386/479-5329
                                          www.napri.org

National Constable's Association   215/547-6400
                      www.angelfire.com/la/nationalconstable

Robert Scott, P.I.

National Center for Women and
Policing   213/651-2532
www.feminist.org/police/ncwp

National District Attorney's
Association   703/549-9222
www.ndaa.org

National Drug Enforcement
Officers Association   202/2989653
www.ndeoa.org

National Police Officers Association
of America   502/451-7550

National Organization of Black
Law Enforcement Executives   703/658-1529
www.noblenatl.org

National Narcotics Officers
Associations Coalition   805/290-2834
www.natlnarc.org

National Sheriffs' Association   703/836-7827
www.sheriffs.org

National Tactical Officers
Association   800/279-9127
www.ntoa.org

National Troopers Coalition   317/636-0929
www.nat-trooperscoalition.com

Police Marksman Association   334/271-2010
www.policemarksman.com

Police Women's Association   809/627-5217

Polish-American Police Association   773/235-0506
www.ponetwork.com/PAPA

United States Police K-9
Association   888/371-4014
www.uspcak9.com

Women in Federal Law
Enforcement   703/548-9211
www.wifle.com

LAW LIBRARIES
The single largest law in the world is the *Library of Congress, Law Library*.

202/707-5065
www.lcweb.loc.gov

178

Library, Supreme Court of the United
States   202/479-3177
www.supremecourtus.gov

For links to online law libraries, visit:
www.findlaw.com

FOREIGN LAW:
The Library of Congress, Law Library, maintains two
foreign law divsions:
www.lcweb.loc.gov/rr/law

Eastern Law includes Poland, Russia, Turkey, Iran, Iraq,
the Middle East, South Africa, China, the Far East, and
others.
           202/707-5085

Western Law includes Britain, Canada, Australia, Europe,
India, Pakistan, Mexico, South America and others.

           202/707-5077
For Canadian law, see:

           http://jurist.law.utoronto.ca/locate.htm

LEADERSHIP LIBRARY, THE
See...*YELLOW BOOKS.*

LEXIS-NEXIS
See...*DATABASE PROVIDERS.*

LIBRARIES
 It's 3 a.m. Got a reference desk at a library
you can call for information on a hard-to-
find piece of information? *The University of
Arizona* library is open 24/7 with a reference librarian on
duty. Ask for the *Reference Desk* when calling.

           520/621-6441
dizzy.library.arizona.edu

The U.S. Dept. of Commerce Library reference desk will
check standard business reference publications for basic
background information on businesses.
           202/482-5511

American Library Association   312/944-6780
           www.ala.org

NASA Headquarters Library is a good starting point for
space and flight-related inquiries.
           202/358-0168
           www.nasa.gov

Library of Congress	202/707-5000
	www.lcweb.loc.gov
Library of Congress, Law Library	202/287-5065
	www.lcweb.loc.gov
Library of Congress, Telephone Reference Service	202/707-5522
Library, Supreme Court of the United States	202/479-3177
	www.supremecourtus.gov

Special Libraries Association can refer you to a library in one of many specialty areas.

202/234-4700
www.sla.org

The Academy of Motion Picture Arts & Sciences library contains a wealth of information on movie credits.

310/247-3000
310/247-3020
www.oscar.org

Environmental Protection Agency, Library   202/260-5922

www.epa.gov

The National Library of Medicine is the largest medical library in the world, located in Bethesda, Maryland:

Health Professional Inquiries	301/594-5983
Public Information	301/496-6308
	www.nlm.nih.gov

The largest collection of gambling-related literature in the world can be found at the *University of Nevada, Las Vegas Special Collections Department*.

702/895-2234
www.library.nevada.edu/speccol

For crime-related research, see...*NATIONAL CRIMINAL JUSTICE REFERENCE SERVICE*.

Also see...*NATIONAL TRANSPORTATION LIBRARY*.

LIFE INSURANCE LOCATOR

 Finding the life insurance policy of a decedent when the identity of the insurer is unknown can be a daunting task. Of course, the check register of the decent can always be checked for record of premium payments. But what happens when this is not available? *Life Benefits Search, Inc.* is an Internet-based service that has automated the search process. In essence, you provide them with the information on the decedent and they mass mail inquiries to a lengthy list of life insurance companies. If a policy is found, a claim can then be filed. Cost is $150 per search.

800/770-2485
www.lifesearch.net

Also try contacting *The American Council of Life Insurance*. Its members will search their policyholders for a modest charge.

800/942-4242
www.acli.com

LOBBYISTS

 Lobbyists registered at the Senate's *Public Records Office* can be viewed at the *Political Money Line* website.

www.tray.com

Also see...*FOREIGN AGENT REGISTRATIONS.*

LYCOS 411

 Ever been out in the field on a case and desperately in need of a computer to check your e-mail, do an online lookup or get driving instructions? As of our publication date, web portal *Lycos* was offering just such a service. You call them and one of their operators will go online and then relay the information to you. There's a free 10-call trial. If you like the service, subscriptions start as low as $4.95 per month.

800/WWW-LYCOS
800/999-5926
www.voice.lycos.com

MAIL DROPS

 A mail drop database consisting of over 9,000 mailbox and packaging stores can be searched on the Internet for free. Visit *Black Book Online* (*www.crimetime.com/online.htm*) and click the "Mail Drop" button or go directly to the site below:

www.bnl.com/mb/

Loss Control Technologies is the creator of a mail drop database called the Suspect Address Database. They advertise it as the most comprehensive mail drop database available. The data is available for sale/license to qualified business users.

888/666-6444
www.lct123.com

Also see...*REVERSE MAIL DROPS*.

MAIL FRAUD
The United States Postal Service operates its *Mail Fraud Complaint Center*.

800/372-8347

Also see...*POSTAL INSPECTORS, U.S.*

MAPS – TOPOGRAPHIC
The U.S. Geological Survey maintains topographic maps of the entire United States:

	www.usgs.gov
Eastern Region	703/648-4000
Central Region	303/202-4200
Western Region	650/853-8300

Or try the central USGS information clearinghouse, called the *Earth Science Information Center*.

888/ASK-USGS
www.askusgs.gov

MARINE CORPS PERSONNEL LOCATOR
The Marine Corps World Wide Locator provides military address information for active-duty personnel. The information is available by phone only to family members and government/military officials. All others must submit a written request. Include the service member's full name, date of birth, Social Security Number and a MOS, if possible. Include payment in the amount of $3.50 made payable to the United States Treasury.

HQ U.S. Marine Corps
Personnel Management Support Branch (MMSB-17)
2008 Elliot Road
Quantico, VA 22134-5030
Telephone: 703/784-3942
www.usmc.mil/marinelink/ind.nsf/locator

On the Internet, there are a number of privately run websites which contain contact information of both active and retired Marine Corps personnel. This information should be viewed as unofficial and typically contains information voluntarily submitted.

GIBuddies.com
MarineCorps.com
Military.com

Also see...*MILITARY PERSONNEL*.

MARINE INDEX BUREAU
The Marine Index Bureau is a bodily injury claim database for maritime workers. "Maritime" includes both ocean-

going vessels as well as those that travel inland lakes and waterways. Included are commercial fishing boats, cruise ships, offshore drilling platforms and riverboat casinos. Also included are property claims for hull and machinery losses for the commercial fishing industry. Around since 1937, the *MIB* is now owned and operated by Insurance Services Office, Inc. — the same people behind *ISO Claim-Search*.

800/888-4476
www.iso.com

MARITIME INFORMATION SYSTEM
The Maritime Information System is a CD-ROM containing several databases culled from Coast Guard files and other sources. Included is a database of boating accidents, another of vessel recall and defect notices, another database of federally registered boat owners and more.

800/325-8061
www.boatman.com

MARKET RESEARCH.COM
NEW! Massive collection of over 10,000 reports on a variety of highly specific business, product and market research topics. Samples include *The U.S. Organic Food Market; Private Label Credit Card Markets;* and *Internet Retailing*. The reports are not inexpensive — averaging from a few hundred to a few thousand dollars each. This will be of most interest to investigators specializing in competitive intelligence. Their catalog is available online at the below URL or as a printed catalog.

800/298-5699
212/807-2716
www.marketresearch.com

MEDICAL DEVICES
The Food & Drug Administration, Center for Devices and Radiological Health regulates medical devices.

800/638-2041
www.fda.gov

MEDICAL DOCTORS
HOT! A free background check on MDs and chiropractors can be performed at *SearchPointe*. The search scans AMA, Dept. of Health and Human Services, DEA and 67 state medical and osteopathic board records. For an additional fee, a "License/Sanction Report" can be obtained.

888/275-6334
www.searchpointe.com

AMA Physician Select is a database of the *American Medical Association* that contains address, biographical and disciplinary information on every physician in the United States.

312/464-5000
www.ama-assn.org

Discipline history, license status, and key biographical facts can be found on medical doctors through their state's disciplinary or medical licensing board:

Alabama	334/242-4116
Alaska	907/269-8160
Arizona	877/255-2212
Arkansas	501/296-1802
California	916/263-2388
Colorado	303/894-7690
Connecticut	860/509-7648
Delaware	302/739-4522
District of Columbia	202/442-9200
Florida	904/488-3622
Georgia	404/656-3913
Hawaii	808/586-3000
Idaho	208/327-7000
Illinois	312/814-4500
Indiana	317/232-2960
Iowa	515/281-5171
Kansas	913/296-7413
Kentucky	502/429-8046
Louisiana	504/524-6763
Maine	207/287-3601
Maryland	410/764-4777
Massachusetts	617/727-3086
Michigan	517/373-6873
Minnesota	612/617-2130
Mississippi	601/987-3079
Missouri	314/751-0098
Montana	406/444-4284
Nebraska	402/471-2118
Nevada	702/688-2559
New Hampshire	603/271-1203
New Jersey	609/826-7100
New Mexico	505/476-7120
New York	518/402-0855
North Carolina	919/326-1100
North Dakota	701/328-6500
Ohio	614/466-3934
Oklahoma	405/848-6841
Oregon	503/229-5770
Pennsylvania	717/787-2381
Rhode Island	401/222-3855
South Carolina	803/896-4500
South Dakota	605/334-8343
Tennessee	615/532-4384

Texas	512/305-7010
Utah	801/530-6628
Vermont	802/828-2673
Virginia	804/662-9908
Washington	360/236-4800
West Virginia	304/558-2921
Wisconsin	608/266-2112
Wyoming	307/778-7053

A useful website with links to the professional licensing boards websites in all states is *docboard.org*.

www.docboard.org

Questionable Doctors, published annually, lists doctors, dentists, and chiropractors who have been disciplined by various licensing agencies.

202/588-1000
www.citizen.org

The Federation of State Medical Boards of the United States, Inc. is the nationwide organization for state medical licensing authorities.

817/868-4000
www.fsmb.org

When doctors default on government-backed student loans, they're liable to find their names posted on the *Defaulted Docs* website put up by the *Department of Health and Human Services*. Search it here:

www.mars.psc.dhhs.gov/defaulteddocs

National Board of Chiropractic
Examiners 970/356-9100

National Commission for the
Certification of Acupuncturists 703/548-9004

Also see...*NATIONAL PRACTITIONER DATA BANK*.

Also see...*HEALTH CARE FRAUD*.

MEDICAL EXAMINERS
See...*CORONERS*.

MEDICAL INFORMATION BUREAU
Mega database of confidential health insurance claim information on millions of Americans. Available only to member insurance companies. However, an individual can request a copy of his or her own file:

617/426-3660
In Canada, call: 416/597-0590
www.mib.com

MEDICAL REFERENCE INFORMATION
The National Library of Medicine is the largest medical library in the world, located in Bethesda, Maryland.

Health Professional Inquiries   301/594-5983
Public Information   301/496-6308
www.nlm.nih.gov

Medline is a mega database of nearly 9 million articles from medical journals dating back to 1966. It's searchable, for free, over the Internet.
410/563-2378
www.ncbi.nlm.nih.gov/PubMed/

MEGAN'S LAW
See...*SEX OFFENDER REGISTRIES*.

MERLIN INFORMATION SERVICES
See...*DATA PROVIDERS*.

MEXICAN INVESTIGATIONS
Gaslamp Quarter Investigations, located in San Diego, offers south of the border investigations in Mexico and throughout Latin America. In countries where information doesn't always flow freely, you'll want to rely upon a company like *Gaslamp*.
619/239-6991
619/238-1985
www.gqi.net

San Diego-based *Interpoint Group, Inc.* offers corporate due diligence, competitor intelligence, risk assessment and money-laundering awareness services in Mexico.

619/233-1954

Mexico-based *mexicoinvestigations.com* advertises themselves as English-speaking and American-thinking.

011-52-415-27757
www.mexicoinvestigations.com

Stanley M. Moos of *Pan American Investigations* knows Latin America. He has over 20 years investigative/ intelligence experience, residing and operating in Mexico, Central America and the Caribbean. He is also a Certified Fraud Examiner.
520/297-9318

San Diego-based *AM-MX Investigations* specializes in Mexican investigations with an accent on Baja California.

619/417-8414
www.am-mx.com

MICROSOFT CERTIFICATIONS

NEW! Microsoft Certified (MCSE/MCP) computer-types have to pass training and tests established by *Microsoft Corporation*. If they do, they'll likely boast this MCSE designation on their business card, resume or brochure. But are they really blessed by Bill Gates and Company? To find out, call this number to verify the certification.

800/688-0496

MILITARY – CRIMINAL INVESTIGATIONS

NEW! *The Department of Defense* has designated liaisons for law enforcement agencies who need contact/assistance with military criminal investigators. Organized by service branch.

ARMY LAW ENFORCEMENT LIAISONS:

Criminal Investigation Command	703/806-0305
	703/806-0374
Georgia	706/545-2509
Hawaii	808/655-2396
Kansas	913/239-3933
Kentucky	502/798-7247
National Capital Area	703/696-3496
New Jersey	609/562-5006
North Carolina	910/396-7516
Texas	915/568-5905
Texas (Fort Hood District)	817/287-5039
Washington State	206/967-7859

For areas not listed above, contact the *Criminal Investigation Command.*

NAVY AND MARINE CORPS LAW ENFORCEMENT LIAISONS:

Naval Criminal Investigative Service Headquarters	202/433-9234
Northern California, Colorado, Nevada, Utah and Wyoming	510/273-4158
Central California	909/985-2264
Southern California, Arizona, New Mexico and West Texas	619/556-1364
Georgia, South Carolina, Central America and South America	803/743-3750
Hawaii and Pacific Islands	808/474-1218
Maryland, Northern Virginia and Washington, D.C.	202/433-3658
Tidewater, Virginia	804/444-3139
Northwest Washington State	360/396-4660
New England and Bermuda	401/841-2241
North Central United States	708/688-5655
South Central United States	904/452-4211

Southeastern United States, Cuba
and Puerto Rico   904/270-5361

AIR FORCE LIAISON:
Air Force Investigative Operations
Center, Major Crimes Investigations   202/767-5192
After hours, call   202/767-5450

MILITARY PERSONNEL
LOCATING ACTIVE PERSONNEL:
See...*AIR FORCE PERSONNEL LOCATOR*.

Also see...*ARMY PERSONNEL LOCATOR*.

Also see...*COAST GUARD, U.S.*

Also see...*MARINE CORPS PERSONNEL LOCATOR*.

Also see...*NAVY PERSONNEL LOCATOR*.

Department of Defense Operator is for locating civilian
DOD employees.
                        703/545-6700

When you have the name of a military base, but not a
location, visit the military website of AT&T. You'll find
links to military bases for all five branches of the armed
services.
          www.att.com/mil/bases.html

Defense Prisoners Military Operations Center tracks U.S.
POWs and MIAs for all branches of the armed services.

                  703/602-2102
               www.dtic.mil/dpmo

Also see...*DEERS SYSTEM*.

DESERTERS / CONSCIENTIOUS OBJECTORS:
Each branch of the military operates an investigation unit
for locating deserters. Here's the contact numbers:
Air Force   210/652-3727
Army   317/510-3711
Marines   703/696-2031
Navy   847/688-2106
Coast Guard   202/493-6600

Department of Defense, Amnesty
Programs   703/697-3387

Department of Defense, Deserter
Programs   703/697-3387

Conscientious Objectors   510/465-1617

MILITARY SERVICE RECORDS:

The primary document that authenticates a person's military service is *DD Form 214, Report of Separation.* It will include such items as length of service and reason and character of separation. DD Form 214s are archived at the National Personnel Records Center in St. Louis approximately 6 months after military service is completed. *Full records are only released with the authorization of the service person, next of kin, or legal guardian. However, the form can be sent to any address designated by the authorizing party. (Example: If the subject of the investigation is cooperative, he or she can sign the release and have the DD Form 214 sent directly to an investigator.)* However...an edited version of this same information may be released to third parties when the subject of the investigation is not cooperative and no authorizing signature can be obtained. In this situation, combine your request with a Freedom of Information Act request (see *Reference Guide*). Direct your request to: *National Personnel Records Center, Attn.: FOIA Officer (Military Records), 9700 Page Avenue, St. Louis, MO 63132-5100.*

To request a military person's DD Form 214 (with or without his or her permission), you need to obtain and complete a request *Standard Form 180* from the National Archives and Records Administration. This is available as an Adobe Acrobat .pdf document that can be downloaded off of the Internet at: *www.nara.gov/regional/mprsf180. html.* If you don't have access to the Internet, but do have access to a fax machine, call the NARA's fax-on-demand system at 301/713-6905 and select document number 2255. Or you can call the NARA and request a copy of the form be sent to you.

> 314/538-4261
> 314/538-4243
> 314/538-4141

Each branch of the military also offers a Certificate of Record of Military Service. See...*AIR FORCE PERSONNEL LOCATOR...ARMY PERSONNEL LOCATOR...MARINE CORPS PERSONNEL LOCATOR... NAVY PERSONNEL LOCATOR.*

Interested in determining the pay scale & benefits for active and/or retired military personnel? Visit this website:

www.dfas.mil

UNOFFICIAL SERVICE VERIFICATION:

Website *militaryusa.com* offers free access to a number of databases that might be helpful in determining whether or not a person really did serve in the military. Includes Korean, Vietnam and Desert Storm wars.

www.militaryusa.com

Private, subscription-based data providers *Lexis-Nexis* and *AutoTrackXP* both offer an U.S. military personnel lookup. See *AutoTrackXP* and *Lexis-Nexis* in our *DATABASE PROVIDERS* section.

The American War Library is a notable private effort to document every service person, past and present, who has ever served in the U.S. armed forces. The information comes from a variety of sources. One possible use of it is to verify a person's claim of past military service. Unfortunately, the information-delivery system of the *American War Library* is very user-unfriendly. Available by computer only, direct dial-in software (such as Hyper-Terminal) or a software download at their site will be necessary to view data. Ouch! Couldn't there just be a simple web page to log into?

310/532-0634
www.members.aol.com/veterans

WAR HERO VERIFICATION:
Phony war heroes will often try to pass themselves off as a former Navy SEAL. One place these phonies are exposed on is the online *Navy SEALS Wall of Shame*.

www.cyberseals.org

The Medal of Honor is the nation's highest military honor. The act of bravery must be above and beyond the call of duty and witnessed by at least two persons. Claiming to be a Medal of Honor winner when you're not is a federal crime that will be actively investigated and prosecuted by the *FBI*. For information on this, visit this special page at the *FBI* website:

www.fbi.gov/majcases/medal/medal2.htm

Contact the *Congressional Medal of Honor Society* to learn if a particular person really is a MOH recipient.

843/884-8862

Or you can browse this *U.S. Army* website which lists the 3,400 plus MOH winners.

www.army.mil/cmh-pg/moh1.htm

To determine if a person is a former *Vietnam-era POW*, visit this website:

http://lcweb2.loc.gov/pow/powquery.html

Korean War POW records   703/604-0831
www.korea50.army.mil

DECEASED VETERANS:
Need to know where a veteran is buried? If it is in a VA cemetery, the U.S. Department of Memorial Affairs will provide location information.

800/697-6947
www.cem.va.gov

A searchable database of WWII veterans who were buried in our cemeteries, missing in action, or lost at sea can be found at this American Battle Monuments Commission website. It does not contain the names of all Americans returned to the U.S. for burial, however.

www.americanwardead.com/searchww.htm

MISSING CHILDREN
Nationwide assistance is available through the *National Center for Missing and Exploited Children*. See... *NATIONAL CENTER FOR MISSING AND EXPLOITED CHILDREN*.

800/THE-LOST
www.missingkids.org

National Runaway Hotline:
Nationwide   800/621-4000
www.nrscrisisline.org

In addition, each state has a clearinghouse to assist in missing children matters:

Alabama	334/260-1172
	800/228-7688
Alaska	907/269-5497
	800/478-9333
Arizona	602/223-2158
Arkansas	501/682-1323
	800/448-3014
California	916/227-3290
	800/222-3463
Colorado	303/239-4251
Connecticut	860/685-8260
	800/367-5678
Delaware	302/739-5883
District of Columbia	202/576-6771
Florida	850/410-8585
	888/356-4774
Georgia	404/244-2554
	800/282-6564
Hawaii	808/586-1449
Idaho	208/884-7130
	888/777-3922
Illinois	217/785-4341
	800/843-5763
Indiana	317/232-8310
	800/831-8953

Iowa	515/281-7958
Kansas	785/296-8200
	800/572-7463
Kentucky	502/227-8799
	800/543-7723
Louisiana	225/342-4011
Maine	207/624-8705
Maryland	410/290-1620
Massachusetts	508/820-2130
	800/622-5999
Michigan	517/336-6100
Minnesota	651/642-0627
Mississippi	601/987-1592
Missouri	573/751-3452
	800/877-3452
Montana	406/444-2800
Nebraska	402/479-4019
	402/479-4938
Nevada	702/486-3539
	800/992-0900
New Hampshire	603/271-2663
	800/852-3411
New Jersey	609/882-2000
	800/709-7090
New Mexico	505/827-9191
New York	518/457-6326
	800/346-3543
North Carolina	919/733-3914
	800/522-5437
North Dakota	701/328-9921
	800/472-2121
Ohio	614/644-8066
	800/325-5604
Oklahoma	405/879-2645
Oregon	503/378-3720
	800/282-7155
Pennsylvania	717/783-5524
Puerto Rico	787/729-2697
Rhode Island	401/444-1125
	800/546-8066
South Carolina	803/737-9000
	800/322-4453
South Dakota	605/773-3331
Tennessee	615/744-4000
Texas	512/424-2810
	800/346-3243
Utah	801/965-4500
	888/770-6477
Vermont	802/241-5352
Virginia	804/674-2026
	800/822-4453
Washington	360/586-0030
	800/543-5678
West Virginia	304/558-1467

	800/352-0927
Wisconsin	608/266-1671
	800/THE-HOPE
Wyoming	307/777-7537

In Canada, contact the
Missing Children's Registry.   877/318-3576

Also see...*INTERNATIONAL CHILD ABDUCTION*.

MISSING PERSONS

Central Registry of the Missing distributes publications with profiles of missing persons to law enforcement agencies and other interested parties.

201/288-4445
www.id-wanted.org

The Department of State, Overseas Citizen Services, helps locate U.S. citizens missing in foreign lands.

202/647-5226
www.state.gov

The *FBI* does not search for missing persons. However, at the request of other law enforcement agencies they will post a stop notice on NCIC. As of January 2001, there were approximately 103,000 missing persons on record.

202/324-3000
www.fbi.gov

The Social Security Administration will forward a letter to a missing person if the reason is of "great importance" or to inform the person about a sizeable amount of money due him or her. There is no charge for forwarding letters of a humanitarian nature. There's a $25 fee for forwarding a letter advising the person that they are due money. Generally, the letter is forwarded to the last employer on file for the missing person, unless the person is receiving benefits. The letter must be sent to the SSA in a stamped, unsealed (as it will be reviewed by the SSA), blank envelope. Include with this as much of the following information as possible: The missing person's full legal name; name of his/her parents; Social Security Number; date of birth; place of birth; and last known address. The SSA office does not have a published telephone number. Direct requests to: *Social Security Administration, Office of Earnings Operations, P.O. Box 33003, Baltimore, MD 21290-3003.*

The *Internal Revenue Service* offers a similar service. Send your request to: *Internal Revenue Service, Office of Disclosure Operations, 1111 Constitution Avenue NW, Washington, D.C. 20224.*

The National Association for Search and Rescue is an organization of paid and volunteer searchers dedicated to finding and aiding people in distress. They're known to assist in missing children investigations.

703/222-6277
www.nasar.org

Know a family with a missing person who can't afford reward money? *The Carole Sund/Carrington Memorial Reward Foundation* donates reward money to families without economic means.

888/813-8389
www.carolesundfoundation.com

Also see...*MISSING CHILDREN.*

Also see...*SALVATION ARMY MISSING PERSONS BUREAU.*

Also see...*INTERNATIONAL CHILD ABDUCTION.*

MONEY LAUNDERING

Money Laundering Alert is written primarily for businesses, such as banks and casinos, that are subject to misuse by money launderers. There's a heavy emphasis on compliance with government "Know Thy Customer" rules. The monthly newsletter costs $345 a year. There's also online access to the newsletter and its archives (going back to 1994) for $875 per year (and up, depending on number of users). Individual reports are also online with Lexis-Nexis (by file name MLA). They also offer a Spanish-language version of their website.

305/530-0500
www.moneylaunderingalert.com
www.lavadodinero.com

An e-mail based newsletter with a more European outlook is *The World Money Laundering Report*. Free sample available.

www.vortexcentrum.com/wmlrinf.htm

Also see...*OFFICE OF FOREIGN ASSETS CONTROL.*

Also see...*FINANCIAL CRIMES ENFORCEMENT NETWORK.*

MOTOR VEHICLE RECORDS
See...*DRIVER RECORDS.*

Also see...*VEHICLE IDENTIFICATION NUMBERS.*

MOVIES
See...*ACADEMY OF MOTION PICTURE ARTS & SCIENCES LIBRARY.*

Also see...*CELEBRITY LOCATES.*

Also see...*VIDEOTAPE PIRACY.*

MUTILATED U.S. CURRENCY
Partially mutilated, burned, mildewed or otherwise destroyed money can be submitted to the *Department of Treasury* for redemption:

202/874-2361
www.treas.gov/usss/money_damaged.htm

MVR DECODER DIGEST/MVR BOOK
NEW! *MVR* (Motor Vehicle Record) *Decoder Digest* decodes driver's license records from all fifty states. Sells for $19.95. Its companion book, *The MVR Book*, details the privacy restrictions, access procedures and regulations for driver and vehicle records in all states. See our *Reference Guide* for the formats of drivers licenses in each state, courtesy of the MVR Book.

800/929-3811
www.brbpub.com

NAMEBASE
Namebase is a unique database of persons who have been named in at least one of hundreds of investigative journalism books. Altogether, it includes over one-quarter million citations. If the subject of your investigation travels in the upper circles of business, organized crime, politics, the CIA, unions or the military, you should check *Namebase* to learn of possible past associations and activities. Many investigative journalists know about and use Namebase. Far fewer private investigators do. Fee-based service, but some searching can be done for free at their website.

Public Information Research   210/509-3160
www.namebase.org

NAPPS
See...*NATIONAL ASSOCIATION OF PROFESSIONAL PROCESS SERVERS.*

NARCOTICS AND DANGEROUS DRUGS INFORMATION SYSTEM (NADDIS)
NEW! Top secret database of the *Drug Enforcement Agency*. Includes names of people, businesses, vessels and airstrips previously identified in DEA investigations. Highly

controversial because no arrest or conviction is necessary for a person to have his or her name memorialized here.

202/307-4190
www.usdoj.gov/dea/foia/naddis.html

NATIONAL ASSOCIATION OF BUNCO INVESTIGATORS

 The movements and activities of many "Bunco" artists are tracked through a private organization called *The National Association of Bunco Investigators*, which includes both street-level law enforcement officers and private sector investigators among its members. Their newsletter contains names, photos and M.O.s of known and suspected fraud perpetrators.

410/752-8150

NATIONAL ASSOCIATION OF LEGAL INVESTIGATORS

The National Association of Legal Investigators is the largest national professional organization for private investigators. Be forewarned, though, membership is limited to investigators who devote a majority of time to conducting investigations for plaintiffs (in civil cases), or for the defense (in criminal cases). Nevertheless, it's a respected and important organization.

800/266-6254
www.nali.com

NATIONAL ASSOCIATION OF PROFESSIONAL PROCESS SERVERS

NAPPS is a nationwide network of process servers and public record retrievers. However, many investigators also belong. The organization's website is *very* useful for locating out-of-town process servers and court researchers.

800/477-8211
www.napps.org

NATIONAL ASSOCIATION OF SECURITIES DEALERS (NASD)

Investors (and others) can now get on the Internet to learn about the disciplinary history of stock brokers. Also included are pending complaints and past complaints that have been settled for over $10,000. The same information is also available by telephone.

800/289-9999
License Status   301/590-6500
www.nasdr.com

NATIONAL CENTER FOR MISSING & EXPLOITED CHILDREN

There are many organizations set up to aid in the search for missing children. Only one has quasi-governmental status which includes partial access to NCIC and other law enforcement resources. *The National Center for Missing and Exploited Children* is active in not only the recovery of abducted children, but also in the prevention of various types of sexual exploitation. Assistance offered to law enforcement includes photograph and poster preparation, technical case assistance and forensic services. *NCMEC* collaborates with the U.S. Secret Service's Forensic Division to provide handwriting, polygraph, fingerprint and other technical forensic assistance.

24-Hour Hotline	800/THE-LOST
General Information	703/235-3900
	www.missingkids.org

REGIONAL CENTERS:

NCMEC/CA	714/508-0150
NCMEC/NY	716/242-0900
NCMEC/FL	561/848-1900
NCMEC/SC	803/750-7055

NATIONAL COUNCIL OF INVESTIGATIVE AND SECURITY SERVICES

NCISS is the primary...and sometimes *only*...voice in national legislative matters that might affect the private investigation industry. When new legislation is introduced in Washington that seeks to trim back our right to investigate, *NCISS* is there. Don't look at your membership fee as a business expense — look at it as an investment in the future.

800/445-8408

www.nciss.org

NATIONAL COUNTERINTELLIGENCE CENTER

NEW! Federal quasi-spy agency that seeks to identify and counter foreign intelligence threats to national and economic security. Previously, much of this information was available only in government circles. It provides the infrastructure for sharing some information with the private sector. Look for this agency to be primarily active when foreign concerns are trying to spy on U.S. business interests.

General Information	703/874-4123
Threat Assessment Office	703/874-4119
	www.nacic.gov

NATIONAL CRIME INFORMATION CENTER

See...*CRIMINAL RECORDS*.

Robert Scott, P.I.

NATIONAL CRIMINAL JUSTICE REFERENCE SERVICE

Publications library of the *National Institute of Justice*. Contains huge library of criminal justice related studies and reports.

> 800/851-3420
> 301/519-5500
> *www.ncjrs.org*

RELATED RESOURCES:

Juvenile Justice Clearinghouse	800/638-8736
Bureau of Justice Statistics	800/732-3277
National Victims Resource Center	800/627-6872
Bureau of Justice Assistance	800/688-4252

NATIONAL DIRECTORY OF LAW ENFORCEMENT ADMINISTRATORS

This is the best directory of law enforcement agencies we have been able to locate. It's massive at 785 pages. Includes local police departments, sheriff departments, state police agencies, correctional agencies and federal law enforcement agencies. Sells for $99, including S&H. A web version is available for $119.

> 800/647-7579
> *www.safetysource.com*

NATIONAL DIRECTORY OF PUBLIC RECORD VENDORS, THE

See...*PUBLIC RECORD RESEARCH.*

NATIONAL DRIVER REGISTER

National Driver Register is a database of the most dangerous drivers in America. Typically, they've had their licenses suspended or revoked for serious violations including driving while impaired on alcohol or drugs. Administered by the NHTSA, the purpose of this federal program is to keep problem drivers who have had their licenses yanked in one state from getting a new one elsewhere. The database is restricted to persons wanting their own information, prospective employers (with a signed release from the applicant), the FAA, the FRA (Federal Railroad Administration), U.S. Coast Guard, state and federal driver's license officials and federal accident investigators.

> 202/366-4800
> *www.nhtsa.dot.gov*

NATIONAL DRUG INTELLIGENCE CENTER

National intelligence center that gathers data from domestic law enforcement agencies, foreign intelligence and open sources to identify general trends and specific drug threats. Its primary product is the *National Drug Threat Assessment* which is circulated among key policymakers throughout the government. This is a U.S. Department of Justice agency.

814/532-4601
www.doj.gov/ndic

NATIONAL FISH & WILDLIFE FORENSIC LAB

The U.S. Department of Fish & Game's National Fish & Wildlife Forensic Lab has been called the first full-service wildlife crime lab in the world.

541/482-4191
www.lab.fws.gov

NATIONAL INFRASTUCTURE PROTECTION CENTER
See...*COMPUTER CRIME.*

NATIONAL INSTANT CRIMINAL BACKGROUND CHECK SYSTEM (NICS)

■☞ [NEW!] Effective November 30, 1998, persons purchasing firearms were required to undergo instant criminal background checks. *NICS* includes records on persons who are disqualified from owning a gun and includes but is not limited to the FBI's National Crime Information Center index and Interstate Identification Index (III). The system is available to federally licensed gun dealers making a transaction and law enforcement *only. Unauthorized access to the system is a violation of federal law.*

How it works: When a gun customer seeks to purchase a firearm, the gun dealer, who must hold a Federal Firearm License, uses a computer or telephone to contact the NICS Information Center at FBI headquarters in Clarksburg, West Virginia. The gun dealer provides his FFL number and a password which is then checked against Bureau of Alcohol, Tobacco and Firearm FFL files for authentification. The gun dealer then provides the customer's name and date of birth. The search is conducted by the NICS Information Center and one of three answers is provided to the gun dealer: "Proceed," "Delayed" or "Denied." In no circumstance shall any other information other than these three one word responses be provided to the gun dealer. "Proceed" means no disqualifying information has been found. "Delayed" means more research time is needed. NICS then has three business days to get back to the gun dealer with a Proceed or Denied response. If no response is received back from NICS after three business days, the gun dealer can transfer the firearm. "Denied" means at least one hit was found in the NICS index, NCIC or III.

NICS Information Center is open 7 days a week (except Christmas and Thanksgiving), 9 a.m. to 2 a.m. Eastern time:

877/FBI-NICS

NICS Administrative Information   877/444-6427
www.fbi.gov/programs/nics/nicsfact.htm

NATIONAL INSURANCE CRIME BUREAU
The National Insurance Crime Bureau (NICB) is *the* insurance industry funded investigative agency to combat insurance fraud. Although it is a private organization, most of its agents are former law enforcement officers.

Headquarters	800/447-6282
	708/430-2430
Tip Line	800/TEL-NICB
	www.nicb.org

FIELD OFFICES:

Area 1: Chicago Office *(IA, IL, KS, NW IN, MN, MO, ND, NE, SD, WI)*	800/447-6282
Area 2: Seattle Office *(AK, CO, ID, MT, OR, UT, WA, WY)*	888/241-8130
Area 3: Los Angeles Office *(AZ, CA, HI, NV)*	888/815-9064
Area 4: Dallas Office *(NM, OK, TX)*	888/241-8127
Area 5: Tampa Office *(AL, FL, GA, LA, MS & Puerto Rico)*	888/241-8270
Area 6: Washington, D.C. Office *(D.C., DE, MD, NC, PA, SC, VA, WV)*	888/241-7159
Area 7: New York Office *(NJ & Metro NY City)*	888/241-8280
Area 8: Columbus Office *(AR, IN, KY, MI, OH, TN)*	888/241-7158
Area 9: Hartford Office *(CT, MA, ME, NH, Upstate NY, RI, VT)*	888/306-7710

NATIONAL PASSPORT INFORMATION CENTER
In 1996, the federal government privatized telephone information on how to obtain or renew a passport and how to check on the status of a pending passport. Information on obtaining an emergency passport can also be obtained here. The call center is financed by user fees — 35 cents per minute for automated information and $1.05 per minute for operator assistance.

Billed to your phone:	900/225-5674
Billed to your credit card:	888/362-8668
	http://travel.state.gov/npicinfo.html

NATIONAL PERSONNEL RECORDS CENTER
Located in St. Louis, Missouri, the *National Personnel Records Center* is the primary repository and archive for United States government employee records. Much of the information is restricted by the Privacy Act.

301/457-7000
www.nara.gov

NATIONAL PRACTITIONER DATA BANK
NPDB is the little known and even less understood nationwide database that maintains background information on virtually every doctor (and 39 other categories of health care providers) in the United States. It features doctors who have been professionally disciplined and/or the target of malpractice complaints. There are very tight restrictions on who can access the data.

800/767-6732
www.npdb.com

NATIONAL REFERENCE CENTER
The National Reference Center is a free program of the Library of Congress that maintains a huge database of experts and organizations on virtually every technical or scientific subject.

202/707-5522
www.lcweb.loc.gov/faq/research

NATIONAL TRANSPORTATION LIBRARY
NEW! *The National Transportation Library* is home to documents and databases related to transportation issues. Includes statistical, engineering, government, company and legal information. Operated by the Department of Transportation and accessible over the Internet. Specialized research services are also available on a fee basis.

202/366-0752
www.bts.gov/ntl/

NATIONAL WHITE COLLAR CRIME CENTER
The National White Collar Crime Center fights economic crime through prevention, education, investigation and prosecution. This DOJ organization primarily assists law enforcement agencies in conducting investigations of advance loan fee schemes, credit card fraud, computer fraud and other economic crimes. It also maintains a *Criminal Information Pointer* database that names persons and businesses suspected of economic criminal activity. The database is confidential and subjected to the same privacy provisions as NCIC.

804/323-3563
www.nw3c.org

NAVY PERSONNEL LOCATOR
The Navy Worldwide Locator will provide current location information for active-duty personnel. However, the requestor must be a family member or military/government employee conducting official business. Privacy act restrictions forbid providing address information to other parties.

901/874-3388

All other parties can have a letter forwarded to an active Navy service person for a $3.50 fee. Information is not available by telephone. Send a check or money order payable to the United States Treasurer; the person's full name; rate or rank; and Social Security Number, if known, to the address below:

Naval Personnel Command
PERS 312F
5720 Integrity Drive
Millington, TN 38055-3120

Certain Navy personnel may be located through the *Navy Directory Service*. Personnel who are overseas or in sensitive or routinely deployable units are NOT accessible from this site.

http://directory.navy.mil

To obtain a certificate of service or nonservice, include a check for $5.20 made payable to United States Treasurer for each certificate requested; full name; rank; and Social Security Number, if known, to the Naval Personnel Command address above.

To have a letter forwarded to a *former* service member, mail a letter requesting this service and include the individual's full name; Social Security Number, if known; approximate dates of service; and a check or money order payable to the United States Treasurer for $3.50 to:

National Personnel Records Center
9700 Page Avenue
St. Louis, MO 63132

Contacting an active member of the *U.S. Navy* while at sea can be difficult; especially when the matter is not an emergency and/or the cooperation of family members is not available. Did you know that every ship in the *U.S. Navy* has its own unique "FPO" mailing address. Just mail a letter to the enlisted person at the ship's FPO address and the letter should make its way there. Find a list of Navy ships and their mailing addresses here:

www.chinfo.navy.mil/navypalib/ships/lists/ship-fbo.html

The *U.S. Navy* has set up e-mail links to a number of Navy ships. Visit this website to see if the proper ship can be found, then use the online form to send a message.

www.spear.navy.mil/shipmail/form.asp

Also see...*MILITARY PERSONNEL*.

NAZI WAR CRIMINALS

Office of Special Investigations, Criminal Division, Dept. of Justice investigates suspected Nazi war criminals believed to be living in the United States.

202/616-2492
www.usdoj.gov/criminal/osi.html

For background information on the Holocaust, contact *The Simon Wiesenthal Center.*

310/553-8403
www.wiesenthal.org

Also see...*WAR CRIMES.*

NECROSEARCH

Necrosearch is a nonprofit organization of law enforcement investigators and scientists dedicated to finding clandestine gravesites through numerous scientific techniques including botany, ground-penetrating radar and aerial imagery.

303/734-5187
303/795-4772
www.necrosearch.com

NET DETECTIVE

NEW! If you have an e-mail address, you've undoubtedly received spam with such enticing subject lines as "Find Out Anything About Anyone!" advertising a computer "program" called *Net Detective.* Unfortunately, the information in *Net Detective* is so stale it has more mold growing on it than that half-eaten sandwich your kid tossed under his bed a few months back. What's not outdated is so light on content that it couldn't possibly be of interest to any professional investigator. Sells for $29.

www.jeanharris.com/Detective/

NEVADA BROTHELS

NEW! Of the 17 counties in Nevada, 10 have legalized prostitution. To register for a permit and work card (which includes an identifying photograph), a prostitute must fill out an application, undergo a health exam, and pay a fee ranging from $5 to $100. These permits are public record. Name checks can usually be done by phone or mail, depending on county.

Churchill County	775/423-3116
Elko County	775/777-7310
Esmeralda County	775/485-6367
Humbolt County	775/623-6396
Lander County	775/635-2860

Lyon County	775/463-6600
Mineral County	775/945-2434
Nye County	775/482-8110
Storey County	775/847-0959
White Pine County	775/289-2430

NEWSPAPERS

Options for conducting news searches are many. Among them are pay services like *Lexis-Nexis*; free Internet search sites like *onlinenewspapers.com*; and of course, phoning the morgue of any specific paper. Of them all, *Lexis-Nexis* is the most potent option for the truly serious investigator. No account with *Lexis-Nexis* is necessary to conduct a news search on their system. Just have a credit card handy and visit their website. Once there, click the "pay as you go" option.

www.lexis-nexis.com

A close second is *The Wall Street Journal's Factiva* service. See...*FACTIVA.COM*.

These Internet sites provide links to newspapers with online archives. Some charge a small fee to view the actual article. All allow basic searching for no fee:

www.newslibrary.com
www.newspapers.com
www.onlinenewspapers.com
www.ibiblio.org

If you're looking for the phone number of a newspaper that doesn't appear in the list below, try the *N-Net* website. It's also searchable by geographic area in case the name of the paper isn't known. The site contains a huge databank of newspapers, large and small.

www.n-net.com

Many of these newspapers will search their archives for articles.

Akron Beacon Journal	330/996-3000
Albuquerque Journal	505/823-3800
Arizona Republic (Phoenix)	602/444-8000
Arkansas Democrat Gazette	501/378-3400
Atlanta Journal/Constitution	404/526-5151
Austin American-Statesman	512/445-3500
Baltimore Sun	410/332-6000
Boston Globe	617/929-2000
Buffalo News	716/849-3434
Charlotte Observer	704/358-5000
Chicago Tribune	312/222-3232
Cincinnati Enquirer	513/651-4500
Cleveland Plain Dealer	216/999-4500
Columbus (OH) Dispatch	614/461-5000

Daily Oklahoman	405/475-3311
Dallas Morning News	214/977-8222
Denver Post	303/820-1010
Des Moines Register	515/284-8000
Detroit Free Press	313/222-6600
Florida Times Union (Jacksonville)	904/359-4111
Fort Lauderdale Sun-Sentinel	954/356-4000
Fresno Bee	559/441-6111
Honolulu Star-Bulletin	808/529-4747
Indianapolis News/Star	317/633-1240
Kansas City Star	816/234-4300
Las Vegas Review-Journal	702/383-0211
Los Angeles Times	800/788-8804
Louisville Courier-Journal	502/582-4011
Memphis Commercial Appeal	901/529-2211
Miami Herald	305/350-2111
Milwaukee Journal Sentinel	414/224-2000
Minneapolis Star & Tribune	612/673-4000
Nashville Tennessean	615/259-8000
Newark Star-Ledger	973/392-4141
New Haven Register	203/789-5200
New York Post	212/930-8000
New York Times	212/556-1234
Oakland (CA) Tribune	510/208-6300
Orange County (CA) Register	714/835-1234
Philadelphia Inquirer	215/854-2000
Pittsburgh Post Gazette	412/263-1100
Portland Oregonian	503/221-8327
Raleigh (NC) News & Observer	919/829-4500
Richmond (VA) Times Dispatch	804/649-6000
Sacramento Bee	916/321-1000
St. Louis Post Dispatch	314/340-8000
Salt Lake Tribune	801/237-2045
San Antonio Express News	210/225-7411
San Diego Union-Tribune	619/299-3131
San Francisco Chronicle	415/777-1111
San Jose Mercury News	408/920-5000
Seattle Post-Intelligencer	206/448-8000
Tampa Tribune	813/259-7711
The Times-Picayune (New Orleans)	504/826-3279
USA Today	703/276-3400
Washington Post	202/334-6000

Also see...*ALTERNATIVE PRESS INDEX*.

Also see...*ASSOCIATED PRESS*.

Also see...*BROADCAST TRANSCRIPTS*.

Also see...*NAMEBASE*.

Also see...*VIDEO MONITORING SERVICE OF AMERICA*.

Robert Scott, P.I.

NICB
See...*NATIONAL INSURANCE CRIME BUREAU.*

**OCCUPATIONAL SAFETY & HEALTH
ADMINISTRATION**
General Information   800/321-6742
                                       www.osha.gov

OSHA's *Office of Management of Data Systems* maintains a
database of all OSHA workplace inspections made since
1972. The database is searchable by company name, but not
by injured worker.

                           202/693-1700
                  www.osha.gov/cgi-bin/est/est1

Also see...*OSHADATA.COM.*

ODOMETER FRAUD
Odometer tampering is a federal offense. Contact the
Odometer Fraud Staff of the *National Highway Traffic
Safety Commission.*

                           202/366-4761
                           www.nhtsa.gov

OFAC
See...*OFFICE OF FOREIGN ASSETS CONTROL.*

> DOB 1958; POB Jeddah, Saudi Arabia, All POB
> Yemen (individual) [SDT] [SDGT]
> BIN LADIN, Osama (a.k.a. BIN LADIN, Usama bin
> Muhammad bin Awad; a.k.a. BIN LADEN, Osama;
> a.k.a BIN LADEN, Usama; a.k.a. BIN LADIN,
> Osama bin Muhammad bin Awad; a k a. BIN
> LADIN, Usama), Afghanistan; DOB 30 Jul 57; Alt.
> DOB 1958; POB Jeddah, Saudi Arabia; All. POB
> Yemen (individual) [SDT] [SDGT]
> BIN LADIN, Osama bin Muhammad bin Awad
> (a.k.a BIN LADIN, Usama bin Muhammad bin
> Awad, a.k.a. BIN LADEN, Osama; a.k.a. BIN
> LADEN, Usama; a.k.a. BIN LADIN, Osama; a.k.a.
> BIN LADIN, Usama), Afghanistan; DOB 30 Jul 57;
> Alt DOB 1958; POB Jeddah, Saudi Arabia. Alt.
> POB Yemen (individual) [SDT] [SDGT]
> BIN LADIN, Usama (a.k.a. BIN LADIN, Usama bin

*Above: Terrorist Osama bin Laden's place on the OFAC
list. He was a regular long before September 11, 2001. The
list also includes narcotic traffickers and other undesirables.*

OFFICE OF FOREIGN ASSETS CONTROL (OFAC)
OFAC is a little known Department of the Treasury agency
whose mission is to quash commerce between the United
States and foreign narcotic traffickers, terrorists and
unfriendly nations. *OFAC* maintains a black list, known as
Specially Designated Nationals and Blocked Persons,
containing all of the above. Banks, insurance company and
all other businesses and persons are forbidden from doing

business with these parties. A copy of the list can be downloaded at the OFAC website.

202/622-2490
800/540-OFAC
www.treas.gov/ofac/

OFAC also has a bilingual hotline, located in Miami, for issues related to the Cuban embargo.

305/810-5140

OFFSHOREBUSINESS.COM

NEW! When the trail of a financial investigation goes offshore, it's not unusual for otherwise-competent investigators to find themselves lost-at-sea. One resource that persons in this situation should know about — especially when fraud or potential fraud is involved — is *Offshore Business News and Research, Inc.* This Miami-based firm specializes in coverage of financial dealings and misdealings in Caribbean financial havens. Their products include Offshore Alert, a newsletter that includes coverage of legal actions against offshore financial companies, as well some rare, searchable databases such as court indices from the Grand Cayman Islands and the Bermuda Supreme Court. Also offered are lists of suspended corporations from the Bahamas, Bermuda and elsewhere. Annual subscription costs $595.

305/859-8945
www.offshorebusiness.com

ORGANIZED CRIME

Organized Crime & Racketeering
Section, Criminal Division,
Department of Justice   202/514-3595
www.usdoj.gov/criminal/ocrs.html

The *Chicago Crime Commission* is a not-for-profit organization that has been gathering information on mobsters since 1919.

312/372-0101
www.chicagocrimecommission.org

Jane's Conferences sponsors an annual seminar on *TransNational Organized Crime*. Focus is on groups from Russia, Asia and Latin America.

703/683-3700
conference.janes.com

The *U.S. Department of State* has published "Issues in Global Crime" which focuses on threat analysis of various transnational crime groups and issues including "Cargo Theft in Mexico" and "Nordic Motorcycle Gangs." Get it online:

www.ds.state.gov/publications/keepingsafe.htm

OSHADATA.COM

NEW! *OSHAdata.com* offers more than just rehashed OSHA reports, despite their name.

They've complied a number of public record databases from a variety of federal agencies who regulate businesses into a single, searchable source. Data sources include EEOC Employment Act violators; Health and Human Service's Cumulative Sanctions; and the GSA's Excluded Party List. Most of this information is available for free on the Internet or by contacting the agencies directly. However, *OSHAdata.com* makes them all available with a single search. Subscription-based service.

973/378-8011
www.oshadata.com

OUT OF BUSINESS DATABASE

NEW! Getting information on closed businesses, including executive names, number of employees and other details can be obtained through *InfoUSA's* "Out of Business" database. Not commercially available in many places, it can be found at Lexis-Nexis in their Company Library section. See... *DATABASE PROVIDERS*...for Lexis-Nexis contact information.

OVERSEAS SECURITY ADVISORY COUNCIL

NEW! American firms doing business overseas need current and authoritative information about overseas security conditions. The *State Department* has established an electronic database (available over the Internet) containing this advisory information. To be eligible for access, you must be an American corporation who does business overseas, or a consultant or private sector security firm sponsored by an American corporation with substantial overseas business. Interested parties should send a letter of application to *Executive Director, Overseas Security Advisory Council, Department of State, SA-3, Washington, D.C. 20522-1003*.

202/663-0533
http://ds.state.gov/publications/osacpubs.htm

PACER

Pacer is the computerized indexing system for most of the federal court system. Included is the nationwide index of all but two bankruptcy courts, *most* federal civil and criminal courts, and eight of twelve appelate courts. (See the *Reference Guide* of this book for a list of nonparticipating courts.) Now available on the Internet, with a subscription.

800/676-6856
http://pacer.uspci.uscourts.gov

PALADIN PRESS

Paladin Press has certainly earned its controversial reputation. Titles in this Boulder, Colorado publisher's extensive book and video catalog include "Homemade Grenade Launchers," "Secrets of a Super Hacker" and "Hit Man, A Tactical Manual for Independent Contractors."

Order Department   800/392-2400
Customer Service   303/443-7250
www.paladin-press.com

PAROLE COMMISSION, U.S.

The U.S. Parole Commission controls parole of federal prisoners.

301/492-5990
www.usdoj.gov/uspc

PASSPORTS

See...*NATIONAL PASSPORT INFORMATION CENTER.*

PATENTS

Patents issued by the U.S. Patent and Trademark Office from 1790 through the present can now be researched on the Internet at the USPTO website. Recent patent applications can also be researched here. The days of paying outside services to do basic patent searches appear to have come to a close.

800/786-9199
www.uspto.gov

Over 25,000 attorneys are registered to practice in front of the Patent Trademark Office. Search the registry here:

www.uspto.gov/web/offices/dcom/olia/roster/

PENTAGON LOCATOR

The *Pentagon* locator finds Pentagon civilian employees. (This number is <u>not</u> for locating military personnel.)

703/545-6700
www.defenselink.mil/pub/pentagon

PHONE BOOKS

Worldwide Books specializes in finding phone books from around the world.

800/792-2665
www.worldwide.com

The Directory Source from Qwest can provide telephone books from anywhere in the United States, Canada and over 100 hundred other countries.

800/422-8793
www.directorysource.com

The Pacific Bell Directory Smart Resource Center also sells phone books from throughout the country. Costs range from $6 to $50 each and delivery time is around 2 weeks.

800/848-8000

Over 8,000 different phone books can be purchased at the website of telephone mega-company Verizon.

www2.gte.com/OrderBook/index.cfm

The Sherman Foundation Library is a unique private library that houses an enormous collection of old phone books and city directories. Due to a staff shortage, they have a strictly limited policy on doing checks by phone.

949/673-1880

The U.S. Dept. of Commerce has a collection of foreign phone books and might do lookups over the phone if you ask in a very nice way.

202/482-5511
www.doc.gov

Also contact the business liaison office of any embassy listed in our *EMBASSY* section — they usually have phone books from their home countries and often will often offer assistance by phone.

PHONE DISGUISER

Local Presence is a unique service that will be invaluable to investigators who conduct undercover phone investigations and need to disguise their true location. Establishes a phone number in any one of numerous area codes throughout the country — but when the number is called, the call is routed through to your own desk. Just $9.95 a month! Sign up online at their website.

888/647-4373
800/835-5710
http://lp.voicenet.com

PHYSICIANS
See...*MEDICAL DOCTORS*.

PILR
See...*ISO CLAIMSEARCH*.

P.I. MAGAZINE
P.I. Magazine is the most read *independent* publication for private investigators. Each issue contains useful information on investigative techniques and resources. Also included are marketing ideas for investigators who are

growing a new practice. Subscription cost is $39 per year, which includes six issues. Find a free sample issue online at their website.

419/382-0967
www.pimag.com

POCKET PARTNER

Think of *Pocket Partner* as *The Investigator's Little Black Book* for street cops. It's very compact, jammed with reference information...and sells for the ridiculously low price of $9.95. You'll find it fat with crime scene investigation checklists, a mini-Spanish phrase book, a hazardous materials guide and more. Available through *Calibre Press*.

800/323-0037
www.calibrepress.com

POISON - INFORMATION

The FDA maintains a database of known poisonous substances:

Poison Control Branch   301/827-4573
                                     www.fda.gov
American Association of Poison
Control Centers   202/362-7217
                                     www.aapcc.org

Also see...*CRIME LABS*.

Also see...*TOXIC CHEMICALS*.

POLICE COMPLAINT CENTER, THE

The Police Complaint Center advertises itself as a national nonprofit organization that provides assistance to victims of police misconduct. They've received plenty of media exposure by conducting undercover stings of police departments who refuse to take complaints from minorities.

850/894-6819
www.policeabuse.com

POLICE REPORTS

Regional Report Services, Inc. specializes in retrieving police reports on a nationwide basis.

800/934-9698
www.rrsinfo.com

POLITICIANS

Public Records Section, Federal Election Commission, maintains a database of financial information disclosed by all federal candidates and contributors since 1977.

800/424-9530
www.fec.gov

The best site on the Internet with FEC information on political donations can be found at *Political Money Line*. Includes a search to look up campaign donations by donor. Also found at the site are Lobbyists registered at the Senate's Public Records Office.

www.tray.com

Project Vote Smart is a nonprofit voter information service that maintains information on over 13,000 elected officials, on both the federal and state level. Information available includes issue position, voting records, and PAC funding.

General Information	800/622-7627
Voter Research Hotline	888/868-3762

www.vote-smart.org

The Reporter's Source Book is relied upon by political journalists and includes an extensive listing of special interest groups, experts and think tanks. Free for political reporters & PVS members, but can also be purchased for $10.

800/622-7627
www.vote-smart.org

Laird Wilcox Editorial & Research Service is relied upon by journalists for information on fringe political groups – of both the right and left.

913/829-0609
www.lairdwilcox.com

For campaign finance information and other money trail clues, visit the *CampaignFinance.org* website from Investigative Reporters & Editors.

www.campaignfinance.org

Biographical, voting record and other information on American politicians can be found in *The Almanac of American Politics*. Lookups can be done online for free. The complete book can be purchased for $56.94 (soft cover) or $75.95 (hard cover). This is bread-and-butter stuff for political junkies.

800/356-4838
202/739-8400
http://nationaljournal.com/members/almanac/

CQ Washington Alert is an online information service specializing in congressional information — from bills currently pending, to profiles of House/Senate members and more.

800/432-2250
www.library.cq.com

To learn what bills are pending in Congress on any given topic, call the *Office of Legislative Information and Bill Status*. They'll do a free keyword search of their computerized database which contains information on all legislation pending in both the House and Senate.

202/225-1772
www.house.gov

Also see...*YELLOW BOOKS*.

POLYGRAPH

There are two national organizations for polygraph examiners. The websites of both contain names and contact information for local polygraph examiners.

The National Polygraph Association is geared specifically for private sector examiners.

877/NPA-POLY
www.nationalpolygraph.com

The American Polygraph Association also includes polygraph examiners from the criminal justice system:

423/892-3992
800/272-8037
www.polygraph.org

Polygraph Place also has an online lookup for locating a polygraph examiner anywhere in the United States.

www.polygraphplace.com

A critical look at polygraph practices and its underlying science can be found here:

www.antipolygraph.com

Another website, aimed primarily at stinging polygraph tests is:

www.polygraph.com

Ed Gelb is considered by many to be one of the leading polygraph examiners in the world.

323/932-0200
www.polygraphexpert.com

National Training Center of
Polygraph Science   212/755-5241

Also see...our *Privacy Law Survival Guide* for polygraph law information.

POSTAL INSPECTORS, U.S.
The *U.S. Postal Inspectors* investigate the criminal usage of mail — from mail bombs to mail fraud:

Complaint Line	800/654-8896

www.usps.gov/postalinspectors

FIELD OFFICES:

Atlanta Division	404/608-4500
Boston Division	617/464-8000
Charlotte Division	704/329-9120
Chicago Division	312/983-7900
Denver Division	303/313-5320
Detroit Division	313/226-8184
Ft. Worth Division	817/317-3400
Houston Division	713/238-4400
Los Angeles Division	626/405-1200
Miami Division	954/436-7200
Newark Division	973/693-5400
New York Division	212/330-3844
Philadelphia Division	215/895-8450
Pittsburgh Division	412/359-7900
St. Louis Division	314/539-9300
San Francisco Division	415/778-5800
Seattle Division	206/442-6300
Tampa Division	954/436-7200
Washington, D.C. Division	202/636-2300

Also see...*REWARDS OFFERED* for information on reward money posted by the *USPS*.

POSTAL SERVICE
24-Hour General Information, including zip code lookups and identifying the carrier station for any given address:

800/ASK-USPS
www.usps.gov

For inquiries relating to lost, stolen or unclaimed Postal money orders, contact the *U.S. Postal Office, Money Order Branch*.

800/868-2443

To verify the employment of a person with the *U.S. Postal Service*, call this number and when prompted by the automated attendant, punch in his or her Social Security Number.

800/276-9850

Watchdog group *Postalwatch.org* is every postal bureaucrats worst nightmare. Their website is full of scathing scrutiny of the Post Office.

www.postalwatch.org

Looking for insight into the mind of the postal employee? Try *disgruntledpostalemployees.com*. Let's hope they're not giving away guns at this year's Christmas party.

www.disgruntledpostalemployees.com

Also see...our *Privacy Law Survival Guide* for Post Office release of customer information guidelines.

PRESIDENTIAL PARDONS
All requests for presidential pardons are to be submitted to *Pardon Attorney, Department of Justice*. Don't send cash!

202/616-6070
www.usdoj.gov/pardon/

PRISON HISTORIES, FEDERAL

Sentry (*not* an acronym) is the *Federal Bureau of Prison's* database that keeps track of the location and status of current and former (going back to 1982) federal inmates. Much of the information was formerly available to the public via phone. Now an Internet lookup will be needed to learn the status/location of a current or former inmate. Exceptions include defense attorneys, victims and prisoner family members. These parties may call for information. At the website, click the Inmate Information link.

	202/307-3126
Pre-1982 Information	202/307-2934
	www.bop.gov

For *Fast* Access to Online Prison Inmate Lookups for All Available States, Visit

BLACK BOOK ONLINE
found only at
www.crimetime.com

PRISONS
Bureau of Prisons (Federal)
General Information — 202/307-3198
www.bop.gov

STATE DEPARTMENT OF CORRECTIONS:
Alabama Dept. of Corrections — 334/240-9500
Alaska Department of Corrections — 907/465-4652
Arizona Department of Corrections — 602/542-5536
Arkansas Department of Correction — 870/267-6999

California Department of Corrections	916/445-7682
Colorado Department of Corrections	719/579-9580
Connecticut Dept. of Corrections	860/692-7780
Delaware Department of Corrections	302/739-5601
District of Columbia D.O.C.	202/673-7316
Florida Department of Corrections	904/488-5021
Georgia Department of Corrections	404/656-4593
Hawaii Department of Public Safety	808/587-1288
Idaho Department of Correction	208/658-2000
Illinois Department of Corrections	217/522-2666
Indiana Department of Correction	317/232-5715
Iowa Department of Corrections	515/242-5705
Kansas Department of Corrections	785/296-3317
Kentucky Department of Corrections	502/564-4726
Louisiana D.O.C.	225/342-6633
Maine Department of Corrections	207/287-4360
Maryland D.O.C.	410/585-3300
Massachusetts Office of Public Safety	617/727-7775
Michigan Department of Corrections	517/373-0720
Minnesota Dept. of Corrections	612/342-0200
Mississippi Dept. of Corrections	601/359-5621
Missouri Department of Corrections	573/751-2389
Montana Department of Corrections	406/444-3930
Nebraska Dept. of Correctional Services	402/471-2654
Nevada Department of Prisons	775/887-3285
New Hampshire Dept. of Corrections	603/271-5600
New Jersey Dept. of Corrections	609/292-9860
New Mexico Corrections Department	505/827-8709
New York Dept. Correctional Services	518/457-8126
North Carolina Dept. of Correction	919/716-3700
North Dakota D.O.C. and Rehabilitation	701/328-6390
Ohio Dept. of Rehab. & Correction	614/752-1159
Oklahoma Dept. of Corrections	405/425-2500
Oregon Department of Corrections	503/945-0920
Pennsylvania Dept. of Corrections	717/975-4925
Rhode Island Dept. of Corrections	401/462-2611
South Carolina Dept. of Corrections	803/896-8500
South Dakota Dept. of Corrections	605/773-3478
Tennessee Dept. of Correction	615/741-1000
Texas Dept. of Criminal Justice	936/295-6371
Utah Department of Corrections	801/265-5500
Vermont Department of Corrections	802/241-2442
Virginia Department of Corrections	804/674-3000
Washington Dept. of Corrections	360/753-1573
W. Virginia Dept. of Military Affairs & Public Safety	304/558-2037
Wisconsin Department of Corrections	608/266-4548
Wyoming Department of Corrections	307/777-7405
Corrections Information Center	800/877-1461
	303/682-0213
	www.nicic.org

PRIVATE INVESTIGATION LICENSES

Most states license private investigators. A handful of states offer no licensing — relying on either local registration or no licensing at all.

Alabama	205/532-3316
Alaska	by local gov.
Arizona	602/223-2361
Arkansas	501/618-8600
California	800/952-5210
Colorado	by local gov.
Connecticut	860/685-8290
Delaware	302/736-5900
District of Columbia	202/671-0500
Florida	904/488-5381
Georgia	404/656-2282
Hawaii	808/586-3000
Idaho	by local gov.
Illinois	847/352-1500
Indiana	317/232-2980
Iowa	515/281-3211
Kansas	913/296-8200
Kentucky	by local gov.
Louisiana	225/925-4704
Maine	207/624-8775
Maryland	410/799-0191
Massachusetts	978/538-6128
Michigan	517/336-3425
Minnesota	612/215-1753
Mississippi	by local gov.
Missouri	by local gov.
Montana	406/444-3728
Nebraska	402/471-2554
Nevada	775/684-1147
New Hampshire	603/271-3575
New Jersey	609/882-2000
New Mexico	505/827-7172
New York	518/474-4429
North Carolina	919/662-4387
North Dakota	701/224-3063
Ohio	614/466-4130
Oklahoma	405/425-2775
Oregon	503/731-4359
Pennsylvania	610/268-4162
Puerto Rico	809/781-0227
Rhode Island	401/277-2000
South Carolina	803/737-9000
South Dakota	800/829-9188
Tennessee	615/741-6382
Texas	512/463-5545
Utah	801/965-4461
Vermont	802/828-2837
Virginia	804/786-4700
Washington	360/664-1400

West Virginia	304/558-6000
Wisconsin	608/266-0829
Wyoming	by local gov.

For links to licensing agency websites containing specifics of licensing requirements in most states, visit:

www.crimetime.com/licensing.htm

PRIVATE INVESTIGATOR INSURANCE
See...*INSURANCE FOR INVESTIGATORS*.

PROCESS SERVERS
These websites allow lookups of process servers throughout the U.S.

National Association of
Professional Process Servers   *www.napps.com*

United States Process
Servers Association   *www.usprocessservers.com*

Public Record Retriever
Network   *www.brbpub.com*

Also see...*FOREIGN SERVICE OF PROCESS*.

PRODUCT SAFETY
Consumer Product Safety Commission, National Inquiry Information Clearinghouse maintains a database on product-related injuries.

800/638-2772
301/504-0424
www.cpsc.gov/about/clrnghse

Auto Safety Hotline, Dept. of Transportation, maintains information on auto safety related information, including auto recalls.

800/424-9393
www.nhtsa.dot.gov

Underwriter's Laboratories can provide information on any product marked "UL Approved."

847/272-8800
www.ul.com

PROFNET
See...*EXPERT WITNESSES*.

PROPERTY INSURANCE LOSS REGISTRY
Property Insurance Loss Registry (PILR) no longer exists as a separate database. Rather, this insurance industry database of property claims can now be found within *ISO ClaimSearch*. See...*ISO CLAIMSEARCH*.

PROSTITUTION
See...*NEVADA BROTHELS*.

PUBLIC RECORD RESEARCH
 NEW! Looking for an out-of-town attorney service to make a courthouse run for copies of public records? Finding one can be much easier with *The National Directory of Public Record Vendors*. Searchable by county and state. Fatter than most phone books, this extensive directory sells for $59.95. Like all good reference books, it more than pays for itself in saved time.

800/929-3811
www.brbpub.com

Washington Document Service is a private company that specializes in retrieving public documents from federal agencies in Washington, D.C.

800/728-5201
www.wdsdocs.com

Also see...*SOURCEBOOK TO PUBLIC RECORD INFORMATION, THE*.

Also see...*PROCESS SERVERS*.

QUESTIONED DOCUMENT EXAMINATION
Need a questioned document examiner? These professional associations offer name and contact information for members:

American Association of Questioned
Document Examiners   312/558-1684
www.asqde.org

American Board of Forensic Docu-
ment Examiners   713/784-9537
www.asqde.org/abrefpg

RAILROADS
Jane's World Railways has reference information on over 450 railway systems in 120 countries. Information includes routes, organizational structures, political and financial information, locomotive and rolling car inventory and more. Available in book form, diskette and CD-ROM ($390 - $975).

Jane's Information Group   703/683-3700
www.janes.com

Federal Railroad Administration   202/493-6024
Rail Accidents   202/632-3125
www.fra.dot.gov

Amtrak National Communications Center is a good place to start if you're looking for information on passenger reservation histories, contractors, vendors, employees or incident reports. For most of this you'll need to be law enforcement or have an appropriate subpoena in hand.

General Information	800/331-0008
FOIA Requests	202/906-3000
	www.amtrak.com

Railroad maps are available through *Deskmap Systems*.

512/863-6886
www.deskmap.com

Association of American Railroads	202/639-2100
	www.aar.org

International Association of Railway Police	877/203-1120
	www.iarpolice.org

National Association of Railroad Safety Consultants and Investigators	615/255-6288
	www.narsci.com

RAND CORPORATION

RAND (an acronym for research and development) is an elite think tank where over 500 research professionals, most holding doctorate degrees, study subjects from national defense to criminal justice. The end goal is producing clear information to aid public policy makers. The Internet was conceived by *RAND* researcher Paul Baran in 1962.

RAND Headquarters	310/393-0411
Washington, D.C. Office	703/413-8111
	www.rand.org

REAL ESTATE INFORMATION

Experian offers online access to real estate ownership information in several states, including California, Hawaii, Colorado, Nevada, Michigan, Ohio, Alabama, Georgia, Mississippi, North Carolina, South Carolina, Tennessee, New York, Illinois, Minnesota, Montana, Wisconsin, New Jersey, Oklahoma, Texas, Maryland, Virginia, D.C. Metro, Delaware, Connecticut, Pennsylvania, Oregon, Washington and Utah. Data is available by property address or by owner's name.

Consumer Relations	714/385-7333
	888/397-3742
	www.experian.com

Also available from *Experian* are comparable worth lookups. Learn the last sales price of a property plus the most recent sales price of four neighboring properties. No subscription is necessary. Cost is $9.95 per search.

www.experian.com/ecommerce/

A similar free search offering less data is also available through the real estate section of Internet portal *Yahoo!*

http://list.realestate.yahoo.com/re/homevalues/

Dataquick is also a major compiler and re-seller of real estate ownership information from 46 states and the District of Columbia. Much of the same or similar information is available a la carte through the major database companies (see *DATABASE PROVIDERS*). Still, for those in need of this type of information on a frequent basis, a direct account might be of interest.

888/604-DATA
www.dataquick.com

Land Registry Information does real estate ownership searches throughout England.

011-44-1812-881418
www.landreg.gov.uk

Also see...our *Master List of Commercially Available Public Record Databases*...which details areas in which real estate ownership searches are available.

Also see...*DATABASE PROVIDERS*.

Also see...*DATATREE*.

RESEARCH PAPERS
University Microfilms has over one half million doctoral dissertations on file. There's a computerized index system to search by subject.

800/521-0600
www.umi.com

Academic Research, Inc. has over 20,000 research files on file, available by fax or overnight delivery. Prices are $7.95 per page for papers already in their catalogue and $40 per page for custom reports. They also offer dissertation, consultation and research services.

800/47-RESEARCH
201/939-0189
www.greatpapers.net

Over 18,500 research papers are available on variety of subjects.

310/477-8226
www.researchassistance.com

National Technical Information Service (NTIS) maintains a computerized database of over one million reports on a wide range of technical subjects such as "Concealed Weapons Detection Technologies" and "Automated Security Response Robot."

800/553-NTIS
www.ntis.gov

RETAIL THEFT
See...*UNITED STATES MUTUAL ASSOCIATION.*

REVERSE DIRECTORIES
Reverse lookups are available in both real time and as stored data. The advantage of the real time lookups is that the information is continually updated. There are three noteworthy real time services—*Experian, Haines MetroNet* and *AT&T "00" Info.* (The latter provides reverse checks on phone numbers only, and doesn't include address reverses.) The next best option are CD-ROM editions of the reverse directory. Despite quarterly updates, most of this information is at least a year old due to lag time in reporting new data by regional Bell companies. Taking up the rear are free Internet searches. Know the saying, "You get what you pay for"? Well, believe it when it comes to the free Internet-based reverse lookups — data is old, missing and usually incomplete.

REAL TIME SERVICES:
Experian (formerly Cole Products) offers its National Lookup Service for reverse directory checks. Coverage is nationwide. The source of information is Experian's proprietary data, electronic directory assistance and their own Criss-Cross books. Also available are historical searches going back to 1992. The service is available by subscription, or through a 900 pay-per-call line which costs $3 for the first minute and $2 for each additional minute.

Subscription Information   800/809-8680
Pay-Per-Call   900/288-3020
www.experian.com

Haines MetroNet offers stiff competition to Experian in the reverse lookup arena. Information is available by both computer and by call-in service. Significant cost savings are found with the online service. In addition, more detailed information is readily available including other co-habitants at an address and wealth rating information based on census data. New published phone numbers make it into their database as soon as two weeks after start of service. The online service has a $50 monthly minimum and a cost of 50 cents per search. Their National Lookup Service offers phone access for a $20 monthly minimum and $2 per lookup.

Subscription Information   800/843-8452
www.haines.com

AT&T's "00" Info now includes two reverse checks per call. Available for reversing published phone numbers only — they don't reverse addresses. Cost is $1.99 per call for up to two listings. There are two ways to reach AT&T "00" Info. If AT&T is your long distance company, just dial zero twice. If not, dial 10-10-ATT-00.

10-10-ATT-00

CD-ROMs:
PowerFinder offers most of the published phone numbers in the United States in a CD-ROM or DVD multi-disc set, totaling 115,000,000 listings. Easy to use, the discs also work as a reverse directory. You can enter a phone number, and get back an address; or enter an address and get back a phone number. The regular edition costs around $265. For around $300, you'll get the Commercial version.   Both include quarterly updates for the year.

800/321-0869
www.infousa.com

FREE INTERNET LOOKUPS:
Free Internet-based reverse lookups tend to come and go. For the current best available, visit *Black Book Online.*

www.crimetime.com/online.htm

REVERSE MAIL DROPS

NEW! A mail drop is a commercial mail receiving service, such as *Mailboxes, Etc.*
A reverse mail drop is a service that will mail a letter from their location for you, no questions asked. Here's one in Orlando, Florida:

www.orlandomaildrop.com

REWARDS OFFERED

WeTip is a nonprofit anti-crime group that offers rewards, nationwide, to any informant whose tip leads to the arrest and conviction of a perpetrator of a felony or serious misdemeanor. A reward is then paid in an amount of $50 to $1,000. The reward program is available in all fifty states and there are no restrictions on the type of crime reported. *WeTip* also offers "extraordinary" rewards for select high profile or unusually serious crimes. The organization will also act as a safe keeper for reward money that has been posted by an interested party.

800/78-CRIME

www.wetip.com

The Internal Revenue Service has a reward program for snitching on tax cheats. Depending on the quality of information provided, and the money recovered, reward payments can be up to $100,000. For specific information leading to recovery, the reward will be ten percent of the first $75,00 recovered, and 5% of the next $25,000, tapering down to 1% of any additional recovery, capped at $100,000 in total reward money. Be sure to cite Section 7623 of the IRS Code and ask for form 211 to file your claim. Your information should be directed to the Criminal Investigative Division in the office of any District Director, or the Criminal Investigative Branch of any IRS Service Center. See...*INTERNAL REVENUE SERVICE* for a listing of criminal investigation offices.

Stop an act of espionage against the United States and you're entitled to a reward of up to $500,000 as set forth by federal law (Title 18, U.S.C., Section 3071). The reward money is controlled by the United States Attorney General. To report the suspected espionage, contact your nearest FBI office and speak with its ANSIR (Awareness of National Security Issues and Response) coordinator. See...*FEDERAL BUREAU OF INVESTIGATION* for a list of branch offices.

Stop an act of terrorism against American citizens and/or property and you may be eligible for a reward of up to 5 million dollars through a program funded by the U.S. Department of State in conjunction with the Airline Pilots Association and the Air Transport Association. Call this number to hear a recorded message by Charlton Heston for more details.

800/HEROES-1

The *United States Postal Service* offers a variety of rewards for information leading to the arrest and conviction of any person for committing any one of numerous crimes. The largest reward offered is $100,000 for information leading to an arrest and conviction where an USPS employee has been murdered. Other crimes and their rewards:

Assault on employee:	$15,000
Mailing bombs or explosives:	$50,000
Postage or meter tampering:	$50,000
Robbery:	$25,000
Burglary of a post office:	$10,000
Money laundering:	$10,000
Offenses involving postal money orders:	$10,000
Theft/destruction of mail:	$10,000

Child pornography through mail: $10,000
Poisons/controlled substances through mail: $10,000

Contact the Postal Inspector in charge at the nearest division office. (See...*POSTAL INSPECTORS, U.S.*) Or:

Chief Postal Inspector   202/636-2300
    www.usps.gov

Security Information Center, Crime Reward Money branch offers rewards for information concerning various North American crimes. For more information contact their office or visit their website.

    416/425-0576
    www.yesic.com

ASH (Action in Smoking) offers a $25,000 reward for information leading to the arrest and conviction of current and former tobacco industry executives for felonies such as perjury, obstruction of justice, false swearing and conspiracy.

    202/659-4310
    www.ash.org

The World's Most Wanted offers various rewards for information leading to the arrest of fugitives and unsolved crimes. Visit their website for more information.

    www.mostwanted.org/rewards

The Carole Sund/Carrington Memorial Reward Foundation donates money to help families without economic means to offer rewards.

    888/813-8389
    www.carolesundfoundation.com

The *FBI* offers rewards ranging from $50,000 to $5 million dollars for information leading to the arrest of persons listed on the *Top Ten Most Wanted Fugitives List*. For specific information visit their website.

    202/324-3000
    www.fbi.gov/mostwant/topten

The *FBI* also offers rewards for specific art theft crimes:

    202/324-4192
    www.fbi.gov/hq/cid/arttheft

Fur Crime offers a rewards of $25,000 for providing them with information that helps them criminally convict an American fur rancher or employee of engaging in animal cruelty.

    888/882-6462
    www.furcrime.com

Rewards for Justice is a program run by the Diplomatic Security Service of the U.S. Department of State. They offer specific rewards leading to the arrest or conviction of those responsible for specific crimes against humanity and war crimes. For more information visit their website.

800/437-6371
www.dssrewards.net

ROLEX WATCHES
The Rolex database includes dates of service when a watch has been worked on at one of two authorized Rolex service centers (New York and Dallas). Also included in the database is the serial numbers of watches reported stolen. If a stolen watch is brought into an authorized service center for service, it will be confiscated. Information from the database is available to persons with a legitimate need to know, including law enforcement, insurance investigators, jewelers and others. Telephone requests are not honored. There is no master registry of Rolex ownership. Fax your request on company letterhead to:

Rolex (fax)   212/980-2166
Rolex (telephone)   212/758-7700
www.rolex.com

RUNAWAYS
See...*MISSING CHILDREN*.

SAFE DEPOSIT BOXES
The American Safe Deposit Box Association can assist in locating the safe deposit boxes of deceased persons.

317/738-4432
www.americansafedeposit.com

Screenshot: The SAFER website — a payload of background information on interstate trucking companies and truckers.

SAFER DATABASE

The federal government keeps close watch on interstate truckers and trucking companies through roadside inspections. This information is culled into a central database called *SAFER* (Safety and Fitness Electronic Records). Here's the great news — this information is freely available on the Internet. Lookups can be done by firm name, owner name or MC (Motor Carrier) or DOT (Department of Transportation) number. (These are the numbers stenciled onto the side of truck cabs.) Information returned includes the firm's physical and mailing addresses, insurance carrier, number of prior accidents, inspections and more.

703/288-8386
www.safersys.org

SALVATION ARMY MISSING PERSONS BUREAU

The Salvation Army's Missing Persons Program may be one of the few options for persons who cannot afford the services of a traditional private investigation agency. Private investigators should know about this service as it provides them a place to refer would-be clients who simply can't afford their services. The service is only for persons trying to locate missing family members who have not been heard from for six months or longer. The privacy of the missing person who does not wish to be located will be maintained. Searches will not be done for legal, adoption or genealogical purposes or when the missing person is under 18 years of age. There's a $25 application fee. If the case is accepted, the investigation is done free of charge. (If the party seeking help simply cannot afford the $25 application fee, it is waived.) Nationwide, thousands of cases are taken every year. There are four regional missing persons bureaus:

Eastern Territory:	800/315-7699
	www.salvationarmy-usaeast.org
Southern Territory:	800/939-2769
	www.salvationarmysouth.org
Central Territory:	847/294-2088
	www.usc.salvationarmy.org
Western Territory:	800/698-7728
	www.salvationarmy.usawest.org

SCAMBUSTERS.ORG

Private website dedicated to exposing Internet schemes, scams and viruses. Also includes a free e-mail based newsletter.

828/265-0400
www.scambusters.org

SCOTLAND YARD, NEW
(aka METROPOLITAN POLICE SERVICE)
General Information   011-44-207-230-1212
                          www.met.police.uk

Metropolitan Police Service Computer Crime Unit deals with crimes such as hacking and computer-based fraud.

                          011-44-207-230-1177

SCREEN ACTOR'S GUILD
Screen Actor's Guild, also known as *SAG*, is the primary union of film and television actors. Through the union's representation office, agents or representatives of the actor can often be identified.

                          323/954-1600
                          www.sag.com

SEARCH AND RESCUE DATABASE
The *U.S. Coast Guard* maintains a database of past search and rescue operations.

                          202/267-2229
                www.uscg.mil/hq/g-o/g-opr/sar.htm

SECRET SERVICE, U.S.
Headquarters   202/406-8000
                          www.ustreas.gov/usss

Contact the *USSS Investigative Support Division* for information regarding fugitives wanted by the U.S. Secret Service.

                          877/CIC-DESK
                www.treas.gov/usss/wanted.htm

SECRET SERVICE FIELD OFFICES:

Albany, GA	912/430-8442
Albany, NY	518/436-9600
Albuquerque, NM	505/248-5290
Anchorage, AK	907/271-5148
Atlanta, GA	404/331-6111
Atlantic City, NJ	609/487-1300
Austin, TX	512/916-5103
Baltimore, MD	410/962-2200
Bangkok, Thailand	011-662-255-1959
Baton Rouge, LA	225/389-0763
Birmingham, AL	205/731-1144
Boise, ID	208/334-1403
Bonn, Germany	11-49-228-339-2587
Boston, MA	617/565-5640
Buffalo, NY	716/551-4401
Charleston, SC	843/747-7242
Charleston, WV	304/347-5188
Charlotte, NC	704/442-8370
Chattanooga, TN	423/752-5125

Cheyenne, WY	307/772-2380
Chicago, IL	312/353-5431
Cincinnati, OH	513/684-3585
Cleveland, OH	216/706-4365
Colorado Springs, CO	719/632-3325
Columbia, SC	803/765-5446
Columbus, OH	614/469-7370
Concord, NH	603/626-5631
Dallas, TX	972/868-3200
Dayton, OH	937/225-2900
Denver, CO	303/866-1010
Des Moines, IA	515/284-4565
Detroit, MI	313/226-6400
El Paso, TX	915/533-6950
Fresno, CA	209/487-5204
Grand Rapids, MI	616/454-4671
Great Falls, MT	406/452-8515
Greenville, SC	864/233-1490
Honolulu, HI	808/541-1912
Houston, TX	713/868-2299
Indianapolis, IN	317/226-6444
Jackson, MS	601/965-4436
Jacksonville, FL	904/724-6711
Kansas City, MO	816/460-0600
Knoxville, TN	423/545-4627
Las Vegas, NV	702/388-6571
Lexington, KY	606/233-2453
Little Rock, AR	501/324-6241
London, England	011-44-171-499-9000
Los Angeles, CA	213/894-4830
Louisville, KY	502/582-5171
Lubbock, TX	806/472-7347
Madison, WI	608/264-5191
McAllen, TX	210/630-5811
Melville, NY	631/249-0404
Memphis, TN	901/544-0333
Miami, FL	305/629-1800
Milwaukee, WI	414/297-3587
Minneapolis, MN	612/348-1800
Mobile, AL	334/441-5851
Montgomery, AL	334/223-7601
Nashville, TN	615/736-5841
Newark, NJ	973/656-4500
New Haven, CT	203/865-2449
New Orleans, LA	504/589-4041
New York, NY	212/637-4500
Norfolk, VA	757/441-3200
Oklahoma City, OK	405/810-3000
Omaha, NE	402/965-9670
Orlando, FL	407/648-6333
Paris, France	011-33-1-4312-7100
Philadelphia, PA	215/861-3300
Phoenix, AZ	602/640-5580
Pittsburgh, PA	412/395-6484

Portland, ME	207/780-3493
Portland, OR	503/326-2162
Providence, RI	401/331-6456
Raleigh, NC	919/790-2834
Reno, NV	775/784-5354
Richmond, VA	804/771-2274
Riverside, CA	909/276-6781
Roanoke, VA	540/345-4301
Rochester, NY	716/263-6830
Sacramento, CA	916/930-2130
Saginaw, MI	517/752-8076
Salt Lake City, UT	801/524-5910
San Antonio, TX	210/472-6175
San Diego, CA	619/557-5640
San Francisco, CA	415/744-9026
San Jose, CA	408/535-5288
San Juan, PR	787/277-1515
Santa Ana, CA	714/246-8257
Savannah, GA	912/248-4401
Scranton, PA	717/346-5781
Seattle, WA	206/220-6800
Shreveport, LA	318/676-3500
Sioux Falls, SD	605/330-4565
Spokane, WA	509/353-2532
Springfield, IL	217/492-4033
Springfield, MO	417/864-8340
St. Louis, MO	314/539-2238
Syracuse, NY	315/448-0304
Tampa, FL	813/228-2636
Toledo, OH	419/259-6434
Trenton, NJ	609/989-2008
Tucson, AZ	520/670-4730
Tulsa, OK	918/581-7272
Tyler, TX	903/534-2933
Ventura, CA	805/339-9180
Washington, D.C.	202/406-8000
West Palm Beach, FL	561/659-0784
White Plains, NY	914/682-6300
Wichita, KS	316/269-6694
Wilmington, DE	302/573-6188
Wilmington, NC	910/815-4511

SPECIALIZED UNITS:

Intelligence Division	202/435-5000
Public Information Office	202/406-5708

Direct Freedom of Information Act requests to: *United State Secret Service, Freedom of Information Request, 1800 G Street NW, Washington, D.C. 20223.*

Financial Crimes Division investigates bank fraud, access device fraud involving credit and debit cards, telecommunications and computer crimes, fraudulent identification, fraudulent government and commercial securities, and electronic funds transfer fraud. The division also oversees money laundering investigations.

202/406-5850

Counterfeit Division   202/406-5756

Forensic Services Division   202/435-5926

Chief Counsel   202/406-5843

Special Investigations & Security   202/435-5830

Presidential Protective Division   202/395-4112

Vice Presidential Protective Division   202/634-5890

SECURITIES AND EXCHANGE COMMISSION

The *SEC* regulates the interstate sale of stocks and bonds and also monitors the financial markets against insider trading and other potential abuses.

800/SEC-0330
202/942-8088
www.sec.gov

Investor Information Service Public Reference Desk will do name lookups for licensing status on stock brokers:

202/942-8090

FOIA Office	202/942-4320
Insider Trading, Enforcement	202/942-4542
Public Affairs	202/942-0020
Los Angeles Office	323/965-3998
New York Office	212/748-8000

FYI: *The Securities and Exchange Commission* publishes its own phone directory, with over 7,000 employees listed. The phone book is available through the Government Printing Office. Or try calling this *SEC Personnel Locator* number to locate a *SEC* employee.

Personnel Locator   202/942-4150

Financial statements, insider trading information and executive compensation packages of publicly owned companies are complied by the SEC into a massive database called *EDGAR* (which stands for Electronic Data Gathering, Analysis and Retrieval). The EDGAR database can be searched for free on the Internet at the SEC's website (*www.sec.gov*) but a much better way to search this data is through a private company called *Edgar Online*. They've crunched the SEC's EDGAR information into a more user-friendly website. For more details, see...*EDGAR ONLINE*.

Hard copy of SEC filings made by publicly owned companies are available through *Disclosure*, a private information provider.

800/638-8241
www.disclosure-investor.com

Washington Service Bureau also sells SEC filings. They also publish *SEC Today*.

202/508-0600
800/955-5219
www.wsb.com

Also see...*NATIONAL ASSOCIATION OF SECURITIES DEALERS*.

SECURITIES FRAUD
See...*SECURITIES AND EXCHANGE COMMISSION*.

Also see...*STANFORD SECURITIES CLASS ACTION CLEARINGHOUSE*.

Also see...*INSIDER TRADING*.

Also see...*STOCK BROKERS*.

SECURITIES – LOST & STOLEN
The Securities Information Center, Inc. maintains a computerized database of lost, stolen, counterfeit and forged securities. Used by investment professionals, access to *SIC* is restricted and is not available directly to the general public. *SIC* is overseen by the Securities and Exchange Commission.

617/345-4900
www.secic.com

The Bureau of Public Debt maintains information on who purchased and/or redeemed certain U.S. Savings Bonds and other securities. If U.S. Savings Bonds have been stolen, lost or destroyed, an application for relief can be made to this agency.

304/480-6112
www.publicdebt.treas.gov

Have a decedent but his or her life insurance policy can't be located? Contact *The American Council of Life Insurance*. Its members will search their policyholders for a modest charge.

800/942-4242
www.acli.com

Direct inquiries or claims relating to lost, stolen or

unclaimed postal money orders to the *U.S. Post Office Money Order Branch*.

> 800/868-2443
> *www.usps.com/missingmoneyorders/*

Have you come across some old stock certificates and believe they may have value? *Stock Search International* will research the value of the certificates for a modest fee.

> 800/537-4523
> *www.stocksearchintl.com*

SELECTIVE SERVICE REGISTRATION

All male U.S. citizens and male immigrant aliens must register with the Selective Service System within 30 days of their 18th birthday. These registrations can be verified online or by phone.

> 847/688-6888
> *https://www4.sss.gov/regver/verification1.asp*

SENATE, U.S.
General Information   202/224-3121
Senate Staff Locator   202/224-3207
> *www.senate.gov*

SERVICE OF PROCESS
See...*CT CORPORATION*.

Also see...*PROCESS SERVERS*.

Also see...*FOREIGN SERVICE OF PROCESS*.

SEX OFFENDER REGISTRIES
All fifty states and the District of Columbia now have a sex offender registration and community notification law in place. These laws are often collectively referred to as Megan's Law, named after Megan Kanka, a seven-year-old New Jersey girl who was murdered by a recently released rapist. Although each state has its own Megan's Law, implementation of the law in each state varies greatly. Some states make the information readily available; others keep it closely guarded. Likewise, some states offer name lookups. Others offer community searches — where a list of offenders in a given area is provided. Still others offer both. Most states also categorize their offenders as either offenders or sexual predators. As a rule of thumb, the term "sexual predator" refers to a sex offender who is either a repeat offender, a violent offender, or one who victimizes children. *Investigators should pay careful attention to the registration effective dates when relying on checks of sex offender registries for background checks. Several states only include offenders who were convicted as of a very recent date. For example, in Louisiana, only offenders*

convicted after July 1, 1997, are included. An offender with a long list of offenses prior to this time would come up clean in a check of the state's registry.

ALABAMA

Alabama releases the names of its sex offenders — but only if they were released after June 30, 1998. On the Internet, visit the Alabama Department of Public Safety website where searches can be done by offender name, city or state. In addition, local police and sheriff stations maintain a publicly available file of prior community notification flyers. Neighbors of a released offender are to receive community notification flyers. The registry may also include juveniles, who are also subject to community notification based upon their risk to the community. Offenders must register for 25 years; repeat offenders for life.

Alabama Bureau of Investigation
Attn.: Sex Offender Database
2720 Gunter Park Drive West #A
Montgomery, AL 36109
Telephone: 334/260-1100
www.gsiweb.net

ALASKA

Alaska offers wide access to its sex offender registry through the Internet, by mail and in-person. On the Internet, both name and community searches are available. Each Alaska State Trooper post also maintains a copy of the statewide registry, which is available for public inspection. Name lookups and community searches are also available by mail. Includes persons convicted of certain sex offenses that were incarcerated, on probation, on parole or convicted on or after July 1, 1984. First-time offenders must register for 15 years, second-time offenders for life.

Screenshot: The Alaska sex offender registry on the Internet. The site includes photos, addresses and other information on registrants.

Alaska State Troopers
Permits and Licensing Unit
5700 E. Tudor Road
Anchorage, AK 99507
Telephone: 907/269-0396
www.dps.state.ak.us/nSorcr/htm/searchframe.htm

ARIZONA

Information on some but not all offenders is released to the public through a website as well as community notification flyers. Available is information on high and moderate risk offenders that were released from incarceration or supervision on or after June 1, 1996, or who were sentenced on or after this date. Searches can be done by name or community. Local law enforcement agencies may also make community notifications. For low-risk offenders, only other members of the household are notified. For medium and high-risk offenders, the neighborhood and other at-risk parties are notified through flyers and other means. Phone and mail requests for offender information are not available. All offenders must register for life.

Arizona Dept. of Public Safety
Attn.: Sex Offender Community Notification Unit
P.O. Box 6638
Phoenix, AZ 85005-6638
Telephone: 602/255-0611
www.azsexoffender.org

ARKANSAS

Information available to the public in Arkansas is very limited and consists of arbitrary law enforcement notification. Neither name nor community searches are available. Release of information typically includes flyers with offender information. Stalking is also included as a registerable offense. Offenders must register for fifteen years; sexual predators for twenty.

Arkansas Crime Information Center
One Capital Mall
Little Rock, AR 72201
Telephone: 501/682-2222
www.acic.org/registration

CALIFORNIA

California has the largest registry of sex offenders in the nation and is accessible by phone and in-person. All but 12,419 are public record. Many police and sheriff stations have a public access computer containing a CD-ROM with information on the state's "serious offenders" and "high-risk offenders" — the worst of the worst. (These two categories account for approximately 72,550 of the state's 85,350 registrants.) It's updated four times a year. Offender zip codes, but not street addresses, are included. Photos are posted for approximately 65% of the offenders. Both name and community searches are available. Users must show identification and sign a form before accessing the CD-ROM. Note: California's official sex offender registry is NOT available on the Internet. Beware of unofficial sites with unofficial and incomplete information. *The Sex Offender Identification Line* is a "900" pay-per-call line which also allows the statewide sex offender registry to be checked. (Previously it was limited to child molesters only.) The cost is $10 per call; two names can be checked per call. Information is for "protecting persons at risk" only and is prohibited from being used for insurance, loan, credit, employment, education, housing or business purposes. Law enforcement agencies may also proactively notify the community with flyers and other means when a serious or high-risk offender is present. All offenders must register for life.

California Dept. of Justice
Attn.: Sex Offender Reg. Program
P.O. Box 944255
Sacramento, CA 94244-2550
Telephone: 900/448-3000 ($10 per call)
www.caag.state.ca.us/megan

COLORADO

Public access to Colorado's sex offender registry is very limited. Statewide name searches are not available. However, local law enforcement agencies are authorized to release information on offenders registered in their jurisdiction. Includes offenders convicted of certain sex offenses on or after July 1, 1994. Before hiring new employees, nursing care facilities must have the Colorado Bureau of Investigation check the registry. Depending on the severity of the original offense, registrants are required to be registered for 5, 10 or 20 years.

Colorado Bureau of Investigation
Attn.: Sex Offender Registry
690 Kipling Street., Suite 3000
Lakewood, CO 80215
Telephone: 303/239-4222
cdpsweb.state.co.us

CONNECTICUT

The state's sex offender registry is not open to the public per a May 18, 2001, U.S. District Court ruling. Prior to the court ruling, the sex offender registry was available on the Internet. The registry contains names of persons convicted of certain sex offenses who were released into the community on or after October 1, 1988. Offenders must register for ten years; sexual predators for life.

Department of Public Safety
Sex Offender Registry Unit
P.O. Box 2794
Middletown, CT 06457
Telephone: 860/685-8060
www.state.ct.us/dps/Sor.htm

DELAWARE

Delaware makes its sex offender registry available to the public via the Internet only. Searches can be done by name, city, development or zip. It includes offenders convicted after June 24, 1994. Local police may also go door-to-door with flyers if a high risk offender is present. All offenders must register for life.

State Bureau of Investigation
Sex Offender Central Registry
P.O. Box 430
Dover, DE 19903
Telephone: 302/739-5882
www.state.de.us/dsp/sexoff/index.htm

DISTRICT OF COLUMBIA

The nation's capital finally has a sex offender registration program in effect — but be forewarned it offers little real protection because of its late starting date. Information is available both online and in-person. On the Internet, lookups can be done of Class A sex offenders — the most serious group. Information on the less serious Class B & C offenders can be obtained by viewing a MPDC registry book at select police locations. Offenders who live, work or attend school in D.C. must register if they were convicted of an offense or on parole after August 1997. The MPD cannot guarantee that offenders convicted before that date are registered. Offenders must register for ten years; sexual predators for life.

Metropolitan Police Department
Sex Offender Registry Unit
300 Indiana Avenue, N.W.
Washington, D.C. 20001
Telephone: 202/727-4407
www.mpdc.org/Registry/default.htm

FLORIDA

Florida offers one of the very best versions of Megan's Law in the country. On the Internet, conduct name or community searches at the Florida Department of Law Enforcement's website. To access offender information by phone, call 888/FL Predator (888/357-7332). (If you're outside of Florida, call 850/410-8572.) To receive a free list of offenders in one particular zip code, mail or telephone your request to the FDLE. Includes "Predators" whose offense occurred on or after October 1, 1993; and

"Offenders" who were released from incarceration, probation or parole on or after October 1, 1997. Offenders must register for 20 years, sexual predators, indefinitely unless relieved by a court.

Florida Dept. of Law Enforcement
Sexual Offender/Predator Unit
P.O. Box 1489
Tallahassee, FL 32302-1489
Telephone: 888/FL Predator
(From Outside Florida:) 850/410-8572
www.fdle.state.fl.us/Sexual_Predators/index.asp

GEORGIA

Georgia's sex offender registry is open to the public, online and in-person. On the Internet, the registry is searchable by offender name, city, county or zip code. Information on locally registered offenders is also kept on file at local sheriff's departments for viewing by the public. Phone or mail requests are not available. Includes offenders released from prison, probation or parole after July 1, 1996. Offenders are required to register for 10 years; sexual predators for life.

Georgia Bureau of Investigation
Attn.: GCIC
P.O. Box 370748
Decatur, GA 30037-0748
Telephone: 404/244-2601
www.ganet.org/gbi/sorsch.cgi

HAWAII

Hawaii's sex offender registry is public record and can be searched on the Internet and elsewhere. However, pre-1997 information may be incomplete. Includes both name and community searches. Public-access computer terminals are also available at the Hawaii Criminal Justice Data Center as well as at main county police stations. For a fee of $10, mail-in requests are also accepted. Send the name of the person to be checked to the address below. All offenders must register for life in Hawaii.

Hawaii Criminal Justice Data Center
465 S. King Street, Room 101
Honolulu, HI 96813
Telephone: 808/587-3100
www.ehawaiigov.org/HI_SOR/

IDAHO

Idaho's sex offender registry is open to the public by mail or in-person. Name or community searches can be run at local sheriff's departments, but persons requesting this information must provide their name; address; and driver's license number or SSN. By mail, names will be checked when submitted to the Bureau of Criminal Identification. (See address below.) Be sure to include the offender's name and as many identifiers as possible, including date of birth, Social Security Number and address. If possible, requests should be made on the form entitled *Central Sex Offender Registry Request for Public Information*, which can be obtained at local sheriff's offices or by calling 208/884-7305. Offender photos can be obtained for an additional $5. The registry includes persons who were incarcerated or on probation or parole as of July 1, 1993, or were convicted after this date. Registrants who have been arrest free for 10 years are eligible to apply for relief from registration.

Idaho State Police
Bureau of Criminal Identification
P.O. Box 700
Meridian, ID 83680-0700
Telephone: 208/884-7305
www.isp.state.id.us

ILLINOIS

The Illinois sex offender registry is available to the public via the Internet and in-person at select local police agencies. The data is searchable by city, county, zip or offender name. Neither mail nor phone lookups of offender information are available. The registry includes persons convicted of certain sex offenses who were released from prison, probation or parole within the past 10 years. The list is also distributed to local schools and child care facilities. Offenders must register for 10 years, sexual predators for life.

Illinois State Police
Attn.: Sex Offender Reg. Unit
400 Iles Park Place, Suite 140
Springfield, IL 62718
Telephone: 217/785-0653
http://samnet.isp.state.il.us/ispso2/sex_offenders/

INDIANA

Indiana's sex offender registry is widely open to the public via the Internet, phone and mail. Name searches can be run, but not community searches. Name lookups can be done by calling 317/232-1233. Lookups can also be requested by mail at the address below. The list of sex offenders is also mailed out to local schools, child care facilities, libraries and other organizations. Includes offenders convicted of certain sex offenses who were released from incarceration, probation or parole since 1989. Prior to 1989, the registry includes State Police records going back 75 years. Offenders must register for ten years; sexual predators indefinitely.

Indiana Department of Correction
302 West Washington Street
Room E334
Indianapolis, IN 46204
Telephone: 317/232-1233
www.in.gov/serv/indcorrection_ofs

IOWA

The statewide Iowa sex offender registry is open for inspection on the Internet in limited form and by visiting local sheriff stations for more complete information. On the Internet, only "at-risk" to re-offend offenders who were convicted after July 1, 1995, can be found. The Iowa sex offender registry can also be searched at local police and sheriff stations. This information includes all registrants, regardless of risk status or date of registration. You'll have to complete form DCI-150 (*Request for Registry Information*) and provide the name and one of three identifiers — address, Social Security Number or date of birth — of the person you are investigating. Authorities will indicate a "hit" only if both the offender name and address on file match with the offender name and address you provide. Includes offenders who were convicted, incarcerated, or on probation or parole on or after July 1, 1995. Offenders are required to register for 10 years, sexual predators and second offenders, indefinitely.

Sex Offender Registry
Iowa Div. of Criminal Investigation
Wallace State Office Building
Des Moines, IA 50319
Telephone: 515/281-5138
www.iowasexoffender.com

KANSAS

The Kansas sex offender registry is open to the public via the Internet, by mail or phone, and in-person. On the Internet, information is searchable by name, city, county or zip code. Name lookups can be obtained by calling 785/296-6656. Mail requests for offender information can be obtained by writing to the address below. Every sheriff's station also maintains public information on offenders registered locally in that particular county. Offenders who committed their offenses after April 14, 1994, are included. All offenders must register for 10 years, but can apply to a court for release from registration prior to this.

Kansas Bureau of Investigation
Crime Data Information Center
1620 S.W. Tyler
Topeka, KS 66612-1837
Telephone: 785/296-6656
www.ink.org/public/kbi/kbisexpage.html

KENTUCKY

Kentucky offers one of the weakest Megan's Laws in the nation. Offender information is not available by phone or mail, and is available via Internet only for those offenders released and registered after April 11, 2000. Sheriffs are authorized to release information on high-risk offenders to the news media and "interested persons" in the community. Includes persons convicted of certain sex offenses who were released from incarceration on or after January 15, 1999. Offenders must register for a minimum of 10 years.

Kentucky State Police
Attn.: Records Section
1250 Louisville Rd.
Frankfort, KY 40601
Telephone: 502/227-8700
http://kspsor.state.ky.us

LOUISIANA

Louisiana's sex offender registry is open to the public via phone and mail. Name lookups can be obtained by calling 800/858-0551 between 8 a.m. and 4:30 p.m. Name searches can also be done by mail. (See address below.) Includes offenders convicted since July 1, 1997. Offenders must register annually for ten years; sexual predators must register every 90 days for life.

Louisiana State Police
Bureau of Criminal Identification and Information
P.O. Box 66614
Mail Slip #18
Baton Rouge, LA 70896
Telephone: 800/858-0551
www.lasocpr.lsp.org/socpr

MAINE

The Maine sex offender registry is open to the public, but has serious limitations and only contains 300 names. Name searches are available by calling 207/624-7009. Information is also available by mail — single name lookups or the state's entire registry can be requested. (Include a 9" x 12" SASE for the complete registry.) The City of Bangor maintains a telephone message line with offender names. Call 207/947-7382, then press *104. The recording ends with an invitation to view the city's registered sex offender book in-person. The state's sex offender registry is limited to offenders sentenced on or after June 30, 1992, for Gross Sexual Assault when the victim was under 16 years of age *or* offenders sentenced after September 18, 1999, for any one of a number of sex-related or violent crimes. Offenders sentenced between 6-30-92 and 9-17-99 must register for 15 years. Offenders sentenced after 9-17-99 must register for 10 years; sexual predators every 90 days for life.

Maine State Police
State Bureau of Identification
36 Hospital Street
Augusta, ME 04330
Telephone: 207/624-7009

MARYLAND
The Maryland sex offender registry is open to the public but it only includes persons convicted after October 1, 1995 (for offenses against children) and/or October 1, 1997 (for offenses against adults). Written requests for name checks and community checks should be made to the Department of Public Safety and Correctional Services. (See address below.) The request must contain your name, address, phone number *and* reason for the request. Local law enforcement agencies also maintain the registry on file for public inspection. Contact your local police or sheriff's station for details. In Prince George's County, information is available by calling 301/985-3660. Local law enforcement is also required to notify area schools when an offender is released. Sex offenders must register for 10 years; sexual predators for life, or until relieved of the duty by a court.

Dept. of Public Safety
Crimes Against Children &
Sex Offender Registry
P.O. Box 5743
Pikesville, MD 21282-5743
Telephone: 410/764-5665
www.dpscs.state.md.us

MASSACHUSETTS
Public access to the statewide sex offender registry in Massachusetts is available for offenders classified by the SORB as Level 2 or 3. Information may be obtained from local police departments or directly from the Sex Offender Registry Board. Both name and community searches are available for locally registered offenders. Moderate and high-risk offenders will be identified to members of the public who inquire at a local police station. Law enforcement will proactively notify the community through flyers and other means when a high-risk offender is released. Internet, phone or mail requests for offender information are not available. Includes any offender who was convicted, or released from custody or parole, since October 1, 1981. Offenders must register for 20 years after their release from supervision; sexual predators, for life.

Sex Offender Registry Board
200 Arlington Street
Chelsea, MA 02150
Telephone: 617/660-4600
www.state.ma.us/sorb

MICHIGAN

The Michigan sex offender registry is open to the public, but only community searches are available, not name searches. On the Internet, the state's registry can be searched by zip code only. Local police agencies also maintain information on locally registered offenders for public inspection. Phone and mail requests for name or community searches are not available. Re-distributing information from the sex offender registry to any third party is a misdemeanor and, in addition, allows the person whose name was released to sue for damages. Includes offenders who were convicted, or were on probation, parole or incarcerated, on or after October 1, 1995. First-time offenders must register for 25 years; repeat offenders, for life.

Michigan State Police
Investigative Resources Section
Violent Crimes Unit
2911 Eyde Parkway, Suite 130
East Lansing, MI 48824
Telephone: 517/336-6292
www.mipsor.state.mi.us

MINNESOTA

Minnesota makes very little information available to the public from its sex offender registry. Level 3 offenders, which represent about 14 percent of all registrants, can be identified at the website below. Other community notification may be made when a Level 3 offender is released. When a moderate-risk offender is released, area schools, child care facilities and other groups may be notified. Only other law enforcement agencies will be notified upon the release of low-risk offenders. Includes offenders released after January 1, 1997. All offenders must register for a period of ten years.

Bureau of Criminal Apprehension
Attn.: Predatory Offender Registry Unit
1246 University Avenue
St. Paul, MN 55104
Telephone: 651/603-6748
www.doc.state.mn.us/level3/countysearch.htm

MISSISSIPPI

The sex offender registry in Mississippi is open to the public by mail, Internet and in-person. Internet checks can be made by name, city and county. For information via mail, send $5 per name and a SASE to the address below. The state has 14 days to respond. Local sheriff departments maintain information on locally registered offenders for public viewing. Offenders must register for 10 years, at which time they can apply to the courts for relief from registration.

Mississippi Dept. of Public Safety
Sex Offender Registry
P.O. Box 958
Jackson, MS 39205-0958
Telephone: 601/368-1740
www.sor.mdps.state.ms.us

MISSOURI
The sex offender registry in Missouri is open to the public
in limited form only. Police and sheriff departments
maintain a list of locally registered offenders for public
review. Local newspapers occasionally publish a list of
locally registered offenders, too. No Internet, phone or mail
requests for offender information are presently available.
Includes offenders convicted of a felony sexual assault or
child kidnapping since July 1, 1979. Both sex offenders
and sexual predators must register for life.

Missouri State Highway Patrol
Criminal Records and Identification Division
1510 E. Elm Street
P.O. Box 568
Jefferson City, MO 65101
Telephone: 573/526-6153

MONTANA
The Montana sex offender registry is open to the public by
phone, Internet, mail or in-person. To check a name by
phone, call 406/444-9479 or 406/444-3875. To check a
name by mail, send your request to the address below. To
conduct a community search, visit your local law
enforcement agency where information on offenders
registered in that particular jurisdiction can be viewed.
Local law enforcement agencies may also notify the news
media when a high-risk offender is released into the
community. The state's entire 2,000-plus name registry can
also be purchased. Photocopying and handling fees apply.
The registry includes offenders convicted, incarcerated or
on probation or parole for certain sex offenses on or after
July 1, 1989, or for certain violent offenses after October 1,
1995. Offenders are required to register for life, but certain
offenders can petition the courts for relief after 10 years if
they do not have a second conviction.

Montana Department of Justice
Div. of Criminal Investigation
P.O. Box 201417
Helena, MT 59620-1417
Telephone: 406/444-9479
or 406/444-3875
www.svor.doj.state.mt.us

NEBRASKA

Information on high risk offenders is available on the Internet but information on low and moderate risk offenders is not public record with limited exceptions. The registry includes offenders who were convicted after January 1, 1997, or were incarcerated, or on probation or parole as of this date. Offenders must register for ten years; sexual predators for ten years and then they are eligible to apply for relief from registration.

Nebraska State Patrol
Attn.: Sex Offender Registry
P.O. Box 94907
Lincoln, NE 68509
Telephone: 402/471-4545
www.nsp.state.ne.us/sor/find.cfm

NEVADA

Nevada offers open access to its sex offender registry by phone or mail. Name searches are available; community searches are not. Names can be checked by calling the Nevada Highway Patrol at 775/687-1600. There's an $8 charge per name checked. (They'll bill you.) Results should come back the same day. Name searches can also be done by mail — direct your request to the address below and include $8 per name and a SASE or a telephone number. (They'll call you with the results.) When sexual predators or other high-risk offenders are released, law enforcement may notify the community. For moderate-risk offenders, only schools and other child care organizations are notified. Only law enforcement is notified about the release of low-risk offenders. The registry includes offenders convicted of any one of 20 sex-related crimes since July 1, 1956. Registration is required for life, although removal from registry can be applied for after 15 years.

Nevada Highway Patrol
Records & Identification Services
808 W. Nye Lane
Carson City, NV 89703
Telephone: 775/687-1600
http://ag.state.nv.us/sex_offenders/home.htm

NEW HAMPSHIRE

Limited sex offender information is available to the public in New Hampshire. The state offers a confusing, patchwork Megan's Law that offers very little real protection to the public. Only the names of offenders whose victims were under age 13, 17 or 18 (depending on the crime) are public record — this is roughly 17% of the state's total registered sex offender population. The rest are known to law enforcement only. Local police stations maintain files on locally registered offenders. The file is public record, but a form must be filled out and identification shown prior to viewing. Community and name searches are of limited value as they only include offenders whose victims were under 13, 17 or 18 years of age, depending on the crime committed. TV station WMUR has independently obtained the state's list of publicly identified offenders and posted them on the Internet at the URL below. The registry includes offenders convicted of certain sex offenses who, depending on the crime, were incarcerated, on parole, on probation or convicted on or after January 1, 1988, or January 1, 1996. Offenders must register for ten years; sexual predators, for life.

New Hampshire State Patrol
Attn.: Special Investigations Unit
10 Hazen Drive
Concord, NH 03305
Telephone: 603/271-2663
www.wmur.com/sex-offenders/home.htm

NEW JERSEY
Sex offender information is available in New Jersey through community notifications by local law enforcement and on the Internet. On the Internet, searches can be conducted by name or area. Information returned includes offender name, photo, address, modus operandi and more. The New Jersey State Police website includes Tier 2 & 3 offenders. However, some first-time Tier 2 offenders may petition for removal from the online registry in the case of incest (to protect family member/victims), juveniles, and statutory rape. A case-by-case determination is made on these possible exceptions. Through flyer distribution, local law enforcement can notify the community when high and moderate-risk offenders are released. Schools and other youth organizations may be notified when a moderate-risk offender is released. When low-risk offenders are released, only the victim and law enforcement agencies are notified. There is no phone or mail access to offender information. The registry includes any person convicted since October 31, 1994, of certain sex offenses or any person diagnosed since 1976 as being a "repetitive and compulsive" offender. Offenders must register annually for 15 years, at which point they can then apply for relief from registration.

NJ Division of Criminal Justice
25 Market St.
P.O. Box 085
Trenton, NJ 08625
Telephone: 609/984-2814
www.state.nj.us/lps/dcj/megan1.pdf
Online Searches: *www.njsp.org*

NEW MEXICO
New Mexico makes a limited amount of information available to the public. Name searches can be conducted

via the Internet or by calling the New Mexico Department of Public Safety at 505/827-9181. Name or community searches can also be obtained by sending a written request to the DPS address below. The registry includes any offender who was convicted of certain sex offenses after July 1, 1995. All offenders must register for life.

New Mexico Dept. of Public Safety
Attn.: Sex Offender Registry
P.O. Box 1628
Santa Fe, NM 87504-1628
Telephone: 505/827-9181
www.nmsexoffender.dps.state.nm.us

NEW YORK

New York's sex offender registry is open to the public by phone (pay-per-call) and in-person. Name lookups are available but meaningful community searches are not. Name searches of the state's nearly 9,500 registered sex offenders can be made at 900/288-3838. There's a charge of $.50 for up to five names checked and the caller must provide the offender's name and at least one personal identifier. A statewide subdirectory of sexual predators is also distributed semi-annually via the Internet and to local police agencies for public viewing. The registry includes any offender who was convicted, on probation or on parole on or after January 21, 1996. Pre-1996 registration information may be unreliable. Low and moderate risk offenders must register for 10 years; sexual predators for life.

New York State Division of Criminal Justice Services
Attn.: Sex Offender Registry Unit
4 Tower Place
Stuyvesant Plaza
Albany, NY 12203
Telephone: 518/457-6326
Name Lookups Pay-Per-Call: 900/288-3838
www.criminaljustice.state.ny.us/nsor/index.htm

NORTH CAROLINA

North Carolina makes information from its sex offender registry available over the Internet and in-person. On the Internet, the statewide registry can be searched by name, city, county or zip code. The sheriff in each county also maintains a registry of locally registered offenders that can be viewed by the public. By submitting a written request, a member of the public can also obtain a copy of the entire county's registry. A copy of the state's entire sex offender registry can be requested by contacting the agency below. No phone or mail-in lookups are available. The registry includes persons convicted on or after January 1, 1996, of certain sex offenses and/or child kidnapping/abduction or felonious restraint when the perpetrator is not the child's parent. Offenders must register for 10 years; sexual predators must register indefinitely, but can apply for relief from registration after ten years.

North Carolina State Bureau of Investigations
Division of Criminal Information
407 N. Blount Street
Raleigh, NC 27601
Telephone: 919/733-3171
sbi.jus.state.nc.us/sor

NORTH DAKOTA

North Dakota has two different sex offender registries. The smaller, official one (which complies with the federal Megan's Law) allows for public notification of the community only when a high-risk offender is released. The second one, called the *Non-Registrant List*, is larger and is wholly available upon request. The official Megan's Law list, which complies with federal guidelines, can be accessed for name or community searches. On the Internet, only high-risk and lifetime registrants can be searched. By phone, all registrants can be searched. The Non-Registrant List can be requested in whole or single name checks can be obtained by sending a written request to the ND Bureau of Criminal Investigation. Both the Megan's Law list and the Non-Registrant List include offenders convicted or incarcerated on or after August 1, 1985. "Sexual Predators" and those convicted of a second offense must register for life. All other offenders must register for 10 years.

North Dakota Bureau of Criminal Investigation
P.O. Box 1054-A
Bismarck, ND 58502
Telephone: 701/328-5500
www.ndsexoffender.com

OHIO

Ohio offers limited information to the public from its sex offender registry. There is no public access to the statewide registry. Visit your nearest sheriff's office to conduct a countywide check. Several counties (Hamilton, Butler, Clermont, Fayette, Highland, Licking, Montgomery, Stark, Green, Franklin, Clark and Summit) and one city (Cincinnati) have also posted their locally registered offenders on the Internet. Find these links at *Black Book Online* (*www.crimetime.com/online.htm*) and click on the "Sex Offender" button. Law enforcement agencies should notify next-door neighbors when high or medium-risk offenders are present. The surrounding neighborhood and community may *not* be notified. Local school boards, child care centers, institutions of higher learning and others are also notified. Who must register? Any offender who was incarcerated as of January 1, 1997, or who was convicted

248

on or after January 1, 1997, or who was required to register under the prior sex offender registration law. Sexual Predators must register for life; "Habitual Sex Offenders" for twenty years; all others, for ten years.

Ohio Attorney General
Attn.: S.O.R.N.
Box 1580
State Route 56
London, OH 43140
Telephone: 614/466-8204 ext. 224

OKLAHOMA

The Oklahoma sex offender registry is open to the public via the Internet, in-person inquiry and by mail. Phone lookups are not offered. On the Internet, a website has been hosted by TV station KWTV. Both name and community searches are available. The entire statewide registry can be viewed and copied at the Oklahoma Department of Corrections in Oklahoma City. Name searches can be done by mail here, too. Police and sheriff departments maintain information on locally registered offenders which is available for public viewing. Copies are available to schools and other child care organizations. Local law enforcement has great leeway in making community notifications. Some police departments, such as the Tulsa PD, release the information to newspapers for publication. Offenders who were convicted on or after November 1, 1989, must register as sex offenders. An offender who receives a second conviction after November 1, 1997, is to be designated as a sexual predator. Sexual predators must register for life; sex offenders for ten years.

Oklahoma Dept. of Corrections
Attn.: Sex Offender Registry
3400 Martin Luther King Avenue
Oklahoma City, OK 73136
Telephone: 405/425-2872
csextra.doc.state.ok.us
Registry Search: *www.kwtv.com/crime/sex_offenders/*
sex-offenders-map.htm

OREGON

Oregon's sex offender registry is open to the public by phone or mail. Single names can be checked by calling 503/378-3720. Ask for Sex Offender Registration. Community searches can also be requested by phone, but the results will be mailed back. Send your request to the Oregon State Police address below. The Oregon State Police or other law enforcement agencies may proactively notify the community with flyers and press releases when a high-risk offender is present. The registry includes offenders who were incarcerated or convicted on or after October 3, 1989, for certain sex offenses. All offenders must register for life, although after 10 years they can apply for relief from registration.

Oregon State Police
Attn.: Sex Offender Reg. Unit
Public Service Building, Room 400
Salem, OR 97310
Telephone: 503/378-3720
www.osp.state.or.us/orec/index

PENNSYLVANIA

Pennsylvania offers a very, very limited Megan's Law. It's an on-again, off-again effort that has had more than one courtroom.set back. It now appears to be on again, effective July 8, 2000. The statewide sex offender registry is available to law enforcement only. A very small subsection of the main database, sexually violent predators, is made available to the public via notification flyers. This includes distribution of flyers to neighbors as well as local schools and child service agencies. There is no community notification for regular sex offenders. There is no Internet, phone or mail-in request available. Residents can visit local law enforcement agencies to see flyers on prior community notifications. Offenders who were convicted or released after May 21, 1996, are required to register. Offenders must register for 10 years; sexually violent predators and repeat offenders must register every 90 days for life, unless relieved of the duty by a court.

Pennsylvania State Police
Attn.: Megan's Law Unit
1800 Elmerton Avenue
Harrisburg, PA 17110
Telephone: 717/783-4363
www.meganslaw.state.pa.us

RHODE ISLAND

Sharply limited Megan's Law information is available to the public in Rhode Island. Phone, mail, or Internet lookups are not available. Only law enforcement can access the state's entire sex offender registry. Local law enforcement may notify at-risk persons in the community upon the release of moderate and high-risk offenders. Includes persons convicted of certain sex crimes who were convicted or incarcerated on or after July 1, 1992. Also includes persons who committed additional Megan's Law offenses, such as child kidnapping by a non-parent, when the crime was committed on or after July 24, 1996. Offenders must register for 10 years; sexual predators for life.

Rhode Island Attorney General
150 S. Main Street
Providence, RI 02903
Telephone: 401/274-4400 ext. 2288

SOUTH CAROLINA

South Carolina's sex offender registry is open to the public via the Internet and at local sheriff stations. Mail and phone inquiries are not available. On the Internet, the state's sex offender registry can be searched by offender name, city, county or zip code. Information returned includes offender photograph, name and address. Local sheriff stations also maintain information on locally registered offenders, including photographs. Community notifications are not made in South Carolina. Includes any offender convicted or released from prison after January 1, 1995, for certain sex offenses. Includes juvenile offenders as young as 12 years of age. All offenders must register for life.

S.C. Law Enforcement Division
Attn.: Sex Offender Registry
P.O. Box 21398
Columbia, SC 29221
Telephone: 803/896-7051
www.scattorneygeneral.org

SOUTH DAKOTA

The South Dakota sex offender registry is open to the public in limited form. A statewide check of the database is *not* available. However, local law enforcement agencies maintain information on offenders registered in their own county and this information is available for public inspection. Includes persons who were convicted of felony sex crimes prior to July 1, 1994. Offenders must register for life, but can apply for relief from registration.

South Dakota Division of Criminal Investigations
Attn.: Sex Offender Registry
East Highway 34
c/o 500 E. Capitol Avenue
Pierre, SD 57501-5070
Telephone: 605/773-3331
www.state.sd.us/attorney/divisions/dci/administration/id/
sexoffender/index.htm

TENNESSEE

Tennessee offers public access to its statewide sex offender registry through both the Internet and by phone. Visit the website below or call 888/837-4170 to conduct a search by offender name, county or zip code. The registry is limited to offenders whose crimes were committed on or after July 1, 1997. However, if an offender committed his crime prior to this date *and* is deemed a significant threat to the community, information *may* be released. Offenders must register for life, but can apply for relief from registration after ten years.

Robert Scott, P.I.

Tennessee Bureau of Investigation
Attn.: Criminal Intelligence Div.
1148 Foster Avenue
Nashville, TN 37210
Telephone: 615/741-0430
Name Searches: 888/837-4170
www.tbi.state.tn.us/SEX_ofndr/search_short.asp

TEXAS

The Texas sex offender registry is public record and is available over the Internet, by mail and by walk-in service. On the Internet, the registry can be searched by a person's name, city or zip code. Names can also be checked by mail at the address below. Include a $10.00 fee. Be sure to include all available personal identifiers. Local law enforcement agencies shall notify the community by media releases when an offender with a prior child victim is released. They also maintain information on registered offenders for public viewing. Telephone lookups are not available. Includes adult and juvenile offenders convicted of certain sex offenses who were incarcerated or under supervision on or after September 1, 1997, for crimes committed after September 1, 1970. Offenders must register for 10 years, sexual predators for life.

Crime Records Service
Texas Dept. of Public Safety
5805 N. Lamar Boulevard, Building G
(mail requests to:) P.O. Box 4143
Austin, TX 78765
Telephone: 512/424-2479
http://records.txdps.state.tx.us

UTAH

The Utah sex offender registry is available over the Internet or by mail. On the Internet, a search can be run by zip code, city or offender name. For those without Internet access, a written request can be made to the address below. Residents can request a list of offenders in one zip code plus one neighboring zip code. All written requests must include the requester's name, address and phone number. Includes offenders convicted of certain sexual offenses after April 29, 1996. All offenders must register for 10 years.

Utah Department of Corrections
Sex Offenders Registry Program
6100 155 East, Room 100
Murray, UT 84107
Telephone: 801/265-5500
www.cr.ex.state.ut.us

VERMONT

Vermont has a very restrictive Megan's Law, offering little information to the public. Checks of the statewide registry are not possible. However, the public may visit local police stations to conduct a name search of locally registered offenders *only. WARNING: If the offender being checked is not registered or is registered in another jurisdiction, he will come up clean.* Further, state law provides that local law enforcement agencies *may* release the information, not *shall.* Law enforcement does not conduct community notifications in Vermont. Includes offenders convicted of certain sex offenses who were under the supervision of the Department of Corrections as of July 1, 1996, or were convicted after this date. Offenders must register for 10 years; sexual predators for 10 years, when they can then petition for relief from registration.

Vt. Criminal Information Center
103 S. Main Street
Waterbury, VT 05671
Telephone: 802/244-8727
www.dps.state.vt.us/cjs/s_registry

VIRGINIA

Virginia's sex offender registry is open to the public via the Internet and by mail. Phone lookups are not available. The state's registered sex offender population is divided into two groups: Sexually Violent Offenders and Sex Offenders. The former is searchable on the Internet only, the latter by mail only. On the Internet, visit the Virginia State Police website where information is available on the more dangerous sexually violent offenders. *The website does NOT include regular sex offenders.* Searchable by name, zip code, county or city. Also at the VSP website, schools, other child care organizations and foster homes can register to receive electronic notification about locally registered sex offenders and sexually violent offenders. By mail *only,* name searches can be conducted of the regular sex offenders. Cost is $15 per search. Form 266 must be used. Obtain it at any law enforcement agency or on the Internet at *www.vsp.state.va.us* by clicking the State Police Forms button. Includes offenders convicted, incarcerated or on probation or parole on or after July 1, 1994, for certain sex offenses. Sex offenders must register for 10 years, sexually violent offenders for life.

Virginia State Police
Attn.: Sex Offender Registry
P.O. Box 27472
Richmond, VA 23261
Telephone: 804/674-2147
http://sex-offender.vsp.state.va.us/cool-ICE

WASHINGTON

Washington's sex offender registry is open to the public — for those who know how to access information through the state's public disclosure law. The state's entire sex offender registry can be obtained in totality in only one way: by contacting the Public Records Office of the Washington State Patrol. Some counties offer Internet searches by name, city and zip code of level 2 and 3 offenders. Upon written request, the entire registry, almost 17,000 names, will be sent to you on diskette. It's updated monthly. First-time users must sign a declaration that the information will be used for non-commercial purposes. Send your request to *Washington State Patrol, Attn.: Public Records Office, P.O. Box 42600, Olympia, WA 98504*; 360/753-5966. Local law enforcement may notify the community when moderate and high-risk offenders are released. Includes offenders convicted of certain sex offenses who were in custody, or on probation or parole, on or after July 28, 1991. Depending on the seriousness of their crime, offenders must register for ten or fifteen years. The most serious offenders must register for life, or until relieved of the duty by a court.

Washington State Patrol
Attn.: Criminal History &
Identification
P.O. Box 42633
Olympia, WA 98504
Telephone: 360/705-5100

WEST VIRGINIA
West Virginia makes public some of its statewide sex offender registry. The identity of the worst offenders are made public, but those of less serious offenders are not. The West Virginia State Police will also release information on locally registered offenders to the county superintendent of schools and to community or religious organizations. The state's registry is gradually being posted online, one county at a time. *Only lifetime registrants are included in Internet postings; less serious offenders will not be identified here.* Both name and community searches can be done online. Offender information is not available by phone or mail. Includes offenders convicted of certain sex offenses going back decades. Offenders must register for ten years, sexual predators for life.

West Virginia State Police
Attn.: Sex Offender Registry
725 Jefferson Road
South Charleston, WV 25309
Telephone: 304/746-2133
www.wvstatepolice.com/sexoff/

WISCONSIN
The Wisconsin sex offender registry is open to the public, with dissemination through a toll-free telephone hotline and by mail. Wisconsin offers a state-of-the-art telephone information line for name checks. If the name you are checking is found, you'll need one of these identifiers to

confirm the information: date of birth, Social Security Number, or driver's license number. Names can also be checked by mail. Form *Registry Public Inquiry* should be used. It's available from local law enforcement agencies and from the Wisconsin DOC. Call them at 608/266-3831 to have a blank form faxed or mailed. Community searches are also available. Names of offenders registered in a specific geographic area will be released to bona fide neighborhood watch groups, who are then free to openly disseminate the information. Start by obtaining a *Neighborhood Watch Request for Information Form* from your local law enforcement agency. Includes offenders convicted of certain sex offenses who were incarcerated or on probation or parole, on or after December 25, 1993. Offenders must register for 15 years; those labeled sexually violent persons and repeat offenders must register for life.

Department of Corrections
Attn.: S.O.R.P.
3099 E. Washington Avenue
P.O. Box 7925
Madison, WI 53707
Telephone: 608/266-3831
Name Searches: 800/398-2403
www.public-sor.doc.state.wi.us/static

WYOMING
The Wyoming sex offender registry is open to the public in limited form via community notifications and a website limited to high-risk offenders. Unfortunately, information on low and moderate-risk offenders is not widely disseminated. Telephone, mail or other requests for offender information are not available. Law enforcement agencies are authorized to notify neighbors who live within 750 feet of moderate and high-risk offenders. Includes offenders convicted of certain sex offenses committed after January 1, 1985. Offenders must register for 10 years; sexual predators for life.

Division of Criminal Investigation
Attn.: WSOR
316 W. 22nd Street
Cheyenne, WY 82002-0001
Telephone: 307/777-7181
www.state.wy.us/~ag/so/so_registration.html

SHARK ATTACKS

When sharks attack humans, one of the first places the media turns to for information is *The International Shark Attack File*. It's a database of more than 3,200 documented shark attacks from around the world. Direct access to the case files by both the public and the media is prohibited as they contain sensitive information such as autopsy reports and medical records of victims. However, statistical analysis of the data is available on the Internet including a breakdown of attacks by area, species and conditions. *The International Shark Attack File* is jointly administered by the American Elasmobranch Society and the Florida Museum of Natural History.

352/392-1721
www.flmnh.ufl.edu/fish/Sharks/ISAF/ISAF.htm

SHIP INFORMATION

Ownership of vessels registered with the U.S.C.G. can be identified through the *Coast Guard's National Vessel Documentation Center*. Products available include Abstracts of Title ($25) and Certificates of Ownership ($125).

800/799-8362
304/271-2400
www.uscg.mil

Also see *Black Book Online* and click the "Vessels" button for online USCG lookups of vessel ownership records.

www.crimetime.com/online.htm

Lloyd's of London remains one of the most authoritative sources of information on ocean-going vessels. Data includes voyage records, casualty data, registered owners and more.

800/423-8672
203/359-8383
www.lmis.com

The *U.S. Coast Guard* maintains a database of past search and rescue operations.

202/267-2229
www.uscg.mil/hq/g-o/g-opr/sar.htm

The Centers for Disease Control inspects cruise ships for health code violations and posts their ranking on the Internet.

888/232-6789
www2.cdc.gov/nceh/vsp/vspmain.asp

Thousands of tugboat workers are out on the rivers and waterways of America at any one time. Sometimes, they're gone for weeks at a time. *Water-Com* is a phone company that will place a call for you directly to anyone of the tugboats. You only need to know the name of the tugboat.

800/258-9329

Todd & Associates is a Southern California based marine surveying and investigative firm that specializes in boat theft cases, relying on not only good old fashioned gum shoe investigation, but also high tech information gathering. They operate a website where stolen boats are posted with rewards offered for information leading to the safe recovery of the vessel.

800/325-8061
www.boatman.com

The International Association of Marine Investigators is a network of sleuths who specialize in investigations of marine theft and marine-related insurance fraud. Over 2,000 members.

978/392-9292
www.iamimarine.org

The American Bureau of Shipping is one of the world's leading ship classification societies. Its primary purpose is to inspect the structural fitness of ships and offshore platforms. An extended list of suspended vessels can be found at their website.

281/877-5800
www.eagle.org

Also see...*MARITIME INFORMATION SYSTEM*.

SHOMER-TEC
                    Shomer-Tec's catalog of law enforcement and military equipment stands out for its bold selection of merchandise. Sure, you'll find the usual stuff like flashlights and holsters here. But dig deeper and you'll find some very unique, and potentially wicked, products, too. The catalog's phone section includes devices called "The Hold Invader" and "The Informer." Other products include a universal garage door opener and a peephole reverser. Certain items are restricted for sale to law enforcement only.

360/733-6214
www.shomer-tec.com

Also see...*SPY GEAR*.

SHOPLIFTING
See...*UNITED STATES MUTUAL ASSOCIATION*.

NEW! SHREDDING SERVICES

Shred-it
(Nationwide and Canada)   800/69-SHRED
                                           (800/697-4733)
                                           www.shredit.com

Instashred Security Services
(Nationwide)   800/96SHRED
                                           (800/967-4733)
                                           www.instashred.com

Accurate Document Destruction
(Northern Illinois, Quad Cities,
Milwaukee and NW Indiana)   800/40-SHRED
                                           (800/407-4733)
                                           www.shredd.net

All-Shred
(Colorado and parts of Wyoming)   303/791-5171
                                           800/747-3365
                                           www.all-shred.com

All-Shred Inc.
(Maryland and Tri-State area)   877-2SHREDD
                                           (877/274-7333)
                                           www.allshredmd.com

American Security Shredding
(New York City and Long Island)   516/766-2997
                                           800/882-1979
                                     www.americanshredding.com

Confidential Shredding Services
(Indiana)   219/486-1713
                                     www.confidentialshred.com

Docu-Shred
(Oregon and Southwest Washington)   503/638-2800
                                     www.docu-shred.com

Mobile Document Shredding
(Texas)   972/221-5744
                                     www.docshredding.com

Mobile Shred
(New Jersey)   877/638-5300
                                     www.mobile-shred.com

SHRED-RITE
(Arizona)   480/969-2323
                                     www.shredrite.com

Shred-X
(Illinois)   800/474-7337
                          www.shred-x.com

SIC CODES
See...*STANDARD INDUSTRIAL CLASSIFICATION.*

SOCIAL SECURITY NUMBERS
Social Security Administration   800/772-1213
                          www.ssa.gov

 The only true way to verify a Social
Security Number is through the *Social
Security Administration*. However, the *SSA*
will only verify if a Social Security Number is legitimate to
an employer seeking to verify the validity of an employee's
Social Security Number. The employer must be prepared to
provide his or her company's Employer Identification
Number and then the full name, Social Security Number
and date of birth of the person in question. The SSA
employee will then respond "match" or "no match." No
other information will be provided. This is the *SSN
Verification Line* that is for up to five requests by
employers:

                          800/772-6270

All investigators know about Social Security Numbers
("SSNs"), and most know about Employer Identification
Numbers ("EINs"), which is the taxpayer identification
system for businesses. Did you know that there is a THIRD
numbering system? *Individual Taxpayer Identification
Numbers* (ITINs) are a taxpayer identification numbering
system for resident and non-resident aliens who have a U.S.
federal income tax responsibility, but who are ineligible to
obtain valid SSNs. *ITINs* are configured like SSNs, but
always begin with the digit "9": 9XX-XX-XXXX. Be
aware: If you come across a SSN in the future that begins
with "9" — don't automatically assume that it's a
fraudulent number. It may be an *ITIN*.

To report fraudulent usage of a Social Security Number,
call the *Social Security Administration's Fraud Hotline*:

                          800/269-0271

In the *Reference Guide* of this book, and published widely
elsewhere, is a Social Security Number identification chart.
It decodes the first three digits of a Social Security Number
to identify the original state where it was issued.

For the latest information on the highest number issued
sub-sets of Social Security Numbers, visit this SSA
website:

                www.ssa.gov/foia/highgroup.htm

There are a lot of urban legends when the *Social Security Administration* will issue a new SSN. In fact, the SSA has a clearly announced policy on this which can be found in SSA publication number 05-10002. In short, they'll dole out a fresh set of nine-digits if the person is a victim of identity theft; if the person is the victim of domestic violence and is attempting to establish a new identity, or if the person has a superstitious or religious objection to the assigned number. (For example, Christians who receive an SSN containing "666.") Find the publication online here:

www.ssa.gov/pubvs/englist.html

Or call and request a copy by mail: 800/772-1213

Now, here's a notable *Social Security Number*: 078-05-1120. This number appeared on a dummy social security card that was distributed in thousands of wallets as a filler in the 1950's and 1960's. Inevitably, the number has been used (illegally) by many people. We recently ran a credit header search on the number and found two dozen people still using it!

For the record, the government has set aside the following dummy Social Security Numbers for use in advertisements: 987-65-4320 through 4329.

Once a person has died and appears in the *Social Security Death Index* (also known as the Death Master File), some personal information, previously protected by the Freedom of Information Act, becomes publicly available. Included in this is Social Security Administration's Form SS-5. This is the name of the original application for a Social Security Number. See DEATH INVESTIGATIONS for full details.

The SSA's master death index is public record and searchable for free on the Internet. Click the "Death Records" button at *Black Book Online*.

www.crimetime.com/online.htm

Also see...*EIN IDENTIFIER*.

SOFTWARE COPYRIGHT VIOLATIONS
Microsoft Anti-Piracy Hotline   800/RU-LEGIT
www.microsoft.com/piracy/

Business Software Alliance operates this snitch line for pirated software. No rewards offered.

888/NO PIRACY
www.bsa.org

Software Publishers Association seeks to prevent the

violation of copyrights on software.

202/452-1600
www.spa.org

SOURCEBOOK TO PUBLIC RECORD INFORMATION, THE

 This heavy-duty reference book is vital stuff for any investigator who needs to research public records. Includes contact information and access procedures for thousands of government agencies in all fifty states. Sections include civil and criminal courts, corporations, UCC filings, vital records and lots more. A bargain at $74.95. Don't go out on the paper trail without it.

800/929-3811
www.brbpub.com

Also check out *publicrecordsources.com*, a subscription-based online service with the same information, also from BRB Publications.

SOUTHERN POVERTY LAW CENTER
See...*HATE GROUP INVESTIGATIONS*.

SPECIAL INVESTIGATION UNITS
International Association of
Special Investigation Units   410/931-8100
www.iasiu.com

SPORTS ORGANIZATIONS
Each of these major professional sports associations has a in-house investigation unit.

National Basketball Association   212/407-8000
National Football League   212/450-2000
National Hockey League   212/789-2000
Major League Baseball   212/931-7800

Also see...*BOXING*.

Also see...*HORSES AND HORSERACING*.

SPY GEAR
Interested in spy gear? Get information on virtually every product out there in Lee Lapin's book, *Extreme Covert Catalog*. See...*EXTREME COVERT CATALOG*.

A fast-growing company for hidden cameras, P.I. books and other spy stuff is *Spy Tech Agency*. Be sure to visit their showroom when in L.A. Otherwise, go to their online superstore.

310/657-6333
www.spytechagency.com

Also see...*SHOMER-TEC*.

Also see...*HIDDEN CAMERAS*.

SPYWARE

"*Spyware*" is a general term meant to describe software that, when installed on a computer, lets you eavesdrop on how the computer is being used in the future. To the best of our knowledge, simple possession of this software is not a crime; however, use of it may be — especially when used to secretly record chat room, e-mail and other communications. Nevertheless, there are a number of free hacker and commercial spyware programs on the market. Two of the most widely used such programs are from software firm, *Spectorsoft*:

Spector is a program that, once installed on a personal computer, lets the user see a series of screen shots of past activity on the computer. This includes websites visited, chat room conversations, keystrokes typed and e-mails viewed. A companion software, called *eBlaster* does likewise, but has the added feature of e-mailing the results secretly to an outside computer for review. Both programs require physical access to the computer being spied upon for installation. Legal uses of these programs may include parents monitoring web habits of their children and employers doing likewise with employees.

888/598-2788
561/234-2340
www.spectorsoft.com

STALKING & THREAT ASSESSMENT
A leading firm for threat management and risk assessment is the *Omega Group*, operated by John Lane who helped develop the LAPD's anti-stalker squad, Threat Management Unit. He's also the founder of the Association of Threat Assessment Professionals.

310/551-0007

Gavin de Becker is widely considered to be a leading expert in the subject of stalking, and in particular, in the stalking of celebrities, politicians, and other high profile persons. His company, *Gavin de Becker, Inc.* has assessed and managed over 19,000 cases, including the case of Tina Marie Ledbetter who is alleged to have sent over 6,000 death threats to actor Michael J. Fox. His firm maintains a library containing over 350,000 pieces of threatening and/or obsessive letters.

818/505-0177
www.gdbinc.com
www.gavindebecker.com

Dr. Park Dietz is a well known forensic psychiatrist who directed a five-year study for the U.S. Department of Justice on mentally disordered persons who threaten and stalk public figures. His firm, *Threat Assessment Group,* is active in the assessment and management of stalkings for businesses, lawyers and celebrities.

949/644-3537
www.taginc.com

Los Angeles is home to the stars — and stalkers. The *LAPD Threat Management Unit* investigates threats against both the well known and just average citizens.

213/473-7488

Also see...*ASSOCIATION OF THREAT ASSESSMENT PROFESSIONALS.*

STANDARD & POOR'S ONLINE REGISTRY
Standard & Poor's Online Registry is a database of information on publicly and privately owned companies, their owners and key executives.

800/237-8552
www.standardandpoor.com

STANDARD INDUSTRIAL CLASSIFICATION
SIC codes can be looked up online at this OSHA website.

www.osha.gov/oshstats/sicser.html

STANFORD SECURITIES CLASS ACTION CLEARINGHOUSE
The Stanford Securities Class Action Clearinghouse provides detailed information on all federal class action securities fraud lawsuits filed since passage of the Private Litigation Reform Act of 1995. Data includes not only index data, but also complaints, briefs and other filings. Provided by the *Stanford Law School* and available online for free.

http://securities.stanford.edu

STATE BAR ASSOCIATIONS
All fifty states have a state bar association which licenses attorneys and provides discipline, when necessary. Other background information typically available is basic biographical data, such as school attended.

Alabama	334/269-1515
Alaska	907/272-7469
Arizona	602/252-4804
Arkansas	501/375-4606
California	415/538-2100

Colorado	303/660-1115
Connecticut	860/721-0025
Delaware	302/658-5279
D.C.	202/737-4700
Florida	850/562-5600
Georgia	800/422-0893
Hawaii	808/537-1868
Idaho	208/334-4500
Illinois	217/525-1760
Indiana	800/266-2581
Iowa	515/243-3179
Kansas	785/234-5696
Kentucky	502/564-3795
Louisiana	800/421-LSBA
Maine	207/622-7523
Maryland	410/837-7878
Massachusetts	617/338-0500
Michigan	517/346-6300
Minnesota	612/333-1183
Mississippi	601/948-4471
Missouri	573/635-4128
Montana	406/442-7660
Nebraska	800/927-0117
Nevada	702/382-2200
New Hampshire	603/224-6942
New Jersey	732/214-8500
New Mexico	505/271-9706
New York	518/463-3200
North Carolina	800/662-7407
North Dakota	701/255-1404
Ohio*	800/282-6556
Oklahoma	405/416-7000
Oregon	503/620-0222
Pennsylvania	717/238-6715
Rhode Island	401/421-5740
South Carolina	803/799-6653
South Dakota	605/224-7554
Tennessee	615/741-3096
Texas	512/463-1463
Utah	801/531-9077
Vermont	802/223-2020
Virginia	804/775-0500
Washington	800/945-WSBA
West Virginia	304/558-2456
Wisconsin	608/257-3838
Wyoming	307/632-9061

* State bar membership in Ohio is voluntary. However, all attorneys must register through the Supreme Court's *Attorney Registration Unit*.

614/466-1553

Also see...*ATTORNEYS*.

STATE DEPARTMENT, U.S.

General Information   202/647-4000
                                   www.state.gov

Counter Terrorism Programs
Office   202/647-8941
International Narcotics Matters   202/647-8464

For passport information, including information on obtaining an emergency passport, contact the *National Passport Information Center*. (Pay-per-use service, billed to your phone at 35 cents per minute.)

Billed to your phone: 900/225-5674
Billed to your credit card: 888/362-8668

Contact *Overseas Citizen Services* for any situation involving the death, robbery, arrest or disappearance of an American abroad.

                                   202/647-5225

Contact the *Office of Children's Issues* for matters involving international parental child abduction and international adoptions. There's also recorded information on custody and adoptions.

                                   202/736-7000

The State Department also operates the *Children's Passport Issuance Alert Program* which will alert a parent if a passport is applied for for his or her child, or if a currently valid passport exists. A Passport Alert form can be downloaded off the Internet.

                                   202/736-7000
                   http://travel.state.gov/paf_print.html

Contact *Visa Services* for inquiries about visa cases and the application process.

                                   202/663-1225

For validation of passports for travel to Libya and Iraq; and inquiries regarding issuance or denial of passports to minors in certain circumstances such as adoptions or abductions.

                                   202/955-0232

For information on obtaining death certificates of Americans who have died abroad or on the high seas, see... *DEATH INVESTIGATIONS*.

STATE HOTLINES

Trying to locate a particular state agency or office through regular directory assistance can often be frustrating. Every state now has a general information operator:

Alabama	334/242-8000
Alaska	907/465-2111
Arizona	602/542-4900
Arkansas	501/682-3000
California	916/322-9900
Colorado	303/866-5000
Connecticut	860/566-4200
Delaware	302/739-4000
D.C.	202/727-1000
Florida	850/488-1234
Georgia	404/656-2000
Hawaii	808/586-2211
Idaho	208/334-2411
Illinois	217/782-2000
Indiana	317/232-3140
Iowa	515/281-5011
Kansas	785/296-0111
Kentucky	502/564-2500
Louisiana	225/342-6600
Maine	287/624-9494
Maryland	410/974-3591
Massachusetts	617/727-7030
Michigan	517/373-1837
Minnesota	651/296-6013
Mississippi	601/359-1000
Missouri	573/751-2000
Montana	406/444-2511
Nebraska	402/471-2311
Nevada	775/687-5000
New Hampshire	603/271-1110
New Jersey	609/292-2121
New Mexico	505/827-9632
New York	518/474-2121
North Carolina	919/733-1110
North Dakota	701/328-2000
Ohio	614/466-2000
Oklahoma	405/521-2011
Oregon	503/986-1388
Pennsylvania	717/787-2121
Rhode Island	401/222-2000
South Carolina	803/896-0000
South Dakota	605/773-3011
Tennessee	615/741-3011
Texas	512/463-4630
Utah	801/538-3000
Vermont	802/828-1110
Virginia	804/786-0000
Washington	360/753-5000
West Virginia	304/558-3456
Wisconsin	608/266-2211
Wyoming	307/777-7011

STATE POLICE AGENCIES AND HIGHWAY PATROLS

Alabama Dept. of Public Safety	334/242-4371
Alaska State Troopers	907/248-1410
Arizona Dept. of Public Safety	602/223-2000
Arkansas State Police	501/618-8000
California Highway Patrol	916/657-7261
Colorado State Police	303/239-4500
Connecticut State Police	860/685-8000
Delaware State Police	302/739-5901
Florida Highway Patrol	904/758-0515
Georgia Dept. of Public Safety	404/657-9300
Idaho State Police	208/884-7200
Illinois State Police	217/782-6637
Indiana State Police Department	317/232-8248
Iowa State Patrol	515/281-5824
Kansas Highway Patrol	785/296-6800
Kentucky State Police	502/695-6300
Louisiana State Police	225/925-6006
Maine State Police	207/624-7000
Maryland State Police	410/486-3101
Massachusetts State Police	508/820-2300
Michigan State Police	517/332-2521
Minnesota State Patrol	651/297-3935
Mississippi Highway Safety Patrol	601/987-1212
Missouri State Highway Patrol	573/751-3313
Montana Highway Patrol	406/444-3780
Nebraska State Patrol	402/471-4545
Nevada Highway Patrol	775/687-5300
New Hampshire State Police	603/271-3636
New Jersey Division of State Police	609/882-2000
New Mexico State Police	505/827-9000
New York State Police	518/457-6811
North Carolina State Highway Patrol	919/733-7952
North Dakota State Highway Patrol	701/328-2455
Ohio State Highway Patrol	614/799-9241
Oklahoma Dept. of Public Safety	405/425-2424
Oregon State Police	503/378-3720
Pennsylvania State Police	717/783-5599
Rhode Island State Police	401/444-1000
South Carolina State Highway Patrol	803/896-0300
South Dakota Highway Patrol	605/773-3105
Tennessee Department of Safety	615/741-3181
Texas Department of Public Safety	512/424-2000
Utah Highway Patrol	801/965-4518
Vermont Department of Public Safety	802/244-8727
Virginia Department of State Police	804/674-2000
Washington State Patrol	360/753-6540
West Virginia State Police	304/746-2100
Wisconsin State Patrol	608/266-3212
Wyoming Highway Patrol	307/777-4301

STOCK BROKERS
See...*NATIONAL ASSOCIATION OF SECURITIES DEALERS*.

Also see...*INSIDER TRADING*.

Also see...*SECURITIES —LOST & STOLEN*.

Also see...*COMMODITY FUTURES*.

Also see...*STANFORD SECURITIES CLASS ACTION CLEARINGHOUSE*.

STOCK DETECTIVE
NEW! Everybody loves a good stock tip — until the stock heads south. Website *Stock Detective* keeps track of questionable stocks that are promoted by boiler-room outfits. Learn about stock schemes such as pump and dump and more.

www.financialweb.com/stockdetective/

STOLEN VEHICLE INVESTIGATIONS
The National Insurance Crime Bureau (NICB) is an insurance industry funded investigative agency formed to combat insurance fraud. They are very active in combating vehicle theft.

708/430-2430
www.nicb.org

International Association of Auto
Theft Investigators   941/697-2480
www.iaati.org

Also see...*TRUCKS AND TRUCKING*.

Also see...*VEHICLE IDENTIFICATION NUMBERS*.

STREET GANGS
See...*GANG INVESTIGATIONS*.

■☞ NEW! STUDENT LOANS

DEPARTMENT OF EDUCATION:
Debt Collection Service   800/621-3115
Loan Consolidation Center   800/557-7392
www.1800iwillpay.com

Student Loan Marketing Association   888/272-5543

STUDENT RECORDS
See...our *Privacy Law Survival Guide* for information on the release of student records.

SUPREME COURT, U.S.

General Information	202/479-3000
Public Information Office	202/479-3211
Library	202/479-3177

www.supremecourtus.gov

If you know either the Supreme Court case number, or the name of one of the parties to the case, the case status can be learned through this automated touchtone information line:

202/479-3034

TAPE RECORDINGS
See...*AUDIO/VIDEO ENHANCEMENT.*

TAX-EXEMPT ORGANIZATIONS
See...*CHARITABLE ORGANIZATIONS.*

TELEPHONE BOOKS
See...*PHONE BOOKS.*

TELEPHONE SECURITY
One phone scam to be on the look out for is 9-0-#. If someone calls under the guise of being a phone company technician and asks you to press 9-0-# and hang up, the party will be able to make a long distance phone call — on your dime.

Another scam to look out for are any callback requests to area code 809 — this is a Caribbean exchange that may charge rates of $20 per minute or more. The scam frequently involves paging an 809 area code as a call back number, and other variations. Also look out for collect calls from unknown destinations — it could be from a Caribbean boiler room in this area code.

Also see...*CELL PHONE COMPANIES.*

Also see...*COMMUNICATIONS FRAUD CONTROL ASSOCIATION.*

Also see...*DEBUGGING.*

Also see...*AUTOMATIC NUMBER IDENTIFICATION.*

Also see...*INTERACTIVE INFORMATION SYSTEMS.*

Also see...*SPY GEAR.*

TELE-TRACK
Tele-Track could be called the "Fourth Credit Bureau." It's a great source for locating hard to find low income and transient persons. *Tele-Track* collects information from what are referred to as "Sub-Prime" businesses such as

rent-to-own furniture stores, check cashing facilities, used car dealers, secured credit card issuers, cable TV companies and others.

800/729-6981
770/449-8809
www.teletrack.com

TELEVISION – INVESTIGATIVE

America's Most Wanted   800/CRIME-TV
www.amw.com

CNN   404/827-1500
www.cnn.com

Dateline, NBC TV,
30 Rockefeller Plaza, #408,
New York, NY 10112   212/664-7501
www.dateline.msnbc.com

Inside Edition   800/457-5546
www.insideedition.com

Twenty-Twenty prefers that story ideas be mailed to: *Story Editor, 20/20, ABC News, 147 Columbus Ave, New York, NY 10023*. To send an e-mail, direct your correspondence to *2020@ABC.com*

212/456-2020
www.abcnews.go.com

Sixty Minutes prefers that story ideas be mailed to: *Don Hewitt, Executive Producer, 60 Minutes, CBS-TV, 524 West 57th Street, New York, NY 10019*

212/975-3249
www.cbsnews.com

TELEVISION NEWS ARCHIVES

The Television News Archives at *Vanderbilt University* is the world's most extensive collection/archive of TV news history. Contains over 30,000 broadcasts. Abstracts are searchable over the Internet. Actual video is available upon request.

tvnews.vanderbilt.edu

TENANT SCREENING COMPANIES

Trans Registry Limited is a tenant screening organization that links the records of 4,100 member subscribers to track problem tenants. Database is available online or by call in service to apartment building owners.

301/881-3400
www.residentscreening.com

Unlawful Detainer Registry maintains a database of persons who have been evicted from rental housing in California, Nevada and Arizona. Available to landlords.

213/873-5014
818/785-4025
www.udregistry.com

National Tenant Network offers coverage in several states. Service is available to landlords.

503/635-1118
www.e-screening.net

TERRORISTS AND TERRORISM

To report a terrorist threat, contact your local FBI office and ask for the Weapons of Mass Destruction Coordinator or ANSIR coordinator. See...FEDERAL BUREAU OF INVESTIGATION for a list of field offices.

The National Laboratory Response Network for Bioterrorism is a task force of the FBI, Centers for Disease Control and other agencies. Report an event or threat to the FBI first, and then the CDC. The website below also contains substantial reference information on bio-threats.

CDC   770/488-7100
www.bt.cdc.gov

For information specific to the Anthrax threat, visit this Department of Defense website:

www.anthrax.osd.mil

The National Domestic Preparedness Office is a clearinghouse for weapons of mass destruction information and assistance. Charter agencies include the FBI, FEMA, DOD, EPA and other agencies.

202/324-9026
www.ndpo.gov

Anyone who encounters a stranger or suspicious person who is attempting to purchase ammonium nitrate for criminal purposes is requested to discreetly obtain the person's physical description and vehicle license plate number and immediately call the *Bureau of Alcohol, Tobacco and Firearms*:

800/800-3855

ATF Bomb Hotline   888/ATF-BOMB

Foreign terrorists and their organizations are forbidden from doing business with any U.S. business including banks and insurance companies. See...*OFFICE OF FOREIGN ASSETS CONTROL*.

ANSIR (Awareness of National Security Issues and Response) is the FBI's public voice for issues of national security including terrorism and espionage. Each FBI field office has an assigned ANSIR coordinator. ANSIR provides non-classified threat information to private sector security directors and others via e-mail and fax. To request inclusion, send an e-mail containing your name and firm contact information to *ansir@leo.gov*.

www.fbi.gov/hq/nsd/ansir/ansir.htm

Pinkerton Risk Assessment Services monitors political, terrorist and other threats in foreign lands and publishes a daily bulletin.

703/525-6111
pgis.pinkerton.com

NCIC 2000 (National Crime Information Center) includes a file of terrorists. Restricted to law enforcement only. See... *CRIMINAL RECORDS*.

Intelligence Resource Program is a private web-based collection of profiles of foreign terrorist groups from the Federation of American Scientists.

202/546-3300
www.fas.org/irp/world/para/index.html

Stop an act of terrorism against American citizens and/or property and you may be eligible for a reward of up to 5 million dollars through a program funded by the U.S. Department of State in conjunction with the Airline Pilots Association and the Air Transport Association. Call this number to hear a recorded message by Charlton Heston for more details.

800/HEROES-1

THOMAS PUBLICATIONS
Thomas Publications' catalog is the mother of all investigative catalogs — and then some. Virtually every (and we do mean *every*) book that has been published for investigators in the last several years will be found inside.

512/420-9292
www.thomaspub.com

THOMPSON FINANCIAL PUBLISHING
Major publisher of reference information for the banking and finance industries. Their products may be of interest to serious financial investigators. Publications include the *ABA Financial Institutions Directory*, the *ABA Key to Routing Numbers*, and *ACH Participant Directory*.

800/321-3373
847/933-8073
www.tfp.com

TIME

The *Naval Observatory Master Clock* offers the most accurate time available, broken down to 370 trillionths of a second.

202/762-1401
www.tycho.usno.navy.mil

TIRE TRACK EXPERTS

FBI Lab, Tire Impression Section   202/324-4492
www.fbi.gov

International Association for Identification Footwear, Tire Track Subcommittee Latent Print Unit

410/653-4518

TOLL-FREE CARRIER IDENTIFIER

 All toll-free numbers in the United States (800, 877, 866, etc.) are managed by the *800 Service Management System*. When calls are made to a toll-free number, the 800 SMS figures out what phone carrier (or Responsible Organization, in their terminology) should pay for the call. The phone carrier then, in turn, will bill its customer to whom the toll-free line is registered. The 800 SMS therefore maintains a database of all toll-free numbers and knows what phone company operates each. They don't maintain information on the actual customer to whom the line is registered by the phone company. If asked properly, the 800 SMS customer help section will tell you what phone company handles any particular phone line. What is the value of this to investigators? For one thing, when a subpoena is in hand for phone records, this will help determine where it should be served.

888/SMS-3300
www.sms800.com

 But wait — have a case of laryngitis and can't speak? Don't call 800 SMS direct and speak with their customer service department. Rather, call this automated "Responsible Organization" line from *Ameritech*. You'll punch in the 800 number and hear back the name of the carrier!

800/337-4194

TOXIC CHEMICALS

The Registry of Toxic Effects of Chemical Substances (RTECS) is a mega-master list of all known toxic substances. Produced by the National Institute for Occupational Health and Safety, the database currently contains 133,000 chemicals, and the concentrations at which toxicity is known. The database is available through several commercial information vendors, including:

Chemical Information Systems   410/243-0797
www.nisc.com
Silver Platter Information   800/343-0064
www.silverplatter.com

Or look it up for free: *ccinfoweb.ccohs.ca/rtecs/search*

The *National Institute for Occupational Safety and Health* publishes *The Pocket Guide to Chemical Hazards.*

800/356-4674
www.cdc.gov/niosh

The *Environmental Protection Agency Library* maintains reference material on toxic substances.

202/260-5922
www.epa.gov

Chemtrec is the chemical industry's emergency hotline for chemical spills.

800/424-9300
www.chemtrec.org

Chemical Accident Reconstruction Services is an Arizona based firm specializing in analysis of chemical spills.

800/645-3369
www.chemaxx.com

The *National Hazardous Material Information Exchange* includes the participation of FEMA and DOT (Department of Transportation).

630/252-8023
www.dis.anl.gov/disweb/hmixtt

National Pesticides Telecommunications Network   800/858-PEST
nptn.orst.edu

To report an oil or chemical spill, call the Coast Guard's *National Response Center.*

800/424-8802
202/267-2675
www.nrc.uscg.mil

Also see...*NFPA Hazardous Material Symbols* in our *Reference Guide.*

Also see...*ENVIROFACTS.*

Also see...*ENVIRONMENTAL INVESTIGATIONS.*

Also see...*ENVIRONMENTAL PROTECTION AGENCY.*

TRADEMARK INFORMATION

Trademarks issued by the U.S. Patent and Trademark Office can now be researched on the Internet at the USPTO website. The days of paying outside services to do basic trademark searches appear to have come to a close.

U.S. Patent and Trademark Office   800/786-9199
                                        www.uspto.gov

U.S. Patent and Trademark Office Status Library provides information on pending registrations.

                                        703/305-8747
                                        www.uspto.gov

International Trademark Association will answer questions regarding usage of trademarks.

                                        212/768-9886
                                        www.inta.org

Government Liaison Services, Inc. offers hand searches of paper records at the Trademark Research Library.

                                        800/642-6564
                                        703/524-8200
                                        www.trademarkinfo.com

Canadian trademarks are searchable online at the website of the *Canadian Intellectual Property Office*.

                        http://strategis.ic.gc.ca/cgi-bin/
                        sc_consu/trade-marks/search_e.pl

TRANSCRIPTION SERVICE (BY PHONE)

NEW! Need to get a report out and you're away from your office? One option is to use this dictation by phone service. You'll call their 800 number, dictate your report, then download it by computer a day or two later. Cost is roughly $4 per page.

Gerger-Moretti Sten-Tel   800/536-0804

TRANSLATORS

NEW! *The National Association of Judiciary Interpreters and Translators* has over 800 members with significant court room experience. Looking for an interpreter who is certified to practice in the federal courts? Did you know only three languages require federal court certification? Haitian Creole, Navajo and Spanish. Useful website.

                                        212/692-9581
                                        www.najit.org

Also see...*AT&T LANGUAGE LINE.*

TRANSPORTATION
See...*NATIONAL TRANSPORTATION LIBRARY*.

Also see...*RAILROADS*.

Also see...*SHIP INFORMATION*.

Also see...*AUTO SAFETY HOTLINE*.

Also see...*TRUCKS AND TRUCKING*.

TRANSUNION
See...*CREDIT BUREAUS*.

TRAP LINES
See...*INTERACTIVE INFORMATION SYSTEMS*.

TRAUMA CLEANUP SERVICES
See...*CRIME SCENE CLEANUP SERVICES*.

TRAVEL ADVISORIES
U.S. Department of State Travel
Advisory Hotline   202/647-5225
        http://travel.state.gov/travel_warnings.html

Centers for Disease Control,
Traveler's Health Hotline   877/394-8747
                                   (877/FYI-TRIP)
                                   www.cdc.gov/travel/

Pinkerton Risk Assessment Services monitors political, terrorist, and travel threats in foreign lands. Publishes daily bulletin.

                                   703/525-6111
                                   www.pinkertons.com

TRAVELER'S CHECKS – LOST OR STOLEN
Although this *American Express* number is for merchant verification, they will tell if a traveler's check is reported lost or stolen.

                                   800/221-7282

Visa International will also verify their traveler's checks.

                                   800/227-6811

TRUCKS AND TRUCKING
Contact information on over 13,000 licensed truck/freight brokers can be obtained on the Internet for free at *The Dispatch*.

                                   www.thedispatch.net

Mercedes-Benz Corporation is a major financier of big rig trucks and in particular, Freightliners. By calling this automated line at their national truck office, a VIN can be run for account status.

800/222-4221

Also see...*SAFER*.

Also see...*DAC SERVICES*.

Also see...*VEHICLE IDENTIFICATION NUMBERS*.

TRW CREDIT BUREAU
See...*EXPERIAN*.

TSCM
See...*DEBUGGING*.

UNCLAIMED FUNDS
Unclaimed funds can have many faces including unclaimed bank accounts, stocks, bonds and insurance pay outs. Various laws seek to protect the rights of the owners of these funds, which are kept in the unclaimed property offices in each state. The identity of the rightful owners is public information. Typically, the state unclaimed property offices will make available for free, or sell, a list of the names. Some enterprising investigators have found it worthwhile to locate and reunite these persons with their money, in exchange for a commission-based fee.

The National Association of Unclaimed Property Administrators is the national organization of the state unclaimed property offices and is a central repository for legal and other questions relating to unclaimed funds.

859/244-8150
www.unclaimed.org

Missingmoney.com is a website sponsored by the NAUPA which allows users to search the unclaimed money funds of 27 states at once. The states are Arizona, Colorado, Delaware, District of Columbia, Florida, Iowa, Kansas, Kentucky, Maine, Maryland, Massachusetts, Michigan, Minnesota, Missouri, Montana, Nebraska, New Hampshire, New Mexico, North Carolina, Oklahoma, South Carolina, South Dakota, Utah, Vermont, Virginia, West Virginia and Wisconsin. Free.

www.missingmoney.com

STATE OFFICES:
Here are the phone numbers for each state's unclaimed property office. For websites, visit *unclaimed.org*.

Alabama	334/242-9614
Alaska	907/465-4653

Arizona	602/542-4643
Arkansas	501/682-9174
	800/252-4648
California	916/445-8318
Toll free, within California	800/992-4647
Colorado	303/894-2443
Connecticut	860/702-3050
Delaware	302/577-3349
District of Columbia	202/442-8181
Florida	850/488-7777
Georgia	404/656-4244
Hawaii	808/586-1589
Idaho	208/334-7623
Illinois	217/785-6995
Indiana	317/232-6348
Iowa	515/281-5367
Kansas	785/296-4165
Kentucky	502/564-4722
Louisiana	504/925-7407
Maine	207/287-6668
Maryland	410/767-1700
Massachusetts	617/367-0400
Michigan	517/335-4327
Minnesota	800/925-5668
Mississippi	601/359-3600
Missouri	573/751-0840
Montana	406/444-2425
Nebraska	402/471-2455
Nevada	702/486-4140
New Hampshire	603/271-2649
New Jersey	609/984-8234
New Mexico	505/827-0767
New York	518/474-4038
North Carolina	919/508-5979
North Dakota	701/328-2805
Ohio	614/644-4433
Oklahoma	405/521-4275
Oregon	503/378-3805
Pennsylvania:	
Claims Inquiries	800/222-2046
Reporting Questions & Instructions	800/379-3999
Rhode Island	401/222-6505
South Carolina	803/737-4771
South Dakota	605/773-3378
Tennessee	615/741-6499
Texas	512/463-3610
Utah	801/320-5360
Vermont	802/828-2407
Virginia	800/468-1088
Washington	360/586-2736
West Virginia	304/340-5020
Wisconsin	608/267-7977
Wyoming	307/777-5590

OTHER SOURCES:

To search for unclaimed money at a failed or closed bank that was FDIC insured, visit this website:

www2.fdic.gov/funds/index.asp

The Swiss Bankers Association is actively attempting to identify owners or heirs to dormant Swiss bank accounts, opened before the end of World War II.

011-41-1-298-5454
www.dormantaccounts.ch

Unclaimed bank accounts at the Bank of Canada can be searched online.

*ucbswww.bank-banque-canada.ca/
scripts/search_english.asp*

Pension Benefit Guaranty Corporation is an agency of the federal government that seeks to reunite missing persons with their pensions. Typically, either the pensioner has moved and left no forwarding address, or the pension fund or company itself became financially troubled and was taken over by government caretakers.

800/326-LOST
www.pbgc.gov

The Bureau of Public Debt maintains information on who purchased and/or redeemed certain U.S. Savings Bonds and other securities. If U.S. Savings Bonds have been stolen, lost or destroyed, an application for relief can be made to this agency.

304/480-6112
www.publicdebt.treas.gov

Have you come across some old stock certificates and believe they may have value? *Stock Search International* will research the value of the certificates for a modest fee.

800/537-4523
www.stocksearchintl.com

To make a claim or inquiry about a lost or uncashed postal money order, contact the *U.S. Post Office Money Order Branch*.

800/868-2443
www.usps.gov

Victims of the Holocaust and their survivors may be entitled to insurance claims if a life, education or dowry policy was in effect during the relevant period (1920-1945). Using information from insurance company lists and from various public record sources, *The International*

Commission on Holocaust Era Insurance Claims seeks to unite beneficiaries with insurance settlements. Visit their website to check a name to see if benefits are owed.

www.icheic.org

A database of persons owed refunds by the IRS can be found at the MSNBC website. These are for people who moved and didn't update the IRS with their new address. Includes names and cities but no dollar amounts.

www.msnbc.com/news/592125.asp

Also see...*LIFE INSURANCE LOCATOR.*

UNDERWRITER'S LABORATORIES
Underwriter's Laboratories can provide information on any product marked "UL Approved."

847/272-8800
www.ul.com

UNIONS
See...*LABOR UNIONS.*

Also see...*Unions* in our *Privacy Law Survival Guide.*

UNITED NATIONS, THE
Public Inquiries   212/963-4475
U.S. Mission   212/415-4000
www.un.org

UNITED STATES MUTUAL ASSOCIATION
◼◗ NEW! *USMA* is a screening company that conducts pre-employment investigations for more than 900 retail companies around the country. The firm maintains a unique database called the *USMA Theft Database*. It contains information on both shoplifters and employees previously implicated in theft. No criminal conviction is necessary to end up in the database. If the accused signs an admission, retribution or other document, he or she will be entered into the database. Started in 1994, the database now contains over 700,000 cases of reported theft. Member companies include The Gap, Blockbuster, Sears and many others. Unfortunately, the database is not commercially available to non-retail companies, such as private investigators.

888/338-USMA
www.usmutual.com

◼◗ NEW! **U.S. ATTORNEY OFFICES**

Alabama Middle District   334/223-7280
Alabama Northern District   205/244-2001

Alabama Southern District	334/441-5845
Alaska	907/271-5071
Arizona	602/514-7500
Arkansas Eastern District	501/324-5342
Arkansas Western District	501/783-5125
California Central District	213/894-2434
California Eastern District	916/554-2700
California Northern District	415/436-7200
California Southern District	619/557-5610
Colorado	303/454-0100
District of Columbia	202/514-7566
Connecticut	203/821-3700
Delaware	302/573-6277
Florida Middle District	813/274-6000
Florida Northern District	850/942-8430
Florida Southern District	305/961-9000
Georgia Middle District	912/752-3511
Georgia Northern District	404/581-6000
Georgia Southern District	912/652-4422
Guam	671/472-7332
Hawaii	808/541-2850
Idaho	208/334-1211
Illinois Central District	217/492-4450
Illinois Northern District	312/353-5300
Illinois Southern District	618/628-3700
Indiana Northern District	219/322-8576
Indiana Southern District	317/226-6333
Iowa Northern District	319/363-6333
Iowa Southern District	515/284-6257
Kansas	316/269-6481
Kentucky Eastern District	606/233-2661
Kentucky Western District	502/582-5911
Louisiana Eastern District	504/680-3000
Louisiana Middle District	225/389-0443
Louisiana Western District	318/676-3600
Maine	207/780-3257
Maryland	410/209-4800
Massachusetts	617/748-3100
Michigan Eastern District	313/226-9100
Michigan Western District	616/456-2404
Minnesota	612/664-5600
Mississippi Northern District	662/234-3351
Mississippi Southern District	601/965-4480
Missouri Eastern District	314/539-2200
Missouri Western District	816/426-3122
Montana	406/657-6101
Nebraska	402/221-4774
Nevada	702/388-6336
New Hampshire	603/225-1552
New Jersey	973/645-2700
New Mexico	505/346-7274
New York Eastern District	718/254-7000
New York Southern District	212/637-2200
New York Western District	716/551-4811

North Carolina Eastern District	919/856-4530
North Carolina Middle District	336/333-5351
North Carolina Western District	704/344-6222
North Dakota	701/297-7400
Ohio Northern District	216/622-3600
Ohio Southern District	614/469-5715
Oklahoma Eastern District	918/684-5100
Oklahoma Northern District	918/581-7463
Oklahoma Western District	405/553-8700
Oregon	503/727-1000
Pennsylvania Eastern District	215/861-8200
Pennsylvania Middle District	570/348-2800
Pennsylvania Western District	412/644-3500
Puerto Rico	787/766-5656
Rhode Island	401/528-5477
South Carolina	803/929-3000
South Dakota	605/330-4400
Tennessee Eastern District	865/545-4167
Tennessee Middle District	615/736-5151
Tennessee Western District	901/544-4231
Texas Eastern District	409/839-2538
Texas Northern District	214/659-8600
Texas Southern District	713/567-9000
Texas Western District	210/384-7100
Utah	801/524-5682
Vermont	802/951-6725
Virgin Islands	340/774-5757
Virginia Eastern District	703/299-3700
Virginia Western District	540/857-2250
Washington Eastern District	509/353-2767
Washington Western District	206/553-7970
West Virginia Northern District	304/234-0100
West Virginia Southern District	304/345-2200
Wisconsin Eastern District	414/297-1700
Wisconsin Western District	608/264-5158
Wyoming	307/772-2124

U.S. COURT DIRECTORY

The United States Court Directory is published by the Government Printing Office and contains address and other pertinent information on the individual courts of the federal court system. It's 612 pages and sells for $51.

866/512-1800
202/512-1800
http://bookstore.gpo.gov

Ever wonder who keeps all the various federal courts organized? It's the *Administrative Office of the United States Courts.*

202/502-1504
www.uscourts.gov

U.S. COURT OF INTERNATIONAL TRADE

NEW! One of the most obscure and specialized courts around is the *U.S. Court of International Trade*. It's a federal court established solely to resolve international trade disputes and there's just one courthouse, which is located in New York City. There are nine judges, and each is a lifetime presidential appointment. Name checks are not currently possible, but will be in the future.

212/264-2800
www.uscit.gov

U.S. CUSTOMS SERVICE
See...*CUSTOMS SERVICE, U.S.*

U.S. GOVERNMENT MANUAL

The U.S. Government Manual is over 900 pages long and details bureaus, divisions, services, offices and departments within the Federal government. Cost is $33; available through the Government Printing Office.

866/512-1800
202/512-1800
http://bookstore.gpo.gov

It can also be viewed on the Internet, for free. Both current and past years are available.

www.access.gpo.gov/nara/nara001.html

U.S. HOUSE OF REPRESENTATIVES
General Information   202/225-3121
www.house.gov

U.S. IDENTIFICATION MANUAL

NEW! *The U.S. Identification Manual* is a super-book of identification cards. Includes driver's licenses, license plates, military identification, credit cards and more. The primary use of this resource is to authenticate identification and to spot counterfeits. Sell for $149.

800/227-8827
www.driverslicenseguide.com

U.S. INVESTIGATIONS SERVICES, INC.

NEW! *USIS* is one of the largest private investigation agencies in the U.S. — thanks to help from the federal government. The company is the result of the mid-1990s privatization of a background checking service previously run by the Office of Personnel Management. The company continues to specializes in background checks of potential federal employees, conducting over 400,000 investigations a year. Company headquarters are in Pennsylvania, with regional headquarters in Philadelphia, Chicago and San Francisco.

888/794-USIS
www.usis.com

U.S. MARSHALS SERVICE
The *U.S. Marshals Service* is responsible for providing protection for the federal judiciary, transporting federal prisoners, protecting endangered federal witnesses and managing assets seized from criminal enterprises. In addition, the men and women of the Marshals Service pursue and arrest 55 percent of all federal fugitives, more than all other federal agencies combined.

Headquarters   202/307-9000
www.usdoj.gov/marshals

Contact the *Communications Center* of the *U.S. Marshals Service* to report federal fugitives from justice:

202/307-9100

DISTRICT OFFICES:

Birmingham, AL	205/731-1712
Montgomery, AL	334/223-7401
Mobile, AL	205/690-2841
Anchorage, AK	907/271-5154
Phoenix, AZ	602/379-3621
Little Rock, AR	501/324-6256
Fort Smith, AR	501/783-5215
San Francisco, CA	415/436-7677
Sacramento, CA	916/930-2030
Los Angeles, CA	213/894-6820
San Diego, CA	619/557-6620
Denver, CO	303/844-2801
New Haven, CT	203/773-2107
Washington, D.C.	202/353-0600
Washington, D.C.	202/616-8600
Wilmington, DE	302/573-6176
Tallahassee, FL	904/942-8400
Tampa, FL	813/274-6401
Miami, FL	305/536-5346
Atlanta, GA	404/331-6833
Macon, GA	912/752-8280
Savannah, GA	912/652-4212
Hagatna, Guam	011-671-477-7827
Honolulu, HI	808/541-3000
Boise, ID	208/334-1298
Chicago, IL	312/353-5290
Springfield, IL	217/492-4430
East St. Louis, IL	618/482-9336
South Bend, IN	219/236-8291
Indianapolis, IN	317/226-6566

Cedar Rapids, IA	319/362-4411
Des Moines, IA	515/284-6240
Topeka, KS	785/295-2775
Lexington, KY	606/233-2601
Louisville, KY	502/582-5141
New Orleans, LA	504/589-6079
Baton Rouge, LA	225/389-0364
Shreveport, LA	318/676-4202
Portland, ME	207/780-3355
Baltimore, MD	410/962-2220
Boston, MA	617/748-2500
Detroit, MI	313/226-4922
Grand Rapids, MI	616/456-2438
Minneapolis, MN	612/664-5900
Oxford, MS	601/234-6661
Jackson, MS	601/965-4444
St. Louis, MO	314/539-2212
Kansas City, MO	816/512-2000
Great Falls, MT	406/453-7597
Omaha, NE	402/221-4781
Las Vegas, NV	702/388-6355
Concord, NH	603/225-1632
Newark, NJ	973/645-2404
Albuquerque, NM	505/346-6400
Syracuse, NY	315/448-0341
Brooklyn, NY	718/254-6700
New York, NY	212/637-6000
Buffalo, NY	716/551-4851
Raleigh, NC	919/856-4153
Greensboro, NC	336/333-5354
Asheville, NC	828/271-4651
Fargo, ND	701/297-7300
Garpan, Saipan, MP 96950	011-670-234-6563
Cleveland, OH	216/522-2154
Columbus, OH	614/469-5540
Tulsa, OK	918/581-7738
Muskogee, OK	918/687-2523
Oklahoma City, OK	405/231-4206
Portland, OR	503/326-2209
Philadelphia, PA	215/597-7273
Scranton, PA	570/346-7277
Pittsburgh, PA	412/644-3351
Hato Rey, PR	809/766-6000
Providence, RI	401/528-5302
Columbia, SC	803/765-5821
Sioux Falls, SD	605/330-4351
Knoxville, TN	615/545-4182
Nashville, TN	615/736-5417
Memphis, TN	901/544-3304
Dallas, TX	214/767-0836
Beaumont, TX	409/839-2581
Houston, TX	713/718-4800
San Antonio, TX	210/472-6540
Salt Lake City, UT	801/524-5693

Burlington, VT	802/951-6271
St. Thomas, VI	340/774-2743
Alexandria, VA	703/274-2013
Roanoke, VA	703/857-2230
Spokane, WA	509/353-2781
Seattle, WA	206/553-5500
Clarksburg, WV	304/623-0486
Charleston, WV	304/347-5136
Milwaukee, WI	414/297-3707
Madison, WI	608/264-5161
Cheyenne, WY	307/772-2196
U.S. Marshals Employment Info	202/307-9600
Justice Prison and Alien Transportation System	816/374-6060

U.S. MERIT SYSTEMS PROTECTION BOARD

It can be very difficult to fire a federal employee. One of the reasons why is because federal employees have the right to an appeal in front of the *U.S. Merit Systems Protection Board*. The Board maintains indices on employee-litigants going back to at least 1994. Name searches can be done on either the Internet or by phone. If a case is found, details can be obtained, including the nature of the firing, such as for workplace drug use or theft.

Headquarters	800/209-8960
Name Searches (Clerk of the Board)	202/653-7200
	www.mspb.gov

U.S. PARTY/CASE INDEX
See...*PACER*.

U.S. POSTAL SERVICE
See...*POSTAL SERVICE*.

U.S. TAX COURT
When the Internal Revenue Service files a Notice of Deficiency against a taxpayer, the taxpayer has three options: Pay the taxes; don't pay the taxes and become delinquent, or sue the IRS in *U.S. Tax Court* and seek to overturn the tax bill. Why should investigators care about this? Because when a person or business takes on the IRS in Tax Court, they put their once private financial affairs into the realm of public record. Many of the U.S. Tax Court cases will include the tax returns of the filing party. Tax Court will do name checks over the phone, limited to one name per call.

202/606-8764
www.ustaxcourt.gov

After you've found a case in Tax Court that's of interest, you'll want to obtain a copy of it. One local Washington, D.C., public record retrieval company that is familiar with the U.S. Tax Court is *Federal Document Retrieval*.

> 800/874-4337
> *www.itsdoc.com*

VEHICLE IDENTIFICATION NUMBERS

NEW! *Vehicle Identification Numbers*, commonly referred to as VINs, can be decoded on the Internet at two websites. Visit *www.carfax. com* or *www.e-autohistory.com*. Both sites work essentially the same way — for free, the VIN can be decoded into model year, manufacturer and model. For a small additional charge, information specific to the history of the vehicle can be found, such as state of registration. No personal address or owner information is included as the information is restricted by the Driver's Privacy Protection Act. Also see the *Reference Guide* of this book for *Anatomy of a VIN*.

> *www.carfax.com*
> *www.e-autohistory.com*

Also available on the Internet is software that will do basically the same thing. Find it at

> *www.vinpower.com*

Published by the National Insurance Crime Bureau, the pocket-sized *Passenger Vehicle Identification Manual* is an invaluable reference manual to understanding and decoding VINs. Distribution of the book is free to NICB and Law Enforcement, but can also be purchased by professional investigators for $10. Also available for $10 is "Commercial Vehicle Identification Manual" which covers heavy duty trucks and equipment. Send your request on company letterhead, or with a business card, to: *National Insurance Crime Bureau, 10330 South Roberts Road, Palos Hills, IL 60465, ATTN: Operations Support Department*.

> 708/430-2430
> *www.nicb.org*

In Georgia, lien holders can call this number with a VIN number to determine the current license plate on the vehicle. No account is necessary and the lookup is free.

> 404/362-6500

Mercedes-Benz Corporation is a major financier of big rig trucks and in particular, Freightliners. By calling this automated line at their national truck office, a VIN can be run for account status.

> 800/222-4221

VEHICLES
See...*STOLEN VEHICLES*.

Also see...*VEHICLE IDENTIFICATION NUMBERS*.

Also see...*TRUCKS AND TRUCKING*.

VETERAN'S AFFAIRS, DEPARTMENT OF
General Information   800/827-1000
                                          www.va.gov

Need to know where a veteran is buried? If it is in a VA
cemetery, the U.S. Department of Memorial Affairs will
provide location information.
                                          800/697-6947
                                          www.cem.va.gov

**VICTIM INFORMATION AND NOTIFICATION
EVERYDAY (VINE)**
The second biggest fight (after mere
survival) most victims of crime engage in
is to regain peace of mind. Knowing the
incarceration status of their victimizer and being notified of
his or her release date can go along way toward providing
this. The *VINE* system is a fully automated notification
system set up to do just this. It links inmate records with a
telephone call center so that victims can inquire about the
status of their attacker. In addition, after (anonymous)
registration, the victim will be notified (by phone, pager or
e-mail) when there is a change in the offender's status such
as escape, transfer, release or death. Currently 650 counties
in 35 states use VINE. Statewide systems are in place in
Alaska, Arkansas, Kentucky, Montana, Ohio and
elsewhere. Call this number to learn if VINE is available in
your area.
                                          800/865-4314
                                          www.vineco.com

VICTIM'S RESOURCES
National Criminal Justice Reference
Service Office for Victims of Crime   800/627-6872
                        http://www.ojp.usdoj.gov/ovc/

National Organization for Victim
Assistance (NOVA)   202/232-6682
                                          www.try-nova.org

VIDEO ENHANCEMENT
See...*AUDIO/VIDEO ENHANCEMENT*.

VIDEO MONITORING SERVICE OF AMERICA
Video Monitoring Service of America is a news clipping
service for television. VMS records and monitors thousands
of hours of TV and radio broadcast news in over 100 top

U.S. and international markets every day. Their news database includes immediate access to detailed summaries of what is seen and said in more than 1,500,000 news stories every month. If it's appeared on local TV in the last thirty days — or on network TV in the last sixty days — there's a good chance this company can provide a copy of it.

323/993-0111
www.vidmon.com

VIDEOTAPE PIRACY

The Motion Picture Association of America initiates 60,000 investigations per year into pirated movies. A reward may be paid for information that leads to the arrest and conviction of persons engaged in piracy. The lab must have 30 or more VCRs at one location used to produce unauthorized copies of MPAA member company motion pictures.

800/NO-COPYS
www.mpaa.org/anti-piracy/

National Anti-Piracy Association (NAPA) is a privately owned company that specializes in the investigation of pirated pay-per-view programming. They hire investigators, on a commission basis, to ID commercial establishments who are showing the programming without authorization. Interested? Call *NAPA* and request their information packet.

888/USA-NAPA
www.pimall.com/nais/n.napa

VINs
See...*VEHICLE IDENTIFICATION NUMBERS.*

VITAL RECORDS

NEW! *Vital Records* is a term that generally includes birth, death, marriage and divorce records. However, not all states maintain all of these records at state level. This is particularly true of divorce records.

Alabama	334/206-5418
Alaska	907/465-3391
Arizona	602/255-3260
Arkansas	501/661-2336
California	916/445-2684
Colorado	303/756-4464
Connecticut	860/509-7897
Delaware	302/739-4721
D.C.	202/442-9009
Florida	904/359-6900
Georgia	404/656-4900
Hawaii	808/586-4533
Idaho	208/334-5988

Illinois	217/782-6553
Indiana	317/233-2700
Iowa	515/281-4944
Kansas	785/296-1400
Kentucky	502/564-4212
Louisiana	504/568-5152
Maine	207/287-3184
Maryland	410/764-3038
Massachusetts	617/753-8600
Michigan	517/335-8656
Minnesota	612/676-5120
Mississippi	601/576-7450
Missouri	573/751-6400
Montana	406/444-4228
Nebraska	402/471-2871
Nevada	775/684-4280
New Hampshire	603/271-4654
New Jersey	609/292-4087
New Mexico	505/827-2338
New York (Except NYC)	518/474-3075
New York City	212/788-4520
North Carolina	919/733-3526
North Dakota	701/328-2360
Ohio	614/466-2531
Oklahoma	405/271-4040
Oregon	503/731-4095
Pennsylvania	724/656-3100
Rhode Island	401/222-2811
South Carolina	803/898-3630
South Dakota	605/773-3355
Tennessee	615/741-1763
Texas	512/458-7111
Utah	801/538-6105
Vermont	802/863-7275
Virginia	804/225-5000
Washington	360/236-4300
West Virginia	304/558-2931
Wisconsin	608/266-1371
Wyoming	307/777-7591

OTHER TERRITORIES:

American Samoa	684/633-1222
	ext. 214
Guam	671/734-4589
North Mariana Islands	670/234-6401
	ext. 15
Puerto Rico	787/728-7980

Now, if you don't mind paying a small service fee, you'll want to consider *VitalChek* for obtaining vital records. The company will fulfill your request for vital records. Orders are taken by phone, fax or online. In addition, their website contains quite a bit of free information about the specifics for obtaining vital records in any given state.

800/255-2414
www.vitalchek.com

For information on obtaining vital records in Canada, visit website *www.archives.ca*.

VOTER REGISTRATION RECORDS
Voter registration records have become less and less available from both government agencies and commercial database providers. One such company that still offers voter registration records from 20 states is Loc8fast.com. See... *DATABASE PROVIDERS*...for further information.

WANTS AND WARRANTS

Information contained in the FBI's NCIC computer is tightly restricted — and available to law enforcement only (with the exception of a person who wants to obtain his or her own criminal record). However, there's one highly noteworthy exception to this. The "Wants and Warrants" file of NCIC is available to private investigators, pre-employment screening firms and other private companies for pre-employment, tenant screening and other background reasons. The information doesn't come directly from the FBI though. Through a quirk of law, the police department in Duluth, Georgia, makes this information available to non-law enforcement agencies. The cost is $5 per name run. The permission of the person whose name is being run is not needed. *UPDATE: Effective February, 2002 this service was discontinued.*

770/623-2770 ext. 254
Fax 770/623-9424
www.duluthpd.com

WAR CRIMES
The Nazi War Criminal Records Interagency Working Group was established in 1999 to locate, inventory, recommend for declassification and make available to the public all classified Nazi war criminal records throughout the United States government so that Nazis who have naturalized in the U.S. can be deported and to aid in the identification of assets of Holocaust victims. Administered by a five-person staff at the National Archives and Records Administration.

301/713-7230
www.nara.gov/iwg

Victims of the Holocaust and their survivors may be entitled to insurance claims if a life, education or dowry policy was in effect during the relevant period (1920-1945). Using information from insurance company lists and from various public record sources, *The International Commission on Holocaust Era Insurance Claims* seeks to unite beneficiaries with insurance settlements. Visit their website to check a name to see if benefits are owed.

www.icheic.org

The Coalition for International Justice (CIJ) is an international, nonprofit organization working to support the international war crimes tribunals for Rwanda and the former Yugoslavia. CIJ provides support through advocacy, fundraising, working with other Non-Governmental Organizations (NGO's) and by providing legal assistance.

202/662-1595
www.cij.org

Rewards for Justice is a program run by the Diplomatic Security Service of the U.S. Department of State. They offer specific rewards leading to the arrest or conviction of those responsible for specific crimes against humanity and war crimes. For more information visit their website.

800/437-6371
www.dssrewards.net

WAR HERO VERIFICATION
See...*MILITARY PERSONNEL*.

WEATHER
PRIVATE SERVICES:
Metro Weather Service, Inc.   800/488-7866
www.metroweather.com

Continental Weather &
Earth Sciences, Inc.   800/843-7246
www.continentalweather.com

Falconer Weather Information
Service   800/428-5621
518/399-5388
www.wxscape.com/fwis

Compu Weather, Inc.   800/825-4445
www.compuweather.com

Intellicast   *www.intellicast.com*

Fleet Weather   *www.fleetweather.com*

Weather Underground   *www.wunderground.com*

GOVERNMENT SERVICES:
National Oceanic &
Atmospheric Administration   202/482-6090
                                 www.noaa.gov

National Climatic Data Center   828/271-4800
                               www.ncdc.noaa.gov

National Weather Service   301/713-0622
                               www.nws.noaa.gov

NOAA information products relevant to insurance claims
(such as freeze/frost data) can be found at

www.nndc.noaa.gov/phase3/insuranceaccm.htm

The National Severe Storms Laboratory is the federal
government's research lab for improving severe weather
warnings and forecasts. Headquartered in Norman,
Oklahoma, with staff in Colorado, Nevada, Washington,
Utah and Wisconsin.

                               405/360-3620
                              www.nssl.noaa.gov

For lightning related information, including prediction and
historical data, visit the website of *Global Atmospherics*:

www.lightningstorm.com

Or contact the *National Lightning Detection Network,*
which has 150 stations which detect lightning strikes
throughout the U.S. Information dates back to 1988.
Operated by the *Global Hydrology and Climate Center* in
Huntsville, Alabama.

                             256/961-7932
           wwwghrc.msfc.nasa.gov/uso/readme/gai.html

WE TIP HOTLINE
See...*REWARDS OFFERED*.

WHITE HOUSE, THE
General Information   202/456-1414
                             www.whitehouse.gov

WIRETAPS
For statistical information on quantity and location of
federally approved wiretaps, visit *www.uscourts.gov*.

Also see...our *Privacy Law Survival Guide* for *Wiretaps*.

WORK NUMBER, THE

One very useful source for employment verifications is *The Work Number*. It's a private company to which many large corporations have outsourced their employment verifications. Over 600 major corporations are currently using *The Work Number*, covering a whopping 40 million employees. (Visit their website for a list of participating employers.) There are a number of plans for subscribing to the service based on monthly volume. Verifications cost $8 and up. Of most interest to investigation agencies who only conduct only an occasional verification is an 800 number that allows single verifications using a credit card. Basic verifications here are $10 each and include most recent start/termination date, total time at company and job title.

General Information	800/996-7566
	314/214-7000
Pay-Per-Call	800/367-5690

www.theworknumber.com

WORKPLACE VIOLENCE
See...*STALKING & THREAT ASSESSMENT*.

WORLD FACTBOOK, THE
The *World Factbook* is published by the CIA and contains a factual profile of each of the world's nations. Available for free on the Internet and for purchase as a book.

Online version:	*www.cia.gov*
Purchase copies:	866/512-1800
	202/512-1800

http://bookstore.gpo.gov

WORLD JUSTICE INFORMATION NETWORK
Internet site/community for sharing open source information on crime. Includes a virtual library of criminal justice publications and a news-clipping library to keep up on crime trends here and abroad. Looking for background info on an organized crime group? You might want to take a look-see here.

www.justinfo.net

YAHOO – SERVICE OF PROCESS
Need to serve a subpoena on web mega-portal *Yahoo* to obtain e-mail account holder info or other information? Try directing it here: *Yahoo, Attn.: Custodian of Records, 3420 Central Expressway, 2nd Floor, Santa Clara, CA 95051.*

408/616-3760

YELLOW BOOKS

NEW! Known collectively as *The Leadership Library*, there are fourteen Yellow Books which provide biographical and contact information on America's elite. The categories are Congressional, Federal, State, Municipal, Federal Regional, Judicial, Corporate, Financial, News Media, Associations, Law Firms, Government Affairs, Foreign Representatives and Nonprofit Sector. Updated quarterly. Available as a book or over the Internet or on CD-ROM. Price varies from $290 for a single directory to $2,700 for full web access to all directories. Need just a single lookup and don't want to spend your hard-earned money? Try visiting their website — as of our publication date, they were offering a free trial subscription.

212/627-4140
www.leadershipdirectories.com

ZIP CODE INFORMATION

Need to know a zip code for a given address or what area a given zip code corresponds to? The *U.S. Postal Service* now has a single 800 number for all of the above.

24-Hour   800/ASK-USPS
www.usps.gov

THE INVESTIGATOR'S LITTLE BLACK BOOK 3

REFERENCE GUIDE

REFERENCE GUIDE

Table of Contents

Directory of North American Area Codes   300

Directory of International Telephone Country Codes   309

U.S. Postal Service Official Abbreviations*   313

Airport Codes: United States Airports*   315

Internet Abbreviations   319

U.S. Military Internet Abbreviations*   323

Calendars (2002—2007)*   325

Social Security Number Decoder   332

Employer Identification Number Decoder   335

Anatomy of a Check   337

Federal Reserve Codes   339

Lawful Bank Account Sources*   340

Financial Investigation Checklist*   344

Background Investigation Checklist*   346

Common Personal Identifiers*   348

Master List/Public Record Databases*   349

PACER: Missing Courts*   365

International Business Type Abbreviations*   367

Anatomy of a VIN*   371

NCIC Vehicle Manufacturer Codes*   376

Drivers License Formats*   379

NFPA Hazardous Material Symbols*   381

Phonetics   383

26 Warning Signs of Electronic Eavesdropping*   384

State Laws: Recording Phone Calls*   387

Caliber Comparison Chart   389

State by State Guide to Concealed Weapons*   391

Sample Miranda Warning   393

Beyond a Reasonable Doubt   394

The Death Penalty: State by State Profile   395

Interpol Member States*   398

Diplomatic Immunity*   400

DEA Schedules of Controlled Substances*   402

Key Department of Justice Databases*   405

New section not appearing in previous editions.

DIRECTORY
OF
NORTH
AMERICAN
AREA CODES

BY AREA CODE:

201 New Jersey	269 Michigan
202 District of Columbia	270 Kentucky
	276 Virginia
203 Connecticut	281 Texas
204 Manitoba	283 Ohio
205 Alabama	284 British Virgin Islands
206 Washington	
207 Maine	289 Ontario
208 Idaho	301 Maryland
209 California	302 Delaware
210 Texas	303 Colorado
212 New York	304 West Virginia
213 California	305 Florida
214 Texas	306 Saskatchewan
215 Pennsylvania	307 Wyoming
216 Ohio	308 Nebraska
217 Illinois	309 Illinois
218 Minnesota	310 California
219 Indiana	312 Illinois
224 Illinois	313 Michigan
225 Louisiana	314 Missouri
227 Maryland	315 New York
228 Mississippi	316 Kansas
229 Georgia	317 Indiana
231 Michigan	318 Louisiana
234 Ohio	319 Iowa
240 Maryland	320 Minnesota
242 Bahamas	321 Florida
246 Barbados	323 California
248 Michigan	330 Ohio
250 British Columbia	331 Illinois
	334 Alabama
251 Alabama	336 North Carolina
252 North Carolina	337 Louisiana
253 Washington	339 Massachusetts
254 Texas	340 U.S. Virgin Islands
256 Alabama	
260 Indiana	345 Cayman Islands
262 Wisconsin	347 New York
264 Anguilla	351 Massachusetts
267 Pennsylvania	352 Florida
268 Antigua & Barbuda	360 Washington
	361 Texas

380 Ohio	505 New Mexico
385 Utah	506 New Brunswick
386 Florida	507 Minnesota
401 Rhode Island	508 Massachusetts
402 Nebraska	509 Washington
403 Alberta	510 California
404 Georgia	512 Texas
405 Oklahoma	513 Ohio
406 Montana	514 Quebec
407 Florida	515 Iowa
408 California	516 New York
409 Texas	517 Michigan
410 Maryland	518 New York
412 Pennsylvania	519 Ontario
413 Massachusetts	520 Arizona
414 Wisconsin	530 California
415 California	540 Virginia
416 Ontario	541 Oregon
417 Missouri	551 New Jersey
418 Quebec	557 Missouri
419 Ohio	559 California
423 Tennessee	561 Florida
424 California	562 California
425 Washington	563 Iowa
434 Virginia	567 Ohio
435 Utah	570 Pennsylvania
438 Quebec	571 Virginia
440 Ohio	573 Missouri
441 Bermuda	574 Indiana
443 Maryland	575 New Mexico
445 Pennsylvania	580 Oklahoma
450 Quebec	585 New York
456 Inbound Int'l	586 Michigan
464 Illinois	600 Canadian
469 Texas	Services
470 Georgia	601 Mississippi
473 Grenada	602 Arizona
475 Connecticut	603 New Hampshire
478 Georgia	604 British
479 Arkansas	Columbia
480 Arizona	605 South Dakota
484 Pennsylvania	606 Kentucky
500 Personal Comm.	607 New York
Service	608 Wisconsin
501 Arkansas	609 New Jersey
502 Kentucky	610 Pennsylvania
503 Oregon	612 Minnesota
504 Louisiana	613 Ontario

614 Ohio	724 Pennsylvania
615 Tennessee	727 Florida
616 Michigan	731 Tennessee
617 Massachusetts	732 New Jersey
618 Illinois	734 Michigan
619 California	740 Ohio
620 Kansas	754 Florida
623 Arizona	757 Virginia
626 California	758 St. Lucia
630 Illinois	760 California
631 New York	763 Minnesota
636 Missouri	765 Indiana
641 Iowa	767 Dominica
646 New York	770 Georgia
647 Ontario	773 Illinois
649 Turks & Caicos	774 Massachusetts
650 California	775 Nevada
651 Minnesota	778 British
660 Missouri	Columbia
661 California	780 Alberta
662 Mississippi	781 Massachusetts
664 Montserrat	784 St. Vincent/
667 Maryland	Grenada
670 Northern	785 Kansas
Mariana Islands	786 Florida
671 Guam	787 Puerto Rico
678 Georgia	800 Toll-Free
682 Texas	801 Utah
700 IC Services	802 Vermont
701 North Dakota	803 South Carolina
702 Nevada	804 Virginia
703 Virginia	805 California
704 North Carolina	806 Texas
705 Ontario	807 Ontario
706 Georgia	808 Hawaii
707 California	809 Dominican
708 Illinois	Republic
709 Newfoundland	810 Michigan
710 U.S. Gov't	812 Indiana
712 Iowa	813 Florida
713 Texas	814 Pennsylvania
714 California	815 Illinois
715 Wisconsin	816 Missouri
716 New York	817 Texas
717 Pennsylvania	818 California
718 New York	819 Quebec
719 Colorado	828 North Carolina
720 Colorado	830 Texas

831 California	914 New York
832 Texas	915 Texas
835 Pennsylvania	916 California
843 South Carolina	917 New York
845 New York	918 Oklahoma
847 Illinois	919 North Carolina
848 New Jersey	920 Wisconsin
850 Florida	925 California
856 New Jersey	928 Arizona
857 Massachusetts	931 Tennessee
858 California	936 Texas
859 Kentucky	937 Ohio
860 Connecticut	939 Puerto Rico
862 New Jersey	940 Texas
863 Florida	941 Florida
864 South Carolina	947 Michigan
865 Tennessee	949 California
866 Toll-Free	952 Minnesota
867 Yukon, NW	954 Florida
Territories and	956 Texas
Nunavut	959 Connecticut
868 Trinidad and	970 Colorado
Tobago	971 Oregon
869 St. Kitts and	972 Texas
Nevis	973 New Jersey
870 Arkansas	975 Missouri
872 Illinois	978 Massachusetts
876 Jamaica	979 Texas
877 Toll-Free	980 North Carolina
878 Pennsylvania	984 North Carolina
880 Paid Toll-Free	985 Louisiana
881 Paid Toll-Free	989 Michigan
882 Paid Toll-Free	
888 Toll-Free	
900 Premium	
Services	
901 Tennessee	
902 Nova Scotia	
903 Texas	
904 Florida	
905 Ontario	
906 Michigan	
907 Alaska	
908 New Jersey	
909 California	
910 North Carolina	
912 Georgia	
913 Kansas	

BY PLACE:

Place	Code	Place	Code
Alabama	205	California	760
Alabama	251	California	805
Alabama	256	California	818
Alabama	334	California	831
Alaska	907	California	858
Alberta	403	California	909
Alberta	780	California	916
Anguilla	264	California	925
Antigua	268	California	949
Arizona	480	Cayman Islands	345
Arizona	520	CNMI	670
Arizona	602	Colorado	303
Arizona	623	Colorado	719
Arizona	928	Colorado	720
Arkansas	479	Colorado	970
Arkansas	501	Connecticut	203
Arkansas	870	Connecticut	475
Bahamas	242	Connecticut	860
Barbados	246	Connecticut	959
Barbuda	268	Delaware	302
Bermuda	441	D.C.	202
British Columbia	250	Dominican Rep.	809
British Columbia	604	Dominica	767
British Columbia	778	Florida	305
British Virgin Is.	284	Florida	321
California	209	Florida	352
California	213	Florida	386
California	310	Florida	407
California	323	Florida	561
California	408	Florida	727
California	415	Florida	754
California	424	Florida	786
California	510	Florida	813
California	530	Florida	850
California	559	Florida	863
California	562	Florida	904
California	619	Florida	941
California	626	Florida	954
California	650	Georgia	229
California	661	Georgia	404
California	707	Georgia	470
California	714	Georgia	478

AREA CODES (BY PLACE)

Place	Code	Place	Code
Georgia	678	Maryland	227
Georgia	706	Maryland	240
Georgia	770	Maryland	301
Georgia	912	Maryland	410
Grenada	473	Maryland	443
Guam	671	Maryland	667
Hawaii	808	Massachusetts	339
Idaho	208	Massachusetts	351
Illinois	217	Massachusetts	413
Illinois	224	Massachusetts	508
Illinois	309	Massachusetts	617
Illinois	312	Massachusetts	774
Illinois	331	Massachusetts	781
Illinois	464	Massachusetts	857
Illinois	618	Massachusetts	978
Illinois	630	Michigan	231
Illinois	708	Michigan	248
Illinois	773	Michigan	269
Illinois	815	Michigan	313
Illinois	847	Michigan	517
Illinois	872	Michigan	586
Indiana	219	Michigan	616
Indiana	260	Michigan	734
Indiana	317	Michigan	810
Indiana	574	Michigan	906
Indiana	765	Michigan	947
Indiana	812	Michigan	989
Iowa	319	Minnesota	218
Iowa	515	Minnesota	320
Iowa	563	Minnesota	507
Iowa	641	Minnesota	612
Iowa	712	Minnesota	651
Jamaica	876	Minnesota	763
Kansas	316	Minnesota	952
Kansas	620	Mississippi	228
Kansas	785	Mississippi	601
Kansas	913	Mississippi	662
Kentucky	270	Missouri	314
Kentucky	502	Missouri	417
Kentucky	606	Missouri	557
Kentucky	859	Missouri	573
Louisiana	225	Missouri	636
Louisiana	318	Missouri	660
Louisiana	337	Missouri	816
Louisiana	504	Missouri	975
Louisiana	985	Montana	406
Maine	207	Montserrat	664
Manitoba	204	Nebraska	308

Place	Code	Place	Code
Nebraska	402	Ohio	513
Nevada	702	Ohio	567
Nevada	775	Ohio	614
New Brunswick	506	Ohio	740
New Hampshire	603	Ohio	937
New Jersey	201	Oklahoma	405
New Jersey	551	Oklahoma	580
New Jersey	609	Oklahoma	918
New Jersey	732	Ontario	289
New Jersey	848	Ontario	416
New Jersey	856	Ontario	519
New Jersey	862	Ontario	613
New Jersey	908	Ontario	647
New Jersey	973	Ontario	705
New Mexico	505	Ontario	807
New Mexico	575	Ontario	905
New York	212	Oregon	503
New York	315	Oregon	541
New York	347	Oregon	971
New York	516	Pennsylvania	215
New York	518	Pennsylvania	267
New York	585	Pennsylvania	412
New York	607	Pennsylvania	445
New York	631	Pennsylvania	484
New York	646	Pennsylvania	570
New York	716	Pennsylvania	610
New York	718	Pennsylvania	717
New York	845	Pennsylvania	724
New York	914	Pennsylvania	814
New York	917	Pennsylvania	835
Newfoundland	709	Pennsylvania	878
North Carolina	252	Puerto Rico	787
North Carolina	336	Puerto Rico	939
North Carolina	704	Quebec	418
North Carolina	828	Quebec	438
North Carolina	910	Quebec	450
North Carolina	919	Quebec	514
North Carolina	980	Quebec	819
North Carolina	984	Rhode Island	401
North Dakota	701	Saskatchewan	306
Nova Scotia	902	South Carolina	803
Ohio	216	South Carolina	843
Ohio	234	South Carolina	864
Ohio	283	South Dakota	605
Ohio	330	St. Kitts & Nevis	869
Ohio	380	St. Lucia	758
Ohio	419	St. Vincent &	
Ohio	440	Grenada	784

Tennessee	423	Wisconsin	414
Tennessee	615	Wisconsin	608
Tennessee	731	Wisconsin	715
Tennessee	865	Wisconsin	920
Tennessee	901	Wyoming	307
Tennessee	931	Yukon, NW	
Texas	210	Territory &	
Texas	214	Nunavut	867
Texas	254		
Texas	281		
Texas	361		
Texas	409		
Texas	469		
Texas	512		
Texas	682		
Texas	713		
Texas	806		
Texas	817		
Texas	830		
Texas	832		
Texas	903		
Texas	915		
Texas	936		
Texas	940		
Texas	956		
Texas	972		
Texas	979		
Trinidad & Tobago	868		
Turks & Caicos Is.	649		
U.S. Virgin Is.	340		
Utah	385		
Utah	435		
Utah	801		
Vermont	802		
Virginia	276		
Virginia	434		
Virginia	540		
Virginia	571		
Virginia	703		
Virginia	757		
Virginia	804		
Washington	206		
Washington	253		
Washington	360		
Washington	425		
Washington	509		
West Virginia	304		
Wisconsin	262		

DIRECTORY
OF
INTERNATIONAL
TELEPHONE
COUNTRY
CODES

93	Afghanistan	269	Comoros and
355	Albania		Mayotte
213	Algeria	242	Congo
684	American Samoa	682	Cook Islands
376	Andorra	506	Costa Rica
244	Angola	385	Croatia
54	Argentina	53	Cuba
374	Armenia	357	Cyprus
297	Aruba	42	Czech Republic
247	Ascension Island	45	Denmark
61	Australia	246	Diego Garcia
672	Australian	253	Djibouti
	External	593	Ecuador
	Territories	20	Egypt
43	Austria	503	El Salvador
994	Azerbaijan	240	Equatorial
973	Bahrain		Guinea
880	Bangladesh	291	Eritrea
375	Belarus	372	Estonia
32	Belgium	251	Ethiopia
501	Belize	500	Falkland Islands
229	Benin	298	Faroe Islands
975	Bhutan	679	Fiji
591	Bolivia	358	Finland
387	Bosnia and	33	France
	Herzegovina	590	French Antilles
267	Botswana	594	French Guiana
55	Brazil	241	Gabon
673	Brunei	220	Gambia
	Darussalm	995	Republic of
359	Bulgaria		Georgia
226	Burkina Faso	49	Germany
257	Burundi	233	Ghana
237	Cameroon	350	Gibraltar
238	Cape Verdi	30	Greece
236	Central African	299	Greenland
	Republic	671	Guam
235	Chad	502	Guatemala
56	Chile	224	Guinea
86	China (People's	245	Guinea-Bissau
	Republic)	592	Guyana
886	China (Taiwan)	509	Haiti
57	Colombia	504	Honduras

852 Hong Kong	230 Mauritius
36 Hungary	52 Mexico
354 Iceland	691 Micronesia
91 India	373 Moldova
62 Indonesia	377 Monaco
98 Iran	976 Mongolia
964 Iraq	212 Morocco
353 Ireland	258 Mozambique
972 Israel	95 Myanmar
39 Italy	264 Namibia
225 Ivory Coast	674 Nauru
81 Japan	977 Nepal
962 Jordan	31 Netherlands
254 Kenya	599 Netherlands
855 Khmer Republic	Antilles
(Cambodia/	687 New Caledonia
Kampuchea)	64 New Zealand
686 Kiribati Republic	505 Nicaragua
(Gilbert Islands)	227 Niger
82 Korea - South	234 Nigeria
850 Korea - North	683 Niue
965 Kuwait	670 North Mariana
996 Kyrgyz Republic	Islands (Saipan)
371 Latvia	47 Norway
856 Laos	968 Oman
961 Lebanon	92 Pakistan
266 Lesotho	680 Palau
231 Liberia	507 Panama
370 Lithuania	675 Papua New
218 Libya	Guinea
352 Luxembourg	595 Paraguay
853 Macao	51 Peru
389 Macedonia	63 Philippines
261 Madagascar	48 Poland
60 Malaysia	351 Portugal
265 Malawi	(includes Azores)
60 Malaysia	974 Qatar
960 Maldives	262 Reunion (France)
223 Mali	40 Romania
356 Malta	7 Russia
692 Marshall Islands	250 Rwanda
596 Martinique	378 San Marino
222 Mauritania	239 Sao Tome and

	Principe	58	Venezuela
966	Saudi Arabia	84	Viet Nam
221	Senegal	681	Wallis and
381	Serbia and		Futuna
	Montenegro	685	Western Samoa
248	Seychelles	969	Yemen
232	Sierra Leone	967	North Yemen
65	Singapore	243	Zaire
42	Slovakia	260	Zambia
386	Slovenia	263	Zimbabwe
677	Solomon Islands		
252	Somalia		
27	South Africa		
34	Spain		
94	Sri Lanka		
290	St. Helena		
508	St. Pierre &		
	Miquelon		
249	Sudan		
597	Suriname		
268	Swaziland		
46	Sweden		
41	Switzerland		
963	Syria		
689	Tahiti		
255	Tanzania		
66	Thailand		
228	Togo		
690	Tokelau		
676	Tonga		
216	Tunisia		
90	Turkey		
688	Tuvalu (Ellice		
	Islands)		
256	Uganda		
380	Ukraine		
971	United Arab		
	Emirates		
44	United Kingdom		
598	Uruguay		
678	Vanuatu (New		
	Hebrides)		
379	Vatican City		

Dialing Other Countries from the U.S. or Canada:

Dial 011 for international access. Then...
...the country code;
...the city code*;
...the local telephone number.

* Don't have the city code? See our section, COUNTRY CODE LOOKUPS in the main book.

U.S. POSTAL SERVICE OFFICIAL ABBREVIATIONS

ALABAMA	AL
ALASKA	AK
AMERICAN SAMOA	AS
ARIZONA	AZ
ARKANSAS	AR
CALIFORNIA	CA
COLORADO	CO
CONNECTICUT	CT
DELAWARE	DE
DISTRICT OF COLUMBIA	DC
FED. STATES OF MICRONESIA	FM
FLORIDA	FL
GEORGIA	GA
GUAM	GU
HAWAII	HI
IDAHO	ID
ILLINOIS	IL
INDIANA	IN
IOWA	IA
KANSAS	KS
KENTUCKY	KY
LOUISIANA	LA
MAINE	ME
MARSHALL ISLANDS	MH
MARYLAND	MD
MASSACHUSETTS	MA
MICHIGAN	MI
MINNESOTA	MN
MISSISSIPPI	MS
MISSOURI	MO
MONTANA	MT
NEBRASKA	NE
NEVADA	NV

NEW HAMPSHIRE	NH
NEW JERSEY	NJ
NEW MEXICO	NM
NEW YORK	NY
NORTH CAROLINA	NC
NORTH DAKOTA	ND
NORTH. MARIANA ISLANDS	MP
OHIO	OH
OKLAHOMA	OK
OREGON	OR
PALAU	PW
PENNSYLVANIA	PA
PUERTO RICO	PR
RHODE ISLAND	RI
SOUTH CAROLINA	SC
SOUTH DAKOTA	SD
TENNESSEE	TN
TEXAS	TX
UTAH	UT
VERMONT	VT
VIRGIN ISLANDS	VI
VIRGINIA	VA
WASHINGTON	WA
WEST VIRGINIA	WV
WISCONSIN	WI
WYOMING	WY

Military "State" Abbreviations

Armed Forces Africa	AE
Armed Forces Americas (except Canada)	AA
Armed Forces Canada	AE
Armed Forces Europe	AE
Armed Forces Middle East	AE
Armed Forces Pacific	AP

AIRPORT CODES: UNITED STATES AIRPORTS

(Alphabetized by Code)

ABE	ALLENTOWN, PA
ABQ	ALBUQUERQUE,NM
ABI	ABILENE, TX
ACT	WACO,TX
ALB	ALBANY, NY
AMA	AMARILLO, TX
ANC	ANCHORAGE, AK
ATL	ATLANTA, GA
ATW	APPLETON, WI
AUS	AUSTIN, TX
AVP	WILKES BARRE, PA
AZO	KALAMAZOO, MI
BDL	HARTFORD, CT
BFL	BAKERSFIELD, CA
BGR	BANGOR, ME
BHM	BIRMINGHAM, AL
BIL	BILLINGS, MT
BMI	BLOOMINGTON, IL
BNA	NASHVILLE, TN
BOI	BOISE, ID
BOS	BOSTON, MA
BPT	BEAUMONT/PORT ARTHUR, TX
BTR	BATTON ROUGE, LA
BTV	BURLINGTON, VT
BUF	BUFFALO, NY
BUR	BURBANK, CA
BWI	BALTIMORE, MD
CAE	COLUMBIA, SC
CAK	AKRON/CANTON, OH
CHA	CHATTANOOGA, TN
CHS	CHARLESTON, SC
CID	CEDAR RAPIDS, IA
CLE	CLEVELAND, OH
CLT	CHARLOTTE, NC
CMH	COLUMBUS,OH
CMI	CHAMPAIGN/URBANA, IL
COS	COLORADO SPRINGS, CO
CRP	CORPUS CHRISTI, TX
CVG	CINCINNATI, OH
CWA	WAUSAU/STEVENS POINT, WI
DAY	DAYTON, OH
DBQ	DUBUQUE, IA
DCA	WASHINGTON DC/NATIONAL

DEN DENVER, CO
DET DETROIT, MI./CITY
DFW DALLAS/FT.WORTH, TX
DRO DURANGO, CO
DSM DES MOINES, IA
DTW DETROIT, MI./METRO
DUT DUTCH HARBOR, AK
EGE VAIL, CO
ELP EL PASO, TX
EUG EUGENE, OR
EVV EVANSVILLE, IN
EWR NEWARK, NJ
EYW KEY WEST, FL
FAI FAIRBANKS, AK
FAT FRESNO, CA
FLL FT. LAUDERDALE, FL
FLO FLORENCE, SC
FNT FLINT, MI
FSD SIOUX FALLS, SD
FSM FORT SMITH, AR
FWA FORT WAYNE, IN
FYV FAYETTEVILLE, AR
GEG SPOKANE, WA
GJT GRAND JUNCTION, CO
GRB GREEN BAY, WI
GRR GRAND RAPIDS, MI
GSO GREENSBORO, NC
GSP GREENEVILLE/SPARTANBURG, SC
GUC GUNNISON, CO
HLN HELENA, MT
HNL HONOLULU, HI
HOU HOUSTON, TX/HOBBY
HPN WESTCHESTER COUNTY, NY
HRL HARLINGEN, TX
HSV HUNTSVILLE, AL
HVN NEW HAVEN, CT
IAD WASHINGTON DC/DULLES
IAH HOUSTON,TX/
     INTERCONTINENTAL
ICT WICHITA, KS
ILM WILMINGTON, NC
IND INDIANAPOLIS, IN
ISP ISLIP, NY
ITH ITHACA, NY
JAC JACKSON HOLE, WY
JAX JACKSONVILLE, FL
JAN JACKSON, MS
JFK NEW YORK, NY/KENNEDY
LAN LANSING, MI
LAS LAS VEGAS, NV
LAX LOS ANGELES, CA
LBB LUBBOCK, TX
LCH LACK CHARLES, LA
LEX LEXINGTON, KY

LFT	LAFAYETTE, LA
LGA	NEW YORK, NY/LA GUARDIA
LGB	LONG BEACH, CA
LIH	LIHUE, KAUAI, HI
LIT	LITTLE ROCK, AR
LNK	LINCOLN, NE
LSE	LA CROSSE, WI
MAF	ODESSA/MIDLAND
MCI	KANSAS CITY, MO
MCO	ORLANDO, FL
MDT	HARRISBURG, PA
MDW	CHICAGO, IL/MIDWAY
MEM	MEMPHIS, TN
MFE	MCALLEN, TX
MFR	MEDFORD, OR
MGM	MONTGOMERY, AL
MHT	MANCHESTER, NH
MIA	MIAMI, FL
MKE	MILWAUKEE, WI
MKG	MUSKEGON, MI
MKK	MOLOKAI, MOLOKAI, HI
MLB	MELBOURNE, FL
MLI	MOLINE, IL
MOB	MOBILE, AL
MQT	MARQUETTE, MI
MRY	MONTEREY, CA
MSN	MADISON, WI
MSP	MINNEAPOLIS, MN
MSY	NEW ORLEANS, LA
MYR	MYRTLE BEACH, SC
OAK	OAKLAND, CA
OGG	MAUI, HI
OKC	OKLAHOMA CITY, OK
OMA	OMAHA, NE
ONT	ONTARIO, CA
ORD	CHICAGO, IL/O'HARE
ORF	NORFOLK, VA
OWB	OWENSBORO, KY
OXR	OXNARD, CA
PBI	WEST PALM BEACH, FL
PDX	PORTLAND, OR
PHL	PHILADELPHIA, PA
PHX	PHOENIX, AZ
PIA	PEORIA, IL
PIT	PITTSBURGH, PA
PNS	PENSACOLA, FL
PSC	PASCO, WA
PSP	PALM SPRINGS, CA
PVD	PROVIDENCE, RI
PWM	PORTLAND, ME
RDU	RALEIGH-DURHAM, NC
RIC	RICHMOND, VA
RNO	RENO, NV
ROA	ROANOKE, VA

ROC ROCHESTER, NY
RST ROCHESTER, MN
RSW FT.MYERS, FL
SAN SAN DIEGO, CA
SAT SAN ANTONIO, TX
SAV SAVANNAH, GA
SBA SANTA BARBARA, CA
SBN SOUTH BEND, IN
SDF LOUISVILLE, KY
SEA SEATTLE, WA
SFO SAN FRANCISCO, CA
SGF SPRINGFIELD, MO
SHV SHREVEPORT, LA
SJC SAN JOSE, CA
SJT SAN ANGELO, TX
SJU SAN JUAN, PR
SLC SALT LAKE CITY, UT
SMF SACRAMENTO, CA
SNA ORANGE COUNTY, CA
SPI SPRINGFIELD, IL
SRQ SARASOTA, FL
STL ST. LOUIS, MO
SVS WICHITA FALLS, TX
SWF NEWBURGH/STEWARD FIELD, NY
SYR SYRACUSE, NY
THL TALLAHASSEE, FL
TOL TOLEDO, OH
TPA TAMPA, FL
TRI TRI-CITY, TN
TUL TULSA, OK
TUS TUCSON, AZ
TVC TRAVERSE CITY, MI
TYS KNOXVILLE, TN
VPS FORT WALTON BEACH, FL

INTERNET ABBREVIATIONS

The most common abbreviations found after an internet address are:

.COM (For commercial organizations)

.NET (For network infrastructure machines and organizations)

.EDU (For 4-year, degree-granting universities and colleges. Schools, libraries and museums register under country domains.)

.GOV (For United States federal government agencies. State and local governments register under country domains.)

.ORG (For miscellaneous, usually non-profit, organizations)

.MIL (For U.S. military organizations)

Internet addresses may contain a two-letter country code:

AFGHANISTAN	AF
ALBANIA	AL
ALGERIA	DZ
AMERICAN SAMOA	AS
ANDORRA	AD
ANGOLA	AO
ANGUILLA	AI
ANTARCTICA	AQ
ANTIGUA & BARBUDA	AG
ARGENTINA	AR
ARMENIA	AM
ARUBA	AW
AUSTRALIA	AU
AUSTRIA	AT
AZERBAIJAN	AZ
BAHAMAS	BS
BAHRAIN	BH
BANGLADESH	BD
BARBADOS	BB
BELARUS	BY
BELGIUM	BE
BELIZE	BZ
BENIN	BJ
BERMUDA	BM
BHUTAN	BT
BOLIVIA	BO
BOSNIA & HERZEGOWINA	BA
BOTSWANA	BW
BOUVET ISLAND	BV
BRAZIL	BR
BRIT. INDIAN OCEAN TERRITORY	IO
BRUNEI ARUSSALAM	BN
BULGARIA	BG
BURKINA FASO	BF
BURUNDI	BI

CAMBODIA	KH	POLYNESIA	PF
CAMEROON	CM	FRENCH SOUTHERN	
CANADA	CA	TERRITORIES	TF
CAPE VERDE	CV	GABON	GA
CAYMAN IS.	KY	GAMBIA	GM
CENTRAL AFRICAN		GEORGIA	GE
REPUBLIC	CF	GERMANY	DE
CHAD	TD	GHANA	GH
CHILE	CL	GIBRALTAR	GI
CHINA	CN	GREECE	GR
CHRISTMAS IS.	CX	GREENLAND	GL
COCOS (KEELING)		GRENADA	GD
ISLANDS	CC	GUADELOUPE	GP
COLOMBIA	CO	GUAM	GU
COMOROS	KM	GUATEMALA	GT
CONGO	CG	GUINEA	GN
COOK ISLANDS	CK	GUINEA-BISSAU	GW
COSTA RICA	CR	GUYANA	GY
COTE D'IVOIRE	CI	HAITI	HT
CROATIA	HR	HEARD &	
CUBA	CU	MC DONALD	
CYPRUS	CY	ISLANDS	HM
CZECH REPUBLIC	CZ	HONDURAS	HN
DENMARK	DK	HONG KONG	HK
DJIBOUTI	DJ	HUNGARY	HU
DOMINICA	DM	ICELAND	IS
DOMINICAN		INDIA	IN
REPUBLIC	DO	INDONESIA	ID
EAST TIMOR	TP	IRAN (ISLAMIC	
ECUADOR	EC	REPUBLIC OF)	IR
EGYPT	EG	IRAQ	IQ
EL SALVADOR	SV	IRELAND	IE
EQUATORIAL		ISRAEL	IL
GUINEA	GQ	ITALY	IT
ERITREA	ER	JAMAICA	JM
ESTONIA	EE	JAPAN	JP
ETHIOPIA	ET	JORDAN	JO
FALKLAND ISLANDS		KAZAKHSTAN	KZ
(MALVINAS)	FK	KENYA	KE
FAROE ISLANDS	FO	KIRIBATI	KI
FIJI	FJ	KOREA,	
FINLAND	FI	DEMOCRATIC	
FRANCE	FR	PEOPLE'S REPUBLIC	
FRANCE,		OF	KP
METROPOLITAN	FX	KOREA, REPUBLIC OF	
FRENCH			KR
GUIANA	GF	KUWAIT	KW
FRENCH		KYRGYZSTAN	KG

LAO PEOPLE'S DEMOCRATIC REPUBLIC	LA
LATVIA	LV
LEBANON	LB
LESOTHO	LS
LIBERIA	LR
LIBYAN ARAB JAMAHIRIYA	LY
LIECHTENSTEIN	LI
LITHUANIA	LT
LUXEMBOURG	LU
MACAU	MO
MACEDONIA, THE FORMER YUGOSLAV REPUBLIC OF	MK
MADAGASCAR	MG
MALAWI	MW
MALAYSIA	MY
MALDIVES	MV
MALI	ML
MALTA	MT
MARSHALL ISLANDS	MH
MARTINIQUE	MQ
MAURITANIA	MR
MAURITIUS	MU
MAYOTTE	YT
MEXICO	MX
MICRONESIA	FM
MOLDOVA	MD
MONACO	MC
MONGOLIA	MN
MONTSERRAT	MS
MOROCCO	MA
MOZAMBIQUE	MZ
MYANMAR	MM
NAMIBIA	NA
NAURU	NR
NEPAL	NP
NETHERLANDS	NL
NETHERLANDS ANTILLES	AN
NEW CALEDONIA	NC
NEW ZEALAND	NZ
NICARAGUA	NI
NIGER	NE
NIGERIA	NG
NIUE	NU
NORFOLK IS.	NF
NORTHERN MARIANA ISLANDS	MP
NORWAY	NO
OMAN	OM
PAKISTAN	PK
PALAU	PW
PANAMA	PA
PAPUA NEW GUINEA	PG
PARAGUAY	PY
PERU	PE
PHILIPPINES	PH
PITCAIRN	PN
POLAND	PL
PORTUGAL	PT
PUERTO RICO	PR
QATAR	QA
REUNION	RE
ROMANIA	RO
RUSSIAN FEDERATION	RU
RWANDA	RW
SAINT KITTS & NEVIS	KN
SAINT LUCIA	LC
SAINT VINCENT & GRENADINES	VC
SAMOA	WS
SAN MARINO	SM
SAO TOME & PRINCIPE	ST
SAUDI ARABIA	SA
SENEGAL	SN
SEYCHELLES	SC
SIERRA LEONE	SL
SINGAPORE	SG
SLOVAKIA	SK
SLOVENIA	SI
SOLOMON ISLANDS	SB
SOMALIA	SO
SOUTH AFRICA	ZA
SOUTH GEORGIA & THE SOUTH SANDWICH ISLANDS	GS

SPAIN	ES	WALLIS & FUTUNA	
SRI LANKA	LK	ISLANDS	WF
ST. HELENA	SH	WESTERN SAHARA	
ST. PIERRE &			EH
MIQUELON	PM	YEMEN	YE
SUDANSD		YUGOSLAVIA	YU
SURINAME	SR	ZAIRE	ZR
SVALBARD & JAN		ZAMBIA	ZM
MAYEN ISLANDS	SJ	ZIMBABWE	ZW
SWAZILAND	SZ		
SWEDEN	SE		
SWITZERLAND	CH		
SYRIA	SY		
TAIWAN	TW		
TAJIKISTAN	TJ		
TANZANIA	TZ		
THAILAND	TH		
TOGO	TG		
TOKELAU	TK		
TONGA	TO		
TRINIDAD &			
TOBAGO	TT		
TUNISIA	TN		
TURKEY	TR		
TURKMENISTAN	TM		
TURKS & CAICOS			
ISLANDS	TC		
TUVALU	TV		
UGANDA	UG		
UKRAINE	UA		
UNITED ARAB			
EMIRATES	AE		
UNITED KINGDOM			
GB			
UNITED STATES	US		
UNITED STATES			
MINOR OUTLYING			
ISLANDS	UM		
URUGUAY	UY		
UZBEKISTAN	UZ		
VANUATU	VU		
VATICAN CITY	VA		
VENEZUELA	VE		
VIET NAM	VN		
VIRGIN ISLANDS			
(BRITISH)	VG		
VIRGIN ISLANDS			
(U.S.)	VI		

U.S. MILITARY INTERNET ABBREVIATIONS

ACOM.MIL	Commander in Chief
AF.MIL	Air Force
ARL.MIL	U.S. Army Research Laboratory
ARMY.MIL	ARMY Signal Command
ARPA.MIL	Advanced Research Projects Agency
ASBCA.MIL	Armed Services
ASSIST.MIL	Defense Information System Agency
BRL.MIL	U.S. Army Ballistic Research Laboratory
CENTCOM.MIL	CENTCOM
DAPS.MIL	Defense Automated Printing Service
DARPA.MIL	Defense Advanced Research Projects Agency
DCAA.MIL	Defense Contract Audit Agency
DECA.MIL	Defense Commissary
DFAS.MIL	Defense Finance and Accounting Service
DIA.MIL	Defense Intelligence Agency
DISA.MIL	DISA Information Systems Center
DLA.MIL	Defense Logistics Agency
DMSO.MIL	Defense Modeling and Simulation Office
DSM.MIL	Defense Systems Management College
DSS.MIL	Defense Security Service
DSWA.MIL	Defense Special Weapons Agency
DTIC.MIL	Defense Technical Information Center
DTRA.MIL	Defense Threat Reduction Agency
EUCOM.MIL	USEUCOM
HPC.MIL	High Performance Computing Modernization Office

IA.MIL	Computer Network Defense
JAST.MIL	Joint Strike Fighter Program
JCS.MIL	Naval Air Warfare Center Aircraft Division
JS.MIL	JSIRMO / Joint Staff
JSC.MIL	DOD Joint Spectrum Center
JSIMS.MIL	JSIMIS Alliance Executive
NAVY.MIL	Navy
NCSC.MIL	National Computer Security Center
NIC.MIL	DOD Network Information Center
NIMA.MIL	National Imagery and Mapping Agency
NIPR.MIL	DOD Network Information Center
NOSC.MIL	Naval Ocean Systems Center
NRO.MIL	National Reconnaissance Office
PACOM.MIL	US Military Pacific Command
PENTAGON.MIL	Single Agency Manager
SOC.MIL	United States Army Special Operations
SOCOM.MIL	US Special Operations Command
SOUTHCOM.MIL	US Southern Command
SPACECOM.MIL	US Space Command
STRATCOM.MIL	US Strategic Command
TRANSCOM.MIL	US Transportation Command
USCG.MIL	US Coast Guard
USMC.MIL	USMC Network Operations Center
USUHS.MIL	Uniformed Services University Health Sciences

CALENDARS

2002 – 2007

2002

2002

JAN
S	M	T	W	T	F	S
		1	2	3	4	5
6	7	8	9	10	11	12
13	14	15	16	17	18	19
20	21	22	23	24	25	26
27	28	29	30	31		

FEB
S	M	T	W	T	F	S
					1	2
3	4	5	6	7	8	9
10	11	12	13	14	15	16
17	18	19	20	21	22	23
24	25	26	27	28		

MAR
S	M	T	W	T	F	S
					1	2
3	4	5	6	7	8	9
10	11	12	13	14	15	16
17	18	19	20	21	22	23
24	25	26	27	28	29	30
31						

APR
S	M	T	W	T	F	S
	1	2	3	4	5	6
7	8	9	10	11	12	13
14	15	16	17	18	19	20
21	22	23	24	25	26	27
28	29	30				

MAY
S	M	T	W	T	F	S
			1	2	3	4
5	6	7	8	9	10	11
12	13	14	15	16	17	18
19	20	21	22	23	24	25
26	27	28	29	30	31	

JUN
S	M	T	W	T	F	S
						1
2	3	4	5	6	7	8
9	10	11	12	13	14	15
16	17	18	19	20	21	22
23	24	25	26	27	28	29
30						

JUL
S	M	T	W	T	F	S
	1	2	3	4	5	6
7	8	9	10	11	12	13
14	15	16	17	18	19	20
21	22	23	24	25	26	27
28	29	30	31			

AUG
S	M	T	W	T	F	S
				1	2	3
4	5	6	7	8	9	10
11	12	13	14	15	16	17
18	19	20	21	22	23	24
25	26	27	28	29	30	31

SEP
S	M	T	W	T	F	S
1	2	3	4	5	6	7
8	9	10	11	12	13	14
15	16	17	18	19	20	21
22	23	24	25	26	27	28
29	30					

OCT
S	M	T	W	T	F	S
		1	2	3	4	5
6	7	8	9	10	11	12
13	14	15	16	17	18	19
20	21	22	23	24	25	26
27	28	29	30	31		

NOV
S	M	T	W	T	F	S
					1	2
3	4	5	6	7	8	9
10	11	12	13	14	15	16
17	18	19	20	21	22	23
24	25	26	27	28	29	30

DEC
S	M	T	W	T	F	S
1	2	3	4	5	6	7
8	9	10	11	12	13	14
15	16	17	18	19	20	21
22	23	24	25	26	27	28
29	30	31				

2003

JAN

S	M	T	W	T	F	S
			1	2	3	4
5	6	7	8	9	10	11
12	13	14	15	16	17	18
19	20	21	22	23	24	25
26	27	28	29	30	31	

FEB

S	M	T	W	T	F	S
						1
2	3	4	5	6	7	8
9	10	11	12	13	14	15
16	17	18	19	20	21	22
23	24	25	26	27	28	

MAR

S	M	T	W	T	F	S
						1
2	3	4	5	6	7	8
9	10	11	12	13	14	15
16	17	18	19	20	21	22
23	24	25	26	27	28	29
30	31					

APR

S	M	T	W	T	F	S
		1	2	3	4	5
6	7	8	9	10	11	12
13	14	15	16	17	18	19
20	21	22	23	24	25	26
27	28	29	30			

MAY

S	M	T	W	T	F	S
				1	2	3
4	5	6	7	8	9	10
11	12	13	14	15	16	17
18	19	20	21	22	23	24
25	26	27	28	29	30	31

JUN

S	M	T	W	T	F	S
1	2	3	4	5	6	7
8	9	10	11	12	13	14
15	16	17	18	19	20	21
22	23	24	25	26	27	28
29	30					

JUL

S	M	T	W	T	F	S
		1	2	3	4	5
6	7	8	9	10	11	12
13	14	15	16	17	18	19
20	21	22	23	24	25	26
27	28	29	30	31		

AUG

S	M	T	W	T	F	S
					1	2
3	4	5	6	7	8	9
10	11	12	13	14	15	16
17	18	19	20	21	22	23
24	25	26	27	28	29	30
31						

SEP

S	M	T	W	T	F	S
	1	2	3	4	5	6
7	8	9	10	11	12	13
14	15	16	17	18	19	20
21	22	23	24	25	26	27
28	29	30				

OCT

S	M	T	W	T	F	S
			1	2	3	4
5	6	7	8	9	10	11
12	13	14	15	16	17	18
19	20	21	22	23	24	25
26	27	28	29	30	31	

NOV

S	M	T	W	T	F	S
						1
2	3	4	5	6	7	8
9	10	11	12	13	14	15
16	17	18	19	20	21	22
23	24	25	26	27	28	29
30						

DEC

S	M	T	W	T	F	S
	1	2	3	4	5	6
7	8	9	10	11	12	13
14	15	16	17	18	19	20
21	22	23	24	25	26	27
28	29	30	31			

2004

JAN
S	M	T	W	T	F	S
				1	2	3
4	5	6	7	8	9	10
11	12	13	14	15	16	17
18	19	20	21	22	23	24
25	26	27	28	29	30	31

FEB
S	M	T	W	T	F	S
1	2	3	4	5	6	7
8	9	10	11	12	13	14
15	16	17	18	19	20	21
22	23	24	25	26	27	28
29						

MAR
S	M	T	W	T	F	S
	1	2	3	4	5	6
7	8	9	10	11	12	13
14	15	16	17	18	19	20
21	22	23	24	25	26	27
28	29	30	31			

APR
S	M	T	W	T	F	S
				1	2	3
4	5	6	7	8	9	10
11	12	13	14	15	16	17
18	19	20	21	22	23	24
25	26	27	28	29	30	

MAY
S	M	T	W	T	F	S
						1
2	3	4	5	6	7	8
9	10	11	12	13	14	15
16	17	18	19	20	21	22
23	24	25	26	27	28	29
30	31					

JUN
S	M	T	W	T	F	S
		1	2	3	4	5
6	7	8	9	10	11	12
13	14	15	16	17	18	19
20	21	22	23	24	25	26
27	28	29	30			

JUL
S	M	T	W	T	F	S
				1	2	3
4	5	6	7	8	9	10
11	12	13	14	15	16	17
18	19	20	21	22	23	24
25	26	27	28	29	30	31

AUG
S	M	T	W	T	F	S
1	2	3	4	5	6	7
8	9	10	11	12	13	14
15	16	17	18	19	20	21
22	23	24	25	26	27	28
29	30	31				

SEP
S	M	T	W	T	F	S
			1	2	3	4
5	6	7	8	9	10	11
12	13	14	15	16	17	18
19	20	21	22	23	24	25
26	27	28	29	30		

OCT
S	M	T	W	T	F	S
					1	2
3	4	5	6	7	8	9
10	11	12	13	14	15	16
17	18	19	20	21	22	23
24	25	26	27	28	29	30
31						

NOV
S	M	T	W	T	F	S
	1	2	3	4	5	6
7	8	9	10	11	12	13
14	15	16	17	18	19	20
21	22	23	24	25	26	27
28	29	30				

DEC
S	M	T	W	T	F	S
			1	2	3	4
5	6	7	8	9	10	11
12	13	14	15	16	17	18
19	20	21	22	23	24	25
26	27	28	29	30	31	

2005

JAN

S	M	T	W	T	F	S
						1
2	3	4	5	6	7	8
9	10	11	12	13	14	15
16	17	18	19	20	21	22
23	24	25	26	27	28	29
30	31					

FEB

S	M	T	W	T	F	S
		1	2	3	4	5
6	7	8	9	10	11	12
13	14	15	16	17	18	19
20	21	22	23	24	25	26
27	28					

MAR

S	M	T	W	T	F	S
		1	2	3	4	5
6	7	8	9	10	11	12
13	14	15	16	17	18	19
20	21	22	23	24	25	26
27	28	29	30	31		

APR

S	M	T	W	T	F	S
					1	2
3	4	5	6	7	8	9
10	11	12	13	14	15	16
17	18	19	20	21	22	23
24	25	26	27	28	29	30

MAY

S	M	T	W	T	F	S
1	2	3	4	5	6	7
8	9	10	11	12	13	14
15	16	17	18	19	20	21
22	23	24	25	26	27	28
29	30	31				

JUN

S	M	T	W	T	F	S
			1	2	3	4
5	6	7	8	9	10	11
12	13	14	15	16	17	18
19	20	21	22	23	24	25
26	27	28	29	30		

JUL

S	M	T	W	T	F	S
					1	2
3	4	5	6	7	8	9
10	11	12	13	14	15	16
17	18	19	20	21	22	23
24	25	26	27	28	29	30
31						

AUG

S	M	T	W	T	F	S
	1	2	3	4	5	6
7	8	9	10	11	12	13
14	15	16	17	18	19	20
21	22	23	24	25	26	27
28	29	30	31			

SEP

S	M	T	W	T	F	S
				1	2	3
4	5	6	7	8	9	10
11	12	13	14	15	16	17
18	19	20	21	22	23	24
25	26	27	28	29	30	

OCT

S	M	T	W	T	F	S
						1
2	3	4	5	6	7	8
9	10	11	12	13	14	15
16	17	18	19	20	21	22
23	24	25	26	27	28	29
30	31					

NOV

S	M	T	W	T	F	S
		1	2	3	4	5
6	7	8	9	10	11	12
13	14	15	16	17	18	19
20	21	22	23	24	25	26
27	28	29	30			

DEC

S	M	T	W	T	F	S
				1	2	3
4	5	6	7	8	9	10
11	12	13	14	15	16	17
18	19	20	21	22	23	24
25	26	27	28	29	30	31

2005

2006

JAN
S	M	T	W	T	F	S
1	2	3	4	5	6	7
8	9	10	11	12	13	14
15	16	17	18	19	20	21
22	23	24	25	26	27	28
29	30	31				

FEB
S	M	T	W	T	F	S
			1	2	3	4
5	6	7	8	9	10	11
12	13	14	15	16	17	18
19	20	21	22	23	24	25
26	27	28				

MAR
S	M	T	W	T	F	S
			1	2	3	4
5	6	7	8	9	10	11
12	13	14	15	16	17	18
19	20	21	22	23	24	25
26	27	28	29	30	31	

APR
S	M	T	W	T	F	S
						1
2	3	4	5	6	7	8
9	10	11	12	13	14	15
16	17	18	19	20	21	22
23	24	25	26	27	28	29
30						

MAY
S	M	T	W	T	F	S
	1	2	3	4	5	6
7	8	9	10	11	12	13
14	15	16	17	18	19	20
21	22	23	24	25	26	27
28	29	30	31			

JUN
S	M	T	W	T	F	S
				1	2	3
4	5	6	7	8	9	10
11	12	13	14	15	16	17
18	19	20	21	22	23	24
25	26	27	28	29	30	

JUL
S	M	T	W	T	F	S
						1
2	3	4	5	6	7	8
9	10	11	12	13	14	15
16	17	18	19	20	21	22
23	24	25	26	27	28	29
30	31					

AUG
S	M	T	W	T	F	S
		1	2	3	4	5
6	7	8	9	10	11	12
13	14	15	16	17	18	19
20	21	22	23	24	25	26
27	28	29	30	31		

SEP
S	M	T	W	T	F	S
					1	2
3	4	5	6	7	8	9
10	11	12	13	14	15	16
17	18	19	20	21	22	23
24	25	26	27	28	29	30

OCT
S	M	T	W	T	F	S
1	2	3	4	5	6	7
8	9	10	11	12	13	14
15	16	17	18	19	20	21
22	23	24	25	26	27	28
29	30	31				

NOV
S	M	T	W	T	F	S
			1	2	3	4
5	6	7	8	9	10	11
12	13	14	15	16	17	18
19	20	21	22	23	24	25
26	27	28	29	30		

DEC
S	M	T	W	T	F	S
					1	2
3	4	5	6	7	8	9
10	11	12	13	14	15	16
17	18	19	20	21	22	23
24	25	26	27	28	29	30
31						

2006

2007

JAN
S	M	T	W	T	F	S
	1	2	3	4	5	6
7	8	9	10	11	12	13
14	15	16	17	18	19	20
21	22	23	24	25	26	27
28	29	30	31			

FEB
S	M	T	W	T	F	S
				1	2	3
4	5	6	7	8	9	10
11	12	13	14	15	16	17
18	19	20	21	22	23	24
25	26	27	28			

MAR
S	M	T	W	T	F	S
				1	2	3
4	5	6	7	8	9	10
11	12	13	14	15	16	17
18	19	20	21	22	23	24
25	26	27	28	29	30	31

APR
S	M	T	W	T	F	S
1	2	3	4	5	6	7
8	9	10	11	12	13	14
15	16	17	18	19	20	21
22	23	24	25	26	27	28
29	30					

MAY
S	M	T	W	T	F	S
		1	2	3	4	5
6	7	8	9	10	11	12
13	14	15	16	17	18	19
20	21	22	23	24	25	26
27	28	29	30	31		

JUN
S	M	T	W	T	F	S
					1	2
3	4	5	6	7	8	9
10	11	12	13	14	15	16
17	18	19	20	21	22	23
24	25	26	27	28	29	30

JUL
S	M	T	W	T	F	S
1	2	3	4	5	6	7
8	9	10	11	12	13	14
15	16	17	18	19	20	21
22	23	24	25	26	27	28
29	30	31				

AUG
S	M	T	W	T	F	S
			1	2	3	4
5	6	7	8	9	10	11
12	13	14	15	16	17	18
19	20	21	22	23	24	25
26	27	28	29	30	31	

SEP
S	M	T	W	T	F	S
						1
2	3	4	5	6	7	8
9	10	11	12	13	14	15
16	17	18	19	20	21	22
23	24	25	26	27	28	29
30						

OCT
S	M	T	W	T	F	S
	1	2	3	4	5	6
7	8	9	10	11	12	13
14	15	16	17	18	19	20
21	22	23	24	25	26	27
28	29	30	31			

NOV
S	M	T	W	T	F	S
				1	2	3
4	5	6	7	8	9	10
11	12	13	14	15	16	17
18	19	20	21	22	23	24
25	26	27	28	29	30	

DEC
S	M	T	W	T	F	S
						1
2	3	4	5	6	7	8
9	10	11	12	13	14	15
16	17	18	19	20	21	22
23	24	25	26	27	28	29
30	31					

2007

SOCIAL SECURITY NUMBER DECODER

The first three numbers of a Social Security Number indicate state of issuance:

001-003	New Hampshire
004-007	Maine
008-009	Vermont
010-034	Massachusetts
035-039	Rhode Island
040-049	Connecticut
050-134	New York
135-158	New Jersey
159-211	Pennsylvania
212-220	Maryland
221-222	Delaware
223-231	Virginia
232-236	West Virginia
232	North Carolina
237-246	North Carolina
247-251	South Carolina
252-260	Georgia
261-267	Florida
268-302	Ohio
303-317	Indiana
318-361	Illinois
362-386	Michigan
387-399	Wisconsin
400-407	Kentucky
408-415	Tennessee
416-424	Alabama
425-428	Mississippi
429-432	Arkansas
433-439	Louisiana
440-448	Oklahoma
449-467	Texas

468-477	Minnesota
478-485	Iowa
486-500	Missouri
501-502	North Dakota
503-504	South Dakota
505-508	Nebraska
509-515	Kansas
516-517	Montana
518-519	Idaho
520	Wyoming
521-524	Colorado
525	New Mexico
526-527	Arizona
528-529	Utah
530	Nevada
531-539	Washington
540-544	Oregon
545-573	California
574	Alaska
575-576	Hawaii
577-579	District of Columbia
580	Virgin Islands
580-584	Puerto Rico
585	New Mexico
586	Guam
586	American Samoa
586	Philippine Islands
587-588	Mississippi
589-595	Florida
596-599	Puerto Rico
600-601	Arizona
602-626	California
627-645	Texas
646-647	Utah
648-649	New Mexico
650-653	Colorado
654-658	South Carolina
659-665	Louisiana
666	Not issued

667-675	Georgia
676-679	Arkansas
680	Nevada
681-690	North Carolina
691-699	Virginia*
700-728	Railroad Retirement
732-763	Not issued
750-751	Hawaii*
752-755	Mississippi*
756-763	Tennessee*
764-765	Arizona
766-772	Florida
773-999	Not issued

Notes

* Numbers allocated but not yet issued as of our publication date

For the latest information on the highest number issued subsets of Social Security Numbers, visit this SSA website *http //www ssa gov/employer/highgroup txt*

Any number beginning with 000 will never be a valid Social Security Number.

Railroad Retirement numbers (700-728) were no longer issued after July 1. 1963

There is now a third taxpayer identification numbering system, called TIPI — Tax Payer Identification Number These numbers are issued by the IRS to parties who may have a federal tax liability, but who are not eligible for a Social Security Number or a Federal Employment Identification Number TIPI's begin with the number 9, and are otherwise in the same configuration as Social Security Numbers. 9XX-XX-XXXX

EMPLOYER IDENTIFICATION NUMBER DECODER

Businesses with employees are required to obtain an Employer Identification Number (EIN). EINs are nine digits long, with the first two digits indicating which IRS district office the number was issued through:

Alabama	Birmingham	63
Alaska	Anchorage	92
Arizona	Phoenix	86
Arkansas	Little Rock	71
California	Laguna Nigel	33
	Los Angeles	95
	Sacramento	68
	San Francisco	94
	San Jose	77
Colorado	Denver	84
Connecticut	Hartford	06
Delaware	Wilmington	51
Florida	Fort Lauderdale	65
	Jacksonville	59
Georgia	Atlanta	58
Hawaii	Honolulu	99
Idaho	Boise	82
Illinois	Chicago	36
	Springfield	37
Indiana	Indianapolis	35
Iowa	Des Moines	42
Kansas	Wichita	48
Kentucky	Louisville	61
Louisiana	New Orleans	72
Maine	Augusta	01
Maryland	Baltimore	52
Massachusetts	Boston	04

Michigan	Detroit	38
Minnesota	St. Paul	41
Mississippi	Jackson	64
Missouri	St. Louis	43
Montana	Helena	81
Nebraska	Omaha	47
Nevada	Las Vegas/Reno	88
New Hampshire	Portsmouth	02
New Jersey	Newark	22
New Mexico	Albuquerque	85
New York	Albany	14
	Brooklyn	11
	Buffalo	16
	Manhattan	13
North Carolina	Greensboro	56
North Dakota	Fargo	45
Ohio	Cincinnati	31
	Cleveland	34
Oklahoma	Oklahoma City	73
Oregon	Portland	93
Pennsylvania	Philadelphia	23
	Pittsburgh	25
Rhode Island	Providence	05
South Carolina	Columbia	57
South Dakota	Aberdeen	46
Tennessee	Nashville	62
Texas	Austin	74
	Dallas	75
	Houston	76
Utah	Salt Lake City	87
Vermont	Burlington	03
Virginia	Richmond	54
Washington	Seattle	91
West Virginia	Parkersburg	55
Wisconsin	Milwaukee	39
Wyoming	Cheyenne	83
Washington, D.C.	Baltimore	52

ANATOMY
OF A
CHECK

Check number

The series of numbers at the bottom of the check is referred to as the *MICR line*, short for *Magnetic Ink Character Recognition*. The MICR line includes the paying bank's ABA (American Banking Association) routing number, the account number of the writer of the check and usually the sequential check number. The dollar amount of the check will be entered on the MICR line by the bank of first deposit as the first step in the processing of the item.

Small type is referred to as the fractional form of the ABA routing number. If the bottom of the check is damaged and the MICR line becomes unreadable, the bank on whom the check was issued can be identified through these numbers.

Amount Field. The dollar amount of the check will be encoded in this area by the bank of first deposit.

Date Code. If present, this optional information indicates the month and year when the account was opened.

Charles Ponzi
123 Scheme St.
Your Town, TX 12345

101
44-44/1199

DATE *April 1, 2002*

PAY *Ponzi Fund for Widows and Orphans* _____ $ | 1000.00/100 |
TO THE

One Thousand Dollars and 00/100 _____ Dollars

06/95

BANK NAME/ADDRESS

Charlie Ponzi

MEMO _____

⑆ 1199 00449 ⑆ 101 ⑈ 9900 33333 ⑈

This 9-digit *Routing Number* may also be referred to as the *Routing and Transit Number* or simply the *ABA Number*. The first 4 digits are the *Fed Routing Symbol*. The first 2 digits identify the Federal Reserve District (see chart, following pages) in which the presentment point of the paying bank is located. A mismatch between the location of the bank and Federal Reserve District could indicate a possible counterfeit check. Digits 5 through 8 constitute the institution identifier and identify the paying institution. The 9th digit is a check digit which allows automated check processing equipment to verify that it has read the first 8 digits correctly. To decode a routing number, see...*ABA ROUTING NUMBERS* in the main book.

This area of the *MICR Line* is used for the printing of the check writer's account number and (usually) the sequential check number and other information. The configuration of this information is not standardized, as it is used only by the paying bank. In this example, the sequential check number is followed by the account number.

FEDERAL RESERVE CODES

01   *Boston*, includes Massachusetts, Maine, New Hampshire, Connecticut, Vermont, Rhode Island.

02   *New York*, includes New York, New Jersey, Connecticut.

03   *Philadelphia*, includes Pennsylvania, Delaware, New Jersey.

04   *Cleveland*, includes Ohio, Pennsylvania, Kentucky, West Virginia.

05   *Richmond*, includes Virginia, Maryland, North Carolina, District of Columbia, South Carolina, West Virginia.

06   *Atlanta*, includes Georgia, Alabama, Florida, Tennessee, Louisiana, Mississippi.

07   *Chicago*, includes Illinois, Michigan, Indiana, Iowa, Wisconsin.

08   *St. Louis*, includes Missouri, Arkansas, Kentucky, Tennessee, Indiana, Illinois, Mississippi

09   *Minneapolis*, includes Minnesota, Montana, North Dakota, South Dakota, Wisconsin, Michigan.

10   *Kansas City*, includes Missouri, Colorado, Oklahoma, Nebraska, Iowa, Wyoming, Kansas, New Mexico.

11   *Dallas*, includes Texas, Arizona, New Mexico, Louisiana.

12   *San Francisco*, includes California, Oregon, Washington, Utah, Hawaii, Alaska, Idaho, Nevada, Arizona.

Note: Other prefixes may be used which indicate any one of a number of special exceptions to the above chart, including checks from thrifts and credit unions, postal money orders and traveler's checks.

LAWFUL BANK ACCOUNT SOURCES

The Financial Privacy Act of 1999 (also known as the Graham-Leach-Bliley Act) made many techniques for obtaining bank account information previously used by private investigators illegal. In essence, the law makes it a federal crime to obtain bank account (and other "financial") information through use of a pretext or "gag." (See following section, "Privacy Law Survival Guide" for more details.)

Not withstanding the new law, there are still lawful methods for obtaining bank account information:

STATUTORY EXEMPTIONS
The law provides limited exemptions to itself. One exempts insurance companies when conducting an insurance investigation into criminal activity, fraud, material misrepresentation or material nondisclosure. Unfortunately though, the law doesn't specifically exempt private investigators working on behalf of insurance companies.

Another exemption relates to child-support enforcement. It allows a state-licensed private investigator to pretext financial information when child-support is delinquent; but only if the pretext has been authorized by a court order. In other words, a deadbeat dad might be warned via a court order that he or his bank is about to be the target of a pretext!

PUBLIC RECORDS
Public records remain a lawful but difficult method for obtaining bank account information.

Let's face it, they're typically far out of date and the debtor would have to be pretty stupid keeping a bank account open that's already appeared in the public record. However, in some cases the target will simply close the publicly known accounts and open new ones at the same institution. This makes lawsuits, divorces, UCC filings and other public records worth a look-see.

A DMV search for vehicle ownership may also be worthwhile as the target of the investigation may have a banking relationship with the vehicle's lien holder. If the lien holder is a credit union, there's a strong probability that the customer will have a depository account at the same institution.

CREDIT REPORTS
Although credit reports don't contain bank account information, they often do contain vital clues about banking relationships. Start in the inquiries section. If the target opened a new checking or savings account, the bank may have run his credit history to verify identity – and left a footprint as an inquiry. In the accounts section of the credit report, check for mortgages and car loans. The customer may also have a checking or saving account at the same institution where he has a home or vehicle loan.

TRASH INSPECTIONS
Dumpster diving remains legal, by case law, not statute, if done properly. The trash must be at the curb; entering private property may constitute invasion of privacy. Be forewarned that some municipalities have local laws prohibiting trash checks.

CASHED CHECKS
Cashed checks made payable to the target of the investigation may provide bank account

information – assuming that the instrument is deposited into the target's bank account and not cashed at a corner liquor store. Rebate gags, formerly used by many P.I.s, are now illegal because they involve a false pretense. However, if the target provides a good or service in kind for the payment, no false pretense is involved. This may be particularly useful when investigating businesses, entrepreneurs and self-employed persons.

SKIPTRACE DEPARTMENTS

Skiptrace departments at companies where the target has charge accounts may also be a viable source of bank account information. Be sure that no pretext is used. If they're in the same boat as you – trying to locate a debtor and/or his bank account – they should be interested in mutual cooperation.

But what if the target has an account with a charge company that isn't delinquent? There is a smooth art to obtaining information this way that a small group of in-the-know P.I.s practice. In essence, they barter favors. They'll still call the skiptrace department and ask for assistance. When told that the customer is in good standing, they'll ask that his or her account information be pulled and in turn a favor is offered. The favor might be an address or court check in the P.I.'s city the next time the charge company's skiptracer needs local assistance.

Of course, if all else fails, consider using the power of subpoena, if available.

THIRD PARTY PRETEXTS

A careful reading of the law suggests that pretexting bank account information from third parties who are *not* financial institutions remains lawful. Although this is likely to only be useful in limited circumstances, it may be viable in certain cases. As an example, a landlord may have a copy of a tenant's rent check that contains bank account information.

SHOTGUN SUBPOENAS

This one is a no-brainer that will require one to burn a fair amount of shoe leather. You'll identify the target's place of residence and business and then serve writs of attachment on every bank and S&L within a five-mile radius. Of course, this assumes that a court judgment is already on the books.

However, this may be easier said then done, depending on which state you are operating in. In California, a writ of attachment is fairly easy to obtain and just requires a filing fee and stamp at the courthouse before becoming valid. In other states, like Texas, you'll need a writ of garnishment which means filing a brand spanking new lawsuit against each bank. If the debtor has no account there, the plaintiff has to pay the bank's legal fees.

PAY DAY SURVEILLANCE

For investigations that are smaller in scope where the subject is a "working person," try a pay day surveillance. Simply tail the subject from work to the bank where he deposits his check. Some advance work will need to be made to determine which day is pay day at the employer. In all likelihood, it will be the second and fourth Friday of the month. Try this one on deadbeat dad cases.

This section adapted from an article by the author which originally appeared in P.I. Magazine. Do you know of other lawful sources or techniques? Please e-mail them to the author at research@crimetime.com.

FINANCIAL INVESTIGATION CHECKLIST

Real Estate Ownership

Vehicle Ownership

Boat/Aircraft Ownership

Business Ownership

Tax Refunds Due

Tax Returns

Stock/Bond Ownership

Retirement Funds

Bank Accounts

Insurance Settlements

Life Insurance Policies

Litigation Settlements

Gambling Winnings

Inheritances

UCC Filings

Accounts Receivable

Foreign Trusts/Accounts

Employment

Art/Collectibles

Government Benefits

Bankruptcies

Tax Liens

Judgments

Professional Licenses

Credit Report

Safe Deposit Boxes

Jewelry

Cash

BACKGROUND INVESTIGATION CHECKLIST

Full Legal Name

Prior Names

Aliases

Social Security Number

Date of Birth

Current Address

Past Addresses

Vehicle/License Plate

Driving History

Litigation History

Criminal History

Sex Offender Check

Bankruptcies

Tax Liens

Judgments

Corporations

Other Business Entities

News Check

Insurance Claims

Associates/Associations

Marital Check

Divorce Check

Internet Check

Death Index Check

UCC Filings

Professional Licenses

Former/Current Employers

Former/Current Neighbors

Former/Current Spouses

Former/Current Partners

Former/Current Landlords

Educational Verification

COMMON PERSONAL IDENTIFIERS

Full Legal Name
Former Names
Aliases
Mother's Maiden Name
Date of Birth
Social Security Number
Driver's License Number
Alien Number
FBI Number
Current Address
Former Addresses
Hair Color
Eye Color
Height/Weight
Tattoos
Physical Abnormalities
Fingerprints
Photograph/Mug Shot

MASTER LIST OF COMMERCIALLY AVAILABLE PUBLIC RECORD DATABASES

Key Codes:

ATXP AutoTrackXP
CPT ChoicePoint
L-N Lexis-Nexis
MER Merlin Information Services

(See *DATABASE PROVIDERS*
for further information.)

NATIONWIDE SEARCHES:

Bankruptcies (L-N, CPT, ATXP, MER)
Tax Liens (L-N, CPT, ATXP)
Judgments (L-N, CPT, ATXP)
Business Credit Reports (L-N, CPT)
Credit Headers (L-N, CPT, ATXP, MER)
DEA Registrants (L-N, ATXP)
Executive Affiliations (L-N)
FAA Pilots (L-N, CPT, ATXP)
FAA Aircraft Ownership By Name (L-N, CPT)
FCC Licenses (L-N, ATXP)
Federal Employer ID Numbers (L-N, CPT, ATXP)
IRS Tax Practitioners & Enrolled Agents (L-N, CPT)
OSHA Inspection Reports (L-N, CPT)
Physician Reports by Medi-Net (CPT)
Reverse Directory Index (CPT)
Significant Shareholders (CPT, ATXP)
SSN Death Records (L-N, CPT, ATXP)
Address Inspector (CPT)
UCC Searches (L-N, CPT, ATXP)
U.S. Coast Guard Vessels (L-N, CPT, ATXP)
U.S. District Civil & Criminal Court Filings (L-N)
Boat Manufacturers (ATXP)
Firearms and Explosives Licenses (ATXP)
Phone Listings (ATXP)
Trademarks (ATXP)
U.S. Military Personnel (ATXP)
Securities Trading (ATXP)
TraceWizard Residential Locator (MER)
TraceWizard Business Locator (MER)
Wingate National PeopleFinder (MER)
National FBNs & New Business Filings (MER)
Probable Carrier (CPT, ATXP)

ALABAMA

Boat Registrations (L-N, ATXP)
Real Property Ownership (L-N, CPT, ATXP)
Fictitious Business Names (L-N)
Motor Vehicle Records (L-N, CPT, ATXP)
Chiropractor Reports (CPT)
Professional Licenses (ATXP)

ALASKA

Boat Registrations (L-N)
Business Licenses (L-N)
Civil Case Filings (L-N)
Criminal Case Filings (L-N)
Fictitious Business Names (L-N)
Fish & Game Licenses (L-N)
Jury Verdicts & Settlements (L-N)
Motor Vehicle Records (L-N, CPT, ATXP)
Permanent Fund Applicants (L-N)
Corporation, LP & LLC Info (L-N, CPT, ATXP)
Real Property Ownership (L-N, CPT, ATXP)
Voter Registrations (L-N)
Chiropractor Reports (CPT)

ARIZONA

Boat Registrations (L-N, ATXP)
Fictitious Business Names – Selected (L-N, CPT)
Liquor Licenses (L-N)
Corporation & LLC Info (L-N, CPT, ATXP)
Real Property Ownership (L-N, CPT, ATXP)
Motor Vehicle Records (CPT)
Chiropractor Reports (CPT)
Federal District Court Searches (CPT)
Superior Court Civil Crim. Filings – Selected (CPT)
Marriage Records Index (CPT)
Maricopa County General Index (CPT)
Professional Licenses (ATXP)

ARKANSAS

Boat Registrations (L-N)
Fictitious Business Name Information (L-N)
Corporation & LLC Info (L-N, CPT, ATXP)
Real Property Ownership (L-N, CPT, ATXP)
Voter Registrations (L-N)
Motor Vehicle Records (CPT)
Chiropractor Reports (CPT)
Professional Licenses (ATXP)

CALIFORNIA

Contractors Licenses (L-N, CPT, MER)
Fictitious Business Names (L-N, CPT, MER)
Liquor Licenses (L-N, MER)
Professional Licenses (L-N, CPT, ATXP, MER)

Real Property Ownership (L-N, CPT, ATXP, MER)
Corporation & LPs (L-N, CPT, ATXP, MER)
Superior Court Civil Cases – Sel. (L-N, CPT, MER)
Superior Court Crim. Cases – Sel. (L-N, CPT, MER)
Municipal Civil Cases – Selected (L-N, CPT)
Municipal Crim. Cases – Selected (L-N, CPT, MER)
Motor Vehicle Records (CPT)
Federal District Court Searches (CPT)
Chiropractor Reports (CPT)
Workers Comp. Appeals Board (CPT)
Marriage Records (CPT, MER)
Death Records (CPT)
State Board of Equalization (CPT, MER)
General Index – Selected (CPT)
UCC Searches (L-N, CPT, ATXP, MER)

COLORADO

Boat Registrations (L-N)
Civil Case Filings (L-N)
Criminal Case Filings (L-N)
Corporation, LP & LLCs (L-N, CPT, ATXP)
State Trademark Information (L-N)
Fictitious Business Names (L-N)
Liquor License (L-N)
Marriage License Records (L-N)
Motor Vehicle Records (L-N, CPT, ATXP)
Real Property Ownership (L-N, CPT, ATXP)
Voter Registrations (L-N)
Professional Licenses (CPT, ATXP)

CONNECTICUT

Boat Registrations (L-N, ATXP)
Criminal Case Filings (L-N, CPT)
Death Records (L-N)
Divorce Records (L-N)
Fictitious Business Names (L-N)
Marriage Licenses (L-N)
Motor Vehicle Records (L-N, ATXP)
Professional Licenses (L-N, CPT)
Corporation, LP & LLCs (L-N, CPT, ATXP)
Real Property Ownership (L-N, CPT, ATXP)
Superior Court Civil Case Index (L-N)
Voter Registrations (L-N)
Chiropractor Reports (CPT)

DELAWARE

Civil Case Filings (L-N)
Fictitious Business Names (L-N)
Motor Vehicle Records (L-N, CPT, ATXP)
Corporation and LPs (L-N, ATXP)
Real Property Ownership (L-N, CPT, ATXP)
Voter Registrations (L-N)
Chiropractor Reports (CPT)
Professional Licenses (ATXP)

DISTRICT OF COLUMBIA

Corporation and LPs (L-N, CPT, ATXP)
Fictitious Business Names (L-N)
Motor Vehicle Records (L-N, ATXP)
Real Property Ownership (L-N, CPT, ATXP)
Voter Registrations (L-N)
Chiropractor Reports (CPT)
Professional Licenses (ATXP)

FLORIDA

Boat Registrations (L-N, ATXP)
Civil Case Filings- Selected (L-N)
Divorce Records (L-N, ATXP)
Fictitious Business Names (L-N, CPT)
Marriage Licenses (L-N, ATXP)
Motor Vehicle Records (L-N, CPT, ATXP)
Professional Licenses (L-N, CPT, ATXP)
Corporation and LPs (L-N, CPT, ATXP)
Real Property Ownership (L-N, CPT, ATXP)
Sweepstakes Registrations (L-N, ATXP)
Incarceration Records (CPT)
Chiropractor Reports (CPT)
Accidents (ATXP)
Attorney Bar Memberships (ATXP)
Banking & Finance Licenses (ATXP)
Beverage Licenses (ATXP)
Boating Citations (ATXP)
Concealed Weapon Permits (ATXP)
Condominiums & Co-ops (ATXP)
Convictions (CPT, ATXP)
Handicap Parking Permits (ATXP)
Hotels & Restaurants (ATXP)
Laboratory Licenses (ATXP)
Medical Malpractices (ATXP)
Professional Claims / Medical & Legal (ATXP)

Salt Water Products (ATXP)
Sexual Predators (ATXP)
Tangible Property (ATXP)
Tobacco Licenses (ATXP)
Unclaimed Property (ATXP)
Worker's Compensation (ATXP)

GEORGIA

Boat Registrations (L-N, ATXP)
Combined Superior Court Civil Filings (L-N)
Divorce Records (L-N)
Fictitious Business Names (L-N)
Marriage Licenses (L-N)
Professional Licenses (L-N)
Corporation and LPs (L-N, CPT, ATXP)
Superior Court Criminal Cases – Selected (L-N)
Real Property Ownership (L-N, CPT, ATXP)
Voter Registrations (L-N)
Chiropractor Reports (CPT)
Residents (ATXP)

HAWAII

Fictitious Business Name Information (L-N)
Real Property Ownership (L-N, CPT, ATXP)
Chiropractor Reports (CPT)

IDAHO

Fictitious Business Names (L-N)
Motor Vehicle Records (L-N, CPT, ATXP)
Corporation and LPs (L-N, ATXP)
Real Property Ownership (L-N, CPT, ATXP)
Chiropractor Reports (CPT)
Professional Licenses (ATXP)

ILLINOIS

Combined Civil Actions – Chicago Area (L-N)
Fictitious Business Names (L-N)
Inmates Index (L-N)
Motor Vehicle Records (L-N, ATXP)
Professional Licenses (L-N)
Corporation Information (L-N, CPT, ATXP)
Real Property Ownership (L-N, CPT, ATXP)
Voter Registrations (L-N)
Chiropractor Reports (CPT)

Professional Licensing Searches (CPT)

INDIANA

Fictitious Business Names (L-N)
Corporation and LPs (L-N, CPT, ATXP)
Real Property Ownership (L-N, CPT, ATXP)
Motor Vehicle Records (CPT)
Chiropractor Reports (CPT)

IOWA

Boat Registrations (L-N, ATXP)
Fictitious Business Names (L-N)
Motor Vehicle Records (L-N, ATXP)
Corporation and LPs (L-N, CPT, ATXP)
Real Property Ownership (L-N, CPT, ATXP)
Chiropractor Reports (CPT)
Professional Licenses (ATXP)

KANSAS

Fictitious Business Names (L-N)
Corporation and LPs (L-N, CPT, ATXP)
Real Property Ownership (L-N, CPT, ATXP)
Voter Registrations (L-N)
Motor Vehicle Records (CPT)
Chiropractor Reports (CPT)
Professional Licenses (ATXP)

KENTUCKY

Boat Registrations (L-N, ATXP)
Death Records (L-N)
Divorce Records (L-N)
Fictitious Business Names (L-N)
Marriage Records (L-N)
Motor Vehicle Records (L-N, CPT, ATXP)
Corporation and LPs (L-N, CPT, ATXP)
Real Property Ownership (L-N, CPT, ATXP)
Chiropractor Reports (CPT)
Professional Licenses (ATXP)

LOUISIANA

Combined Civil Case Filings - Selected (L-N)
Fictitious Business Names (L-N)
Motor Vehicle Records (L-N, CPT, ATXP)

Corporation and LPs (L-N, CPT, ATXP)
Real Property Ownership (L-N, CPT, ATXP)
Chiropractor Reports (CPT)
Professional Licenses (ATXP)

MAINE

Boat Registrations (L-N, ATXP)
Combined Civil Court Filings (L-N)
Fictitious Business Names (L-N)
Motor Vehicle Records (L-N, CPT, ATXP)
Real Property Ownership (L-N)
Corporation and LPs (CPT)
Chiropractor Reports (CPT)
Professional Licenses (ATXP)

MARYLAND

Boat Registrations (L-N, ATXP)
Combined Civil Filings (L-N)
Fictitious Business Names (L-N)
Motor Vehicle Records (L-N, CPT, ATXP)
Corporation, LP & LLC (L-N, CPT, ATXP)
Real Property Ownership (L-N, CPT, ATXP)
Chiropractor Reports (CPT)
Professional Licenses (ATXP)

MASSACHUSETTS

Boat Registrations (L-N, ATXP)
Combined Civil Filings - Selected (L-N)
Fictitious Business Names (L-N)
Motor Vehicle Records (L-N, CPT, ATXP)
Professional Licenses (L-N, ATXP)
Real Property Ownership (L-N, CPT, ATXP)
Corporation & LPs (L-N, CPT, ATXP)
Chiropractor Reports (CPT)

MICHIGAN

Boat Registrations (L-N, ATXP)
Corporation and LPs (L-N, CPT, ATXP)
Fictitious Business Names (L-N)
Inmates Index (L-N)
Motor Vehicle Records (L-N, CPT, ATXP)
Professional Licenses (L-N, CPT)
Real Property Ownership (L-N, CPT, ATXP)
Voter Registrations (L-N)

Chiropractor Reports (CPT)

MINNESOTA

Boat Registrations (L-N, ATXP)
Fictitious Business Names (L-N)
Liquor Licenses (L-N)
Motor Vehicle Records (L-N, CPT, ATXP)
Corporation and LPs (L-N, CPT, ATXP)
Real Property Ownership (L-N, CPT, ATXP)
Voter Registrations (L-N)
Chiropractor Reports (CPT)
Professional Licenses (ATXP)

MISSISSIPPI

Boat Registrations (L-N, ATXP)
Driver License Records (L-N)
Fictitious Business Names (L-N)
Motor Vehicle Records (L-N, CPT, ATXP)
Corporation and LPs (L-N, CPT, ATXP)
Real Property Ownership (L-N, CPT, ATXP)
Chiropractor Reports (CPT)
Professional Licenses (ATXP)

MISSOURI

Boat Registrations (L-N, ATXP)
Fictitious Business Names (L-N)
Motor Vehicle Records (L-N, CPT, ATXP)
Corporation and LPs (L-N, CPT, ATXP)
Real Property Ownership (L-N, CPT, ATXP)
Voter Registrations (L-N)
Chiropractor Reports (CPT)
Professional Licenses (ATXP)

MONTANA

Boat Registrations (L-N, ATXP)
Fictitious Business Names (L-N)
Motor Vehicle Records (L-N, CPT, ATXP)
Corporation and LPs (L-N, CPT)
Real Property Ownership (L-N, CPT, ATXP)
Professional Licenses (ATXP)

NEBRASKA

Boat Registrations (L-N, ATXP)
Fictitious Business Names (L-N)
Gaming Licenses (L-N)
Lottery Sales Agents (L-N)
Motor Vehicle Records (L-N, CPT, ATXP)
Professional Licenses (L-N)
Corporation and LPs (L-N, CPT, ATXP)
Real Property Ownership (L-N, CPT, ATXP)
Chiropractor Reports (CPT)

NEVADA

Boat Registrations (L-N, ATXP)
Fictitious Business Names (L-N)
Motor Vehicle Records (L-N, CPT, ATXP)
Corporation and LPs (L-N, CPT, ATXP)
Real Property Ownership (L-N, CPT, ATXP)
Chiropractor Reports (CPT)
Marriage Records (CPT)
Divorce Records (CPT)
Professional Licenses (ATXP)

NEW HAMPSHIRE

Boat Registrations (L-N, ATXP)
Motor Vehicle Records (L-N, ATXP)
Fictitious Business Names (L-N)
Lottery Sales Agents (L-N)
Corporation and LPs (L-N, CPT, ATXP)
Real Property Ownership (L-N)
Chiropractor Reports (CPT)
Professional Licenses (ATXP)

NEW JERSEY

Combined Civil Filings (L-N)
Fictitious Business Names (L-N)
Gaming Industry Records (L-N)
Liquor Licenses (L-N)
Professional Licenses (L-N)
Real Property Ownership (L-N, CPT, ATXP)
Motor Vehicle Records (CPT)
Corporation and LP Searches (CPT)
Professional Licensing Searches (CPT)
Chiropractor Reports (CPT)

NEW MEXICO

Fictitious Business Names (L-N)
Motor Vehicle Records (L-N, CPT)
Corporation & LLC Information (L-N)
Real Property Ownership (L-N, CPT, ATXP)
Chiropractor Reports (CPT)
Professional Licenses (ATXP)

NEW YORK

Boat Registrations (L-N)
Combined Civil Court Filings – Selected (L-N)
Co. Supreme Court Ind. No. Purchases (L-N, CPT)
Corporation and LPs (L-N, CPT, ATXP)
Liquor Licenses (L-N)
Lottery Sales Agents (L-N)
Motor Vehicle Records (L-N, CPT, ATXP)
Issuers' Allocation Percentages (L-N)
Supreme Court Civil Suits – Selected (L-N)
Real Property Ownership (L-N, CPT, ATXP)
Voter Registrations (L-N)
NYC Cooperatives (L-N)
Judgment Docket & Lien Book (CPT)
Residents (Through 1995) (ATXP)

NORTH CAROLINA

Boat Registrations (L-N, ATXP)
Fictitious Business Names (L-N)
Professional Licenses (L-N)
Corporation and LPs (L-N, CPT, ATXP)
Real Property Ownership (L-N, CPT, ATXP)
Voter Registrations (L-N)
Motor Vehicle Records (CPT)
Chiropractor Reports (CPT)
Professional Licenses (ATXP)

NORTH DAKOTA

Boat Registrations (L-N, ATXP)
Fictitious Business Names (L-N)
Corporation and LPs (L-N, CPT, ATXP)
Real Property Searches (CPT, ATXP)
Motor Vehicle Records (CPT, ATXP)
Chiropractor Reports (CPT)
Professional Licenses (ATXP)

OHIO

Boat Registrations (L-N, ATXP)
Civil Case Filings – Montgomery County (L-N)
Criminal Case Filings – Montgomery County (L-N)
Fictitious Business Names (L-N)
Inmates Index (L-N)
Liquor Licenses (L-N)
Lottery Sales Agents (L-N)
Motor Vehicle Records (L-N, ATXP)
Professional Licenses (L-N, CPT, ATXP)
Corporation and LPs (L-N, CPT, ATXP)
Real Property Ownership (L-N, CPT, ATXP)
Voter Registrations (L-N)
Chiropractor Reports (CPT)
Residents (ATXP)

OKLAHOMA

Fictitious Business Names (L-N)
Motor Vehicle Records (L-N)
Corporation and LPs (L-N, CPT, ATXP)
Real Property Ownership (L-N, CPT, ATXP)
Voter Registrations (L-N)
Professional Licenses (ATXP)

OREGON

Boat Registrations (L-N, ATXP)
Civil Case Filings (L-N)
Criminal Case Filings (L-N)
Fictitious Business Names (L-N)
Lottery Sales Agents (L-N)
Motor Vehicle Records (L-N, CPT, ATXP)
Corporation and LPs (L-N, CPT, ATXP)
Real Property Ownership (L-N, CPT, ATXP)
Voter Registrations (L-N)
Chiropractor Reports (CPT)
Liquor Licenses (ATXP)
Professional Licenses (ATXP)

PENNSYLVANIA

Combined Civil Case Filings – Selected (L-N)
Corporation and LPs (L-N, CPT, ATXP)
Fictitious Business Names (L-N)
Liquor Licenses (L-N)
Philadelphia Common Pleas Civil (L-N, CPT)

Professional Licenses (L-N,CPT, ATXP)
Real Property Ownership (L-N, CPT, ATXP)
State Trademarks (L-N)
Voter Registrations (L-N)
Chiropractor Reports (CPT)

RHODE ISLAND

Fictitious Business Names (L-N)
Corporation and LPs (L-N, CPT, ATXP)
Real Property Ownership (L-N, CPT, ATXP)
Voter Registrations (L-N)
Chiropractor Reports (CPT)
Professional Licenses (ATXP)

SOUTH CAROLINA

Boat Registrations (L-N, ATXP)
Fictitious Business Names (L-N)
Inmates Index (L-N)
Motor Vehicle Records (L-N, ATXP)
Real Property Ownership (L-N, CPT, ATXP)
Corporation and LPs (L-N, CPT, ATXP)
Chiropractor Reports (CPT)
Professional Licenses (ATXP)

SOUTH DAKOTA

Fictitious Business Names (L-N)
Corporation and LPs (L-N, CPT, ATXP)
Chiropractor Reports (CPT)
Professional Licenses (ATXP)

TENNESSEE

Boat Registrations (L-N, ATXP)
Criminal Case Index (L-N)
Fictitious Business Names (L-N)
Motor Vehicle Records (L-N, CPT, ATXP)
Corporation and LPs (L-N, CPT, ATXP)
Real Property Ownership (L-N, CPT, ATXP)
Chiropractor Reports (CPT)

TEXAS

Boat Registrations (ATXP)
Criminal Convictions Database (L-N, CPT, ATXP)
Criminal Case Filings – Sel. (L-N, CPT, ATXP)

Civil Case Filings – Selected (L-N, CPT, ATXP)
Fictitious Business Names (L-N, CPT)
Inmates Index (L-N)
Liquor Licenses (L-N, ATXP)
Lottery Sales Agents (L-N)
Motor Vehicle Records (L-N, CPT, ATXP)
Professional Licenses (L-N)
Corporation and LPs (L-N, CPT, ATXP)
Real Property Ownership (L-N, CPT, ATXP)
Sexual Offender Registrations (L-N)
Voter Registrations (L-N, ATXP)
Sales and Franchise Taxes (CPT)
Chiropractor Reports (CPT)
Death Records (CPT)
Divorce Records (CPT)
Marriage Records (CPT, ATXP)
Trademarks (ATXP)

UTAH

Boat Registrations (L-N, ATXP)
Fictitious Business Names (L-N)
Motor Vehicle Records (L-N, CPT, ATXP)
Corporation and LPs (L-N, CPT, ATXP)
Real Property Ownership (L-N, CPT, ATXP)
Voter Registrations (L-N)
Chiropractor Reports (CPT)

VERMONT

Fictitious Business Names (L-N)
Corporation Information (L-N, CPT, ATXP)
Real Property Ownership (L-N, ATXP)
Motor Vehicle Records (CPT)
Chiropractor Reports (CPT)

VIRGINIA

Boat Registrations (L-N, ATXP)
Fictitious Business Names (L-N)
Liquor Licenses (L-N)
Parolees (L-N)
Professional Licenses (L-N)
Corporation and LPs (L-N, CPT, ATXP)
Real Property Ownership (L-N, CPT, ATXP)
Motor Vehicle Records (CPT)
Chiropractor Reports (CPT)

WASHINGTON

Civil Case Filings (L-N)
Criminal Case Filings (L-N)
Fictitious Business Names (L-N)
Liquor License (L-N)
Corporation and LPs (L-N, CPT, ATXP)
Real Property Ownership (L-N, CPT, ATXP)
Voter Registrations (L-N)
Workers Compensation Decisions (L-N)
Motor Vehicle Records (CPT)
Chiropractor Reports (CPT)

WEST VIRGINIA

Boat Registrations (L-N, ATXP)
Motor Vehicle Records (L-N, ATXP)
Fictitious Business Names (L-N)
Corporation Information (L-N, CPT, ATXP)
Real Property Ownership (L-N, CPT, ATXP)
Chiropractor Reports (CPT)

WISCONSIN

Boat Registrations (L-N, ATXP)
Corporation & Partnership Data (L-N, CPT, ATXP)
Fictitious Business Names (L-N)
Motor Vehicle Records (L-N, CPT, ATXP)
Professional Licenses (L-N)
Real Property Ownership (L-N, CPT, ATXP)
Professional Licenses (CPT)
Chiropractor Reports (CPT)

WYOMING

Fictitious Business Names (L-N)
Motor Vehicle Records (L-N, ATXP)
Corporation and LPs (L-N, CPT, ATXP)
Real Property Ownership (L-N, CPT, ATXP)

FOREIGN SEARCHES:

Australian Aircraft Registrations (L-N)
Austria Aircraft Registrations (L-N)
Belgium Aircraft Registrations (L-N)
Bermuda Aircraft Registrations (L-N)
Brazilian Aircraft Registrations (L-N)
Brazilian Companies Information (L-N)

Brazilian Company Board of Directors (L-N)
Brazilian Company Directory (L-N)
Brazilian Company Properties Info (L-N)
Brazilian Company Shareholder Info (L-N)
Brazilian Company Subsidiaries Info (L-N)
Brazilian People Finder (L-N)
Brazilian Private Company Info (L-N)
Canada Aircraft Registrations (L-N)
Canada – Federal Court (L-N)
Colombia Aircraft Registrations (L-N)
Denmark Aircraft Registrations (L-N)
France Aircraft Registrations (L-N)
Germany Aircraft Registrations (L-N)
Ireland Aircraft Registrations (L-N)
Italy Aircraft Registrations (L-N)
Latin American Company Database (L-N)
Liechtenstein Aircraft Registrations (L-N)
Luxembourg Aircraft Registrations (L-N)
Monaco Aircraft Registrations (L-N)
Netherland Aircraft Registrations (L-N)
New Zealand Aircraft Registrations (L-N)
Northern Mariana Islands District Cases (L-N)
Norway Aircraft Registrations (L-N)
Ontario, Canada Deed Transfers (L-N)
Ontario, Canada Tax Assessor Records (L-N)
Portugal Aircraft Registrations (L-N)
Sweden Aircraft Registrations (L-N)
Switzerland Aircraft Registrations (L-N)
United Kingdom Aircraft Registrations (L-N)
United Kingdom Company Information (L-N)
United Kingdom Disqualified Company Directors
Info (L-N)

For information on current availability of databases, contact the individual database providers. (See *DATABASE PROVIDERS* for contact information.) "Nationwide" searches are available in all or nearly all states. All counties are not available in certain states. "Real Property Ownership" may include tax assessor records, deed transfers and/or mortgage records. "Motor Vehicle Records" may include vehicle registrations and/or drivers license records. Some states, such as California, require registration and approval by state DMV prior to accessing these records.

PACER: MISSING COURTS

PACER, the nationwide index system for federal civil, criminal and bankruptcy courts includes most but not all jurisdictions. Here are the "Missing Courts":

Court of Appeals

U.S. Court of Appeals, 11th Circuit
U.S. Court of Appeals, Federal Court
U.S. Court of Appeals, 5th Circuit
U.S. Court of Appeals, 2nd Circuit
U.S. Court of Appeals, 7th Circuit

Bankruptcy Courts

Florida Middle - Jacksonville
Florida Middle - Orlando
Florida Middle - Tampa
Georgia Southern - Augusta
Georgia Southern - Savannah
Guam
Idaho
Indiana Southern
Montana
Northern Mariana Islands
Tennessee Middle
Virgin Islands - Consolidated
Virginia Eastern - Alexandria
Virginia Eastern - Norfolk
Virginia Eastern - Richmond
Virginia Eastern - Newport News

District Courts

Alaska
Arkansas Western
Guam
Idaho
Indiana Southern
Nevada
Northern Mariana Islands

*Source: Pacer website, http://pacer.psc.
uscourts.gov/*

INTERNATIONAL BUSINESS TYPE ABBREVIATIONS

In the United States, common business type abbreviations would be *Co., Inc.* and *Corp.* Here is a non-exhaustive list of business type abbreviations from other countries.

A. en P.	Mexico
AB	Sweden, Finland
A.C.	Mexico
ACE	Portugal
AD	Bulgaria
AE	Greece
AG	Austria, Germany, Switzerland
AL	Norway
AmbA	Denmark
ANS	Norway
Apb	Finland
ApS	Denmark
ApS & Co. K/S	Denmark
AS	Norway
A/S	Denmark
ASA	Norway
Bpk	South Africa
B.V.	Belgium, Netherlands, Netherlands Antilles
BVBA	Belgium
CA	Ecuador
C.V.	Netherlands
CVA	Belgium
CvoA	Netherlands
DA	Norway
EE	Greece
EEG	Austria
ELP	Bahamas
EPE	Greece

EURL	France
e.V.	Germany
GbR	Germany
GCV	Belgium
GesmbH	Austria
GIE	France
GmbH & Co. KG	Germany
GmbH	Austria, Germany, Switzerland
HB	Sweden
hf	Iceland
IBC	Various Caribbean
I/S	Denmark
KA/S	Denmark
Kb	Sweden, Finland
KDA	Bulgaria
k.d.d.	Slovenia
Kft	Hungary
KG	Austria, Germany
KGaA	Germany
KK	Japan
Kkt	Hungary
Kol. Srk	Turkey
Kom. Srk	Turkey
K/S	Denmark
KS	Norway
Kv	Hungary
Ky	Finland
Lda	Portugal
LDC	Bahamas
Ltd	United Kingdom, Japan
NT	Canada
NV	Netherlands, Netherlands Antilles, Belgium,
OE	Greece
OHG	Austria, Germany
Oy	Finland
OYJ	Finland
P/L	Australia
PC Ltd	Australia

PLC	United Kingdom, Ireland
PMA	Indonesia
PMDN	Indonesia
PrC	Ireland
PT	Indonesia
Pty.	Australia, South Africa
Rt	Hungary
S. de R.L.	Mexico
S. en C.	Colombia, Peru
S. en N.C.	Mexico
S/A	Brazil
S.A.	Brazil
SA	Belgium, France, Greece, Luxembourg, Mexico, Poland, Portugal, Romania
sa	Italy
SA de CV	Mexico
SApA	Italy
Sarl	France, Luxembourg
SAS	Italy
SC	France, Poland
S.C.	Spain
SCA	Belgium, Romania
SCP	Brazil
SCS	Belgium, France, Romania
S.C.S.	Brazil
SENC	Luxembourg
SGPS	Portugal
SK	Poland
SNC	France, Italy, Romania, Spain
SOPARFI	Luxembourg
sp	France
SpA	Italy
SPRL	Belgium
Sp. z.o.o.	Poland
Srl	Chile, Italy, Spain,

	Romania, Mexico
TLS	Turkey
VOF	Netherlands

ANATOMY
OF A
VIN

(Vehicle Identification Number)

In 1981 VINs were standardized at a length of 17 characters. By decoding the 17 characters, vehicle manufacturer, country of origin, model year and other information can be gleaned. (See code charts, following pages.)

VINs include zeros and the number one, but not the letters "o" (as in ocean) or "l" (as in linen).

VINs can be found at several places on most vehicles. Nearly all passenger vehicles manufactured since 1970 have a VIN plate on the driver's side dashboard, visible from outside the windshield.

First character identifies the country of origin. Most common countries: USA (1 or 4), Japan (J), Canada (2), Mexico (3), Korea (K), England (S), Germany (W), Italy (Z). In this example, the first character is "J," indicating the car to be Japanese. Collectively, the first three characters are also referred to as the World Manufacturer Code.

The third character identifies vehicle type or manufacturing division.

The 10th character identifies model year. (See chart.) In this example, the "T" denotes 1996.

Last 6 characters identify the production number of the vehicle.

The 11th place identifies assembly plant.

The 4th through 8th positions identify vehicle features such as body style, restraint system, engine, etc.

J T 2 B F 1 2 K 0 T 0 1 4 6 5 3 6

The second character identifies the vehicle maker. See chart, next page. In this example, the "T" stands for Toyota.

The 9th position is a check digit.

Manufacturer Codes
(2nd Character)

Cars:

Audi	A
BMW	B
Buick	4
Cadillac	6
Chevrolet	1
Chrysler	C
Dodge	B
Ford	F
GM Canada	7
General Motors	G
Honda	H
Jaguar	A
Lincoln	L
Mercedes Benz	D
Mercury	M
Nissan	N
Oldsmobile	3
Pontiac	2 or 5
Plymouth	P
Saturn	8
Toyota	T
VW	V
Volvo	V

World Manufacturer Codes
(First 3 VIN Characters)

Popular Heavy Duty Trucks:

Freightliner	1FU
Isuzu	JAL
Kenworth	1XK
Mack	1M1
Mercedes Benz	1MB
Mitsubishi	JW6
Navistar/International	1HT
Nissan	JNA
Peterbilt	1XP

Popular Heavy Duty Trailers:

Freuhauf	1H2
Great Dane	1GR
Trail King	1TK
Trailmobile	1PT
Utility	1UY

Model Year Code
(10th Character)

Year	Code	Year	Code	Year	Code
1971	1	1981	B	1991	M	2001	1
1972	2	1982	C	1992	N	2002	2
1973	3	1983	D	1993	P	2003	3
1974	4	1984	E	1994	R	2004	4
1975	5	1985	F	1995	S	2005	5
1976	6	1986	G	1996	T	2006	6
1977	7	1987	H	1997	V	2007	7
1978	8	1988	J	1998	W	2008	8
1979	9	1989	K	1999	X	2009	9
1980	A	1990	L	2000	Y	2010	A

NCIC VEHICLE MANUFACTURER CODES

Passenger Cars & Light Trucks

Acura	ACUR
AM General (Hummer)	AMGN
Audi	AUDI
BMW	BMW
Buick	BUIC
Cadillac	CADI
Chevrolet	CHEV
Chrysler	CHRY
Daewoo	DAEW
Dodge	DODG
Eagle	EGIL
Ferrari	FERR
Ford	FORD
Geo	GEO
GM/Canada	PONI
Honda	HONDA
Hyundai	HYUN
Infiniti	INFI
Isuzu	ISU
Jaguar	JAGU
Kia	KIA
Lamborghini	LAMO
Land Rover	LNDR
Lexus	LEXS
Lincoln	LINC
Lotus	LOTU
Mazda	MAZD
Mercedes Benz	MERZ
Mercury	MERC
Mitsubishi	MITS
Nissan	NISS
Oldsmobile	OLDS
Plymouth	PLYM
Pontiac	PONT

Porsche	PORS
Rolls Royce	ROL
Saab	SAAB
Saturn	STRN
Subaru	SUBA
Suzuki	SUZI
Toyota	TOYT
Volkswagen	VOLK
Volvo	VOLV

Motorcycles

Aprilia	APRI
BMW	BMW
Buell	BUEL
Ducati	DUCA
Harley-Davidson	HD
Honda	HOND
Kawasaki	KAWK
Suzuki	SUZI
Triumph	TRUM
Yamaha	YAMA

Medium & Heavy Duty Trucks

Crane Carrier Co.	CCC
Ford	FORD
Freightliner	FHRT
General Motors	GMC
Hino	HINO
International	INTL
Isuzu	ISU
Kenworth	KW
Mack	MACK
Mitsubshi Fuso	MIFU
Navistar	NAVI
Peterbilt	PTRB
Sterling	STRG
UD Truck	NDMC
Volvo	VOLV
Western Star Trucks	WSTR

Truck Trailers

Benson	BENS
City	CITY
Clement	CLEM
Cobra	COBR
Dorsey	DORS
Eager Beaver	EAGR
East	EAST
Fontaine	FONA
Fruehauf	FRUE
Great Dane	GDAN
Heil	HEIL
Kayln Siebert	KALY
Kentucky	KENT
Lufkin	LUFK
Pines	PINE
Ravens	RAVE
Stroughton	STOU
Strick	STRI
Summit	SUMT
Trail King	TRLK
Trailmobile	TRIM
Transcraft	TRAO
Utility	UTIL
Wabash National	WANC
Walker	WALK

Off-Road Equipment
(includes construction and farm equipment)

JI Case	CASE
Caterpillar	CAT
Daewoo	DAEW
Grove Crane	GROV
Ingersoll Rand	INGS
JCB Inc.	JCBE
John Deere	DEER
Komatsu	KOMA
Kubota	KUBO
Melroe Bobcat	MELR
New Holland	NEWH

DRIVERS LICENSE FORMATS

N=number L=Letter
SSN=Social Security Number

Alabama	NNNNNNN
Alaska	N or NN or NNN or NNNN
	or NNNNN or NNNNNN
	or NNNNNNN
Arizona	LNNNNNNNN or SSN
Arkansas	NNNNNNNNN or SSN
California	LNNNNNNNN
Colorado	NNNNNNNNN
	Old: LN or LNN or LNNN
	or LNNNN or LNNNNN
	or LNNNNNN
Connecticut	NNNNNNNNN
Delaware	N or NN or NNN or NNNN
	or NNNNN or NNNNNN
	or NNNNNNN
D.C.	NNNNNNN (permit) or SSN
Florida	LNNNNNNNNNNNN
Georgia	NNNNNNN or NNNNNNNN
	or NNNNNNNNN or SSN
Hawaii	HNNNNNNNN (new)
	or NNNNNNNNN or SSN
Idaho	LLNNNNNNL
	or NNNNNNNNN (old)
Illinois	LNNNNNNNNNNNN
Indiana	NNNNNNNNNN
Iowa	NNNLLNNNN or SSN
Kansas	KNNNNNNNN
Kentucky	LNNNNNNNN or SSN
Louisiana	00NNNNNNN
Maine	NNNNNNN or NNNNNNNX
Maryland	LNNNNNNNNNNNN
Massachusetts	LNNNNNNNN or SSN
Michigan	LNNNNNNNNNNNN
Minnesota	LNNNNNNNNNNNN
Mississippi	NNNNNNNNN or SSN
Missouri	LNNNNN or LNNNNNN
	or LNNNNNNN or LNNNNNNNN
	or LNNNNNNNNN
	or NNNNNNNNN or SSN
Montana	NNNNNNNNNNNNNN
	or LNNNNNNNN or SSN
Nebraska	LN or LNN or LNNN or LNNNN

	or LNNNNN or LNNNNNN
	or LNNNNNNN or LNNNNNNNN
Nevada	NNNNNNNNNN
	or NNNNNNNNNNNNN (old)
New Hampshire	NNLLLNNNNN
New Jersey	LNNNNNNNNNNNNNNN
New Mexico	NNNNNNNNN
New York	NNNNNNNNN
North Carolina	N or NN or NNN or NNNN
	or NNNNN or NNNNNN or
	NNNNNNN or NNNNNNNN
North Dakota	NNNNNNNNN or SSN
Ohio	LLNNNNNN
Oklahoma	NNNNNNNNN or SSN
Oregon	usually NNNNNNN but can be
	N or NN or NNN or NNNN
	or NNNNN or NNNNNN or
	NNNNNNN or NNNNNNNN
Pennsylvania	NNNNNNNN
Rhode Island	NNNNNNN or VNNNNNN
South Carolina	NNNNNNNNN
South Dakota	NNNNNNNNN or SSN
Tennessee	NNNNNNNNN
	or NNNNNNN or NNNNNNNN
Texas	NNNNNNNN
Utah	NNNNNNNNN but can be NNNN
	or NNNNN or NNNNNN or
	NNNNNNN or NNNNNNNN or
	NNNNNNNNN or NNNNNNNNNN
Vermont	NNNNNNNN or NNNNNNNA
Virginia	TNNNNNNNN or SSN
Washington	LLLLLLLNNNNN or
	LLLLLLLNNNLL or
	LLLLLLLNNNLN or
	LLLLLLLNNNNL
West Virginia	LNNNNNN or 1LNNNNN or
	XXNNNNN or NNNNNNN
Wisconsin	LNNNNNNNNNNNNNN
Wyoming	NNNNNNNNN

Source: The MVR Book, reprinted by permission from BRB Publications, Inc.

NFPA* HAZARDOUS MATERIAL SYMBOLS

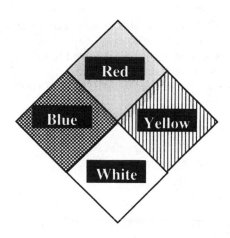

Red—Flammability

4 — **Danger** Flammable Gas or extremely flammable liquid.

3 — **Warning** Flammable liquid flash point below 100° F.

2 — **Caution** Combustible liquid flash point of 100° to 200° F.

1 — Combustible if heated.

0 — Not combustible.

Blue —Health

4 — **Danger** May be fatal on short exposure. Specialized protection equipment required.

3 — **Warning** Corrosive or toxic. Avoid skin contact or inhalation.

2 — **Warning** May be harmful if inhaled or absorbed.

1 — **Caution** May be harmful if inhaled or absorbed.

Yellow — Reactivity

4 — **Danger** Explosive material at room temperature.

3 — **Danger** May be explosive if shocked, heated under confinement or mixed with water.

2 — **Warning** Unstable or may react violently if mixed with water.

1 — **Caution** May react if heated or mixed with water but not violently.

0 — **Stable** Not reactive when mixed with water.

White — Special Notice Key

W — Water reactive

OX — Oxidizing agent

Special Precaution Symbols:

Poison!

Flammable!

Corrosive!

Explosive!

* National Fire Protection Association

PHONETICS

A "Adam"
B "Boy"
C "Charlie"
D "David"
E "Edward"
F "Frank"
G "George"
H "Harry"
I "Ida"
J "John"
K "King"
L "Lincoln"
M "Mary"
N "Nora"
O "Ocean"
P "Peter"
Q "Queen"
R "Robert"
S "Sam"
T "Tom"
U "Union"
V "Victor"
W "Walter"
X "X Ray"
Y "Young"
Z "Zebra"

26 WARNING SIGNS OF ELECTRONIC EAVESDROPPING

1. Others know your confidential business or professional trade secrets.

2. Secret meetings and bids seem to be less than secret.

3. People seem to know your activities when they shouldn't.

4. You have noticed strange sounds or volume changes on your phone lines.

5. You have noticed static, popping or scratching on your phone lines.

6. Sounds are coming from your phone's handset when it's hung up.

7. Your phone often rings and nobody is there, or a very faint tone, or high pitched squeal/beep is heard for a fraction of a second.

8. You can hear a tone on your line when your phone is on the hook (by using an external amplifier).

9. Your AM/FM radio has suddenly developed strange interference.

10. Your car radio suddenly starts "getting weird."

11. Your television has suddenly developed strange interference.

12. You have been the victim of a burglary, but nothing was taken.

13. Electrical wall plates appear to have been moved slightly or jarred.

14. A dime-sized discoloration has suddenly appeared on the wall or ceiling.

15. One of your vendors just gave you any type of electronic device such as a desk radio, alarm clock, lamp, small TV, boom box, CD player and so on.

16. A small bump or deformation has appeared on the vinyl baseboard near the floor.

17. The smoke detector, clock, lamp or exit sign in your office or home looks slightly crooked, has a small hole in the surface, or has a quasi reflective surface.

18. Certain types of items have "just appeared" in your office of home, but nobody seems to know how they got there.

19. White dry-wall dust or debris is noticed on the floor next to the wall.

20. You notice small pieces of ceiling tiles, or "grit" on the floor, or on the surface area of your desk.

21. You notice that "Phone Company" trucks and utilities workers are spending a lot of time near your home or office doing repair work.

22. Telephone, cable, plumbing or air conditioning repair people show up to do work when no one called them.

23. Service or delivery trucks are often parked nearby with nobody (you can see) in them.

24. Your door locks suddenly don't "feel right," they suddenly start to get "sticky" or they completely fail.

25. Furniture has been moved slightly and no one knows why.

26. Things "seem" to have been rummaged through, but nothing is missing (at least that you noticed).

Provided by and used with the permission of James M. Atkinson, Granite Island Group. For further information, visit his website at www.tscm.com.

STATE LAWS: RECORDING PHONE CALLS

Federal law prohibits the recording of a phone call in nearly all circumstances unless at least one party to the call consents to the recording. However, some states require all parties to the call provide their consent.

Alabama	One
Alaska	One
Arizona	One
Arkansas	One
California	All
Colorado	One
Connecticut	All
Delaware	All
District of Columbia	One
Florida	All
Georgia	One
Hawaii	One
Idaho	One
Illinois	All
Indiana	One
Iowa	One
Kansas	One
Kentucky	One
Louisiana	One
Maine	One
Maryland	All

Massachusetts	All
Michigan	All
Minnesota	One
Mississippi	One
Missouri	One
Montana	All
Nebraska	One
Nevada	One
New Hampshire	All
New Jersey	One
New Mexico	One
New York	One
North Carolina	One
North Dakota	One
Ohio	One
Oklahoma	One
Oregon	One
Pennsylvania	All
Rhode Island	One
South Carolina	One
South Dakota	One
Tennessee	One
Texas	One
Utah	One
Vermont	One
Virginia	One
Washington	All
West Virginia	One
Wisconsin	One
Wyoming	One

CALIBER COMPARISON CHART

(Common Handgun Rounds)

Source: *Death Investigator's Handbook by Louis Eliopulos*
(Paladin Press, 1993).

CALIBER COMPARISON CHART

Common Round	Avail- ability	Inch Size	Metric Equiv.	Bullet Diameter
.22	Revolver or Semi-	.22	5.6mm	
.25	Semi- Auto	.25	6.38mm	
.32	Revolver or Semi-	.31	7.65mm	
9mm	Semi- Auto	.356	9mm	
.380	Semi- Auto	.356	9mm	
.357	Revolver	.357	9.1mm	
.38	Revolver	.357	9.1mm	
.40 S&W	Semi- Auto	.40	10.16mm	
.44	Revolver	.429	10.91mm	
.45	Semi- Auto	.451	11.47mm	

STATE BY STATE GUIDE TO CONCEALED WEAPONS

"Shall Issue States"

(Concealed Weapon Permits shall be provided to any person who meets standards set by law.)

Alaska
Arizona
Arkansas
Florida
Georgia
Idaho
Indiana
Kentucky
Louisiana
Maine
Mississippi
Montana
Nevada
New Hampshire
North Carolina
North Dakota
Oklahoma
Oregon
Pennsylvania
South Carolina
South Dakota
Tennessee
Texas
Utah
Virginia
Washington

West Virginia
Wyoming

"May Issue States"
(Concealed Weapon Permits may be provided, subject to the discretion of licensing authority.)

Alabama
California
Colorado
Connecticut
Delaware
District of Columbia
Hawaii
Iowa
Maryland
Massachusetts
Michigan
Minnesota
New Jersey
New York
Rhode Island

"Prohibited States"
(Concealed Weapon Permits not available.)

Illinois
Kansas
Missouri
Nebraska
New Mexico
Ohio
Wisconsin

"No Permit Required"
(Concealed weapons may be carried without a permit.)

Vermont

SAMPLE MIRANDA WARNING

"You have the right to remain silent.

Anything you say can and will be used against you in a court of law.

You have the right to consult with an attorney, and to have an attorney present both before and during questioning.

If you cannot afford to hire an attorney, one will be appointed by the court, free of charge, to represent you before any questioning, if you wish.

You can decide at any time to exercise these rights and not answer any question or make any statements."

To secure a waiver of these rights, the following questions should be asked and an affirmative answer received:

"Do you understand these rights I have just explained to you?

With these rights in mind, are you willing to talk to me now?"

BEYOND A REASONABLE DOUBT

This is the legal definition of "Reasonable doubt" as read to all criminal juries in California. A similar version is used in the 49 other states and in federal criminal cases:

"Reasonable doubt is defined as follows: It is not a mere possible doubt; because everything relating to human affairs, and depending on moral evidence, is open to some or imaginary doubt. It is the state of the case which, after the entire comparison and consideration of all the evidence, leaves the minds of the jurors in that condition that they cannot say they feel an abiding conviction, to a moral certainty, of the truth of the charge."

THE
DEATH PENALTY

STATE BY STATE
PROFILE

DEATH PENALTY: STATE BY STATE

State	Death Penalty?	Lethal Injection	Electrocution	Gas Chamber	Hanging	Firing Squad
AL	Y		Y			
AK	N					
AZ	Y	Y		Y		
AR	Y	Y	Y			
CA	Y	Y		Y		
CO	Y	Y				
CT	Y	Y				
DE	Y	Y			Y	
DC	N					
FL	Y	Y	Y			
GA	Y		Y			
HI	N					
ID	Y	Y				Y
IL	Y	Y				
IN	Y	Y				
IA	N					
KS	Y	Y				
KY	Y	Y	Y			
LA	Y	Y				
ME	N					
MD	Y	Y		Y		
MA	N					
MI	N					
MN	N					
MS	Y	Y				

Source: Death Penalty Information Center

DEATH PENALTY: STATE BY STATE

State	Death Penalty?	Lethal Injection	Electrocution	Gas Chamber	Hanging	Firing Squad
MO	Y	Y		Y		
MT	Y	Y				
NE	Y		Y			
NV	Y	Y				
NH	Y	Y			Y	
NJ	Y	Y				
NM	Y	Y				
NY	Y	Y				
NC	Y	Y				
ND	N					
OH	Y	Y	Y			
OK	Y	Y	Y			Y
OR	Y	Y				
PA	Y	Y				
RI	N					
SC	Y	Y	Y			
SD	Y	Y				
TN	Y	Y	Y			
TX	Y	Y				
UT	Y	Y				Y
VT	N					
VA	Y	Y	Y			
WA	Y	Y			Y	
WV	N					
WI	N					
WY	Y	Y		Y		

INTERPOL MEMBER STATES

Albania - Algeria - Andorra - Angola - Antigua & Barbuda - Argentina - Armenia - Aruba - Australia - Austria - Azerbaijan - Bahamas - Bahrain - Bangladesh - Barbados - Belarus - Belgium - Belize - Benin - Bolivia - Bosnia-Herzegovina - Botswana - Brazil - Brunei - Bulgaria - Burkina-Faso - Burundi - Cambodia - Cameroon - Canada - Cape Verde - Central African Republic - Chad - Chile - China - Colombia - Comoros - Congo - Congo (Democratic Rep.) - Costa Rica - Côte d'Ivoire - Croatia - Cuba - Cyprus - Czech Republic - Denmark - Djibouti - Dominica - Dominican Republic - Ecuador - Egypt - El Salvador - Equatorial Guinea - Eritrea - Estonia - Ethiopia - Fiji - Finland - Former Yugoslav Republic of Macedonia - France - Gabon - Gambia - Georgia - Germany - Ghana - Greece - Grenada - Guatemala - Guinea - Guinea Bissau - Guyana - Haiti - Honduras - Hungary - Iceland - India - Indonesia - Iran - Iraq - Ireland - Israel - Italy - Jamaica - Japan - Jordan - Kazakhstan - Kenya - Korea (Rep. of) - Kuwait - Kyrgyzstan - Laos - Latvia - Lebanon - Lesotho - Liberia - Libya - Liechtenstein - Lithuania - Luxembourg - Madagascar - Malawi - Malaysia - Maldives - Mali - Malta - Marshall Islands - Mauritania - Mauritius - Mexico - Moldova - Monaco - Mongolia - Morocco - Mozambique - Myanmar - Namibia - Nauru - Nepal - Netherlands - Netherlands Antilles - New Zealand - Nicaragua - Niger - Nigeria - Norway - Oman - Pakistan - Panama - Papua New Guinea - Paraguay - Peru - Philippines - Poland - Portugal - Qatar - Romania - Russia - Rwanda - St. Kitts & Nevis - St. Lucia - St Vincent & the Grenadines - Sao Tome & Principe - Saudi Arabia - Senegal - Seychelles - Sierra Leone - Singapore - Slovakia - Slovenia - Somalia - South Africa - Spain - Sri Lanka - Sudan - Suriname - Swaziland - Sweden - Switzerland - Syria - Tanzania - Thailand - Togo - Tonga - Trinidad & Tobago - Tunisia - Turkey - Uganda - Ukraine - United Arab Emirates - United Kingdom - United States - Uruguay - Uzbekistan - Venezuela - Vietnam - Yemen - Zambia - Zimbabwe

Source: www.interpol.int

DIPLOMATIC IMMUNITY

DIPLOMATIC

Diplomatic Agent:
May Be Arrested or Detained - No
May Be Issued Traffic Citation - Yes
Residence May Be Entered[1] - No
May Be Prosecuted - No
May Be Subpoenaed as Witness - No

Member of Administrative and Technical Staff:
May Be Arrested or Detained - No
May Be Issued Traffic Citation - Yes
Residence May Be Entered[1] - No
May Be Prosecuted - No
May Be Subpoenaed as Witness - No

Service Staff:
May Be Arrested or Detained - Yes
May Be Issued Traffic Citation - Yes
Residence May Be Entered[1] - Yes
May Be Prosecuted - No[2]
May Be Subpoenaed as Witness - Yes

CONSULAR

Career Consular Officers:
May Be Arrested or Detained - Yes[3]
May Be Issued Traffic Citation - Yes
Residence May Be Entered[1] - Yes
May Be Prosecuted - No[2]
May Be Subpoenaed as Witness - No[2]

Honorary Consular Officers:
May Be Arrested or Detained - Yes
May Be Issued Traffic Citation - Yes
Residence May Be Entered[1] - Yes
May Be Prosecuted - No[2]

May Be Subpoenaed as Witness - No[2]

Consular Employees:
May Be Arrested or Detained - Yes
May Be Issued Traffic Citation - Yes
Residence May Be Entered[1] - Yes
May Be Prosecuted - No[2]
May Be Subpoenaed as Witness - No[2]

INTERNATIONAL ORGANIZATION
International Organization Staff:
May Be Arrested or Detained - Yes
May Be Issued Traffic Citation - Yes
Residence May Be Entered[1] - Yes
May Be Prosecuted - No[2]
May Be Subpoenaed as Witness - No[2]

Diplomatic-Level Staff of Missions to International Organizations:
May Be Arrested or Detained - No
May Be Issued Traffic Citation - Yes
Residence May Be Entered Entered[1] - No
May Be Prosecuted - No
May Be Subpoenaed as Witness - No

Support Staff of Missions to International Organizations:
May Be Arrested or Detained - Yes
May Be Issued Traffic Citation - Yes
Residence May Be Entered[1] - Yes
May Be Prosecuted - No[2]
May Be Subpoenaed as Witness - No[2]

[1] Subject to ordinary procedures.
[2] No for official acts. Otherwise, yes.
[3] If for a felony and pursuant to a warrant.

Source: Bureau of Diplomatic Security, U.S. Department of State

DEA SCHEDULES OF CONTROLLED SUBSTANCES

Schedule I

- The drug or other substance has a high potential for abuse.
- The drug or other substance has no currently accepted medical use in treatment in the United States.
- There is a lack of accepted safety for use of the drug or other substance under medical supervision.
- Some Schedule I substances are heroin, LSD, marijuana and methaqualone.

Schedule II

- The drug or other substance has a high potential for abuse.
- The drug or other substance has a currently accepted medical use in treatment in the United States or a currently accepted medical use with severe restrictions.
- Abuse of the drug or other substance may lead to severe psychological or physical dependence.
- Schedule II substances include morphine, PCP, cocaine, methadone and methamphetamine.

Schedule III

- The drug or other substance has a

potential for abuse less than the drugs or other substances in Schedules I and II.

- The drug or other substance has a currently accepted medical use in treatment in the United States.
- Abuse of the drug or other substance may lead to moderate or low physical dependence or high psychological dependence.
- Anabolic steroids, codeine and hydrocodone with aspirin or Tylenol, and some barbiturates are Schedule III substances.

Schedule IV

- The drug or other substance has a low potential for abuse relative to the drugs or other substances in Schedule III.
- The drug or other substance has a currently accepted medical use in treatment in the United States.
- Abuse of the drug or other substance may lead to limited physical dependence or psychological dependence relative to the drugs or other substances in Schedule III.
- Included in Schedule IV are Darvon, Talwin, Equanil, Valium and Xanax.

Schedule V

- The drug or other substance has a low potential for abuse relative to the drugs or other substances in Schedule IV.
- The drug or other substance has a currently accepted medical use in

treatment in the United States.

- Abuse of the drug or other substance may lead to limited physical dependence or psychological dependence relative to the drugs or other substances in Schedule IV.
- Over-the-counter cough medicines with codeine are classified in Schedule V.

Controlled Substance Analogues

A new class of substances was created by the Anti-Drug Abuse Act of 1986. Controlled substance analogues are substances which are not controlled substances, but may be found in the illicit traffic. They are structurally or pharmacologically similar to Schedule I or II controlled substances and have no legitimate medical use. A substance which meets the definition of a controlled substance analogue and is intended for human consumption is treated under the CSA as if it were a controlled substance in Schedule I.

Source: Drug Enforcement Administration

KEY DEPARTMENT OF JUSTICE DATABASES

Alien Status Verification Index System

ASVI supports the Systematic Alien Verification for Entitlements (SAVE) Program by providing automated status verification information to Federal, State, and local benefit granting and entitlement agencies. ASVI also provides employment verification information to private employers in various SAVE-sponsored Employment Verification Pilots. (Immigration and Naturalization Service)

Automated Biometric Identification System

IDENT is a client-server system that allows Immigration and Naturalization Service (INS) officers to identify individuals quickly and accurately. IDENT captures the left and right index fingerprints and a photo and enables searches of online databases to identify criminal and non-criminal deportable aliens. (Immigration and Naturalization Service)

Automated Intelligence Records System (Pathfinder)

In general, this system contains computerized and manual intelligence information gathered from DEA and INS investigative records and reports. Specifically, intelligence information is gathered and collated from the following DEA and INS records and reports; (1) DEA Reports of Investigation (DEA-6), (2) DEA and INS

Intelligence Reports, (3) INS Air Detail Office Index (I-92A), (4) INS Operational Activities Special Information System (OASIS), (5) INS Marine Intelligence Index, (6) INS Fraudulent Document Center Index, (7) INS Terrorist Index, (8) INS Reports of Investigation and Apprehension (I- 44, I-213, G-166) and (9) U.S. Coast Guard Vessel 408 file. In addition, data is obtained from commercially available flight plan information concerning individuals known, suspected or alleged to be involved in criminal smuggling activities using private aircraft. (Drug Enforcement Administration)

Central Index System

CIS is the master records management system that collects and distributes automated biographical information on aliens. The system contains the physical status of alien files (A-file) and provides the tracking capability to move these files to various Immigration and Naturalization Service (INS) locations. (Immigration and Naturalization Service)

Confidential Source System

The Confidential Source System (CSS) is a centralized listing of all sources of information utilized by the Drug Enforcement Administration (DEA) in drug trafficking investigations worldwide. (Drug Enforcement Administration)

Controlled Substances Act System

The Controlled Substances Act System (CSA) Database is made up of the following: The CSA Master File (CSAMAST) contains information on active registrants responsible for handling controlled substances. The CSA History File (CSAHIST) contains historic information generated by changes to (transactions) individual information (name, address, etc.) on the Master File. The CSA Table File (CSATABLE) contains code tables used for validation of data entry information, printing of coded information (for reports, and display purpose) and for updating and processing master records. The CSA History Archive contains three years or more of history records from the History File. (Drug Enforcement Administration)

DEA Aviation Unit Reporting System

This system is maintained to monitor the utilization and maintenance of DEA aircraft and the qualifications of DEA pilots in furtherance of DEA enforcement operations conducted pursuant to the Comprehensive Drug Abuse Prevention and Control Act of 1970 (Pub. L. 91-513). (Drug Enforcement Administration)

Deportable Alien Control System

DACS is a mainframe system designed to serve the data entry needs of personnel in the Immigration and Naturalization Service (INS) service processing centers and in Detention and Deportation (D&D) District and Regional offices. DACS automates many of the functions associated with tracking the status of illegal aliens under removal proceedings, including detention status. Information is maintained on the alien's entry and departure status until the alien is either granted a stay, deported or relief granted. If the alien is detained or is jailed for criminal actions, additional information pertinent to the offense is maintained. Records in DACS provide congressional reporting statistics. (Immigration and Naturalization Service)

Domestic Security/Terrorism Investigations Records System

The Domestic Security/Terrorism Investigations Records System (DOSTERS) of the Office of Intelligence Policy and Review (OIPR) is no longer an active information system and has not been augmented or modified since 1993. It is a collection of case summaries pertaining to the U.S. person subjects of FBI domestic security and terrorism investigations opened prior to 1993. Responsibility for reviewing these summaries was transferred to the Department of Justice, Criminal Division, Terrorism and Violent Crimes Section (TVCS) in 1995. While OIPR does not itself conduct investigations, it has retained the DOSTERS summaries reviewed prior to 1994 as a permanently valuable information resource. DOSTERS is a manual system consisting of files indexed alphabetically. (Office of Intelligence Policy and Review)

Drug Testing Program Record System

The Drug Testing Program Record System encompasses all information from the Drug Enforcement Administration Headquarters and field offices regarding the DEA urinalysis drug testing program. The DEA utilizes the system to conduct drug testing of applicants and employees. This system consists of records containing sample collection and drug test results by date and social security number. (Drug Enforcement Administration)

Electronic Surveillance Tracking System

ELSURTS is operated by the Office of Enforcement Operations (OEO). The system tracks all inquiries from federal agencies regarding past subjects of electronic surveillance. (Criminal Division)

Essential Chemical Reporting System

The system contains: (1) Precursor dine reports submitted to DEA pursuant to Pub. L. No. 95-633, (2) Information extracted from precursor reports and maintained on magnetic tape, (3) Reports submitted voluntarily to DEA concerning chemicals essential to the manufacture of controlled substance. (Drug Enforcement Administration)

Fingerprint Identification Records System

The Fingerprint Identification Records System (FIRS) maintains identification and criminal history record information on individuals fingerprinted as a result of law enforcement action; federal employment or military service; and a limited number of persons fingerprinted for alien registration and naturalization purposes and for those desiring to have their fingerprints on record for personal identification purposes. FIRS serves as the nation's centralized repository for identification and criminal history record information functions for criminal justice agencies, authorized non-criminal justice agencies and other authorized entities. (Federal Bureau of Investigation)

Grants of Confidentiality Files (GCF)

Information in these records are utilized for the purpose of investigating applicants prior to the granting of confidentiality. In the course of such investigations, information may be disseminated to state and local law enforcement and regulatory agencies to other federal law enforcement and regulatory agencies. (Drug Enforcement Administration)

Inappropriate Communications/Threat Information System

The IC/TIS system contains identifying information and background data on persons who have directly threatened or pose a violent threat to USMS protectees; information concerning the threat; and threat-related investigative information. (United States Marshals Service)

Information Support System

The National Drug Intelligence Center Information Support System encompasses all centralized records of the National Drug Intelligence Center (NDIC). Records in this system may contain, but are not limited to, personal identification data and any data that may assist law enforcement agencies and agencies of the U.S. foreign intelligence community in executing their responsibility with respect to counter-drug enforcement. The NDIC Information Support System also maintains data which aids in the administration of NDIC resources. (National Drug Intelligence Center)

International Intelligence Database

This system is maintained to further criminal investigations through the collation, analysis and dissemination of intelligence information. This system produces the following reports: (a) Tactical, operational and strategic intelligence reports; (b) Major organizational reports; (c) Network analysis; (d) Trafficker profiles; (e) Intelligence briefs on prior experience with individuals, firms, countries, etc.; (f) Country profiles; (g) Country Intelligence Action Plans; (h) Current Situational reports; (i) Special reports as requests; (j) Drug patterns and trends and drug trafficking from source to U.S. distributors. (Drug Enforcement Administration)

Narcotics and Dangerous Drugs Information System (NADDIS)

A centralized automated file of summaries of reports on subjects of interest to DEA, consisting of over 3,500,000 individuals, businesses, vessels and selected airfields identified through the DEA investigative reporting system, and related investigative records. (Drug Enforcement Administration)

National Automated Immigration Lookout System II

NAILS II is a central mainframe computer system that provides a reliable method of verifying the admissibility of an individual and preventing inadmissible individuals from entering the United States. (Immigration and Naturalization Service)

National Crime Information Center

The National Crime Information Center (NCIC) system provides a computerized database for ready access by authorized users to documented criminal justice information. (Federal Bureau of Investigation)

National DNA Index System

The National DNA Index System (NDIS) maintains data which identifies DNA associations with DNA records obtained during an investigation of a crime or a missing person. The system also contains data used for statistical and identification research. (Federal Bureau of Investigation)

National Drug Pointer Index (NDPIX)

National Drug Pointer Index (NDPIX) greatly enhances coordination among drug law enforcement entities. By accessing the system's database, participating law enforcement agencies will be able to determine quickly whether a current drug suspect is under active investigation by another participating agency. (Drug Enforcement Administration)

National Instant Criminal Background Check System

The National Instant Criminal Background Check System (NICS) provides a method of checking available information to determine whether a person is disqualified from possessing a firearm under federal or state law. The NICS contains records on individuals who are disqualified from possessing a firearm. These records include an individual's name, sex, race, other personal descriptive data, date of birth, state of residence, and sometimes a unique identifying number. The NICS also contains criminal information which may disqualify an individual from possessing a firearm under federal or state law. (Federal Bureau of Investigation)

Security Clearance Forms for Grand Jury Reports

This system of records permits the USAOs and EOUSA to compile, maintain and track information relating to the security clearance status of the individual grand jury reporters employed by the reporting firm under contract with the Justice Department. (Executive Office for United States Attorneys)

Sentry

It is an online, real-time, database management system that monitors the system-wide movement and management of inmates, including sentence computations, work assignments, program assignments, institution designation, administrative remedies, discipline and inmate financial responsibility. SENTRY resides on the Department of Justice Data Center mainframe in Dallas, Texas, and is accessed by about 200 Bureau of Prisons (BOP) and Department of Justice offices that need access to inmate information, including all BOP offices nationwide. (Federal Bureau of Prisons)

System to Retrieve Information From Drug Evidence II

STRIDE consists of six (6) subsystems providing information on drug intelligence, statistics on markings found on pills and capsules, drug inventory, tracking, statistical information on drugs removed from the market place, utilization of laboratory manpower and information on subsystems analyzed outside of the DEA laboratory system where DEA participated in the seizure(s). (Drug Enforcement Administration)

Threat Analysis Information System

The Threat Analysis Information System (TAIS) contains identifying information and background data on persons who have directly threatened or pose a violent threat to USMS protectees, information concerning the threat and threat-related investigative information. (United States Marshals Service)

Warrant Information System

WIN contains the warrant, court records, internal correspondence related to the warrant and other information on individuals for whom Federal warrants have been issued. (United States Marshals Service)

Witness Immunity Tracking System

WITS tracks all requests for individuals seeking witness immunity in criminal cases. (Criminal Division)

Source: U.S. Department of Justice

Privacy
Law
SURVIVAL
Guide

DISCLAIMER

Although every reasonable effort has been made to present accurate and complete information in this guide, errors may be contained in the information presented. THE PURPOSE OF THIS GUIDE IS TO SUMMARIZE FEDERAL PRIVACY LAWS MOST LIKELY TO AFFECT INVESTIGATORS. STATE AND LOCAL PRIVACY LAWS HAVE NOT BEEN INCLUDED. FEDERAL PRIVACY LAWS MAY EXIST WHICH HAVE BEEN OMITTED. THE INFORMATION IN THIS GUIDE SHOULD NOT BE CONSTRUED AS LEGAL ADVICE. Laws and regulations may have been enacted, changed or eliminated since the publication of this report. No warranties, either expressed or implied, are made by the author, publisher or distributors of this publication.

PRIVACY LAW SURVIVAL GUIDE

Table of Contents

Wiretaps	417
Electronic Eavesdropping	418
Recording Phone Calls	420
Surveillance	422
Polygraph Examinations	424
Video Rentals	428
Debt Collection	429
Freedom of Information Act	433
Sample FOIA Letter	436
The Privacy Act	437
Financial Privacy	439
Credit Reports	441
Pre-Employment Investigations	444
Post Office Information	447
Mail Inspection	452
Trash Inspection	454
Economic Espionage	456
Theft of Trade Secrets	458
Student Records	460
Impersonation of a Federal Official	463
Disclosure of Confidential Information	465
Tax Returns	467
Computer Crime	470
Stored Communications	472
Driver Records	473
Medical Histories	475
Union Activities	477
Privacy Law Resources	478

WIRETAPS

SUMMARY:

A wiretap is the unauthorized interception of an electronic communication — phone, pager, cell phone, cordless phone, fax or data transmission. The interception could be recorded or it could simply be listened to, but not recorded. Either way, it's illegal.

PENALTY FOR VIOLATION:

Up to 5 years imprisonment, criminal fines and possible civil liability.

PRACTICAL TIPS:

* Manufacturing, distributing, possessing or advertising of wire, oral, or electronic intercepting *devices* is also a federal crime punishable by fine or imprisonment.

* The law also prohibits illegally intercepted communications from being entered as evidence into a court proceeding.

THE LAW:

18 USC 2510, et seq, *The Electronic Communications Privacy Act of 1986.*

ELECTRONIC EAVESDROPPING

SUMMARY:

The same federal law (18 USC 119) that outlaws wiretaps also makes illegal the interception and disclosure of oral communications. *In plain English, this means it's illegal to use an electronic eavesdropping device to listen to or record other people's private conversations.*

Federal law allows the recording of an oral conversation with the consent of one party. However, certain states may require consent of all parties to the conversation. In states where the permission of just one party is required, investigators are known to secretly record interviews of witnesses and suspects.

Manufacturing, distributing, possessing or advertising of an electronic eavesdropping device is also a federal crime.

PENALTY FOR VIOLATION:

Up to 5 years imprisonment, criminal fines, and possible civil liability.

PRACTICAL TIPS:

- The disclosure of the contents of an illegally recorded conversation is also a federal crime when the person disclosing the contents knew or should have known that they were illegally obtained.

- Don't record sound when conducting videotaped surveillance; the inadvertent recording of a private conversation could be an unlawful recording. Never use parabolic dishes or shotgun microphones.

- Recording of audio in public settings where there is no expectation of privacy is lawful.

THE LAW:

18 USC 2510, et seq, *The Electronic Communications Privacy Act of 1986.*

RECORDING PHONE CALLS

SUMMARY:

Federal law prohibits the covert recording of phone calls unless one of the following two exceptions are met:

- Phone calls can be recorded with the consent of at least one party to the conversation. However, 12 states require that *all* parties to the conversation give their consent. (See our *Reference Guide* for the list of states.)

- The second exception is known as the "business extension" exception. A business may monitor employee phone calls that are business related over a phone extension if the monitoring is part of the "ordinary course of business." Use of a tape recorder or other special equipment (unless provided by the phone company) is not allowed. If the content of the phone conversation is personal, the monitoring must cease.

PENALTY FOR VIOLATION:

Up to 5 years imprisonment, criminal fines, and possible civil liability.

PRACTICAL TIPS:

- Federal Communications Commission regulations (48 C.F.R. Sec. 64.501) require at least one of the following measures be taken when recording an *interstate* phone call:

1. Both parties consent to the recording; or
2. The recording party must give verbal notification before recording; or
3. There must be a regular electronic beep tone during recording.

- Among the states that require the consent of all parties to a recording of a phone call, there are some notable loopholes. For example, in California, a phone call can be recorded with the permission of just one party if the other party is making a criminal threat, such as extortion or blackmail.

- The state statutes can be found at *http://www.rcfp.org/taping/index.html*

THE LAW:

18 USC 2510, et seq, *The Electronic Communications Privacy Act of 1986.*

SURVEILLANCE

SUMMARY:

The right of investigators to conduct surveillance is established by case law, not
statute. High courts have consistently ruled
that when a surveillance is conducted in an
unobtrusive and non-threatening manner
from a public area, there is no invasion of
privacy of the person being observed and/
or photographed. Commonly known as the
"plain view doctrine," this means that surveillance from publicly accessible areas is
acceptable, whereas hiding in bushes on
private property and other trespasses is not.

PENALTY FOR VIOLATION:

Civil liability for invasion of privacy or
harassment if the surveillance is obtrusive,
threatening or otherwise offensive.

PRACTICAL TIPS:

- Never trespass onto private property
  during a surveillance. Don't climb
  trees, roofs or cut holes in bushes.
  Limit your vantage point to "plain
  view."

- If detected by the subject, end the surveillance. Continuation could be
  viewed as harassment or invasion of
  privacy and serve as the grounds for
  civil litigation.

- Don't record audio during surveillance

unless the persons speaking are in a clearly public setting with no expectation of privacy. Recording of private conversations could result in criminal charges for electronic eavesdropping. (See section "Electronic Eavesdropping.")

THE LAW:

Notable case law includes:

Forster v. Manchester [410 PA 192, 189 A2D 147 (1963)] Supreme Court of Pennsylvania ruling that while claimants do have a reasonable expectation of privacy, it is in the best interest of society to allow insurance claims to be investigated so that false claims can be exposed.

McClain v. Boise Cascade [507 P.2d 478 (Colo.1972)] is one of several landmark decisions establishing the taking of photographic surveillance as an appropriate method to obtain evidence to impeach a witness or otherwise defend a lawsuit.

Nader v. General Motors [25 N.Y. 2d 560, 255 NE 2d 765 (1970)] Ruled that mere surveillance does not constitute invasion of privacy. However, when the investigator followed the subject so close as to be able to read the serial numbers on money, it was ruled over zealous and actionable.

POLYGRAPH EXAMINATIONS

SUMMARY:

Federal law bans employers from administering polygraph or "lie detector" examinations to their employees. However, the law is riddled with loopholes which in fact make such polygraph examinations lawful in many circumstances. The law does not regulate the administering of polygraph examinations between any parties outside the employer-employee relationship.

A polygraph may be administered to an employee if *all* of the following conditions are met. (However, the employee's cooperation is purely voluntary — he or she can refuse to take the test at any time and the employer can take no recourse against the employee for the refusal.)

- The test is administered as part of an ongoing theft, embezzlement or other investigation at the company where there is economic loss.

- The employee had access to the property that is the subject of the investigation.

- The employer has reasonable suspicion that the employee was involved in the incident or activity under suspicion.

- The employer provides a written statement before the examination which:

(A) sets forth with particularity the specific incident or activity being investigated and the basis for testing particular employees,

(B) is signed by a person (other than a polygraph examiner) authorized to legally bind the employer,

(C) is retained by the employer for at least 3 years, and

(D) contains at a minimum:

(i) an identification of the specific economic loss or injury to the business of the employer,

(ii) a statement indicating that the employee had access to the property that is the subject of the investigation, and

(iii) a statement describing the basis of the employer's reasonable suspicion that the employee was involved in the incident or activity under investigation.

• The employee must be provided with a written notice of the date, time and location of the test, and of such examinee's right to obtain and consult with legal counsel or an employee representative before the test. This notification must also describe the nature of a polygraph test.

• The employee must be read and then asked to sign a written notice informing him or her that he or she cannot be required to take the test as a condition of employment. That any statement made during the test may be used to make an adverse employment decision against the employee. Of the legal rights and remedies available to the examinee if the polygraph test is administered unlawfully. He or she must also be provided the opportunity to review the test questions before the test and be informed of the right to terminate the test at anytime.

• After the test the employer must further interview the employee on the basis of the test results; provide the employee with a copy of any opinion or conclusion rendered as a result of the test, and a copy of the questions asked during the test along with the corresponding charted responses.

Several industries are exempt from *The Employee Polygraph Protection Act* and can require *mandatory* examinations. These include certain federal government defense agencies, defense contractors, security services (such as armored car personnel and alarm company employees), and companies involved in the manufacturing, distribution or control of prescription drugs.

PENALTY FOR VIOLATION:

Civil liability up to $10,000 per violation plus lost wages, reinstatement, and legal fees incurred by the employee.

PRACTICAL TIPS:

• In most situations, an employee can refuse to take a polygraph examination and the employer can take no adverse action against the employee as a result of the refusal. An employee can also terminate a polygraph examination at any time without consequence.

- Employers cannot take adverse action against an employee based *solely* on the results of a polygraph examination.

- The polygraph examiner must be licensed in the state where the examination occurs (if that state licenses polygraph examiners), cannot conduct more than five examinations a day and each examination must last no less than ninety minutes.

- The results of a polygraph examination arising from an employer-employee relationship are to be held confidential between the examiner, employer, employee and any court, arbitrator, mediator or concerned government agency.

- All employers are required by law to post a notice in the workplace summarizing employee rights under this act.

- The results of polygraph examinations are not admissible in court in criminal trials due to questions over the scientific reliability of the tests.

THE LAW:

29 USC 2001, et seq, *The Employee Polygraph Protection Act of 1988.*

VIDEO RENTALS

SUMMARY:

Records of videotape rentals have special protection under federal law. Firms who rent or sell videotapes cannot release information about these transactions to any third party unless specifically exempted by statute. Exemptions are sharply limited, but do include court orders in a civil proceeding. However, the customer whose records are sought must be given advance notice and the opportunity to quash the court order.

PENALTY FOR VIOLATION:

Aggrieved parties may pursue a remedy in federal court which include both actual and punitive damages. Such action must be brought within two years of date of discovery.

PRACTICAL TIPS:

- Videotape rental companies are required by statute to destroy customer rental records that are over one year old, unless there is a pending need or court order for the records.

THE LAW:

18 USC 2710, *Wrongful Disclosure of Videotape Rental or Sales Records.*

DEBT COLLECTION

SUMMARY:

Enacted to protect consumers from abusive bill collectors, *The Fair Debt Collection Practices Act* (FDCPA) may impact certain activities of private investigators.

The law only applies to the collection of debts that are personal, family, or household in nature. It does *not* apply to business debts. Further, the law only regulates debt collectors who regularly collects debts owed to others. Private investigators who skiptrace to locate debtors, *but who do not demand or accept payments,* are probably *not* covered by the law. Private investigators who regularly demand or collect payments probably *are* debt collectors under the law.

There is one notable exception to the FDCPA that private investigators should know about. When attempting to serve legal process in conjunction with judicial enforcement of any debt, a private investigator (or any party) is automatically exempt from the FDCPA.

The full text of this complex law can be found on the Internet at *www.ftc.gov* or *www.ftc.gov/os/statutes/fdcpajump.htm*.

PENALTY FOR VIOLATION:

Civil liability and monetary fines as levied by the Federal Trade Commission.

PRACTICAL TIPS:

Debt collectors may not harass, oppress or abuse debtors they contact. For example, debt collectors may not:

- use threats of violence or harm;

- publish a list of consumers who refuse to pay their debts (except to a credit bureau);

- use obscene or profane language; or

- repeatedly use the telephone to annoy someone.

Debt collectors may not use any false or misleading statements when collecting a debt. For example, debt collectors may not:

- falsely imply that they are attorneys or government representatives; falsely imply that a debtor has committed a crime;

- falsely represent that they operate or work for a credit bureau;

- misrepresent the amount of a debt; or indicate that papers being sent to a debtor are legal forms when they are not; or

- state that papers being sent to a debtor are not legal forms when they are;

- use any business, company or organization name other than the true name of the debt collector's business, company or organization.

Debt collectors also may not state that:

- a debtor will be arrested if he or she does not pay a debt;

- they will seize, garnish, attach, or sell a property or wages, unless the collection agency or creditor intends to do so, and it is legal to do so; or

- actions, such as a lawsuit, will be taken against a debtor, when such action legally may not be taken, or when they do not intend to take such action.

Debt collectors may not:

- give false credit information about a debtor to anyone, including a credit bureau;

- send you anything that looks like an official document from a court or government agency when it is not; or

- use a false name.

Debt collectors may not engage in unfair practices when they try to collect a debt. For example, collectors may not:

- collect any amount greater than a debt, unless your state law permits such a charge;

- deposit a post-dated check prematurely;

- use deception to make a debtor accept collect calls or pay for telegrams;

- take or threaten to take a debtor's property unless this can be done legally; or

- contact a debtor by postcard.

THE LAW:

15 USC 1692, et seq, *The Fair Debt Collection Practices Act.*

Note: Portions of this section have been copied from FTC public education materials.

FREEDOM OF INFORMATION ACT

SUMMARY:

The Freedom of Information Act (FOIA) allows public access to certain federal government records. It does not apply to the records of state or local governments or of Congress, the courts or the White House. Of the remaining federal agencies, there are nine further exemptions and three exclusions to the release of information. (Exclusions differ from exemptions in that exempt items can still be released by the agency if the release is not prohibited by law and would cause no foreseeable harm. No such discretion exists with the three exclusions.)

The exemptions are:

*   Classified national defense and foreign relations information

*   Internal agency rules and practices

*   Information that is prohibited from disclosure by another law

*   Trade secrets and other confidential business information

*   Inter-agency or intra-agency communications that are protected by legal

privileges

- Information involving matters of personal privacy

- Most law enforcement records

- Information relating to the supervision of financial institutions

- Geological information on wells

The exclusions are:

- Current law enforcement investigations

- Informants in law enforcement investigations

- FBI records relating to terrorism, espionage and foreign intelligence.

FOIA requests must be made in writing and should be directed to the FOIA officer of the individual agency that records are being requested from. (See sample request letter below.) FOIA requests are typically fulfilled at no cost unless unusual research or copying is required. By law, an agency is to reply to a FOIA request within ten days. If a FOIA request is denied, the denial should be appealed with the agency. If the denial is upheld, the last resort is to file a lawsuit in the U.S. District Court.

PENALTY FOR VIOLATION:

None.

PRACTICAL TIPS:

- To obtain FOIA Officer contact information for any federal agency, call the Federal Information Center, 1-800-688-9889. Or see...the *FREEDOM OF INFORMATION ACT* entry in the main book for lists of FOIA contact phone numbers.

- The Freedom of Information Act relates solely to the federal government. However, all states now have their own state-version applicable to state government records.

THE LAW:

5 USC 552, *The Freedom of Information Act.*

Sample FOIA Letter

Date

FOIA Act Request
Agency Head or FOIA Officer
Name of Agency
Agency Address

Re: Freedom of Information Act Request

Dear _____:

Under the Freedom of Information Act, 5 USC subsection 552, and the Privacy Act, 5 USC subsection 552a, I am requesting access to the following records:

(Describe records as specifically as possible)

If there are any fees for searching for or copying the records, please let me know before you fill my request. [Or, please supply the records without informing me of the cost if the fees do not exceed $_____, which I agree to pay.]

If you deny all or any part of this request, please cite each specific exemption you think justifies your refusal and notify me of appeal procedures available under the law.

If you have any questions about handling this request, you may telephone me at _____(home phone) or at _____ (office phone).

Sincerely,
Name
Address

Enclosure: Proof of Identity

Notes: Although the general services administration recommends including proof of identity, such as a copy of a driver's license, many agencies do not require this. If you wish to make an anonymous FOIA request, contact Washington, D.C. based FOIA Group, Inc., at 202/408-7028. Fee-based service.

THE PRIVACY ACT

SUMMARY:

The Privacy Act of 1974 has two main components. First, it allows any citizen to view and amend, if incorrect, any federally maintained information about him or herself that is kept in database form. *The law cannot be used by a third party to obtain information on another individual.* The second purpose of the law is to set forth security and other guidelines for federal agencies to follow when collecting data. Among these are tight restrictions on personal information kept by the government on its own employees, as well as for the general public. The law makes it a criminal offense to obtain protected information from the federal government through false pretense.

PENALTY FOR VIOLATION:

Federal agency employees who improperly release protected information could face criminal penalties including a misdemeanor conviction and fines up to $5,000. A person outside of the government who uses a false pretense to obtain protected information may also be convicted of a misdemeanor and fined up to $5,000. Civil remedies can also be obtained against government agencies that violate the act.

PRACTICAL TIPS:

• None; this law will be seldom if ever
used by most private investigators.

THE LAW:

5 USC 552a, *The Privacy Act of 1974.*

FINANCIAL PRIVACY

(Including Bank Accounts)

SUMMARY:

The Financial Services Modernization Act of 1999, also known as the G-L-B (Graham-Leach-Bliley) Act, tightly restricts the means by which bank account, credit card and other financial information can be obtained. Most relevant is its prohibition against obtaining customer information by false pretense. Specifically, the law makes it a federal crime to pretext or "gag" financial information from either a financial institution *or* a financial institution's customer.

PENALTY FOR VIOLATION:

Criminal penalties including imprisonment and substantial fines; possible civil liability for invasion of privacy and other torts.

PRACTICAL TIPS:

- The law has a very broad definition of what constitutes a "financial institution". In addition to banks, it also includes stock brokerage firms, insurance companies, loan companies, credit card issuers and credit bureaus.

- Certain limited exemptions do apply. Exempted parties include law enforcement agencies, financial institutions, insurance companies conducting claims related investigations, and state-licensed private investigators who are attempting to collect delinquent child support. However, private investigators must also first have a court order in hand authorizing the bank investigation.

• A different federal law, *The Right to Financial Privacy Act (12 USC 35)* regulates release of banking information from financial institutions to government agencies.

• See the section in our *Reference Guide* "Lawful Bank Account Sources."

THE LAW:

Public Law 106-102, *The Financial Services Modernization Act of 1999.*

CREDIT REPORTS

SUMMARY:

Any person's credit report can only be lawfully obtained if a "permissible purpose" under *The Fair Credit Reporting Act* (FCRA) exists. In addition, the party obtaining the credit report may have legal obligations to the subject of the credit report, depending on how it is used. If an adverse employment or credit decision is made based on the report, certain notices and disclosures must be made to the consumer under the FCRA.

The "permissible purposes" under which a credit report can be obtained are:

- By subpoena or other court order.

- With the written permission by the consumer to whom it relates.

- For the extension of credit or for the review or collection of an existing credit account.

- For employment purposes. (See section *Employment Investigations* for further details.)

- For insurance underwriting purposes.

- For the purposes of granting a government license or benefit.

- For assessing the risk associated with an existing credit obligation by a "potential investor, servicer or current insurer."

- For a "legitimate business need" in connection with a transaction that is initiated by the person whose credit report is being obtained.

- For a "legitimate business need" for the information to review an account to determine whether the consumer continues to meet the terms of the account.

PENALTY FOR VIOLATION:

Criminal penalties including imprisonment and substantial fines; possible civil liability for invasion of privacy and other torts.

PRACTICAL TIPS:

- When an adverse credit decision is made in whole or in part on review of a credit report, the person whose credit report was obtained must be provided with notice of the adverse action; the name, address and toll-free phone number of the credit reporting agency that furnished the report; a statement informing the person that the credit reporting agency did not make the adverse action; and a statement that the person can obtain a free copy of his credit report by requesting it from the credit reporting agency. (See the actual text of the FCRA for full details.)

- Further information on the Fair Credit
  Reporting Act and credit reports can be
  found at the Federal Trade Commission's web site, located at *www.ftc.gov*.
  At the site, click on the "business" button, then go to the Fair Credit Reporting Act area. Also noteworthy here are
  FTC staff opinions. These are responses to questions from the private
  sector about credit reports and the
  FCRA.

THE LAW:

15 USC 1681, et seq, *The Fair Credit Reporting Act*.

PRE-EMPLOYMENT INVESTIGATIONS

SUMMARY:

Private investigators and pre-employment screening firms that conduct pre-employment investigations on behalf of employers are regulated by the Fair Credit Reporting Act. The law places on the investigation agency and/or employer a legal duty to provide the applicant certain disclosures, notices and authorizations aimed at protecting him from the reporting of inaccurate information.

In broad overview, these requirements include:

- Notification to the applicant that an investigation will be conducted;

- Obtaining a signed authorization from the applicant authorizing the investigation;

- If adverse action will be taken against the applicant as a result of the investigation, he or she must first be advised that adverse action is pending. At this time, the employee must be provided with a copy of the investigative report; and finally,

- After a "reasonable" waiting period,

the employee must be given notice that adverse action has been taken as a result of the investigation. In addition, the employee must be provided a copy of his rights under the FCRA with all written communications throughout the investigative process.

In addition to federal law, 21 states have mini-FCRA's which may impose additional duties upon the investigation firm. For example, in California, a checkbox must be on the authorization which allows the applicant the right to receive a copy of the investigative report, regardless if it is or is not used to make an adverse hiring decision.

PENALTY FOR VIOLATION:

Government fines and possible civil liability.

PRACTICAL TIPS:

- These requirements only apply to third parties (such as investigation agencies and screening firms) who conduct investigations on behalf of employers. It does not apply to an employer conducting in-house pre-employment screenings. However, if the employer obtains information from a credit reporting agency, then the notices, disclosures and authorizations described above must be provided.

- Instructions, forms, notices and disclosures for conducting pre-employment investigations can be purchased at *crimetime.com. The FCRA Compliance for Employment Investigations* kit sells for $19.95 and can be immediately downloaded for use. However, the kit does not contain information on state law requirements for those states that have their own "mini-FCRA".

2-10-04 Reprint Update: Effective March 31, 2004 investigation firms conducting employee misconduct investigations no longer have a duty to inform the subject of the investigation in advance, and to provide a report releasing details of the investigation afterward. However, if an adverse hiring decision will be made based on the investigation, the subject of the investigation must be provided with a summary from the employer containing the nature and the substance of the communication that lead to the adverse action. The law states that the sources of information used in preparing the report do not need to be disclosed. (The new law is found in Section 603 of the FCRA.)

THE LAW:

15 USC 1681, et seq, *The Fair Credit Reporting Act.*

Warning: Nothing in this summary should be construed as legal advice; consult a qualified attorney before conducting these investigations!

POST OFFICE INFORMATION

SUMMARY:

The United States Postal Service will release information about customers only in these circumstances:

- Information on post office box holders is kept on PS Form 1093, *Application for Post Office Box or Caller Service.* The physical address of a P.O. box holder as it appears on this form will be released if it is for the purpose of service of process and the person requesting the information is empowered to serve legal documents. *See request form at end of this section.*

- When a customer wants his or her mail forwarded to a new address, he or she must complete Postal Service Form 3575. The post office will release information off of this form when the new address is needed for service of process. Again, the person requesting the information must be empowered to serve legal documents. *See request form at end of this section*

- The Post Office will release information about a bulk permit or postage meter holder. One possible use of this might be for an anonymous letter that is stamped by a postage meter.

- If the location of a residence or a place of business of a postal customer is known to a postal employee, the employee may, but need not, disclose the location or give directions to it. This may be useful in instances where an investigator knows the neighborhood, but not the exact residence, of a missing person.

PENALTY FOR VIOLATION:

None.

PRACTICAL TIPS:

- A person who is the subject of a protective order may file the protective order with the post office to prevent release of information as described above.

- Commercial Mail Receiving Agencies, such as Mailboxes, Etc., collect information on Form 1583, *Application of Delivery of Mail Through Agent*. Information collected on the form includes the box holder's physical address, phone number, and a copy of his or her identification. This information is restricted and is not available without a subpoena. (To see a blank copy of this form, go to *www.usps.gov*, then click on "forms," then click on "All Online PDF Forms in Numeric Order," then scroll down to PS Form 1583.)

- Prior to June 21, 2000, the post office would release registration information on the owner of a post office box if the box was being used for business purposes. However, as of this date, this information was no longer being released to protect the privacy of small business owners who work out of their homes.

• All mail delivered to a Commercial Mail Receiving Agency, such as Mailboxes, Etc., must have the box number designated as either "PMB" (Private Mail Box) or with the pound sign (#). The post office will *not* deliver mail marked "Suite," "Apt." or "Unit" number when in fact the mail is going to a private box.

THE LAW:

The primary law regulating release of information by the USPS is the *Code of Federal Regulations, 39CFR265.6 et seq.*

(AGENCY LETTERHEAD)

To: Postmaster,_____

Date:_____

ADDRESS INFORMATION REQUEST

Please furnish this agency with the new address, if available, for the following individual or verify whether or not the address given below is one at which mail for this individual is currently being delivered. If the following address is a post office box, please furnish the street address as recorded on the box holder's application form. I certify that the name and address is needed and will be used solely for service of legal process in connection with actual or prospective litigation.

I am empowered to serve legal process under the following statute:

The names of all known parties to the litigation are:

The case will be held in this court:_____ Docket #:_____

The box holder or postal customer is to be served under the capacity of:

( ) Witness ( ) Defendant

Name: _____

Last Known Address: _____

I certify that all information contained in this request is true:

_____
(Signature of Requesting Party)   (Title)

_____
(Name of Requesting Party)   (Address)

FOR POST OFFICE USE ONLY
[ ].. MAIL IS DELIVERED TO ADDRESS   NEW ADDRESS GIVEN
[ ].. NOT KNOWN AT ADDRESS GIVEN
[ ].. MOVED, LEFT NO FORWARDING
       ADDRESS

                                          BOX HOLDER'S STREET ADDRESS
[ ].. NO SUCH ADDRESS
[ ].. OTHER (SPECIFY):

MAIL INSPECTION

SUMMARY:

Federal law relating to mail theft may apply to investigators in certain circumstances. In essence, it is a crime to "take, steal or abstract" any mail. (*The American Heritage Dictionary* defines abstract as "to remove without permission, to filch.")

Certainly, any investigator that takes the mail of another and opens it has committed a crime. Any investigator who forces open or otherwise opens a locked letterbox without proper authorization has also violated the law.

But what about when an investigator sneaks a peak at mail inside an unlocked mailbox (without removing it) at a home or business to verify occupants at the address? Has he committed a crime? Although this is a gray area of the law, a technical reading of these statutes suggests no law has been broken. *However, proceed at your own risk only after getting qualified legal advice.*

PENALTY FOR VIOLATION:

Criminal penalties include fines and imprisonment up to five years. Possible civil liability for invasion of privacy and related torts, depending on the circumstances involved.

PRACTICAL TIPS:

- Don't remove any mail from any mail-box or letterbox for any reason.

- Don't open any mail without the per-mission of the recipient.

THE LAW:

18 USC 1702, 1708, *Obstruction of Correspondence* and *Theft or Receipt of Stolen Mail.*

TRASH INSPECTION

SUMMARY:

The right of investigators to inspect the trash of persons or businesses is based in case law, not statute. The over-riding case law comes from *California v. Greenwood* in which the U.S. Supreme Court ruled that a person who places his trash at the curb for pick up has no reasonable expectation of privacy over the trash.

The Supreme Court held, "It is common knowledge that plastic garbage bags left on or at the side of a public street are readily accessible to animals, children, scavengers, snoops and other members of the public."

However, several municipalities have enacted local ordinances making curbside trash off limits to anyone but the trash man. In addition, four states (Hawaii, New Jersey, Washington and Vermont) may have state supreme court rulings which conflict with the U.S. Supreme Court ruling on *California v. Greenwood*.

PENALTY FOR VIOLATION:

Criminal penalties are limited and apply only in jurisdictions where local municipalities have passed trash-protection laws. Possible civil and criminal penalties for trespassing and invasion of privacy may apply if trash was recovered improperly.

PRACTICAL TIPS:

- If the trash is at the curb or in a public area, there is no expectation of privacy.

- Do not enter onto private property to obtain trash from the curtilage or any other area.

- There may be limited case law exceptions to the above curtilage rule, although these cases involved police officers, not private investigators. One exception allows trash to come from the curtilage if it is first picked up by the trash company and then turned over to the police. The other allows access to the curtilage if it is in plain view of the public and readily accessible by the public.

THE LAW:

Case law as decided by the United States Supreme Court in *California v. Greenwood*, 486 U.S. 35 (1988).

ECONOMIC ESPIONAGE

SUMMARY:

Obtaining a trade secret from a U.S. business (without authorization) and providing it to a foreign government, agent or company is economic espionage — a federal crime. Investigators performing competitive intelligence investigations for foreign clients need to familiarize themselves with this law.

The law defines trade secrets as *"all forms and types of financial, business, scientific, technical, economic, or engineering information, including patterns, plans, compilations, program devices, formulas, designs, prototypes, methods, techniques, processes, procedures, programs, or codes, whether tangible or intangible, and whether or how stored, compiled, or memorialized physically, electronically, graphically, photographically, or in writing if (A) the owner thereof has taken reasonable measures to keep such information secret; and (B) the information derives independent economic value, actual or potential, from not being generally known to, and not being readily ascertainable through proper means by, the public..."*

PENALTY FOR VIOLATION:

Criminal penalties include imprisonment up to 15 years and fines up to $10,000,000.

Civil liability may also apply.

PRACTICAL TIPS:

- Using pretexts, undercover infiltration, bribes and other means to obtain unauthorized access to trade secrets will constitute a violation of this law.

- Passed in 1996, there have been few prosecutions under this act and none of investigators to date.

- To initiate an investigation into suspected economic espionage on behalf of a client/victim, contact your nearest FBI field office and ask to speak to the ANSIR coordinator.

THE LAW:

18 USC 1831, *The Economic Espionage Act of 1996.*

THEFT OF TRADE SECRETS

SUMMARY:

Obtaining a trade secret from a U.S. business (without authorization) with the intent to convert it for financial gain is a federal crime.

The law defines trade secrets as *"all forms and types of financial, business, scientific, technical, economic, or engineering information, including patterns, plans, compilations, program devices, formulas, designs, prototypes, methods, techniques, processes, procedures, programs, or codes, whether tangible or intangible, and whether or how stored, compiled, or memorialized physically, electronically, graphically, photographically, or in writing if (A) the owner thereof has taken reasonable measures to keep such information secret; and (B) the information derives independent economic value, actual or potential, from not being generally known to, and not being readily ascertainable through proper means by, the public..."*

PENALTY FOR VIOLATION:

Criminal penalties include imprisonment up to 10 years and fines up to $5,000,000. Civil liability may also apply.

PRACTICAL TIPS:

- Using pretexts, undercover infiltration, bribes and other means to obtain unauthorized access to trade secrets will constitute a violation of this law.

THE LAW:

18 USC 1831, *Theft of Trade Secrets.*

STUDENT RECORDS

SUMMARY:

Federal law restricts release of student record information from any educational institution that accepts federal funds. Schools who fail to protect the privacy of student records risk losing federal assistance.

Under the law, student records can only be lawfully released to third parties with the written consent of the student's parent, or, by the student himself if over eighteen years of age. However, there are limited exceptions to the ban on release of information that will be of interest to investigators:

- "Directory information" is not included as protected information. "Directory information" is defined as the student's name, address, telephone listing, date and place of birth, major field of study, participation in officially recognized activities and sports, weight and height of members of athletic teams, dates of attendance, degrees and awards received, and the most recent previous educational agency or institution attended by the student.

- Records can be released via a subpoena upon the condition that the parents and student are notified in advance of compliance with the subpoena by the educational institution.

- Nothing in the law prohibits a post-secondary educational institution from disclosing to an *alleged* victim of any crime of violence the results of any disciplinary proceeding conducted by the educational institution against the alleged perpetrator of such crime with respect to such crime.

PENALTY FOR VIOLATION:

Schools who improperly release student records may lose federal funding. There is no criminal penalty prescribed for persons who improperly receive student record information. There may be civil liability for the unauthorized acquisition and use of student records under invasion of privacy and other torts.

PRACTICAL TIPS:

- The law clearly places student directories in the public record. However, the law is silent on whether or not "directory information" must be actually published to be released. It is under this "directory information" exemption that colleges and universities can verify attendance and degree information to investigators conducting employment verifications.

- Educational institutions are required to maintain in a student's official record information on all individuals or institutions who have previously requested or obtained access to the student's record.

THE LAW:

20 USC 1232g, *Family Educational Rights and Privacy Act.*

IMPERSONATION OF A FEDERAL OFFICIAL

SUMMARY:

Four different federal laws make it illegal to impersonate a federal official:

18 USC 701 makes the manufacture, sale or possession of any badge, identification card or other insignia of a federal agency a crime punishable by imprisonment of up to six months plus a fine.

18 USC 712 prohibits the use of the words "national," "Federal," "United States" or "U.S." in the course of debt collection, private investigation or private security service communications, correspondence, or advertisements. Use of emblems of federal agencies is also prohibited. Punishment includes fines and imprisonment up to one year.

18 USC 913 makes it a federal crime to impersonate a federal officer and effect an arrest or detention. Punishment includes up to three years imprisonment plus fines.

18 USC 912 makes it a federal crime to impersonate a federal officer or official and demand money or anything of value. Punishment includes up to three years imprisonment plus fines.

PENALTY FOR VIOLATION:

Criminal penalties include imprisonment up to three years plus fines.

THE LAW:

18 USC Sections 701, 712, 912 and 913, *Various*.

DISCLOSURE OF CONFIDENTIAL INFORMATION
by a Federal Official

SUMMARY:

Any officer or employee of a federal government agency who releases confidential information not authorized by law is guilty of a federal crime (18 USC 1905). A person who bribes a public official is also guilty of a federal crime (18 USC 201). A person who uses a false pretense to obtain information protected under The Privacy Act may also be convicted of a misdemeanor and fined up to $5,000 (5 USC 552a). In addition, he may have criminal liability for Theft of Government Property (18 USC 641) and (if applicable) False Personation of a Federal Official (18 USC 912).

PENALTY FOR VIOLATION:

For government officials, penalties include imprisonment up to one year, fines and removal from office or employment. For persons bribing government officials, penalties include imprisonment up to ten years.

PRACTICAL TIPS:

- Specific types of protected information are listed in the statute and include income tax returns, income/profit/loss information for individuals and corporations, and trade secrets.

THE LAW:

18 USC 1905, *Disclosure of Confidential Information.*

TAX RETURNS

SUMMARY:

The Internal Revenue Code contains 35 pages regulating the release of tax returns and return information. The vast majority of this material consists of exemptions that allow various government agencies *outside* of the IRS to access tax returns. These government agencies range from law enforcement to the Department of Health and Human Service's *Blood Donor Locator Service*. Of interest to non-government investigators are these exemptions which allow access to tax returns:

- You can obtain a copy of a person's tax return with their consent and a completed IRS Form 4506. To obtain a copy of this form, go to *www.irs.gov* and click on the Forms section.

- A taxpayer who is party to a state civil court case can have his or her tax return lawfully obtained with a subpoena. This is an important exemption, as most federal agencies will not honor a subpoena issued by a state court. Collection of a civil liability is also listed as an acceptable reason for a state court to subpoena an income tax return.

- Tax liens are exempted from confidentiality. Widely available through commercial data providers, this is the legal authority that makes this IRS information public record.

- Returns of charitable organizations that have tax exempt status with the IRS are public record. To request a return, use IRS Form 4506-A. To obtain a copy of this form, go to *www.irs.gov* and click on the Forms section.

- Both parties of a jointly filed tax return have a right to receive copies of the return. This may be of use in marital separations where a joint filing has been made but one party is left without a copy of the filing.

- A person who owns at least one per cent of a corporation has a right to obtain the corporation's tax return.

- All partners in a general or limited partnership have a right to obtain the partnership's tax return.

- The executor or administrator of the estate of a decedent may obtain the decedent's tax return.

PENALTY FOR VIOLATION:

For government officials, penalties include imprisonment up to one year, fines, and removal from office or employment. For persons bribing government officials, penalties include imprisonment up to ten years.

PRACTICAL TIPS:

- Both state and federal government

child support agencies are authorized to access income tax returns.

THE LAW:

26 USC 6103, et seq, *Confidentiality and Disclosure of Returns and Return Information.*

COMPUTER CRIME

SUMMARY:

Unauthorized access into the computer of a government, business or person is a federal crime if the entry includes removal/copy of information, destruction of files or the planting of any code or virus.

PENALTY FOR VIOLATION:

Criminal penalties include up to ten years imprisonment plus fines. In addition, persons harmed by such unauthorized access may sue for compensatory damages and injunctive relief.

PRACTICAL TIPS:

- Computers specifically named include those owned by the United States government; financial institutions, credit card companies and credit bureaus.

- Unauthorized entry into any computer with the intent to defraud and obtain anything of value is also covered by this statute.

- When unauthorized access to a computer occurs and the only fraud is use of the computer itself, and the value of such use is less than $5,000 in any one year, no crime has been committed.

- Trafficking in computer passwords with the intent to defraud is also a crime under this statute.

- Any threat sent via computer with intent to extort money or anything of value is a crime under this statute.

THE LAW:

18 USC 1030, *Fraud and Related Activity in Connection with Computers.*

STORED COMMUNICATIONS

SUMMARY:

Unauthorized access to electronically stored communications — such as e-mail or telegrams — is a federal crime.

PENALTY FOR VIOLATION:

Criminal penalties include fines and imprisonment up to two years. Civil action may be filed by the aggrieved party to recover actual and punitive (if violation was intentional) damages.

PRACTICAL TIPS:

- Civil actions must be filed within two years of date of discovery of the violation.

THE LAW:

18 USC 2701, *Electronic Privacy Communication Act of 1986*.

DRIVER RECORDS

SUMMARY:

The Driver's Privacy Protection Act restricts the dissemination of motor vehicle and driver records for privacy purposes. (The law grew out of the killing of actress Rebecca Schaeffer by a stalker who had obtained her driver's license information.) States must comply with *The Driver's Privacy Protection Act* or they risk losing federal highway funding. The law has always had a number of permissible users of this data, a list that includes private investigators.

The DPPA was amended in 1999. The new version of the law further tightens restrictions on sale of DMV information. Regardless, states may still sell motor vehicle information "for use in connection with any civil, criminal, administrative or arbitral proceeding in any Federal, State or local court or agency or before any self regulatory body, including the service of process, investigation in anticipation of litigation, and the execution or enforcement of judgments and orders, or pursuant to an order of a Federal, State, or local court."

PENALTY FOR VIOLATION:

Under federal law, violation can lead to a criminal fine but not imprisonment. Individual states maintain criminal penalties for unauthorized access to DMV data. Civil liability may also apply for unauthorized access.

PRACTICAL TIPS:

* DMV records remain available to private investigators in most states. However, some states now require the signed authorization of the person whose record is being obtained before releasing his or her information.

THE LAW:

18 USC 2721, *Driver Privacy Protection Act.*

MEDICAL HISTORIES

For pre-employment screening

SUMMARY:

The Americans with Disabilities Act (ADA) places restrictions on what questions a job applicant can be asked regarding his or her medical history or disabilities. The law specifically prohibits asking a job applicant if he or she is disabled. However, it is lawful to make pre-employment inquiries into the ability of an applicant to perform job-related functions. The ADA only applies to companies with 25 or more employees.

PENALTY FOR VIOLATION:

Government fines and civil liability.

PRACTICAL TIPS:

- A company is permitted to require a medical examination after hiring. The hiring would be conditional on the results of the medical examination.

- Also prohibited are pre-employment checks of prior workers compensation claims.

- Complaints over violation of the ADA should be directed to the Equal Employment Opportunity Commission. Their website is at *www.eeoc.gov/laws/*

ada.html.

THE LAW:

42 USC 12112, *The Americans with Disabilities Act.*

UNION ACTIVITIES

SUMMARY:

Enacted into law in 1935, the Wagner Act was passed to prohibit employers from engaging in unfair tactics against unionizing employees. Two aspects of the act should be of concern to investigators: Prohibitions against conducting surveillance of picket activities and infiltration of union activities.

PENALTY FOR VIOLATION:

Government fines.

PRACTICAL TIPS:

* None.

THE LAW:

Public Law 74-198, *The Wagner Act.*

PRIVACY LAW RESOURCES

The full text of the laws cited in this report are easily accessible over the Internet — visit the URL below. The bottom of this web page contains an easy-to-use form — just enter any cited law's Title number and Section number for fast access. (Example: 18 USC 2510 stands for Title 18 of the U.S. Code, Section 2510.)

www4.law.cornell.edu/uscode/

For information on efforts to keep public records open, please visit the web site of the National Council of Investigation and Security Services:

www.nciss.org

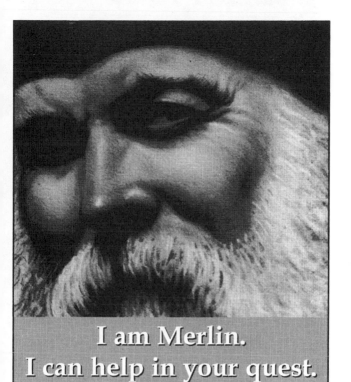

His credit application said "Hotel Management."

Now he's five payments late and nowhere to be found...

www.skipsmasher.com

Skipsmasher.com is the new data service for skiptracers designed by Robert Scott, author of "The Investigator's Little Black Book." This service is not available to the general public.

Phone Numbers

Found a great number for the next edition of *The Investigator's Little Black Book?* Why not let us know about it?! Mail it to: **Black Book c/o Crime Time Publishing Co., 287 S. Robertson Blvd., #224, Beverly Hills, CA 90211** or e-mail it to **research@crimetime.com**

Phone Numbers

Found a great number for the next edition of *The Investigator's Little Black Book?* Why not let us know about it?! Mail it to: **Black Book c/o Crime Time Publishing Co., 287 S. Robertson Blvd., #224, Beverly Hills, CA 90211** or e-mail it to **research@crimetime.com**

Phone Numbers

Found a great number for the next edition of *The Investigator's Little Black Book?* Why not let us know about it?! Mail it to: **Black Book c/o Crime Time Publishing Co., 287 S. Robertson Blvd., #224, Beverly Hills, CA 90211** or e-mail it to **research@crimetime.com**

Phone Numbers

Phone Numbers

Phone Numbers

Found a great number for the next edition of *The Investigator's Little Black Book?* Why not let us know about it?! Mail it to: **Black Book c/o Crime Time Publishing Co., 287 S. Robertson Blvd., #224, Beverly Hills, CA 90211** or e-mail it to **research@crimetime.com**

Phone Numbers

Phone Numbers

Phone Numbers

Phone Numbers